VIETNAMESE
COMMUNISM
1925–1945

HUỲNH KIM KHÁNH

VIETNAMESE COMMUNISM

1925–1945

PUBLISHED UNDER THE AUSPICES OF THE INSTITUTE
OF SOUTHEAST ASIAN STUDIES, SINGAPORE, BY

CORNELL UNIVERSITY PRESS

Ithaca and London

Cornell University Press gratefully acknowledges a grant from the Andrew W. Mellon Foundation that aided in bringing this book to publication.

First published 1982 by Cornell University Press.
First printing, Cornell Paperbacks, 1986.

International Standard Book Number 0-8014-1369-9 (cloth)
International Standard Book Number 0-8014-9397-8 (paper)
Library of Congress Catalog Card Number 81-70696
Printed in the United States of America
Librarians: Library of Congress cataloging information appears on the last page of the book.

The paper in this book is acid-free and meets the guidelines for permanence and durability of the Committee on Production Guidelines for Book Longevity of the Council on Library Resources.

To the "prodigal sons" of Vietnam

PREFACE

This book is a selective history—a history of the transplantation and adaptation of an imported revolutionary ideology in the sociopolitical environment of colonized Vietnam. In the broadest sense it is an analysis of one response to Western imperialism, of Vietnam's prolonged search for teachers, ideas, and techniques to free itself from colonial rule and become a modern society. It is also a history of Vietnamese radicalism—the story of a few thousand young men and women who challenged conventional wisdom, questioned the *raison d'être* of the centuries-old social and political order, and dedicated their lives to regaining Vietnamese independence and rebuilding Vietnamese society. Specifically, this is the story of the Vietnamese Communist movement, from its formation in 1925 until its half-planned, half-accidental victory in August 1945. My aim here is twofold: first to chronicle the internal developments of the Indochinese Communist Party (ICP)—its leadership, organization, ideological orientations, strategies, and tactics, and its relationship with both international communism and Vietnamese society—and second, to assess the reasons for communism's success in 1945.

My discussion of various noncommunist, anticolonial groups is limited to those occasions when they impinged upon or converged with the development of communism. In the late 1920s and early 1940s, for example, the Communists emphasized patriotism and national liberation, and no clear distinction existed between their political orientation and objectives and those of the Vietnamese nation. During the 1930s, however, the Communist party adopted an antinationalist stance; national independence was abandoned as a goal, and throughout the decade there was virtually no convergence between the two historical processes.

Though not neglecting the various non-ICP Marxist-Leninist groups, I have focused on the mainstream of Vietnamese communism: the movement that began with Thanh Nien (Youth) in 1925 and culminated in today's Vietnamese Communist party. My discussion of the short-lived Trotskyist movement and the Trotskyist-Stalinist controversy of the 1930s acknowledges the important role of these groups in the early development of Vietnamese communism. Nevertheless, they constituted only sideshows to the story examined here.

My book is not a biographical study of the men and women who made the Vietnamese revolution. Throughout, I have pointed out the predominant role of Nguyen Ai Quoc (Ho Chi Minh) in the founding and continued existence of the ICP. When appropriate, I have also provided biographical footnotes on individuals who contributed directly to the progress of Vietnamese communism. I am, however, neither a subscriber to the so-called Great Man Theory nor a determinist. In my view, Nguyen Ai Quoc was, to borrow Sidney Hook's terminology, both an "eventful man" and an "event-making man." He appeared on the historical scene because he was part of larger events, and his conduct was partly determined by pressures about him. But he was more than a pawn of historical forces. He impressed his personality on the course of Vietnamese history by his intelligence, vision, will, and ability to influence the Vietnamese masses. To a lesser extent, the same can be said of several other leaders of the Vietnamese Communist movement—individuals who had to make decisions within the confines of historical forces beyond their immediate control.

It is not possible to name or express adequate gratitude to the many individuals who have helped to make this book possible. I owe a large intellectual debt to Professor Sheldon Wolin and to two former teachers who are now personal friends, Robert A. Scalapino and Franz Schurmann. Their interest in this project, as well as their guidance and persistent encouragement, has been an inspiration to me from the beginning. I am obligated to the Center for South/Southeast Asian Studies at the University of California, Berkeley, and its former chairman, Herbert Phillips, for a travel fellowship that enabled me to initiate research for this book. I am grateful to Oey Giok-po, curator of the Wason Collection, Cornell University Library; to Peter Ananda, head of the South/Southeast Asia Library, University of California, Berkeley; and to Monique Pouliquen and the staff members of the Archives Nationales de France, Section Outre-Mer, Paris, for their unfailing assistance. I have unabashedly made full use of the generous help of my colleagues and the staff at the Institute of Southeast Asian Studies, Singapore, especially its director, Kernial S. Sandhu, and its librarian, Patricia Lim Pui Huen. Without their support, it is difficult to imagine how this book could have been completed. I also thank the Association for Asian Studies, Inc., for permission to use, as part of Chapter 6, selections from my article "The Vietnamese August Revolution Reinterpreted," which appeared in the *Journal of Asian Studies*, 30, no. 4 (August 1971), pp. 761–782.

Several of my friends and colleagues have read all or parts of the book at various stages of its composition, though in confronting me with facts, they deprived the world of some startling insights. Professor Tran van Giau wrote a stimulating review of my doctoral dissertation in *Nghien cuu lich su,* raising many questions that are examined here. Philippe Devillers, David G. Marr, Kit G. Machado, Nguyen The Anh, Ong Beng Gaik, George McT. Kahin, Truong Buu Lam, Moffett B. Hall, Deborah Frenkel, Milton Osborne, and Jacqueline Henshall readily offered their help, whenever needed. Finally, I am grateful to Ann Hawthorne, the staff of Cornell University Press, and Sophie Quinn-Judge for their assistance in matters of style and presentation. My shortcomings in these and other respects are not owing to lack of advice.

HUỲNH KIM KHÁNH

Singapore

CONTENTS

ILLUSTRATIONS

ABBREVIATIONS

AOM	Archives Nationales de France, Section Outre-Mer
CCP	Chinese Communist Party
CMTT	*Cach mang thang Tam (Tong khoi nghia o Hanoi va cac dia phuong)*: The August Revolution (The general insurrection in Hanoi and other localities)
CYC	Communist Youth Corps
DDCSD	Dong duong Cong san Dang: Indochinese Communist Party
DKM	*Duong kach menh*: The road to revolution
DRV	Democratic Republic of Vietnam
FLPH	Foreign Languages Publishing House (Hanoi)
ICP	Indochinese Communist Party
KMT	Kuomintang
KUTV	University for the Toilers of the East (Moscow)
NCLS	*Nghien cuu lich su*: Historical studies
NPM	Notes periodiques mensuelles
NXB	Nha xuat ban: Publishing House
PAI	Parti annamite d'indépendence
PCF	French Communist Party
SLOTFOM	Service de Liaison avec les Originaires des Territoires de la France Outre-Mer

TLTK	*Tai lieu tham khao lich su cach mang can dai Viet-Nam*: Research materials on the history of the contemporary Vietnamese revolution
VNQDD	Viet Nam Quoc dan Dang: Vietnamese Nationalist Party
VWP	Vietnam Workers' Party
$	Indochinese piaster

VIETNAMESE
COMMUNISM
1925–1945

PATRIOTISM AND INTERNATIONALISM IN VIETNAM

Communism has achieved remarkable political success in Vietnam since the 1920s. A group of exiled intellectuals engaging in clandestine agitation and experiencing constant persecution by the French colonial rulers was transformed by August 1945 into a party in power. From a cell of nine men in 1925 the Vietnamese Communists grew by December 1976 into a mass party of over 1.5 million members. Since the spring of 1975, the Communist party has held unrivaled power throughout all Vietnam.

This success, paradoxically, was possible largely because of the efforts of France and the United States to destroy the Communist movement in Vietnam. It was under French colonial rule that communism, an ideology originating in Europe, was imported to Vietnam. Colonialist repression was unsuccessful. Instead, it exposed colonialism's violent character and advertised communism's political and social objectives. The French attempt at colonial reconquest during the First Indochina War (1946–1954) further advanced communism's position. By forcing the Viet Minh government to lead national resistance against colonialism, the French inadvertently helped the Communists acquire much-needed legitimacy. Communist success was also assisted by United States intervention (1955–1975). While demonstrating the ineffectiveness, not to say irrelevance, of noncommunist nationalism and revealing the true character of profiteering collaborationism, this intervention confirmed the Communists' claim to be the legitimate representatives of Vietnamese national interests. When the American effort to shape Vietnam's destiny finally collapsed in April 1975, the supremacy of Vietnamese communism was undeniably established.

Given the well-known fraility of most new governments of former European colonies, the ability of Vietnamese Communists to maintain effective power since 1945, to develop a functioning state, and to withstand enormous pressures by foreign powers requires explanation. What factors account for this astounding phenomenon? Vietnamese nationalism? organizational technique? foreign assistance? skillful political management? incompetent opposition? What enabled the Vietnamese Communists to obtain and maintain popular support, while French- and American-backed governments in Vietnam failed? What sources of strength permitted the Vietnamese Communists to accomplish feats rare in Third World states? This book, though not dealing directly with these questions, should help to elucidate the issues that underlie them.

The most outstanding feature in the growth of Vietnamese communism has been its internal fusion of two separate movements: an antiimperialist movement integral with Vietnamese patriotic traditions, and a Communist movement affiliated with, and deeply affected by, developments in the international Communist movement. The Janus face of Vietnamese communism has been the central difficulty of those who seek to identify its nature. So inseparable have these components been that, although it is possible to define certain periods when either patriotism or proletarian internationalism was the dominant feature, any attempt to consider either component the prime feature of Vietnamese communism risks distortion of the true character of the movement.

I view the history of Vietnamese communism as the product of a graft: the union between Vietnamese patriotism and Marxist-Leninist proletarian internationalism. Thus, two essential elements are inherent in Vietnamese communism, one indigenous and one imported. This political hybrid is more than an expression of Vietnamese nationalism or a foreign import. My assumption is that any ideological system, be it Catholicism, democracy, or communism, has a life of its own. When transplanted from its original social, cultural, and political context to another milieu, any system of ideas undergoes a process analogous to that of grafting. In human affairs as in botany, this is a two phase process. The grafting itself involves the insertion of a scion from a foreign plant into the stock of a native plant, followed by either rejection and failure or by adaptation and acceptance. Three conditions are required for a successful graft: first, there should be affinity and compatibility between the two elements; second, both should be in an active stage of growth; and finally, the environment should be favorable for acclimatization. If the second, or "indigenization," phase is successful, the grafted plant usually retains characteristics similar but not identical to those of the original stock. This study deals only with the grafting of Vietnamese communism, not with its indigenization.

The early development of Vietnamese communism can be understood only in the contexts of both world communism and colonized Vietnam's politics between the two world wars. During this period three factors influenced the evolution of Vietnamese communism: the colonial situation of Vietnam, deep-seated Vietnamese patriotic traditions, and the revolutionaries' unshakable commitment to the ideology of international communism. These were the essential determinants, or constants, of the Communist movement. Other factors, such as shifting colonial policies, vacillating strategies of the Comintern, and changing leadership of the ICP, are only variables. This study examines the interplay between two of these constants, the "subjective factors" of Vietnamese communism: the forces of traditional Vietnamese patriotism and of proletarian internationalism.

More specifically, I focus on the two relationships that governed the development of Vietnamese communism: that between the ICP and Vietnamese society—its immediate social and political context—and that between the ICP and the international Communist movement—its organizational reference point. These were complex relationships. To achieve political legitimacy and pursue its social mission, the youthful Communist movement had constantly to maintain a delicate political balance between patriotism and proletarian internationalism; it had to be both Vietnamese and Communist. It had to be accepted in Vietnam's national political life and at the same time retain the purity of its imported ideology. An overemphasis on national independence during the late 1920s

Map 1. Colonial Vietnam

led to neglect of social revolution and to the Party's isolation from the peasantry, whose immediate concerns were physical survival and an end to petty but chronic oppression. On the other hand, an overemphasis on social revolution throughout the 1930s separated the Party from Vietnam's patriotic traditions and alienated the urban petite-bourgeoisie and rural gentry, which had provided the bulk of Party leadership and whose support was much needed in the antiimperialist struggle.

My understanding of Vietnamese communism differs from the official Vietnamese historical interpretation. The latter emphasizes the leading role of the Vietnamese proletariat and the importance of the worker-peasant alliance.[1] I am not convinced that class-oriented analysis is applicable in interpreting the politics of colonized Vietnam, nor that this official interpretation passes the test of historical reality. Unlike Communist movements of industrialized countries in the West, which were born of mature working-class movements and represented a genuine class struggle, the Vietnamese movement was the product of a colonized, predominantly agrarian society in which the native capitalist class was virtually nonexistent and the proletariat infinitesimal. In Vietnam, as in most former European possessions in Asia, those entering the Communist party came from two basic sources: the anticolonial patriotic movement and the antifeudal peasant movement. Party members tended to be urban petit-bourgeois intellectuals and rural peasants. Working-class elements constituted a very small portion of the party and practically none of its leadership. From a class-oriented perspective, early Vietnamese communism was a petit-bourgeois–peasant alliance, organized and led by intellectuals from the urban petite-bourgeoisie and rural gentry.

Two technical aspects of this book require elucidation. The first involves sources. Although I have benefited a great deal from other authors, Vietnamese and foreign, who have written on Vietnamese history, whenever possible I have eschewed secondary sources in order to avoid repeating the many myths that have imbued the

1. For official Communist views on the class character of the ICP, see Le Duan, *The Vietnamese Revolution: Fundamental Problems, Essential Tasks* (Hanoi, 1970), pp. 28–33; also, Truong Chinh, "Ban ve cach mang Viet-Nam" [On the Vietnamese revolution] (1951), in *Cach mang dan toc dan chu nhan dan Viet-Nam* [The people's national democratic revolution in Vietnam], 2 vols. (Hanoi, 1975–76), 1: 70–82.

early history of Vietnamese communism.[2] For this study I have
relied largely on primary source materials. I have, for example,
carefully examined original ICP documents, such as those reprinted in *Buoc ngoat vi dai cua lich su cach mang Viet Nam* [The
great turning point in the history of the Vietnamese revolution];[3]
the twelve-volume *Tai lieu tham khao lich su cach mang can dai
Viet Nam* [Research materials on the history of the contemporary
Vietnamese revolution],[4] and *Chat xieng: Nhung tai lieu lich su tu
chinh bien thang Ba den Cach mang thang Tam 1945* [Breaking our
chains: The historical documents from the political crisis of March
until the August revolution, 1945];[5] and the writings of Communist
leaders such as Lenin and Ho Chi Minh. I have also made extensive use of clandestine and semilegal revolutionary periodicals,
such as the entire collection of *Thanh nien* [Youth], *Bao cong nong*
[Worker-Peasant], *Linh kach menh* [Revolutionary soldier], *Lao
nong* [Toiling peasant], and other ICP and Trotskyist publications
available in the French National Archives, Overseas Section. Finally, I have made full use of the reports of the French Sûreté,
newspaper accounts of the period, and more recent memoirs of
Communist activists. All translations of the primary sources are
my own.

In using these primary materials, I have attempted to avoid being
misled or identifying too closely with the subject. I find, for example, that recent Communist historical accounts of the pre-1945 ICP
tend to gloss over unpleasant facts in the Party's past. Rare, in-

2. Among the secondary source materials, I have found two works most
helpful to understanding the early history of Vietnamese communism: Tran Huy
Lieu, *Lich su tam muoi nam chong Phap* [History of the eighty-year anti-French
resistance], 3 vols. (Hanoi, 1957–61); and Tran van Giau, *Giai cap cong nhan Viet-
Nam: Tu dang cong san thanh lap den cach mang thanh cong* [The Vietnamese
working class: From the formation of the Communist party until the success of the
revolution], 3 vols. (Hanoi, 1962–63).

3. Ban nghien cuu lich su Dang (Commission for the Study of the History of
the Party) (Hanoi, 1961).

4. Tran Huy Lieu, Van Tao, Nguyen Cong Binh, Huong Tan, Nguyen Luong
Bich, and Nguyen Khac Dam, comps. and eds. (Hanoi, 1955–58) (hereafter cited as
TLTK). This twelve-volume compilation contains allegedly all the research materials available in Hanoi by 1958 for the study of the Vietnamese anticolonial and
revolutionary movements from 1883 until 1945.

5. Nguyen van To [Ung Hoe], ed., 2d ed. (Hanoi, 1955).

deed, are accounts of the betrayal of the Party's cause by leaders now deceased, such as Ngo Duc Tri, member of the Standing Committee of the ICP Central Committee, and Duong Hac Dinh and Nghiem Thuong Bien, members of the ICP Bac Ky Regional Commiutee—all of whom acted as informers to the French secret police. Furthermore, Hanoi historians have written nothing about Nguyen Ai Quoc's political eclipse or possible causes for the decline of his influence within the Party in the 1930s.

The French Sûreté reports, too, are only as accurate as their informers' grasp of internal developments in the movement. The voluminous French police reports on Vietnamese communism, which began in 1925, provide detailed information on individual Communist cadres and their activities. But beyond police fascination with personalities, the Sûreté, for lack of understanding of Communist revolutionary concepts, *modi operandi,* and policies, often paid scant attention to or entirely missed events of significance. There is, for instance, no Sûreté analysis of the proletarianization movement of 1928–1930 and its import. Nowhere among the French secret police's reports is there an analysis of the *Political Theses* (1930) of the ICP or of the conflict within the Party between national liberationists and proletarian revolutionaries.[6] Curiously, the Sûreté seems to have been deceived throughout the 1930s by the false reports of Nguyen Ai Quoc's death in 1932; yet confiscated Communist documents in its possession, often attached as appendixes to its own reports, indicated Nguyen's existence.

The second technical aspect requiring consideration is my system of historical periodization, which differs from the official Vietnamese one especially of the early Party history. Official accounts have divided the Party's pre-power history into three periods:[7]

1930–1935: the establishment of the Party; the revolutionary up-

6. See, for example, Commission for the Study of the History of the Vietnam Workers' Party, *An Outline History of the Vietnam Workers' Party (1930–1975)* (Hanoi, 1976).
7. Nguyen Kien Giang. *Les grandes dates du parti de la classe ouvrière du Viet Nam.* Hanoi: FLPH, 1960.

surge of 1930–1931; the destruction of the Party and subsequent struggle to revive Party activities

1936–1939: The Indochinese Democratic Front campaign

1939–1945: the National Liberation Movement and the August Revolution

I have no quarrel with this periodization. My chronology, however, reflects my concept of the Communist movement as a product of both Vietnamese patriotism and revolutionary internationalism and takes into account the importance of events during the years 1925–1930, before the formal establishment of the ICP. I view the years 1925 and 1928 as milestones in the early history of Vietnamese communism. Thus, in this book two chapters deal with the 1925–1930 period as follows:

1925–1927: the eruption of Vietnamese "revolutionary patriotism," during which radical youths rejected reformism and traditional anticolonialism and were actively searching for a new political ideology; communism was systematically introduced to Vietnam by Nguyen Ai Quoc through Thanh Nien (Youth).[8]

1928–1930: the radicalization of Thanh Nien as a consequence of Stalin's Bolshevization of the Communist International; the victory of the radical faction of Thanh Nien, leading to the dissolution of this organization and the emergence of a unified Communist party.

Finally, Vietnamese patriotism and the role it played in the development of Vietnamese communism deserve discussion. In Vietnam the Communists have championed patriotism. Indeed, the political success of communism in Vietnam has been due largely to its ability to identify itself with Vietnamese patriotism. Meanwhile, a succession of foreign-sponsored regimes that styled themselves nationalist were never successful in assuming patriotic leadership and were ultimately rejected by the Vietnamese.

In my view, the motive force of Vietnamese group solidarity in facing external threats is better described as patriotism *(chu nghia ai quoc),* a sentiment shared by Vietnamese of all social strata,

8. For a discussion of Thanh Nien (Youth), see pages 63–88.

than as nationalism *(chu nghia dan toc),*[9] a political expression of the elite. Although in Western political theory the two concepts are not distinct, in Vietnamese experience they are.[10] Patriotism, an inward-looking, kinship-oriented concept with sentimental connotations, reflects the attachment of a people. Nationalism, on the other hand, emphasizes a nation's perceived legitimate rights and is often the political expression of a society's elite elements. An expression of the continuity of the eternal community, Vietnamese patriotism harks back to the nation's physical and cultural heritage and urges fulfillment of an obligation to the community—the protection of patrimony and defense of compatriots.[11] Vietnamese nationalism, on the other hand, relates to the nation's interests and calls for the fulfillment of its requirements of power. In this sense, it may be said that Vietnamese elites—traditional, revolutionary,

9. Until the 1950s the term *nationalism* was usually rendered in Vietnamese as *chu nghia quoc gia.* Although this translation continued to be used in South Vietnam until 1975, scholars of North Vietnam offered in the 1950s a new translation. *Quoc gia* (or, more colloquially, *nha nuoc*) now refers to "state" or "nation-state"; thus, the equivalent of *chu nghia quoc gia* is "statism." *Dan toc* and *chu nghia dan toc* are now equivalents of "nation" and "nationalism," respectively.

10. Perhaps because of their legalistic traditions, most Western political theorists of nationalism have paid scant attention to the importance of patriotism, or even to the phenomenon of patriotism itself. This lack is evident in the voluminous literature on modern nationalism. A recent work, Anthony Smith's *Theories of Nationalism* (London, 1971), provides a case in point. Perhaps the most comprehensive and critical review of the literature on nationalism, Smith's book makes virtually no mention of patriotism. Among the notable exceptions to this tendency is the work of the psychologist Leonard W. Doob, *Patriotism and Nationalism: Their Psychological Foundations* (New Haven, 1964). Doob persuasively demonstrates the distinction between the two concepts and how patriotism is intensified, rather than weakened, under the conditions of alien rule.

11. The language of Vietnamese patriotism was well encapsulated in Phan Boi Chau's declaration to the Hanoi court in the winter of 1925: "In the past as it is in our days, Vietnam ought to be master of its own destiny, and I would like to remake it a nation. . . . Nature has endowed our ancestors and ourselves with forests, precious metals and the sea. In each grain of rice, there is a drop of blood, and for each worn thread of cotton, how many times fingers have been burnt! . . . Houses and temples in our country, gardens inside and ricefields outside, o works of all sorts, how much blood and bone you have cost us!" Quoted in L. Villemotier, "Le patriotisme et le mouvement revolutionnaire en Indochine française," *Mercure de France* 45, no. 872 (15 October 1934), p. 233. This metaphorical language, powerfully recognizing the value and nature of patrimony, was also a reminder: It belongs to us Vietnamese, and is legitimately our property. Take good care of it. Do not let it be taken. Do not squander it; ibid. This language of patriotism pervades the writings of Confucian literati in the late nineteenth and early twentieth centuries.

or otherwise—understand the power of patriotism. These elites often used Vietnam's patriotic traditions for mobilizing the Vietnamese masses to promote nationalist objectives.[12]

As a political concept, patriotism *(chu nghia ai quoc)* is a recent addition to the Vietnamese language. The vocabulary of patriotism, which includes such concepts as *quoc gia* (nation-state), *quoc dan* (nation), *to quoc* (fatherland), and *dong bao* (compatriots), entered the language in the first decade of the twentieth century. Long before this, however, there existed an exhaustive lore evidencing ethnic self-awareness, especially Vietnamese pride in pursuing a political destiny separate from that of China. Vietnamese folk history and schoolbooks tell and retell legends about Giong, the Trung Sisters, Lady Trieu, Ly Thuong Kiet, Tran Hung Dao, Le Loi, and Nguyen Trai defeating the superior Chinese. Every Vietnamese schoolchild knows by heart the inspiring verses of Ly Thuong Kiet, the legendary eleventh-century general, warning the Chinese after a victorious campaign against them:

Over the southern mountains and rivers rules the Emperor of the South;
Such is destiny as written eternally in the Book of Heaven;
How dare you barbarians violate our soil?
Your mad effrontery will undoubtedly end in shameful defeat.

Folk tales about Mac Dinh Chi or Trang Quynh outwitting Chinese emperors or envoys are often recited, arousing ethnic pride. Vietnamese who resisted foreign aggressors are venerated as national heroes; collaborators are reviled as villains to be condemned forever. Behind these stories there is a single theme: The Vietnamese are an indomitable people *(mot dan toc bat khuat);* although we are small in numbers and weak in material terms, we are superior to more powerful foreign aggressors because our cause is just and because we are more skillful, intelligent, adaptable.[13]

12. For a recent Vietnamese discussion of the concept of "patriotism" and its use throughout Vietnamese history, see Thao Giang, "Chu nghia yeu nuoc trong lich su Viet Nam" [Patriotism in Vietnamese history], *Dai doan ket* [Great solidarity], 3, no. 27 (1979), pp. 16–17 and 20; and no. 28 (1979), pp. 20–21.

13. Not all these legends can be categorized as patriotic. Phu Dong Thien Vuong (Giong), for example, was a miraculously born, heaven-sent genie who aided the Vietnamese against the marauding Chinese bandits and returned to heaven upon completion of his task. Its theme is provident justice and divine protection of the Vietnamese people, not patriotism. The Trung Sisters, who led the Vietnamese to rebel against Chinese rule, succeeded in defeating the Chinese and briefly assuming

The Vietnamese concept *ai quoc* (patriotism) as understood today was first defined by anticolonial Confucian literati in the Duy Tan (Renovation) Movement (1905–1908). Before this, the Vietnamese notion of political obligation had been expressed as *trung quan* (loyalty to the king). In this framework, the concept *quoc* (country) was inseparable from the concept *quan* (the king):[14] the country belonged to the king, and the king epitomized the country. Loyalty to the king and loyalty to the country were equivalent.

The introduction of the term *ai quoc,* however, implied a fundamental reconceptualization of the nature of political obligation. In this new formulation, *quoc* became an independent, spiritual entity, a soul *(hon nuoc)* composed of two elements: one in the past, a rich heritage of memories (ancestry, *to tien;* geography, *non song;* history, *lich su*); and one in the present, the desire to live together and make the most of the joint inheritance. Thus, to be faithful to the country or "to love the country" *(ai quoc)* did not presuppose loyalty to the political leadership then in power. Rulers would come and go; the fatherland would always remain. As popularized by the Duy Tan Movement, the concept *ai quoc* signified devotion to one's patrimony: to the heritage, soil, and history that represented the labor of one's ancestors.[15] It also meant protection of and assistance to compatriots *(dong bao)* or those who shared the

------

the government of Vietnam. Their political leadership, however, had been motivated less by patriotism than by conjugal loyalty. The original motive for their rebellion had been to avenge the death of Trung Trac's husband, who had been killed by a Chinese governor. For our purposes, however, the important point is that these legends (and the more recent accounts involving exploits against the French and Americans) became part of the Vietnamese political memory, a valid collective consciousness. Because it has been a guide to Vietnamese political action whenever Vietnamese national independence is threatened, its recognition is important for an understanding of Vietnamese politics.

14. For a discussion of the Confucian concept *quoc* (*kuo* in Chinese), see Joseph R. Levenson, *Modern China and Its Confucian Past* (Garden City, N.Y., 1964), pp. 131–139.

15. The well-known verses of Hoang Trong Mau, which became a popular lullaby, can be roughly translated as follows:

Now let us sing a hymn of patriotism:
What do we love more than our country?
Our ancestors left us a pot of gold,
Which are the vast four fronts of mountain and rivers.
How many kings have opened up and built this country?
Throughout the four thousand years of stormy weather

common heritage.[16] Thus defined, *ai quoc* became the most exalted phrase in the Vietnamese political vocabulary and a battle call to be exploited readily by all political groups.

What, then, explains the intensity of Vietnamese patriotism? Although there are no sure explanations, one partial answer is the ethnic emphasis in the traditional Vietnamese social order. This was expressed in two central elements of traditional Vietnamese social life: ancestor worship, an institution borrowed from China; and the communal cult, apparently a native institution.

Ancestor worship occupied an important place in traditional Vietnamese society. This customary cult was the highest preoccupation of a family; it also formed a significant portion of government activities, in the form of ceremonies for the founder of the country. In ancestor worship, the dead were believed to mingle among, and guide the fortunes of, the living. While departed great men were believed to guide the destiny of the nation, more humble ancestors gave guidance and protection to their living families. As Nguyen Tinh put it: "And thus, the entire throng of the dead themselves fashion the most beautiful creations of the living. In this manner the present is intimately linked to the past—more than just a link: the present lives in the past."[17]

Ancestor worship, more than any major formal religion such as

---

How much labor of those who have gone
Is now seen in each foot of river, each inch of mountain, each melon's pith,
    and each silkworm's innards?

Reprinted in Tran van Giau, *Su phat trien cua tu tuong o Viet Nam tu the ky XIX den cach mang thang Tam* [The development of Vietnamese thought from the nineteenth century to the August Revolution], vol. 2, *He y thuc tu san va su bat luc cua no truoc cac nhiem vu lich su* [Bourgeois thought system and its incapacity in the face of historic tasks] (Hanoi, 1975), p. 75.

16. The following verses, popular in the Duy Tan Movement and reprinted in Tran van Giau, *He y thuc tu san*, pp. 85–86, are illustrative:

Having been born in the same race
In the same country,
Therefore we are the same people.
We ought to live as close as blood relatives;
We ought to protect one another and help one another.
We shall share our fortunes and suffer our woes together.
One same gut, one same innards, let us carve deep the word "together."

17. Nguyen Tinh, "Ordre et anarchie," *La cloche fêlée*, 31 December 1923, p. 1. For a discussion of ancestor worship in Vietnam, see Pierre Huard and Maurice Durand, *Connaissance du Vietnam* (Paris, 1954), pp. 98–99.

Catholicism, Islam, or Buddhism, plays an important role in so-lidifying an ethnic group. Unlike formal religions, which demand faith in the speculative existence of a god, ancestor worship in-volves the veneration of known parents. A religion assembles with-out regard to race and national background all those who believe in its tenets; whereas ancestor worship admits only those who inherit a shared ancestry, those with the same progenitor. Finally, whereas most religions cultivate the self with promises of personal rewards or threats of future punishment, ancestor worship in-volves neither; it emphasizes the eternal continuity of the commu-nity and requires personal obligation to that community. More than just filial piety and *tho cha kinh me* (worship father and revere mother), it demands loyalty to the members of the family, the clan, and others with blood ties or perceived blood ties *(tinh mau mu)*. There is no patriotism without *patria;* ancestor worship, in this sense, may well be the most elementary form of patriotism.

Besides ancestor worship, certain features of the communal cult in the traditional Vietnamese village strengthened ethnic pride and loyalty. In addition to a multiplicity of shrines *(mieu)* for animistic spirits, three formal places of worship were available to Viet-namese at the time of the French conquest: the *van mieu* ("literary shrine" or "temple of literature") was reserved for literati in their veneration of Confucius and other masters; the *chua* (pagoda) served Buddhist devotees who, for some reason, were generally female; and the *dinh* was open to everyone in society. A *van mieu* was most often built at a provincial seat; a *chua* was shared by several villages; but every village had a *dinh*.

At the *dinh* a special feature of the communal cult was instituted that eventually came to play an important role in inculcating ethnic awareness and identity. The *dinh,* a rectangular, multipurpose communal hall, was the center of village life. It served as the meeting place where *ky muc* (notables) discussed issues of impor-tance to the community and where all villagers gathered on feast days. Most important, it was the focal point of the cult of the village guardian spirit *(thanh hoang),* whose protection and bless-ings ensured the village's survival and prosperity. Who were these spirits? In the few villages where a special craft—wood carving, weaving, carpentry—was practiced, the people revered the *tien su* (literally, "first master"), who had taught them their crafts. The majority of villages, however, worshipped national heroes such as Giong, Pham Ngu Lao, Ly Thuong Kiet, Tran Hung Dao, and Le Loi.[18] Virtually all known national heroes of military campaigns against past Chinese aggression were venerated as guardian genies at one *dinh* or another throughout traditional Vietnam. In addition to ancestor worship, this communal cult's exaltation of ethnic attachment and pride may be another source of the intense traditional patriotism that already existed in Vietnam at the time of the French conquest.

The intensity of Vietnamese patriotism is also explained by the unity of the Vietnamese people at the time of the French arrival. Indeed, aside from territorial contiguity and a centralized administrative system, one of the most prominent characteristics of precolonial Vietnam was its virtually monoethnic society. Unlike most other European colonies, by the time of the French invasion Vietnam had developed the social and cultural attributes of a nation—a unified tradition, culture, and language and an effective political and economic system. In confronting French colonial power, the Vietnamese national movement resembled the classic nationalism of Europe (one based on a "nation" or a set of preexisting ethnic and cultural ties) rather than most former colonial possessions in Asia and Africa, which sought to establish independent states on the basis of entirely novel political ties and whose sole bond was their common colonial fate. Both Indonesia and Vietnam, for example, had been colonial possessions and included several component ethnic groups; in both countries the ethnically largest group has played a predominant role in the country's political, economic, and cultural life. In Indonesia, however, it is appropriate to speak of nationalism but not patriotism; whereas Vietnam incorporates both. In Indonesia the dominant Javanese represent approximately 60 percent of the population, and the

18. I am indebted to Mr. Nguyen Ngoc Vy, who took the time to prepare lengthy memos explaining to me the concept behind and practice of the communal cult in Bac Ky and Trung Ky, and especially to call my attention to the worship of national heroes in the *dinh*. For an illuminating essay on the cult of guardian genies and national heroes, read Truong Chinh and Dang Duc Sieu, *So tay van hoa Viet Nam* [Handbook of Vietnamese culture] (Hanoi, 1978), p. 102; see also Nguyen Toai, "Nho lai hoi he dinh dam" [Remembering festivities in the village], *Nghien cuu Viet Nam* [Vietnamese studies] 1 (1973): 38–47.

Javanese *suku* (an ethnic identity) remains distinct from the Indonesian state (a juridical entity). Although it is possible to speak of Javanese, Sundanese, or Batak patriotism, it would be meaningless to refer to Indonesian patriotism. This is not the case with Vietnam. The dominant ethnic group, the lowland Vietnamese, compose nearly 90 percent of the population, and the boundaries between the ethnic group and the state are virtually coterminous. Indonesian national unity was, and remains, the revolutionary objective of a relatively small elite, whereas in Vietnam national unity (the sense of nationhood) was an established precolonial condition. In facing the French, Vietnam was virtually free of divided ethnic loyalties.[19] At least for the dominant ethnic Vietnamese, the protection of the "fatherland," the sacred heritage of their ancestors, was synonymous with defending the interests of their own national community against the common enemy.

Patriotism was an exceedingly important force in the Vietnamese anticolonial struggle. The appeal of this movement was based as much on the xenophobia latent in an ethnically based traditional patriotism as on its call for national independence and revolutionary change. Anti-European feeling intensified Vietnamese solidarity. Vietnamese resistance to earlier Chinese aggression had been mainly political. Though also an expression of ethnic self-awareness, it was essentially an effort to retain political autonomy vis-à-vis a vastly more powerful neighbor. Questions of race, culture, and ideology remained peripheral. If anything, the nineteenth-century mandarin elite—whose motto was "Confucius and Mencius are my masters; the Han Dynasty is my fatherland" *(Khong Manh nga to su, Han duong nga to quoc)*—often identified

19. This is not to say that no ethnically based contradictions existed in precolonial Vietnam. In fact, conflicts between the numerically superior lowland Vietnamese and the ethnic minorities were well known, and the French colonizers sought to make full use of such conflicts in their conquest of the country. See Paul Isoart, *Le phénomène national vietnamien: De l'indépendence unitaire à l'indépendence fractionnée* (Paris, 1961), pp. 153–154; and discussion of this question in Chapter 5 below. At this time there are fifty-four ethnic groups in Vietnam; see "Danh muc cac thanh phan dan toc Viet Nam" [Classification of the ethnic composition of Vietnam], *Tap chi dan toc hoc* [Review of ethnography], no. 1 (1980), pp. 78–86. According to official statistics, the majority people, the lowland Viet, make up 87 percent of the population of Vietnam. See the introduction to "Ethnographic Data," *Vietnamese Studies*, no. 32 (1972), p. 5.

with China, and one of the problems of traditional Vietnamese patriotism was the constant possibility of betrayal by the nation's elite.[20] In the confrontation with French colonial imperialism, however, racialism tended to solidify patriotism; cultural, ideological, and racial distinction sharpened the identification of "we-Vietnamese" versus "they-foreigners." As a people, the Vietnamese appeared to be more united than ever before. This racialist aspect is evident in all Vietnamese anticolonial movements before the August Revolution.

Patriotism, then, was one of the fundamental motive forces of the Vietnamese Communist movement; the other being proletarian internationalism. This book reviews the grafting of those two forces.

20. A popular Vietnamese saying indicated awareness of the possibility of disloyalty by the nation's elite:

> *Trieu Le, ham bon ong Tien si,*
> *Tam ong chan, tam ong nguy,*
> *Tam ong chan nguy. . . .*
> (In the Le Court, there are twenty-four doctoral laureates;
> Eight are loyal, eight disloyal,
> And eight are semiloyal, semidisloyal).

CHAPTER ONE

THE GRAFTING
OF LENINISM

> At first, it was patriotism, not yet communism
> which led me to have confidence in Lenin, in the
> Third International. Step by step, during the course
> of the struggle, by studying Marxism-Leninism
> while engaging in practical activities, I gradually
> understood that only socialism and communism can
> liberate the oppressed nations and the working peo-
> ple throughout the world from slavery.
>
> Ho Chi Minh
> "The Path Which Led Me to Leninism"[1]

In the history of Vietnamese political development the late 1920s
occupy a special place. These pivotal years saw the demise of old
political traditions and the emergence of a new generation of leaders. As the traditional elite of Vietnam watched helplessly from the
sidelines, the Western-educated younger generation was swept up
in an intellectual and political ferment of new ideas and movements. By the end of the decade, a new political tradition had
emerged. The ideas and men who first became known during this
crucial period continued to lead Vietnamese politics for the next

1. Originally published in *Problems of the East*, April 1960; reprinted in Ho
Chi Minh, *Selected Works* (Hanoi, 1977), p. 252.

half century. As successive generations of collaborators served a
variety of foreign masters, these revolutionaries persisted in their
efforts to graft imported values and institutions onto Vietnamese
patriotic traditions. Today, Marxism-Leninism is Vietnam's state
ideology, and members of the generation that emerged in the mid-
1920s, often the same individuals, are defining Vietnam's national
purpose.[2]

A NEW POLITICAL TRADITION

The seminal events of modern Vietnamese politics occurred from 1923 to 1928, when Vietnam experienced intellectual
and political upheaval. The country became the testing ground for
all manner of ideas and movements. Socialism and communism
were discussed along with Gandhism and Sun Yat-sen's *Three
Principles of the People;* the ideas of Tagore found a place next to
those of Piłsudski.[3] Newspapers, periodicals, and pamphlets pro-
liferated; political groups, publishing houses, and Marxist study
groups were organized.[4] This intellectual ferment went hand in
hand with intense political agitation. In the autumn of 1925 the trial
of Phan Boi Chau, the eminent anticolonial Confucian leader who

2. It is worth noting that 214 of the 1,008 delegates who attended the Fourth
Congress of the Vietnamese Communist party, held in Hanoi in December 1976,
had taken part in revolutionary activities before the August Revolution of 1945. Of
these, 25, including Ton Duc Thang, Le Duan, Nguyen Luong Bang, Truong
Chinh, Pham van Dong, Le Duc Tho, Nguyen Duy Trinh, and Vo Nguyen Giap,
had been anticolonial activists in the late 1920s. Voice of Vietnam, Hanoi, 10
December 1976.
3. For a comprehensive treatment of the intellectual and political currents of
Vietnam in the 1920s, see Tran van Giau, *He y thuc tu san.* pp. 421–600.
4. Approximately sixty daily and weekly newspapers appeared during the
1920s; most of them were published during the years 1923–1928. About half of
these could be described as papers of opinion, and the great majority were "opposition" newspapers. In addition, four publishing houses specializing in political pamphlets made their appearance during the period 1925–1928: Nam Dong Thu Xa
(Hanoi), Giac Quan Thu Xa (Hanoi), Cuong Hoc Thu Xa (Saigon), and Ton Viet
Thu Xa (Saigon). Because of differences in colonial policy for the different regions
of Vietnam, most of the opposition newspapers were published in Nam Ky and
most political pamphlets in Bac Ky. See Huynh van Tong, *Lich su bao chi Viet
Nam tu khoi thuy den nam 1930* [History of Vietnamese newspapers from the
beginning until 1930] (Saigon, 1973).

had earlier urged the use of violence as a political instrument, provoked anti-French protest unprecedented in mass spontaneity. In Hanoi and Haiphong, students boycotted classes and held meetings to demand his release. When, in November 1925, the prominent French socialist Alexandre Varenne arrived in Haiphong en route to his new post as governor-general, thousands of young people demonstrated, asking for Phan's release and denouncing "big-stick colonialism."[5] In March 1926, when Bui Quang Chieu, leader of the Constitutionalist party, arrived in Saigon after a lecture tour in France during which he demanded political liberalization in Indochina, 60,000 people went to the Saigon harbor to welcome him home.[6] The funeral of Phan Chu Trinh, leader of the reformist faction of the Confucian literati, also became the occasion for a nationwide protest movement. Virtually all Saigonese wore black armbands as signs of mourning, and 140,000 people from all parts of the country reportedly congregated in Saigon to attend the funeral procession.[7] Memorial services were held by Vietnamese throughout the country and as far away as Vientiane, Laos and Udon, Siam. Shops were closed in Vietnam's cities, and students boycotted schools following an official prohibition of their attempt to organize a "state funeral."

Paradoxically, the very events that launched the new generation of leaders in the national political arena also marked the passing of the traditional anticolonial leadership. Indeed, the activities of 1925–1926 now appear to have served as transitional ceremonies in which the torch of Vietnamese patriotism was passed from one generation to another. Phan Boi Chau's trial, as it turned out, was the final moment of his glory. The young people who had successfully fought for his amnesty through street demonstrations and school boycotts subsequently paid no heed to his advice to proceed slowly and to transform Vietnamese society from within the framework of French colonial rule. From 1926 until his death in

5. Pierre Tedral, *La comédie indochinoise* (Paris, 1926), p. 47.
6. Tran Huy Lieu et al., *TLTK*, 4:98. This figure, however, appears to be exaggerated; according to official statistics Saigon's population at the time was approximately 110,000.
7. Ibid., p. 99.

1941, Phan made no further appreciable contribution to the cause of Vietnamese anticolonialism. Similarly, Bui Quang Chieu's political triumph ended on the very day of his homecoming, following his appeal for Franco-Vietnamese collaboration. Within a short time Bui found himself in political opposition to those who had organized his tumultuous welcome in March 1926. Finally, Phan Chu Trinh's funeral constituted the beginning of a revolutionary career for many. Thousands of students were expelled from schools and countless young office workers and schoolteachers were dismissed from jobs following their attempt to arrange national mourning ceremonies. Such dismissals led in turn to the overseas exodus of several hundred young people to France, Siam, and China in search of teachers and techniques of revolution. Within a few years they were to become Vietnam's leading revolutionaries.

The events of 1925–1926 marked the beginning of a fundamental political disaggregation in Vietnamese society—one that was to characterize Vietnamese politics for several decades. The trial of Phan Boi Chau in 1925 provided the first clear instance of this division. While thousands of young Vietnamese waged a tenacious campaign to obtain his release, a considerable number of older Vietnamese wanted Phan executed as a dangerous revolutionary. At least three provincial mandarins and "more than ten" district mandarins *(tri huyen)* signed a petition to the colonial government, asking for Phan's execution to preempt a future "seditious outbreak."[8] As the political movement gained ground, an open breach developed between the young activists and a group of older, well-established leaders. The latter, who had benefited from the French presence, called for a gradualist approach, nonviolence, and reforms within the framework of colonial rule. The split between the two groups grew wider and mutual antagonism increasingly bitter as the tension between the French and the young became more serious. The latter were now openly contemptuous of the older generation and denounced its resignation, capitulation, and collab-

8. *Dong Phap thoi bao* [The times of French Indochina], 6 January 1926, 18 January 1926. In an excess of zeal, the mandarin who governed Phan's native district, using the argument "like father like son," prevailed upon the local French resident to remove Phan's two adult sons from their homes and make them work under direct French supervision; *Argus indochinois,* 6 January 1926 (with photos).

oration.[9] The older leaders condemned the youth for their impatience, violent language, and arrogance.

By the late 1920s, when most of the surviving anticolonial Confucian literati had withdrawn from the controversy, a confrontation developed between two contending groups of Vietnamese. On the one side stood a sizable group of collaborators, who considered their fortunes intimately bound with continued colonial presence. On the other side stood the revolutionary patriots, who were enemies of foreign imperialism and worked for Vietnamese independence and social transformation. The collaborators, accepting their inferior status vis-à-vis the French, called for sincere Franco-Vietnamese collaboration and hoped for social and economic improvement within the colonial framework. On the other hand, the revolutionaries called for a national revolution, stressing a resolute fight for national liberation and the necessity of a social revolution. The collaborators were to be France's most effective allies in Vietnam; but the revolutionary patriots who emerged for the first time in the mid-1920s were to be the new leaders of the country. This point deserves special notice. To ignore this political division, labeling as nationalists all Vietnamese who during the colonial period expressed their political opinions,[10] is equivalent to ignoring the differences between black American integrationists such as

9. Pham Quynh, the notorious collaborator, was now taunted as "Pham Hot Tay" (Pham the Panderer to the French), and Nguyen van Vinh, editor of *L'Annam nouveau,* as "Nguyen Phan Quoc" (Nguyen the Traitor). The best summary of the feelings of the young activists toward the collaborators is found in a series of interviews with public figures in South Vietnam who had been student activists in the 1920s. See Nguyen van Trung, *Pham Quynh,* vol. 2 (Saigon, 1973), especially interviews with Ho Huu Tuong, pp. 33-37; with Nguyen van Tue, pp. 38–39; and with Pham van Dat, pp. 65–68.

10. William J. Duiker's study *The Rise of Nationalism in Vietnam, 1900–1941* (Ithaca, 1976) is a case in point. Having failed to provide a concept of nationalism, the author considers any Vietnamese who expressed some political opinions a "nationalist." The basic political disaggregation in modern Vietnam and the ideological boundaries between nationalists and Communists are thus ignored. For Duiker, Nguyen van Vinh, the most militant among the enemies of Vietnamese anticolonial nationalism, was a "moderate" nationalist (see note 15, below). Pham Quynh, the "Lord Haw Haw" of Vietnam, is labeled "a significant figure in the history of modern Vietnamese nationalism" (p. 127). In fact, from 1917 until 1934 Quynh was paid by the colonial government to propagate the officially approved line on culture and politics (see note 17, below). Ironically, Duiker chooses to call the Indochinese Communist party a "nationalist party" (p. 230) at its most antinationalist phase, that is, the Nghe Tinh soviet period of 1930–1931 (see chapter 3 below).

Martin Luther King, Jr. and separatists such as Malcolm X. In Vietnam this division persisted throughout the colonial period and, in some forms until 1975.[11]

COLLABORATORS

Two groups of Vietnamese collaborators existed in the 1920s. In Bac Ky they were mainly agents of the colonial government. These middle-aged mandarins had little in common with the members of the traditional elite except their official positions and their external garb. Unlike the earlier, literati mandarins, who were selected by rigorous civil examinations, these government employees obtained their sinecures not by professional competence or devotion to public service, but as rewards for their loyalty to the French. The earlier, literati mandarins were steeped in the traditions of Confucian studies; the French-appointed mandarins had at most some training at the Collège du Protectorat, where interpreters and functionaries were educated, if they had formal training at all.[12] Of shallow cultural roots, whatever they knew of Confucianism and traditional Sino-Vietnamese civilization they had acquired late

11. The continuity of this political division is one of the most remarkable features of modern Vietnamese political development. The same people, Ho Chi Minh, Pham van Dong, Truong Chinh, Vo Nguyen Giap, Le Duan—who had devoted their lives to fighting against French colonial rule also led the "Protracted Resistance" *(Truong Ky Khang Chien)* (1946–1954) against the French attempt at colonial reconquest and, subsequently, against the U. S. intervention (1955–1975). On the other hand, those who had collaborated with the French tended to continue to do so with the Americans. Eight out of fourteen cabinet ministers in the U.S.–sponsored Ngo Dinh Diem regime, for example, had been government functionaries during the colonial period. Also, virtually all the South Vietnamese senior military leaders who fought on the American side and who controlled the fate of South Vietnam from 1964 until 1975 had begun their careers fighting on the side of the French.

12. One of the principal complaints of Vietnamese in Bac Ky and Trung Ky was that the French-appointed mandarins were often "boy-mandarins," many of whom had been elevated to their official positions in reward for loyal service as domestic servants. Often of peasant stock and with no particular administrative training or background, these individuals were notorious for their abuses of power. This corruption of the institution of the mandarinate was the subject of much of Phan Chu Trinh's writing. During the First World War Phan went so far as to accept a proposal by the French minister of colonies to disseminate French propaganda and to recruit Vietnamese soldiers for the French front on the condition that the colonial government would stop making mandarins of former servants and dismiss the boy-mandarins already in office. See Tedral, *Comédie indochinoise*, pp. 62, 116.

through self-education.[13] Meanwhile their notoriety for corruption was rivaled only by their obsequiousness to their French masters.[14]

The Bac Ky collaborators were united in their praise of "Great France" *(Dai Phap)* and their hatred for Vietnamese anticolonialists. This basic position had been their hallmark long before the mid-1920s. During World War I, for example, Nguyen van Vinh had used his French-sponsored *Dong duong tap chi* [Indochina review] to extol French accomplishments in Indochina, urge sincere collaboration, and heap maledictions on anticolonialists. Vinh wrote:

Among the many possible approaches, *our people today should follow only one ideology: the Franco-Vietnamese ideology* [*chu nghia Phap Viet*]. Since we are so fortunate to have Great France as our master, let us try to hang on to our French master. Let us concentrate on our livelihood and our studies. Those scoundrels who encourage stupid things, if arrested, should be put into a wicker basket and rolled into the river *(bo ro lan song).*[15]

Elsewhere Vinh called the anticolonialists "a bunch of famished fellows" and "crazy scoundrels" and urged that "the officials of the

13. Pham Quynh provided a case in point. Quynh learned Chinese characters and read Confucian texts only as an adult, while working as an interpreter at the Ecole française d'extrême-orient (Hanoi). He later reminisced that at age sixteen, the time of his graduation from the Protectorate School, his knowledge of Chinese characters was limited to writing the two characters of his name. See Pham Quynh, "Phap du hanh trinh nhat ky" [Journal of a Trip to France], *Nam phong* [Southern wind], no. 75 (September 1923), pp. 193–194.

14. For a discussion of the decay of the mandarin institution, see Alexander B. Woodside, *Community and Revolution in Modern Vietnam* (Boston, 1976), pp. 18–22.

15. *Dong duong tap chi* [Indochina review], quoted in Tran van Giau, *He y thuc tu san*, p. 499 (Vinh's italics[?]). For a detailed biography of Nguyen van Vinh, see Duiker, *Rise of Nationalism in Vietnam*, pp. 111–116; see also Stephen O'Harrow, "French Colonial Policy toward Vernacular Language Development in Vietnam and the Selection of Pham Quynh," in *Aspects of Vietnamese Language in Asian and Pacific Societies,* ed. Nguyen Dang Liem (Honolulu, 1973), pp. 124, 134. It seems to me that both Duiker, who calls Vinh a "moderate," and O'Harrow, who considers him a "tame nationalist," take Vinh too seriously. A flamboyant and brilliant man, Vinh appeared to have derived a mischievous pleasure from discrediting whatever ideas and institutions he considered "stupid." Though useful to the French, he was nobody's puppet. At the same time, however, he was neither moderate (except, perhaps, as far as the French were concerned) nor tame nor nationalist. Indeed, it is difficult to pin a label on a smart aleck. Vinh reportedly

two countries, France and Annam, should join forces to extermi-nate them."[16] Toward the end of World War I the Bac Ky apologists for French colonial rule grouped themselves into an organization called Khai Tri Tien Duc (Association for the Intellec-tual and Moral Advancement of the Annamese) or AFIMA. Founded at the initiative of Governor-General Albert Sarraut and Louis Marty, director of the Political Bureau (secret police) of the colonial government, this organization was headed by Pham Quynh. Its de facto house organ was the monthly magazine *Nam phong* [Southern wind]. Until at least 1934, when Pham Quynh left Hanoi for Hue to become prime minister in the puppet royal gov-ernment, both *Nam phong* and AFIMA were a sort of native polit-ical front for the colonial government.[17]

---

enjoyed enriching himself at the expense of French officials. His colleagues later recounted how Vinh would "curse the French and take their money," whereas Pham Quynh would "pander to the French to take their money." See interviews with Nguyen Doan Vuong and Phung Tat Dac [pseud. Lang Nhan] by Nguyen van Trung in *Pham Quynh*, 2:45–48. Vinh's favorite trick allegedly was to write up exposés of French scandals, then, for a bribe, to refrain from publishing them. An enemy of feudalism, he showed no mercy to the monarchy. When Emperor Khai Dinh visited Hanoi (1917?), Vinh reportedly welcomed him in a Western dress suit. Holding his colonial hat in one hand, bowing his head à la française, he shook the king's hand, while the other Vietnamese notables, in full traditional regalia greeted the monarch with prostrations. Nguyen van Vinh died sometime in 1936, reportedly while prospecting for gold in Laos.

16. *Dong Duong tap chi*, quoted in Tran van Giau, *He y thuc tu san*, p. 496.

17. Pham Quynh and *Nam phong* have been controversial among Vietnamese intellectual circles during recent years. Was Pham Quynh a "French agent"? In 1972 Saigon students staged a "trial of Pham Quynh," exposing his past association with colonial policies. In 1972–1973 Nguyen van Trung published two volumes on Pham Quynh and *Nam phong*, documenting Quynh's collaboration and harmful influence. Madame Pham thi Ngoan, on the other hand, sought to defend her father's honour and refute the charge that he had been a "French agent" in her 500-page doctoral dissertation, "Introduction au *Nam phong*," published in *Bulletin de la Société des Etudes Indochinoises*, n.s. 48 (1973): 175–473. Pham Quynh himself, however, never denied that he had been a paid agent of the colonial government. (He was paid 400 piasters monthly.) *Nam phong*, too, advertised itself as a propaganda organ of French imperialism. The periodical had a French title, *L'information française*, and its own subtitles, *La France devant le monde—Son role dans la guerre des nations*, which were printed above the Vietnamese title. Beginning with issue no. 39 (Sep-tember 1920) the French title and subtitles disappeared. The Gallic rooster emblem that had appeared on the magazine cover since the first issue was replaced with the stylized logo of AFIMA. According to *Nam phong*, its founder was Louis Marty, director of the Political Bureau (secret police) in the secretariat of the government-general. Heading the list of its sponsors were Emperor Khai Dinh and Governor-General Albert Sarraut. For the origins of *Nam phong*, see the interview given by

The second group of collaborators was an organization called Dang Lap Hien (Constitutionalist party).[18] It was founded in Nam Ky in 1919 and headed by Bui Quang Chieu, an agricultural engineer and native of Nam Ky who had been trained in North Africa and in France. Its leading members included landowners and professionals such as Nguyen Phan Long, Le Quang Liem, and Vuong Quang Nhuong. This was, however, a constitutionalist party without constitutionalism. Acting as a pressure group for the landed and professional bourgeoisie of Nam Ky, this organization, despite its name, never had a constitution of its own, a known membership list, nor procedures for member participation in decision making or selection of leaders. It was, in other words, not a political party but a self-selected group of friends and business associates[19] who had organized themselves to defend their interests. The group was never organized for the purpose of seizing power, whatever the ambitions of certain of its members.

The political objectives of the Constitutionalists somewhat resembled those of integrationist American blacks in the 1950s and 1960s. They wanted protection of their social and economic interests (more educational opportunities, more jobs, higher salaries) and their political freedoms (travel, press, association). Above all they wanted, according to the expression of the time, to be "assimilated" into the French community. One of their constant complaints was that the French had placed obstacles in the way of their naturalization as Frenchmen. By Vietnamese standards at least, they were not nationalists. As cultural and political hybrids (sev-

Pham Quynh to Dao Hung in *Phu nu tan van* [Women's news], 18 June 1931. A particularly revealing report on the objectives, principles, and policies of *Nam phong* exists in a memorandum prepared by Louis Marty, dated 22 August 1917, "Au sujet de la revue *Nam phong*" (AOM, Nouveaux Fonds 11, dossier 56), reproduced in Nguyen van Trung, *Pham Quynh*, vol. 1 (Saigon, 1972), pp. 196–201. For some reason Madame Ngoan's study did not refer to either the Pham Quynh interview mentioned above or Marty's memorandum.

18. For an analysis of the Constitutionalist party see Milton Osborne, "The Faithful Few: The Politics of Collaboration in Cochinchina in the 1920s," in *Aspects of Vietnamese History*, ed. Walter Vella (Honolulu, 1973), pp. 160–190; see also Ralph Smith, "Bui Quang Chieu and the Constitutionalist Party in French Cochinchina, 1917–1930," *Modern Asian Studies* 3 (1969): 131–150; and Megan Cook, *The Constitutionalist Party in Cochinchina: The Years of Decline, 1930–1942* (Clayton, Australia, 1977).

19. According to Nguyen Phan Long, the Constitutionalist party's membership never numbered more than about thirty; *La dépêche*, 6 April 1939.

eral had French citizenship, could speak French better than Vietnamese, and knew more about French than Vietnamese history), they neither took pride in their Vietnamese heritage nor desired national independence. Accepting their inferior status vis-à-vis the French, they strove for more freedom but not for political power. Although both the Nam Ky Constitutionalists and the Bac Ky collaborators were in basic agreement in supporting the French presence, their political approach differed. There was never a "Quynh-Vinh-Long-Chieu clique," despite the allegations of the young revolutionaries of the 1920s and 1930s. Unlike the northern AFIMA members, who groveled before the French, the Constitutionalists were not paid agents of the conquerors. Mostly men of considerable education and private means, they usually did what they could to defend their interests, sometimes even against French nationals, although such class interests were often couched in terms that made them appear to be the interests of the Vietnamese people as a whole.

The attitude of the Constitutionalists toward anticolonial patriotism also differed from that of the northern French agents. Though opting for collaboration with the French, they were not at first antagonistic to anticolonial activists. In fact, typical of reformist bourgeois parties of colonized countries, they initially took a patriotic and progressive stance. At an early stage they even participated in the anticolonial movement. In November 1925, for example, Nguyen Phan Long led eight hundred Vietnamese marchers to present Governor-General Varenne with a *Cahiers des voeux annamites* whose contents reflected the anticolonial Vietnamese sentiments. During the years 1925–1926 students at the Nguyen Phan Long School were required to study inflammatory anticolonial articles by Nguyen Ai Quoc appearing in *Le paria* and by Nguyen The Truyen in *Viet Nam hon* [The soul of Vietnam] as texts for classroom discussion.[20] At least until 1927–1928, newspapers owned by Constitutionalists, such as *Duoc ñha Nam* [The torch of Vietnam] and *La tribune indochinoise,* sided with the anticolonial activists.

The collaborationist character of the Constitutionalists, however, became increasingly apparent toward the end of the decade.

20. Tedral, *Comédie indochinoise,* pp. 28–30.

As the political movement became radicalized and they were forced to take a clear stand between fighting the French for a national revolution and collaborating in order to preserve their interests, the Constitutionalists kept a distance from the revolutionary movement. Constitutionalists no longer marched in demonstrations, and their newspapers increasingly sought to prove their loyalty to the "mother country." By the turn of the decade they had become a mere political lobby representing the interests of the southern bourgeoisie, not the interests of the Vietnamese as a whole. By then the Constitutionalist party had degenerated into an agency dedicated to the transfer of privilege and power from the few white rulers to the few yellow ones—themselves. For a short time during the 1930s Bui Quang Chieu represented Cochin China in the French Chamber of Deputies. In 1939–1940 Bui Quang Chieu, Le Quang Liem, Vuong Quang Nhuong, and other Constitutionalists waged a determined campaign to recruit Vietnamese soldiers for the European front, exhorting Vietnamese to demonstrate their loyalty and "patriotism" to France. Following the August Revolution, Constitutionalists headed the cabinet of a short-lived French-sponsored government, the secessionist Republic of Cochin China (1946–1947). Briefly in 1950, while the Vietnamese nation was engaged in the "Protracted Resistance" *(Truong Ky Khang Chien)* against the French attempt at colonial reconquest, Nguyen Phan Long served as prime minister in the puppet regime of Emperor Bao Dai. By then the Constitutionalist party had ceased to exist.

REVOLUTIONARY PATRIOTS

The constellation of revolutionary patriots was much more complex. Revolutionary patriotic groups appeared in virtually every Vietnamese community. In Bac Ky, for example, the disciples of Sun Yat-sen organized into several groups, the most prominent of which derived its name from its publishing house, the Nam Dong Thu Xa. By December 1927 most of these had united to found a formidable political party, the Viet Nam Quoc Dan Dang (Vietnamese Nationalist Party), usually abbreviated as VNQDD. This party and its role are discussed in the next chapter.

In Trung Ky around 1925–1926, young schoolteachers and university students founded and led an anticolonial organization called the Viet Nam Nghia Doan (Vietnamese Corps for Righteousness). This group subsequently became part of the Dang Phuc Viet (Party for the Restoration of Vietnam), led by Confucianist literati such as Le Huan, Ngo Duc Ke, and Tran Dinh Thanh, who had previously been imprisoned in Poulo Condore prison islands for their involvement in the Tax Protest Movement of 1908. This party was transformed in 1927 into a protocommunist party, the Tan Viet Cach Menh Dang (Revolutionary Party of the New Vietnam), usually abbreviated as Tan Viet (New Vietnam), and was subsequently integrated into the ICP.[21]

In Nam Ky there was organized in March 1926 a Dang Thanh Nien (Youth Party), also known by its French name, Jeune Annam.[22] This group existed for approximately one year. Like its counterparts in Bac Ky and Trung Ky, this party was composed of young schoolteachers, journalists, students, and office workers. Its activities included the organization of demonstrations in Saigon to demand amnesty for Phan Boi Chau, the mobilization of the people for Phan Chu Trinh's funeral and the preparation of a lengthy political program that called for buying back Indochina from the French and terminating French colonial rule in Vietnam. Also in Nam Ky there was a so-called Hoi Kin Nguyen An Ninh (Nguyen

21. For a brief account of the Tan Viet, see Chapter 2.
22. The most detailed account of this party can be found in Tran Huy Lieu's memoirs, *Dang Thanh Nien, 1926–1927* (Hanoi, 1961). Lieu had been one of the party's founders. André Malraux later claimed to be its founder and spiritual leader (see Walter G. Langlois, *André Malraux: The Indochina Adventure* [New York, 1966], p. 58). In his study on Vietnamese nationalism, Duiker calls the newspaper *Jeune Annam* the "propaganda organ" of this party (p. 144). This interpretation attributes too much political sophistication to the group and is also factually inaccurate. Although many adherents of this party may have shared the sentiments expressed in *Jeune Annam,* there was no official connection between the newspaper and the party. In fact, according to Tran Huy Lieu, Dang Thanh Nien found it necessary to publish a public notice in other newspapers, advising the public not to confound the views expressed in *Jeune Annam* with those of the party (*Dang Thanh Nien,* p. 29). In any case, the newspaper edited by Lam Hiep Chau appeared only once, 23 March 1926. Intended as a weekly, it died an early death after its editor was taken to court, fined 100 francs, and jailed for one year for publishing a newspaper while under age (Lam Hiep Chau was twenty in 1926). The real reason for the harsh sentence, however, appeared to be *Jeune Annam's* reprint of two vitriolic tracts of the Phuc Viet party of Trung Ky and of two articles that had previously appeared in *Le paria* (one by Nguyen Ai Quoc and the other by Nguyen The Truyen), attacking French colonialism in general and the appointment of Alexandre Varenne as governor-general in particular.

An Ninh Secret Society), or Thanh Nien Cao Vong Dang (High Aspirations Youth Party), apparently named after a book authored by Ninh. Little is known of this organization except that it was organized by Ninh, that it attempted to use Triad Society operational practices, and that its membership was a mixture of Western-educated youths and rural toughs. By the turn of the decade both these organizations had disintegrated. Their members subsequently swelled the ranks of other revolutionary parties. Tran Huy Lieu, Bui Cong Trung, and Ta Thu Thau, members of Jeune Annam, moved in separate ideological directions. By 1928 Lieu had become head of the Southern Section of the VNQDD and, by the 1930s, a convert to communism. Trung also joined the Communists, was among those sent to Moscow for training, and finally became a notable ICP leader. Thau went to Paris for studies and there became a famous student leader. In the 1930s he was a prominent advocate of Vietnamese Trotskyism. Several members of the Nguyen An Ninh Society also joined the Communists; one of them, Vo van Tan, became an ICP Central Committee member.

Outside the country, too, Vietnamese actively organized into a variety of anticolonial groups. Although such organizations had existed in overseas centers of Vietnamese long before the student movement of the mid-1920s, a massive influx of young people around 1926–1927 gave them new life. (This influx was a result of the reprisals against students and office workers who had been active in mobilizing for Phan Chu Trinh's funeral.) Paris and Aix-en-Provence in France, Canton in China, and Udon and Nong Khai in Siam became the external training grounds for the future leadership of the Vietnamese revolutionary movement. There, young revolutionary activists received their initial tools—revolutionary theory, organizational techniques, and practical experience—to make the revolution in the home country.

Vietnamese revolutionary patriotism of the 1920s was characterized, first, by the youthfulness of its leaders, an interesting phenomenon for a Confucian society, like Vietnam at the time. Up to this point, involvement in national political life had been the preserve of middle-aged or older men. This was particularly true of the leadership of the anticolonial movement of the Confucian literati. In 1904, for example, at the founding of the Duy Tan Hoi (Renovation Society), Phan Boi Chau was already thirty-seven years old, Phan Chu Trinh, thirty-two, Nguyen Ham, forty-one, and Nguyen Thuong Hien, thirty-nine. This was equally true for the collaborators. In 1926, at the height of the political agitation, Pham Quynh was already thirty-four, Nguyen van Vinh, forty-four, and Bui Quang Chieu, fifty-three, to cite just a few. In contrast, the leaders of the political agitation of the mid-1920s were in their early twenties, and the other participants were largely teenagers, still in secondary schools. In 1926 Nguyen An Ninh, the oldest and most eminent among the leaders of this movement, was twenty-six. The others ranged from nineteen to twenty-four (Nguyen Thai Hoc, twenty-four; Tran Huy Lieu and Nguyen Khanh Toan, twenty-three; Bui Cong Trung and Nguyen Trong Hy, twenty-two; Ta Thu Thau, twenty; Pham van Dong and Le Duan, nineteen). Younger, teenage activists included Vo Nguyen Giap, Tran van Giau, Ho Huu Tuong, Pham Hung, and Nguyen Duy Trinh.

The second characteristic of this movement was its urban, petit-bourgeois character. It attracted largely secondary school and university students and young "intellectual workers" such as teachers, journalists, and office clerks.[23] These people, paradoxically, were the products of French colonial rule. As in other societies, the *petits intellectuels (tieu tri thuc)* proved to be the most sensitive to the weakening of the dominant ideology and the harm to their national and cultural pride.[24] Coming from the same social elements that had traditionally been the repository of the public trust and that, three or four decades earlier, would have prepared them either to sit for civil service examinations or to participate in the anticolonial *van than* (literati) movements, they took for granted their responsibility and mission to save the country. Although their educational background was radically different from that of the Confucian literati of the nineteenth century, they retained the public trust and the role of the political vanguard. In the words of Le Duan, one of their number, who is at the time of writing

23. For a discussion of the role of intellectuals in Vietnamese history, see Tam Vu, "Ve vai tro cua tri thuc trong lich su dan toc ta" [On the role of intellectuals in the history of our people], published in three parts in *Dai doan ket* [Great solidarity], nos. 18 (4 June 1977), 20 (18 June 1977), and 21 (28 June 1977).

24. See André Gorz, *Socialism and Revolution* (New York, 1973), p. 17. See also idem, "Mai et la suite," *Les temps modernes*, August–September 1968, on the reasons why students would be the most readily available social sector for ideological subversion and open revolt.

secretary-general of the Vietnamese Communist party, they were "the first ones who lit the fuse of the revolution."[25] Perhaps the most important characteristic of this movement was its radicalism—its complete rejection of established values and institutions and its determined search for substitutes. Unlike the anticolonial literati in the Duy Tan Movement and the Dong Kinh Nghia Thuc (Free School of Dong Kinh) of the first decade of the century, the young activists of the 1920s refused to have anything to do with the value system, institutions, and practical methods of the traditional society. As Nguyen An Ninh put it in a lecture at the Hall of the Cochinchinese Society for Mutual Education on 15 October 1923:

> Today's illness requires today's remedies. The experiences of the past are lost in the faraway mist of history. They no longer have any immediate relevance for today's generation. The weakened voices which remind us of the opinions of the sages of antiquity are only like fading echoes which die at the outer edges of our ears. For today's generation, there must be new ideals—*its own ideals,* a new activity—*its own activity,* new passions—*its own passions.* It is on this condition, and on this condition alone, that the realization of a better future is possible. Life—not only life in Vietnam but life everywhere—must be eternally renewed.[26]

In dealing with the actual situation of Vietnam of the 1920s, members of this movement rejected outright any advice of the older generation, who counseled political patience. Referring, for example, to the appeal for calm from collaborators such as Bui Quang Chieu and Pham Quynh, Nguyen Khanh Toan wrote:

---

25. Le Duan, "Mot vai van de trong khi nghien cuu lich su Dang ta" [Some issues in the study of our party's history], a lecture given at the Nguyen Ai Quoc Party School (1960), reprinted in Le Duan, *Giai cap cong nhan Viet Nam va lien minh cong nong* [The Vietnamese proletariat and the worker-peasant alliance] (Hanoi, 1976), p. 215.

26. Nguyen An Ninh, "L'idéal de la jeunesse annamite," *La cloche fêlée,* 7 January 1923 (Ninh's italics). Nguyen An Ninh was a native of Long Hung, Cholon (Nam Ky). Born 6 September 1900 to a literati, small-landowner family of anticolonial persuasion, he had a formal education that was exclusively Western: primary schooling at the Institution Taberd (Saigon) and secondary schooling at Chasseloup-Laubat (Saigon). After two years of legal studies at the University of Hanoi (1918–1920) he continued his education in France, obtaining a law degree in Paris in 1921. Before returning to Vietnam in 1923 he engaged in anticolonial conspiracy with Nguyen Ai Quoc, Phan Chu Trinh, and Phan van Truong and traveled widely in Europe—Germany, Austria, Switzerland and Italy—trying to learn about and

At a time when, in the political domain, only impatience is the surest guarantee of success, it is more than stupid to subordinate the emancipation of an oppressed people to patience. . . . Those who are supposed to lead the masses love moderation, if not tranquillity. . . . From now on, we shall turn a deaf ear to all the nonsense of our elders in age, but not intellect. It is by freeing ourselves from their tutelage that we shall discharge our duty, all our duty.[27]

The youth reserved their greatest scorn for the traditional elite. All of them blamed the monarchy and the mandarins for having surrendered to the French in order to preserve their positions of prestige and privilege. They condemned these remnants of Vietnam's "feudal" order for subservience to the French and for the predicament in which the country found itself. Indeed, the young people were ready to do away with Vietnam's royalty altogether. Following the death of Emperor Khai Dinh in 1925, as the French colonial government and its Vietnamese collaborators were searching for a new monarch, Nguyen van Pho wrote "in the name of a group of Vietnamese revolutionaries":

The princes of the royal family are all ignorant beings; none of them has sufficient qualities to be king. To seek the will of God and examine the sentiments of the people, one could say that it is the end of royalty in Vietnam. In today's situation in our country, conserving royalty will only have disadvantages. . . .
    Let our compatriots open their eyes and follow the current which

---

understand other societies in the hope of finding an appropriate ideology for Vietnam. From late 1923 until he was arrested in March 1926, Ninh was one of the most prominent intellectual and political leaders in Saigon. *La cloche fêlée,* founded by Ninh in December 1923, was to exemplify the political journey of Vietnamese intellectuals in the mid-1920s. Designed initially to transmit European, especially French, culture to Vietnam and to promote sincere Franco-Vietnamese collaboration, it at first advocated political liberalization by the colonial government and a cultural renaissance among Vietnamese. Ninh quickly discerned the futility of such an endeavor. As Ninh put it, collaboration should be a joint effort of equal partners, but not one between the rider and his horse. By the early months of 1924 his paper had rejected sincere collaboration and begun to discuss the ideas of Gandhi and Tagore. By late 1925 *La cloche fêlée* had become a medium of Communist propaganda, regularly reprinting articles authored by notable international Communist leaders such as Zinoviev, Bukharin, Karl Radek, and Gabriel Péri and previously printed in *L'humanité,* the organ of the French Communist party. Finally, between 29 March and 26 April 1926, the paper published the *Communist Manifesto* in an eight-part series. *La cloche fêlée* ceased publication in May 1926 after Nguyen An Ninh was imprisoned for leading anticolonial demonstrations.
    27. Nguyen Khanh Toan, "Ce que veut la jeunesse annamite," *Le nha que* [The rural hick] no. 1 (January 1927).

has led all the peoples on earth. Let us try to overthrow this old statue. After its demolition, we shall reconstruct the social edifice to give a new life to our country, to demand our rights and our liberty.[28]

In the growing radicalism of the mid-1920s, condemnation of the older generation and the traditional elite went hand in hand with a militant approach to anticolonialism. The youth were united in their hatred for the French colonialists. All the young leaders, including those who had previously advocated sincere Franco-Vietnamese collaboration, were now opposed to continued French rule. Nguyen An Ninh, for example, who throughout 1923–1924 had advocated collaboration and French tutelage for Vietnamese development, now called upon the French to leave the country. At a mass rally on 21 March 1926, Ninh stated:

> There is no point of possible collaboration between Frenchmen and Vietnamese. *The French have nothing more to do here.* Let them return the land of our ancestors to us. Let them quit the country so that we can govern ourselves.
> Our country has given birth to numerous heroes, those people who know how to die for their country. Our race still has no lack of them.[29]

The Vietnamese radicals of the 1920s were distinctive from their counterparts elsewhere. The Western radical, as Daniel Bell portrays him, resembles the proverbial prodigal son, whose quest for independence and thirst for knowledge impel him to leave home.[30] His idealistic impulse exhausted, the son returns, chastened by the world and more willing to accept the old-fashioned but secure shelter of his elders. A resilient society, like wise parents, welcomes the homecoming and, in meeting this challenge to tradition, grows. This extensively observed ritual in human experience is useful for understanding the Vietnamese radical of the 1920s. He, too, left the home of his elders, intellectually and often physically, in search of political knowledge. But here the similarity ends. Instead of leaving on a capricious exploration, the Vietnamese radical de-

28. Nguyen van Pho, "Pour la suppression de la monarchie d'Annam: Proclamation au peuple," *Viet Nam hon* [Soul of Vietnam], January 1926.
29. Quoted in Tedral, *Comédie indochinoise,* pp. 22–23 [Ninh's italics(?)].
30. Daniel Bell, *The End of Ideology* (New York, 1961), especially chapter 13, "The Mood of Three Generations," pp. 299–314.

parted intent on a rescue mission. Unlike his counterparts else-where, he had no home to return to. His inheritance was a home destroyed and a soil desecrated by bandits. His memory was haunted by the shameful resignation of his elders to colonialism. The Vietnamese radical of the 1920s had to face tasks not borne by radicals elsewhere: he had to dislodge the bandits and construct a new home.

This challenge defined and distinguished the Vietnamese radi-calism of the 1920s. Vietnam's colonial experience and the conse-quent philosophic, social, and political dislocations differentiated its radicalism from that of stable, relatively uneventful societies.[31] When confronted with a serious crisis of values, those other societies, too, produce the untypical few who have the daring and energy to challenge conventional wisdoms and to articulate what is typical about their times. Depending on the circumstances, sometimes they succeed briefly in securing national support in their efforts to pose searching questions and propose fundamental changes. Once the crisis has passed, however, the radicals often find themselves overtaken by events and their efforts largely ignored by their own society. Few Americans today care to remember the minority of the 1930s who went into the workshops to organize the CIO, joined the International Brigade to fight Franco in Spain, or demonstrated against war. A similar fate, it seems, awaits the American radicals of the 1960s who marched on the Pentagon, blocked the troop trains, and played an important role in bringing American intervention in Vietnam to an end.

The radicalism of colonized Vietnam more closely resembled that of other societies subjected to foreign domination, such as China and Indonesia.[32] To the extent that they challenged the con-ventions and traditions of the conservative majority and proposed drastic reforms, they remained within the traditions of radicalism. Yet because of the special historical circumstances of their society, the Vietnamese radicals of the 1920s were not regarded as outcasts or misfits, but rather as pathfinders who defined the course and direction of the nation. The *nha cach mang* (respectable revolu-

31. See, for example, Jack Newfield, *A Prophetic Minority* (New York, 1967).
32. Chow Ts'e-tsung, *The May Fourth Movement: Intellectual Revolution in China* (Cambridge, Mass., 1960), especially pp. 92–120; and Hu Shih, *The Chinese Renaissance* (New York, 1963), especially pp. 44–62.

tionaries), as they were named by their contemporaries, were neither untypical in their longings nor unadmired by the majority. When Nguyen An Ninh was arrested in March 1925, shops were closed and workers went on strike in protest against the government. As the Dang Thanh Nien (Youth Party) organized Phan Chu Trinh's funeral, numerous old people rushed to its headquarters to request membership. In an address in October 1927 to the students on the S.S. *Chenonceaux,* en route to France as part of the massive student emigration, Ta Thu Thau included this reminder:

> We students must amass and conquer the education that they deny us in our country. . . . Do you know, my friends, that at each ship departure, some young Vietnamese who have neither relatives nor friends aboard abandon their work in order to be present at the pier? They inform themselves of the number of those leaving and their joy rises with the number of emigrants. . . . These compatriots who thus accompanied us at the departure represent for us Vietnam, and their hopes are those of the fatherland.[33]

For the next fifty years these "prodigal sons" set the tone and orientation of Vietnamese politics. Their appeals were listened to, their orders were taken seriously, and their actions had the support of the nation.

THE INTRODUCTION OF COMMUNISM INTO VIETNAM

Besides the emergence of a new generation of leaders, the arrival of communism was for Vietnam the most consequential event of the mid-1920s. This transplantation was facilitated by two separate historical processes: the quest of the Vietnamese for teachers and techniques for national liberation; and the evolution of a new orientation in the international working-class movement, which brought increasing attention to the problems of revolution in "the East."

From the perspective of Vietnamese history, the arrival of international communism was an incidental result of a long and conscious search for foreign assistance and training to overcome colonial rule. This quest had begun late in the nineteenth century, when

33. *La tribune indochinoise,* 23 December 1927.

some mandarins in the beleaguered Nguyen monarchy sought military aid from China in the hope of overcoming French aggression. It continued, following the capitulation of the court of Hue to the French, when anticolonial Confucian leaders appealed for help to the Japanese government and later to the Chinese Kuomintang, the Soviet delegation in Peking, and even the German legation in Bangkok—in other words, to anyone they believed capable of aiding Vietnam militarily to recover its sovereignty. Phan Boi Chau was a case in point. These literati, however, because of their commitment to Confucian values or their fear of losing sight of the principal objective in their struggle for independence, did not seek an alternative political ideology. This was the case of all such anticolonial movements, including the Can Vuong (Support the King), Dong Du (Eastern Travel), and Dong Kinh Nghia Thuc (Free School of Dong Kinh). As late as 1923 another anticolonial organization, the Tam Tam Xa (Heart-to-Heart Association), still followed a similar approach to anticolonial patriotism.

In the early decades of the twentieth century this quest assumed a new character. The search for teachers, techniques, and material assistance for decolonization became a search for new values and an institutional system that would not only help Vietnam regain its independence but also revitalize Vietnamese society. Following a reexamination of the *raison d'être* of the traditional order, not only were the Confucianist-derived monarchical institutions and its mandarinate discredited because of their collaboration and their failure to safeguard national independence; the Confucian value system itself was undergoing challenge. For young Vietnamese the Confucian traditional order was bankrupt and could no longer serve as a guide for future development; yet to acquiesce in the new order imposed by the French—as most Vietnamese eventually did—would mean the permanent loss of Vietnamese sovereignty. In this general disorientation and frustration, young Vietnamese who earlier would have prepared themselves for positions of leadership in the mandarinate were ready to accept a new anticolonial ideology, *any* anticolonial ideology that was unconnected with the past and the values of colonialism. This was the intellectual and political environment of the country when Marxism-Leninism was transplanted to Vietnam.

THE COMINTERN AND "THE EAST"

The new orientation in the international Marxist movement was also an important factor in the introduction of communism into Vietnam. Until the First World War, European Marxists had paid scant attention to the colonies. Most had believed that the world revolution would occur in Europe, where the conflict of classes was supposed to be most acute and where the proletariat was expected to become numerically superior to all other classes. The subjugated "backward" nations (the colonies) were viewed only as a capitalist hunting ground, marginal to the more interesting and important world, the world of the real agents of history. In the crisis of European socialism that followed the war and Russia's October Revolution, a reexamination of the prospects of capitalist development and the world revolution occurred within the international movement. For the first time, an important minority of socialists began looking to "the East" (the Comintern's designation for the colonial and semicolonial countries of Asia) for new forces capable of assuring victory on a world scale.

Lenin's own theories had a great influence on the evolution of this new orientation. His celebrated pamphlet, *Imperialism, the Highest Stage of Capitalism* (1916),[34] contained one of the earliest statements on the important role of the East in the world revolution. In it Lenin posited the important relation between the antiimperialist struggle for national liberation in the colonies and the overall struggle of the proletariat for liberation. Imperialism, in Lenin's view, gave birth to contrary tendencies. In the mother countries, colonial exploitation became the source of corruption of the proletariat, as the bourgeoisie, enriched by colonial profits, found it possible to encourage "opportunist" (that is, reformist) tendencies within the European working class, thereby "immunizing" workers from revolutionary actions. In the colonies, however, imperialism served to develop antiimperialist nationalist tendencies. Thus, the nationalist struggle in the colonies had to be considered an important part of the worldwide struggle against capitalism.

After the October Revolution Lenin moved increasingly closer

34. V. I. Lenin, *Selected Works*, 3 vols. (Moscow, 1967), 1:673–777.

to the conclusion that the destiny of the world revolution would depend, at least for a time, on revolutionary developments in the East, and tried to convince Europocentric leaders of the international Communist movement accordingly. Of the twenty-one conditions devised by Lenin for admission to the Communist International, which all Communist parties were bound to accept, one required that Communists support the emancipation of the oppressed nationalities and colonial peoples, and that they develop among their own workers fraternal feelings toward the workers of the colonial or oppressed nationalities subject to their own nation. Lenin's "Theses on the National and Colonial Questions,"[35] presented in July 1920 at the Second Congress of the Comintern, though maintaining the prevalent belief among European Communists that revolution would occur first in the West, envisaged an alternative possibility: that if the European revolution did not succeed quickly the Communist strategy would be to support the most radical elements among the colonial national bourgeoisie in the national liberation struggle.[36]

35. For the text, see Lenin, *The National Liberation Movements in the East* (1954; reprint ed., Moscow, 1974), pp. 264–271. Most accounts of the Second World Congress of the Comintern have emphasized the debate on tactics (to what extent Communists ought to collaborate with the national bourgeoisie in the East) and neglected the other, equally important issue at this congress, namely, the discussion of Communist strategy on a world scale. Although three basic positions were represented at the congress (Europocentrism, best represented by Serrati, who insisted on the orthodox position of the primacy of the European revolution; Asiocentrism, represented by M. N. Roy, who argued that the fate of the European revolution depended entirely on the revolution in Asia; and an intermediate position, propounded by Lenin, who saw a close relationship between the Asian and European revolutions), most Comintern leaders at the congress began to look to Asia as a source of new forces capable of assuring victory for the world revolution. The debate on the revolution in "the East" was to be one of the principal topics among Communist leaders in later Comintern congresses. At the Fifth Congress (1924), for example, Nguyen Ai Quoc (Ho Chi Minh) criticized and ridiculed the Europocentric Comintern leaders for their failure to understand the importance of the revolutionary movement in the colonies. For a fuller discussion see Hélène Carrère d'Encausse and Stuart R. Schram, *Marxism and Asia: An Introduction with Readings* (London, 1969), pp. 26–62.

36. Lenin stated at the Third World Congress of the Comintern: "It is perfectly clear that in the impending decisive battles in the world revolution, the movement of the majority of the population of the globe, initially directed towards national liberation, will turn against capitalism and imperialism and will, perhaps, play a much more revolutionary part than we expect. . . . And in spite of the fact that the masses of toilers—the peasants in the colonial countries—are still backward, they will play a very important revolutionary part in the coming phases of the world

These new developments in the European working-class movement led to concrete action in the colonies, making possible the transplantation of communism to Vietnam. In June 1921 the French Communist Party (PCF) fulfilled a Comintern requirement by establishing a *Comité d'études coloniales* within its Central Committee. However reluctant the majority of PCF members may have been to involve themselves with colonial affairs, this committee launched an energetic campaign to denounce colonial exploitation, arouse the French public to colonial malfeasance, and involve anticolonial natives in Communist-sponsored activities. In July the committee founded the Union intercoloniale, with Nguyen Ai Quoc as one of its executive committee members. Through *Le paria,* its organ, the Union intercoloniale made a concerted effort to propagate communism in the colonies. Thus, the reprinting of articles from *Le paria* in *Jeune Annam,* the clandestine circulation of the publication itself, and the formation in 1926–1927 of student circles in Vietnam to discuss Communist ideas were part of the initial step to transplant Marxism-Leninism to Vietnam.

NGUYEN AI QUOC (HO CHI MINH)

No single person played a more important role than Nguyen Ai Quoc in the introduction and adaptation of communism to Vietnam. A patriot and revolutionary, he devoted his entire life to a double cause: the recovery of Vietnamese independence and the creation of a new Vietnamese society. Under the alias Nguyen Ai Quoc (Nguyen Who Loves His Country) he presided over the liquidation of France's "civilizing mission" in Vietnam; then as President Ho Chi Minh (Ho the Most Enlightened), he assumed ultimate responsibility for the construction of Vietnam's new social order. When in 1969 death deprived him of the satisfaction of seeing his country liberated from foreign domination, the ideals that he had lived for had already become a legacy for many Vietnamese. The father of Vietnamese communism, Nguyen Ai Quoc grafted Leninist ideology and Bolshevik revolutionary methods onto the youth-

revolution." V. I. Lenin, "Report on the Tactics of the Russian Communist Party to the Third Congress of the Communist International," in *National Liberation Movements in the East,* pp. 304–305; see also Fernando Claudin, *The Communist Movement: From Comintern to Cominform,* 2 vols. (New York, 1975), 1:63–71.

ful patriotic movement of the 1920s. In 1925 for all practical purposes he single-handedly created the Vietnamese Communist movement. In 1930, after this movement had been riven by internal factionalism, he helped restore unity and founded the first unified Communist party. In 1941, after the Indochinese Communist party had been shattered for a second time by ferocious colonial repression, it was he again who refashioned a new movement out of the debris of the old and led it to a successful seizure of power in the August Revolution. From 1945 until his death he stood at the helm, pursuing his mission of fusing proletarian internationalism with Vietnamese patriotism.

According to official accounts, Nguyen Ai Quoc was born 19 May 1890 to a prominent anticolonial family.[37] His father, Nguyen Sinh Huy, was a doctoral laureate *(pho bang)* who had rejected an official mandarin post as secretary to the ministry of rites in the court of Hue and was considered somewhat of a troublemaker by colonial authorities. Both his older sister, Nguyen thi Thanh (1884–1954), and older brother, Nguyen Sinh Khiem (1888–1950), had had

37. No one is quite sure of Nguyen Ai Quoc's year of birth, to say nothing of his birthdate. In one report, the French secret police indicated that Nguyen Ai Quoc was born on 24 January 1892; in another, that he was born in 1894. In Nguyen Ai Quoc's first visa to the USSR, issued 16 June 1923, his birthdate was given as 15 January 1895 (*Nhan dan,* 3 May 1980, with photo). I suspect that the date 19 May is used to coincide with the anniversary of the formation of the Viet Minh Front (see Huynh Kim Khanh, "The Vietnamese August Revolution Reinterpreted," *Journal of Asian Studies* 30 [August 1971]: 773, n. 56). We are equally at a loss as to the exact number of aliases and literary pseudonyms Nguyen Ai Quoc used during his lifetime. He was born Nguyen Sinh Cung and at age eleven was given another name, Nguyen Tat Thanh. The Soviet film *He Is Ho Chi Minh* claims that he assumed nineteen different names during his revolutionary career (Vuong, Ly Thuy, Song Man-cho, Line, etc.). My own count reveals thirty-two aliases. Historians in Hanoi, however, claim to have discovered seventy-six. (See, for example, Mau Ung, "Ho Chi Minh, ten nguoi tren nhung chang duong lich su cuu nuoc" [Ho Chi Minh, his names in the stages on the road to national liberation], *NCLS,* no. 156 (May–June 1974), pp. 11–18; and The Tap and Thanh Nam, "Ten cua chu tich Ho Chi Minh va cuoc hanh trinh vi dai cua Nguoi" [The names of President Ho Chi Minh and His great odyssey], *Tap chi cong san* [Review of communism], May 1980, pp. 77–85). A recent article in *Nhan dan* [The people], central organ of the Vietnamese Communist party, "Bac Ho viet bao Nhan Dan" [Uncle Ho wrote for *Nhan dan*] (17 May 1980), reports that Ho Chi Minh wrote 1,205 articles in *Nhan dan* from 1951 to 1969 under twenty-three different pseudonyms. In this study I use only two names: Nguyen Ai Quoc and Ho Chi Minh. The first is dominant, for he and his comrades used it throughout the period 1920–1945; the second name became his public identity as of the August Revolution of 1945.

trouble with the law because of their anticolonial activities. His birthplace, the Nghe Tinh region (an abbreviation for the two neighboring provinces of Nghe An and Ha Tinh), was known for its patriotic traditions. These Trung Ky provinces were famous for the quantity and high quality of their heroes and talented individuals. Mai Hac De and Nguyen Hue, two of Vietnam's illustrious kings and military leaders, came from this region, as did some of Vietnam's most respected literary figures, including Nguyen Du, Nguyen Cong Tru, and Ho Xuan Huong. In the long history of Vietnamese resistance to French rule, Nghe Tinh was the source of most of the anticolonial movements and their leaders, including the *van than* (literati) movement of the 1870s and the Can Vuong (Support the King) movement of the 1890s. In 1930–1931 this region was to be the center of Communist agitation.

Nguyen Ai Quoc had had patriotic ambitions from an early age. He told the Soviet poet Mandelstam in 1923, "Around the age of thirteen, I learned of the French phrases: liberty, equality, and fraternity for the first time. . . . Then I wanted to know the French civilization, to see what was hidden behind those phrases."[38] By the age of fifteen he was reportedly working as liaison agent for the anticolonial scholars. In December 1911 young "Teacher Thanh" left Vietnam for France, earning his way by working as a cabin boy on the S.S. *Latouche-Treville*. Prior to departure he reportedly told a close friend, "I want to go abroad, to visit France and other countries. Once I have seen how they did it, I will come back to help our compatriots."[39] Nguyen Ai Quoc's patriotism and his determined search for teachers and techniques to help his country was not unique among Vietnamese of the time. A contemporary slogan of Vietnamese youth illustrates how common this aspiration was: "Go abroad to study to come home to help the country" *(Xuat duong du hoc ve nha giup nuoc)*. What made Nguyen Ai Quoc's journey special was his discovery of Marxism-Leninism and his indomitable will to put the newly discovered revolutionary theory at the service of his compatriots.

38. Mandelstam, "Visiting a Militant of International Communism—Nguyen Ai Quoc," *Iskra* [The spark], no. 39 (23 December 1923); cited in Commission for the Study of the History of the Party, *Chu tich Ho Chi Minh* [President Ho Chi Minh] (Hanoi, 1970), p. 12.
39. Nguyen Khanh Toan et al., *Avec l'Oncle Ho* (Hanoi, 1972), p. 16.

Two important steps in Nguyen Ai Quoc's political education led directly to the introduction of communism into Vietnam. The first was his disillusionment with reformism and Wilsonian idealism. Having discovered that whereas "the French in the colonies are cruel and inhuman," the French at home were good people,[40] Nguyen had placed great trust in the French wartime promises of postwar political liberalization and in the Wilsonian principles of national self-determination. His moderate political proposals at the Paris Peace Conference in 1919, the *Revendications du peuple annamite*, which turned him into a national hero overnight, were a result of that trust. His failure to obtain a hearing at the conference taught him that political freedom is something that must result not from pleas, but from a determined struggle. Versailles radicalized Nguyen Ai Quoc. Before the conference he had the illusion that political liberalization was possible within the framework of the colonial system. In the aftermath, he drew several important conclusions: first, no promises of the colonialists ought to be taken at face value; second, no compromises were possible between the colonizers and the colonized; third, just as colonization had been a violent act, decolonization, too, could be achieved only through political violence; and finally, in their efforts to liberate their countries, the colonized peoples could count only on their own forces. In August 1921 he summarized these lessons in the manifesto of the Union intercoloniale and added, "Applying the formula of Karl Marx, we say to you that your liberation can come only by your own efforts."[41]

Nguyen Ai Quoc's second important step was adherence to the Third International. He discovered Marxism-Leninism during a time of crisis in the international working-class movement. Social democracy, it was clear, had failed and a debate was raging in left-wing French circles about whether to remain with the Second International or join the Comintern, or Third International, recently founded by Lenin (1919). At the Tours Congress in December 1920 Nguyen voted with the majority of the French Socialist party to

---

40. Ibid., p. 25.
41. "Manifeste de l'Union intercoloniale, Association des indigènes de toutes les colonies," in Ho Chi Minh, *Oeuvres choisies,* 4 vols. (Hanoi, 1960), 1:340. I have used the French version of Ho Chi Minh's *Selected Works* for greater linguistic accuracy.

join the Third International, not because of any of the ideological issues involved or because he understood much about the difference between social democracy and communism, but because he knew at that time that

> the Third International is paying considerable attention to the colonial problem. It has promised to help the oppressed peoples to recover their freedom and independence while the Second International has not even mentioned the fate of the colonies. That is why I voted for the Third International.[42]

Forty years later, in 1960, Nguyen Ai Quoc gave a similar explanation for having become a Communist: "I supported the October Revolution only instinctively, not yet grasping all its historic importance. I loved and admired Lenin because he was a great patriot who liberated his compatriots; until then, I had read none of his books."[43]

From the moment he accepted proletarian internationalism, a peculiar mixture of political ideas coexisted within Nguyen Ai Quoc's concept of revolution. This concept embraced both ardent patriotism and devotion to the cause of internationalism. Nguyen Ai Quoc's understanding of proletarian internationalism, even at this stage, was much broader than that of most Eurocentric Marxists. To him, international meant the entire world, not just Europe; and by proletariat, he understood "propertyless," which meant more than industrial workers only. He favored the direct intervention of the international Communist movement in the national liberation movement of "the East" and collaboration between the proletariat of Europe and the national liberationists of the colonies. At the same time, he maintained that every effort must be made to adapt communism creatively to local conditions. As Nguyen saw it, it might be necessary to forgo dogma, and even terms such as *bolshevism* and *communism,* because education, training, and raising the level of political consciousness in the colonies were prerequisites to introducing communism. In an article in *L'humanité* in 1922, Nguyen Ai Quoc stated this view quite bluntly:

> In all the colonized countries, in old Indochina as well as in young Dahomey, no one understands what a class struggle, a proletarian

42. Quoted in Tran Dan Tien, *Glimpses of the Life of Ho Chi Minh* (Hanoi, 1958), pp. 22–23.
43. Ho Chi Minh, *Ecrits (1920–1969)* (Hanoi, 1971), p. 257.

force, . . . a workers' organization, is. In the eyes of the natives, bolshevism . . . signifies either the destruction of everything, or emancipation from the foreign yoke. The first meaning given to this term pushes the ignorant and fearful masses away from us; the second leads them to nationalism. One is just as dangerous as the other.[44]

Disabused of his hope for reform within the colonial framework and buttressed by his adherence to the Third International, Nguyen Ai Quoc now stood ready to transplant communism to Vietnam. Among the obstacles he faced, however, were the ignorance and indifference of the European proletariat and the lackadaisical attitudes of international Communist leaders toward the colonial question, Leninism notwithstanding. In 1922, two years after the founding of the PCF and one year after the creation of the PCF's Section coloniale, Nguyen Ai Quoc found it necessary to chastise the French proletariat for lack of interest in the fate of its colonial counterpart. In *L'humanité* he wrote:

In his theses on the colonial question, Lenin clearly declared that it is incumbent upon the workers in the colonizing countries to give the most active assistance to the liberation movements in the colonies. In order to do so, the worker in the *métropole* must know well what a colony is and must keep abreast of what goes on there, of the suffering—a thousand times sadder than his own—that his brothers, the proletarians of the colonies must endure. . . .

Unfortunately, there are still many militants who believe that a colony is nothing more than a country full of sands below and sunshine above, a few green coconut trees and a few men of color, that's all. And they are completely uninterested.[45]

At the Fifth Congress of the Comintern in 1924 he emphasized to Europocentric Communist leaders the importance of the revolution in the colonies. In his report on the national and colonial questions Nguyen Ai Quoc made an urgent appeal:

In all the French colonies, discontent mounts hand in hand with misery and famine. The uprising of the colonial peasants is imminent. They have already risen up in many colonies, but their revolts have been drowned in blood each time. If at the moment they appear to resign themselves, it is uniquely because of a lack of organization and leaders. The Communist International must work to bring them

44. Idem, *Oeuvres choisies*, 1:13.
45. *L'humanité*, 25 May 1922.

together, provide them with leading cadres, and guide them on the road to revolution and liberation.[46]

During the proceedings, at a point totally unrelated to the colonial question, Nguyen Ai Quoc interrupted the congress with a reproach against Europocentrism:

> I cannot help but observe that the speeches made by the comrades from the mother countries give me the impression that they wish to kill the snake by stepping on its tail. You all know that today the poison and life energy of the capitalist snake is concentrated more in the colonies than in the mother countries. . . . Yet in your discussion of the revolution you neglect to talk about the colonies. . . . Why do you neglect the colonies, while capitalism uses them to support itself, defend itself, and fight you?[47]

In December 1924, half a year after the Fifth Congress, Nguyen Ai Quoc had his opportunity to graft a scion of proletarian internationalism onto Vietnamese patriotism. The product of this graft was the protocommunist group known as Thanh Nien.

THANH NIEN AND THE GRAFTING OF LENINISM

The Viet Nam Thanh Nien Kach Menh Hoi (Vietnamese Revolutionary Youth Association), or Thanh Nien (Youth)[48] for

46. Nguyen Ai Quoc, "Intervention sur la question nationale et la question coloniale au cinquième congrès de l'Internationale communiste," in *Oeuvres choisies,* 1:192.

47. Nguyen Ai Quoc, "The Struggle against Capitalism Lies in the Colonies," in *Protokoll Fuenfter Kongress der Kommunistischen Internationale,* reprinted in Helmut Gruber, *Soviet Russia Masters the Comintern: International Communism in the Era of Stalin's Ascendancy* (New York, 1974), p. 809.

48. Some problems associated with Thanh Nien's formal name require explanations. Most histories published in Vietnam today erroneously refer to this organization as Viet Nam Thanh Nien Kach Menh Dong Chi Hoi (Association of Comrades of Vietnamese Revolutionary Youth). According to the resolutions of the First National Congress of Thanh Nien, held in Hong Kong 1–9 May 1929 ("Resolution on the Subject of the Name of the Association"), before the congress there had been two names for the organization. One was secret and known only among association members: Hoi Viet Nam Cach Menh Dong Chi (Association of Vietnamese Revolutionary Comrades); the other was public: Hoi Viet Nam Cach Menh Thanh Nien (Association of Vietnamese Revolutionary Youth). The congress decided to retain only the organization's publicly known name. (See "Manifesto and Resolutions of the First National Congress of Thanh Nien," in Gouvernement

short, was founded by Nguyen Ai Quoc in the spring of 1925. Typical of Vietnamese revolutionary patriotism of the 1920s, this organization represented both a continuity in and disruption of Vietnam's patriotic traditions. Thanh Nien was a new type of anticolonial organization in that it attempted to unite political with social issues. Earlier patriotic movements had been liberal and exclusively political: their sole object had been freedom from foreign domination, and their political aims had been based on some form of parliamentary liberalism and representative government. None of the previous movements had had a definite social or economic objective for their postindependence programs, assuming they had any. Thanh Nien, however, postulated a new Vietnamese society on the basis of a double revolution, both political ("national independence") and social ("land to the tiller"). From 1925, the cadres, policies, and metamorphoses of Thanh Nien largely determined the course of the Vietnamese revolution. Thanh Nien was the beginning of Vietnamese communism.[49]

Thanh Nien began with Nguyen Ai Quoc's conversion of Tam Tam Xa (Heart-to-Heart Association), an anticolonial organization of Vietnamese residing in southern China, to communism.

Général de l'Indochine, Direction des Affaires politiques et de Sûreté française, *Contribution à l'histoire des mouvements politiques de l'Indochine française,* 5 vols. (Hanoi, 1930–35), vol. 4, supp. 2, p. 68. Also, even among Thanh Nien's documents the organization was sometimes called Hoi Viet Nam Thanh Nien Cach Menh; more often, however, it was Viet Nam Thanh Nien Cach Menh Hoi. This liberal interchange of Vietnamese and Chinese syntaxes was characteristic during the 1920s. Furthermore, the Vietnamese term for revolution in Thanh Nien's documents was spelled variously *cach menh* or *cach mang,* reflecting the regional composition of the organization's membership: northern and southern Vietnamese pronounced the term *cach mang,* whereas central Vietnamese used *cach menh.* Finally, the use of *k* in spelling *kach mang* or *kach menh* deserves notice. This was part of Nguyen Ai Quoc's attempt to simplify the Vietnamese alphabet and render it phonetically logical. When used immediately before vowels, *k* replaces *c, f* replaces *ph, z* replaces *d* or *gi,* etc. These proposed changes were introduced in the early issues of *Thanh nien.* Vietnamese Communists who began their revolutionary career prior to the August Revolution still tend to use this orthography.

49. Today 3 February 1930 is commemorated as the official birthdate of Vietnamese communism, although in fact it was only an important turning point in the history of the Communist movement. On that date the three discordant, rival Communist groups were unified into one revolutionary organization, the Vietnamese Communist party (Dang Cong San Viet Nam). By this time, however, Communist revolutionary theory and techniques had become well-established factors in the Vietnamese anticolonial movement.

Founded in 1923 by a group of seven quasi-intellectuals (mostly elementary-school teachers from the Nghe Tinh region) who had gone to China in search of teachers and techniques to fight the French, this organization differed little from earlier Vietnamese anticolonial groups.[50] Though appearing to favor socialism, it had neither a clear ideological orientation nor a political strategy nor a program of action. The ninth bylaw of Tam Tam Xa stated its objectives as follows:

> Aspirations of the Corps: This period is the initial step of the Corps, as it looks for means to restore the human rights of the Vietnamese people. As to the future political regime, this problem will be decided in the future by all members [of the Corps] and ratified by the majority of the people. Such decisions would be made so as to conform with the international situation and the special circumstances of our country at that time.[51]

50. No one seems to know for certain why this organization was called Tam Tam Xa. A recently recovered Comintern document indicates that it was officially known as Tan Viet Thanh Nien Doan (Youth Corps for a New Vietnam) (see Trung Chinh, "Tam Tam Xa' la gi?" [What was "Tam Tam Xa"] *NCLS,* no. 134 [September–October 1970], pp. 5–6.) Ton Quang Phiet, a revolutionary activist in the 1920s, thinks the name was inspired by a Chinese radical leftist group called Tam Xa (Heart Association), organized by a Luu Su Phuc. Phan Boi Chau reportedly considered this man an "extreme socialist who organized Tam Xa in order to bring about communism; Ton Quang Phiet, *Phan Boi Chau va mot giai doan lich su chong Phap cua nhan dan Viet Nam* [Phan Boi Chau and a period in the history of the anti-French resistance of the Vietnamese people] (Hanoi, 1954), p. 208, n. 1. The seven founders of Tam Tam Xa were: Le Hong Son, alias Le van Phan; Ho Ba Cu, alias Ho Tung Mau; Nguyen Giang Khanh; Dang Xuan Hong; Truong Quoc Huy; Le Cau, alias Tong Giao Cau; and Nguyen Cong Vien, alias Lam Duc Thu. Early in 1924 Tam Tam Xa's membership was enlarged by the addition of two historic figures, Pham Hong Thai and Le Hong Phong. In June 1924 Thai attempted to assassinate Governor-General Merlin. This mission was aborted, and Thai drowned while fleeing from the police. Today, his aborted attempt is often considered the beginning of the anticolonial movement of the 1920s. Le Hong Phong became an important figure in the Vietnamese Communist movement. As a member of Thanh Nien he was admitted to the Whampoa Military Academy in Canton and was later sent to study military aviation in the USSR. During the early 1930s he was in effect the most important leader of the ICP, as head of the Overseas Leadership Committee. In 1936 he was made representative of the Comintern with the ICP. He died on Poulo Condore prison islands in September 1942. Three of the original members of Tam Tam Xa were to play important roles in the vicissitudes of the Vietnamese Communist movement. Le Hong Son (Le van Phan) and Ho Tung Mau (Ho Ba Cu) became members of the Communist Youth Corps in 1925 and guided Thanh Nien duing the late 1920s. Lam Duc Thu (Nguyen Cong Vien) became the most effective agent for the French police within Thanh Nien.

51. See "Dieu Le" [Bylaws] of Tam Tam Xa, Central Party Archives (Hanoi), vol. 5, carton 1, translated from the original version in Chinese in Trung Chinh "Tam Tam Xa la gi?" pp. 5–6.

Little else is known about Tam Tam Xa. Aside from the regulations quoted above and the obvious patriotic zeal of its members, there is no concrete evidence that the organization understood the problems of making a revolution, even though its members reportedly received Communist documents from Soviet advisers in China and discussed Communist theories. Like earlier Vietnamese anticolonial organizations, Tam Tam Xa accepted political violence as part of its *modus operandi*. Its best-known action was the attempt by Pham Hong Thai, one of its members, to assassinate Indochina's Governor-General Merlin, already discussed. When, in December 1924, Nguyen Ai Quoc arrived in Canton from Moscow, ostensibly to work as secretary-interpreter in the Soviet mission led by Michael Borodin, he spoke highly of the patriotic ardor of the members of the existing anticolonial organizations in southern China, particularly Tam Tam Xa, but disparaged their political knowledge and methods of organization. His first report to the Executive Committee of the Communist International (ECCI) stated that these organizations "know nothing about politics, and much less about organizing the masses."[52]

Early in 1925 Tam Tam Xa was reconstructed. Its most trustworthy members were organized into a secret group, the Communist Youth Corps (CYC), or in Vietnamese, Thanh Nien Cong San Doan; others were absorbed into an overt, mass-oriented organization, Thanh Nien. In a report to the Comintern dated 12 February 1925, Nguyen Ai Quoc wrote:

> At the moment I am not a Vietnamese, but a Chinese. Also my name is Ly Thuy and not Nguyen Ai Quoc. . . . We have established a secret group of nine members, two of whom have been sent to the home country, three went to the front (in the Sun Yat-sen Army), and one has a military mission (helping the Chinese Kuomintang). Five among them are now being prepared to be recommended for admission to the Communist party. We have had two who have been admitted to the Komsomol Communist Youth Corps.[53]

From 1925 until the end of 1927 the headquarters of Thanh Nien in Canton was the source of most of the Vietnamese revolutionary

52. Nguyen Ai Quoc to the Executive Committee of the Communist International, 19 December 1924, quoted in Committee for Study, *Chu tich Ho Chi Minh*, p. 32.

53. Trung Chinh, "Thu tim xem Ho Chu tich tiep thu chu nghia Le-nin va truyen ba vao Viet Nam nhu the nao?" [How did President Ho receive Leninism and propagate it in Vietnam?], *NCLS*, no. 132 (May–June 1970), pp. 5–21.

activities in southern China, Siam, and at home. Established at 13 Wang Ming Street, Thanh Nien's headquarters served many functions. The center was, first of all, a meeting place of revolutionaries. Directly supervised by Nguyen Ai Quoc, it received Vietnamese revolutionaries from the interior and from Siam, Chinese Communist Party (CCP) cadres, and sometimes Comintern agents. The center also doubled as a school to train Vietnamese activists in revolutionary theories and practices. In the years 1925–1927 approximately three hundred revolutionaries participated in the Thanh Nien training program.[54] The headquarters also published pamphlets and periodicals on various political subjects. In addition to pamphlets such as *Duong kach menh* [The road to revolution], a handbook of revolutionary theory and techniques for Thanh Nien members, four periodicals appeared regularly:[55] 208 issues of the weekly *Thanh nien* [Youth], from 21 June 1925 until May 1930; the weekly *Bao cong nong* [Worker-Peasant] from December 1926 until early 1928; the biweekly *Linh kach menh* [Revolutionary soldier] from early 1927 until early 1928; and 4 issues of the monthly *Viet Nam tien phong* [Vanguard of Vietnam], in 1927. Finally, Thanh Nien headquarters was the center for underground activities in the home country. All important decisions were made in Canton, and major changes in political tactics in Vietnam had to be referred to Canton for approval. Canton headquarters was also the supreme disciplinary tribunal.

54. For various discussions of the training activities at Thanh Nien headquarters, read Pham van Dong and Commission for the Study of the History of the Vietnam Workers' Party, *President Ho Chi Minh* (Hanoi, 1960), pp. 12–13; Le Manh Trinh, "Nhung ngay o Quang Chau va Xiem" [The days in Canton and Siam], in Le. Manh Trinh et al., *Bac Ho* [Uncle Ho] (Hanoi, 1960), pp. 91–96, and Governement général, 4:15–18.

55. Students of Vietnamese communism, including those in Hanoi, have generally failed to recognize the extent of Thanh Nien's publication program. Vietnamese authors such as Vu Tho and Trung Chinh have contributed substantially to the understanding of the early periods of Vietnamese communism, but for some reason have failed to note the existence of periodicals contemporary with *Thanh nien*, such as *Linh kach menh, Bao cong nong,* and *Viet Nam tien phong*. Western students of Vietnamese communism have tended to repeat and misinterpret Louis Marty's report in Government général, *Contribution*, vol. 4, about *Thanh nien*. Marty reported that eighty-eight issues of *Thanh nien* were published between June 1925 and April 1927 (p. 17). This led some Western writers to conclude that there were in fact only eighty-eight issues (see, for example, Duiker, *Rise of Nationalism in Vietnam*, p. 205). With the exception of a very few issues, AOM has the entire collection of *Thanh nien* (SLOTFOM, vol. 5, carton 16) and a substantial number of issues of *Linh kach menh* and *Bao cong nong*.

REVOLUTIONARY THEORY AND STRATEGY

One of the features that distinguished Thanh Nien from all earlier anticolonial organizations was its emphasis on the importance of a revolutionary theory. Like Lenin, Nguyen Ai Quoc assigned "political consciousness" an extremely important place in a revolutionary movement. He accepted Lenin's dictum that "without a revolutionary theory, there can be no revolutionary movement"[56] and attributed the failure of all the earlier anticolonial organizations in part to their lack of a coherent theoretical perspective. In *Duong kach menh* [The road to revolution] he contended that their "dismal failures" were due not to lack of patriotism or heroism, but to lack of a revolutionary theory: "They all failed because they did not have an ideology, or a plan of action."[57] In *Thanh nien* he contended that a "profound understanding" of theory was indispensable to successful action.

> It is thus indispensable that [revolutionaries] act only after having studied revolutionary doctrines in depth. To act without having a profound understanding of these doctrines, without having examined critically the contents of these doctrines, is to court disaster, to lose one's time and forces, and even to risk one's life unnecessarily. . . . The person who joins a revolutionary party without studying carefully the doctrines of his party resembles a blind man who is abandoned in a street of a big city: he collides with all sorts of obstacles, stumbles, falls down, and even risks being killed. The Vietnamese revolutionaries until today have acted like blind men. They have shed blood for nothing, because they have not studied revolutionary tactics. Their repeated failures have chilled the patriotic sentiments of our people and made them a laughingstock in the eyes of our enemies.[58]

Revolutionary theory had practical relevance for Thanh Nien and for the various Communist organizations into which it

---

56. V. I. Lenin, "What Is to Be Done?" in *Selected Works*, 1:117.

57. Nguyen Ai Quoc, *Duong kach menh* [The road to revolution], a pamphlet published anonymously by A chau Bi Ap buc Dan toc Lien hiep Hoi (League of the Oppressed Peoples of Asia) (n.p., 1926) (hereafter cited as *DKM*). This pamphlet is reprinted in Vu bien soan, Ban tuyen huan trung uong (Editorial section, Central committee for propaganda and education), *Lich su Dang Cong san Viet Nam: Trich van kien Dang* [History of the Vietnamese Communist party: Extracts from Party documents], 3 vols. (Hanoi, 1979), 1:7–16 (hereafter cited as *Van kien Dang*). Vu bien soan, *Van kien Dang*, pp. 7–16. For a recent analytical review of *DKM* see Le Thi, "May van de phuong phap luan cua tac pham 'Duong Kach Menh' cua Ho Chu tich" [On some methodological issues of *Duong kach menh* by Presi-

evolved. Unlike earlier anticolonial organizations, which had depended on sentimental ties and well-known leaders for organizational coherence and continuity, Thanh Nien was, or at least endeavored to be, a movement informed, coordinated, and united by a common theoretical perspective. It would be an exaggeration to say that Thanh Nien went far beyond what Karl Mannheim called "groups of precapitalist origin," which were held together by communal ties, traditions, and sentimental attachments.[59] It would also be an exaggeration to say that Thanh Nien had a self-contained, internally coherent ideological system. It is true, however, that the organization's possession of a more or less consistent revolutionary theory was an important departure from Vietnamese anticolonial traditions. Sentimental ties, Mannheim explained, "are effective only within a limited spatial area, while a theoretical *Weltanschauung* has a unifying power over great distance."[60] Thanh Nien's revolutionary theory was a glue providing coherence in the organization of people of various backgrounds divided by particularistic differences such as geography, traditions, and ethnicity.

There were two practical consequences of Thanh Nien's possession of a revolutionary theory. First, compared with previous anticolonial groups, Thanh Nien had a much wider radius of action. Pre-1925 groups had usually concentrated their activities in one or a few specific localities or had limited their influence to a small circle of people. Their range of activity extended as far as the sentimental ties or personal prestige of specific leaders. In contrast, Thanh Nien's activities covered all three regions of Vietnam and spread among Vietnamese abroad, in Siam, and in southern China. Second, the fact that Thanh Nien depended on a theoretical perspective, not on the personal fortunes of any leader, accounted for its continued existence despite severe repression. Before 1925, anticolonial organizations had been closely identified with one man or group of men. In such circumstances, the removal or political incapacitation of the organization's leadership would (and did) bring about its rapid demise. This was not the case with Thanh Nien. Although it was well known at the time that Nguyen Ai Quoc

dent Ho], *Triet hoc* [Philosophy], no. 28 (March 1980), pp. 22–45.
58. *Thanh nien*, 7 August 1927; SLOTFOM, vol. 5, carton 16.
59. Karl Mannheim, *Ideology and Utopia* (New York, 1963), p. 131.
60. Ibid.

had founded Thanh Nien and his high personal prestige attracted a following, the organization was never tied to his personal fortunes. Thanh Nien and, later, the ICP continued to function (though not too well) despite vicissitudes in the personal careers of Nguyen Ai Quoc and other Communist leaders. Another distinguishing feature of Thanh Nien was its possession of a specific revolutionary strategy. Thanh Nien's preparations for revolution followed Nguyen Ai Quoc's program of action. Designed for an eventual armed insurrection leading to the overthrow of French colonial rule and the establishment of revolutionary power, this program envisaged a three-phase strategy that can be summarized as follows.[61]

Phase One. During the so-called organizatonal phase agitation was to be carried out clandestinely in order to attract anticolonial elements to the revolutionary cause and, when possible, to organize them into revolutionary cells. This initial phase involved the following activities:[62]

OUTSIDE THE HOMELAND:

a. Establish a training center for émigré cadres from the home country;
b. Prepare written propaganda and assure the regular publication of the Party journal, or organ;
c. Create and maintain a liaison network between Vietnam and Communist and other sympathetic revolutionary organizations abroad;
d. Keep all members within Communist orthodoxy and assure discipline within the organization by making the Central Bureau *(Tong Bo)* the supreme tribunal;

---

61. The details of this three-phase revolutionary action program are contained in the lengthy (eighty-five-page) confession *(déclaration)*, extracted under police interrogation, of Nguyen Dinh Tu, one of Thanh Nien's earliest members in Trung Ky. See "Déclarations dernières de Nguyen Dinh Tu, dit provisoirement Pham van Cam, dit Van Cam, sur sa vie depuis juin 1925 jusqu'à son arrestation en date du 5 août 1929 à Ha Tinh," AOM, carton 355, dossier 2690. I am grateful to Martin Bernal for having provided me with a photocopy of this valuable document. Two other contemporary political parties, Tan Viet and VNQDD, later adopted this strategy.
62. This summary appears in Gouvernement général, *Contribution,* 4:18.

PHOTOGRAPHS OF ICP LEADERS

Nguyen Ai Quoc (1890–1969), in USSR ca. 1923; founder of the Communist movement in Vietnam.

Ho Tung Mau (1896–1951), ca. 1928; leader of Thanh Nien, 1925–1929.

Nguyen Duc Canh (1908–1932), ca. 1928; founder of the ICP.

Le Hong Son (1899–1932), ca. 1928; leader of Thanh Nien, 1925–1929.

Le Hong Phong (1902–1942), ca. 1930; Comintern representative with the ICP.

Ngo Gia Tu (1908–1935), ca. 1930; founder of the ICP.

Tran Phu (1904–1931), ca. 1930; ICP secretary general, 1930–1931.

Vo Nguyen Giap (1910–   ), 1933, student in Hanoi; organizer of the Viet Minh guerrilla force. Photograph from Gerard Le Quang, *Giap, ou la guerre du peuple* (Paris: Denoël, n.d.).

Truong Chinh (1907–   ), ca. 1951; ICP
secretary general, 1941–1951.

Pham van Dong (1906–   ), ca. 1951;
organizer of the Viet Minh Front.

Vo Nguyen Giap and Nguyen Ai Quoc with a group of OSS officers in Kunming (China)
in June 1945. Photograph from "Notre guerre d'Indochine," I: "Le Piège" (1945–1951),
Historia, Hors serie, 24, p. 31.

e. Send the young cadres trained in Canton back to the interior to create revolutionary cells.

WITHIN THE HOMELAND:

a. Create numerous revolutionary cells. Each new recruit must in principle become the first element of a new cell;
b. Organize the sections already specified in the statutes of the Party in order to found a homogeneous and well-disciplined Party.

Phase Two. During the so-called agitational or semisecret phase, the revolutionary organizations, having a sufficient number of militants, would initiate political, economic, and sometimes terrorist activities. Workers' strikes, student boycotts of classes, and market strikes were to accompany some bomb throwings, when necessary, in order to excite the masses.

Phase Three. During the insurrectionary phase the revolutionary organization, with cadres in all regions of Indochina and in all social strata, would initiate activities designed to overthrow the government and to organize revolutionary power. The insurrectionary phase was to achieve three successive tasks: first, overthrow the colonial regime and establish a new government; second, disseminate propaganda among segments of the population that remained unaffiliated with revolutionary activities and initiate the masses to revolutionary activities; and finally, reorganize society, including reforms of the educational system, legal system, and the armed forces, according to revolutionary principles.

The training of political activists in revolutionary theories and agitational techniques was another important Thanh Nien activity. To implement the first phase of Nguyen Ai Quoc's action program, the Central Bureau of Thanh Nien created a center at its headquarters in Canton to train cadres.[63] Young activists from Vietnam, mostly students, received intensive training in revolutionary theory and techniques. These short-term, total-immersion courses

63. See Pham van Dong and Commission, *President Ho Chi Minh*, pp. 12–13; and Le Manh Trinh in *Bac Ho*, pp. 91–96.

emphasized propaganda and organizational techniques. The courses had no definite duration: some lasted three weeks, others two months. Some lasted as long as four months, but never longer, for fear of arousing suspicion at home toward those who were absent for too long a period. At the training sessions Nguyen Ai Quoc himself was the principal lecturer. Ho Tung Mau and Le Hong Son were assistant lecturers. After a time, high-echelon CCP cadres also took part in the political education of Thanh Nien trainees. Most of those attending the training sessions ranged in age from seventeen to approximately twenty-five. With the completion of their political education, trainees were taken to the tomb of Pham Hong Thai, where, following a secret-society type of rite and an oath taking, they were admitted to Thanh Nien membership.

The revolutionary theory curriculum included a historical survey of the evolution of human society, with emphasis on the era of capitalism and imperialism; an examination of the history of Western imperialism and the movements of national liberation in Korea, China, and Vietnam; and a critical study of Gandhism, Sun Yat-sen's *Three Principles of the People,* and Marxism-Leninism. Trainees also received instruction on the October Revolution and the history and organizations of the First, Second, and Third Internationals, the Democratic Federation of Women, the Democratic Federation of Youth, the Red Aid International, and the Peasant International. According to an archival document of Thanh Nien, the theoretical part of the curriculum included the following items:[64]

Theory of communism
The ideology of the *Three Principles of the People* (with critique)
Anarchism (with critique)
Party organizational forms, workers' associations, and women's
    liberation associations
Secret operations
Forms of propaganda and agitation
Current events

64. Quoted in Vu Tho, "Qua trinh thanh lap dang vo-san o Viet Nam da duoc dien ra nhu the nao?" [What happened in the process of formation of the proletarian party in Vietnam?], *NCLS*, no. 71 (February 1965), p. 19.

History of the French occupation of Indochina and revolutionary mobilization

The final part of the training program dealt exclusively with the practical aspects of revolutionary activities—mobilizing the workers, organizing workers' unions, and mobilizing and organizing peasants and youths. Trainees were grounded in techniques of public speaking and of preparing propaganda articles, following a situational approach. In the practice sessions in public speaking, for example, student speakers were often confronted by "hecklers" among the listening trainees who would then help the speakers improve the quality of their presentations. Articles prepared by students were also submitted to class discussion for criticism. Additionally, at weekly review sessions each trainee reported on his progress and submitted himself to criticism and self-criticism.

Two paths were open to trainees upon completion of the training session. Most would be sent back to Vietnam, where they were to create propaganda, recruit young anticolonialists for training in Canton, and establish new Thanh Nien cells among workers, peasants, and students. As it turned out, this group became a source of many difficulties for Thanh Nien. Lacking mature leadership within the country and anxious to try their hands at agitational politics, many lost heart, considering the methodical creation of propaganda and organization of revolutionary cells beneath their dignity ("a childish game"); others exhibited a lack of initiative, awaiting an official sign for the agitational phase of the revolution to begin. Meanwhile, the more radical returning trainees were critical of Thanh Nien's Central Bureau for its alleged failure to stay abreast of the rapidly developing revolutionary situation at home and soon defied the leadership. In 1928, after the organization's headquarters had been dislocated by Kuomintang (KMT) repression, the radicals decided to take instructions from the Comintern via the PCF. This was the first step in the schism that led to the disintegration of Thanh Nien in mid-1929.

A small number of trainees were selected for further revolutionary training at either the KMT School of Political and Military Science at Whampoa or the University for the Toilers of the East (KUTV) in Moscow. The Whampoa Military Academy, as the KMT school was usually known, had been established by Soviet advisers Michael Borodin and General Galen on the banks of the muddy Whampoa River about twelve miles from Canton. In the days of the uneasy KMT-CCP alliance, Vietnamese revolution-aries were welcomed among the ranks of the elite Chinese officers trained there. Scattered reports indicate that a large number of Vietnamese were trained at Whampoa and that many later par-ticipated in Chinese military activities, either for the KMT or for the CCP.[65] In addition to those trained at the KMT school, a few Thanh Nien members were selected for training in Moscow. Three among this group—Tran Phu, Le Hong Phong, and Ngo Duc Tri—later held Central Committee leadership positions. Tran Phu be-came the earliest secretary-general of the ICP. In the 1930s Le Hong Phong became the ECCI special representative with the ICP.

ORGANIZATION

The creation of a Leninist organizational system was central in Thanh Nien's preparation for revolution. Herein lay Nguyen Ai Quoc's genius. As a good Leninist, he had begun with the premise that it was not possible to change the world without knowing it thoroughly, and had concluded that it was equally impossible to carry out the revolution without a suitable instrument. Before the creation of Thanh Nien, political organizations in Vietnam had been traditional groupings of political amateurs. These organizations had resembled heads without bodies, relying on the personal repu-tation and prestige of individual leaders. Having neither a concep-tual framework for an analysis of the operative social forces nor an understanding of the political role of the masses, these groups had

65. According to a letter dated 28 December 1927 (no. 5077/SG) from the gover-nor-general of Indochina to the French minister of colonies, not only were numer-ous Vietnamese being trained at Whampoa, but also Vietnamese revolutionaries were employed as training instructors there. Meanwhile, several articles appearing in the *Weekly Review of the Whampoa Academy* in late 1927 indicated that a large number of Vietnamese were being trained there. In an article entitled "The Wham-poa Military Academy and the Vietnamese Revolution," Wou Hai Tsieou stated: "The Whampoa School has existed for three years and it has had five promotions. During that time, there have been Vietnamese revolutionary comrades who braved danger to enter the school to take part in its life, augmenting its military force and developing its spirit. The ones having left the school, the other arrived. . . . From one promotion to another, their number has been enlarged. . . ." (Supplement 2 to letter 1380/SG of 15 March 1928, SLOTFOM, vol. 3, carton 49).

thought of recovering Vietnamese independence in Blanquist terms, as involving a conspiracy of the elite. Consequently, they had never developed an organizational apparatus that would involve large numbers of Vietnamese in the political process. Thanh Nien was different. Whereas previous anticolonial groups had relied on the personal followings of their leaders, Thanh Nien emphasized agitation, propaganda, and organization. Whereas previous groups had ignored the masses, Thanh Nien emphasized the important role of the masses. Whereas previous organizations, in line with traditional Vietnamese thinking, had celebrated the place of the individual hero in history, Thanh Nien, imitating the Bolsheviks, stressed the importance of the collective hero, the Party, as an organized force in the service of a scientifically prepared revolution.

Thanh Nien was only part of an organizational system and not the first or the only, or conceptually the most important, organization founded by Nguyen Ai Quoc during this period.[66] In the typical Leninist pattern, this organizational complex included a nucleus—the CYC—and several auxiliary organizations. Perhaps a branch of the Communist Youth International,[67] the CYC acted as the link between the other Vietnamese organizations and the international Communist movement via its representative in East Asia, the Bureau of the East, located in Shanghai. Composed of the most promising Thanh Nien activists, this secret nucleus originally had nine members in 1924. By the time of Thanh Nien's dissolution in May 1929, the CYC reportedly had twenty-four members, who

66. The first revolutionary organization established by Nguyen Ai Quoc in Canton was the A chau Bi Ap-buc Dan-toc Lien-hiep Hoi (League of the Oppressed Peoples of Asia). Founded in 1924 under the sponsorship of the Comintern, this organization was intended to be a coordinating body for all Asian anticolonial organizations. Its membership reportedly included revolutionaries from India, Korea, Java, Formosa, China, and other countries. There is, however, no evidence of its activities except for several pamphlets in Vietnamese published under its imprimatur. In 1929 this organization was formally transformed into the Dong Phuong Phan-de Dong-Minh Hoi (Antiimperialist League of the Orient). See *Thanh nien,* May 1930.

67. The Communist Youth International was founded at a youth meeting in Berlin from 20 to 26 November 1919. This organization quickly expanded its influence among the youth of several European countries. Within a few years it became possibly the strongest organization within the Comintern. For a brief history of this organization, see Witold S. Sworakowski, ed., *World Communism: A Handbook, 1918–1965* (Stanford, 1973), pp. 92–94.

were the object of envy by the other Thanh Nien members.[68] In addition to the CYC, a network of three "mass organizations" was also created: Thanh Nien, Nong Hoi (Peasants' Association), and Cong Hoi (Workers' Association). Thanh Nien was designed primarily for students and intellectuals, although it also accepted nonstudents, such as Ly Tu Trong and Nguyen Luong Bang. The organizations for the workers and peasants were created sometime in 1927 but they do not appear to have been active until sometime in 1928. In addition, there seems to have been some organizing among women and soldiers in the French army. In the weekly *Thanh nien,* for example, there was a special "Women's Column," whose articles appealed directly to Vietnamese women to organize themselves. The biweekly *Linh kach menh,* which appeared in 1927, discussed military and political affairs and was directed to Vietnamese soldiers.

IDEOLOGICAL ORIENTATION

Because the prime concern of Nguyen Ai Quoc and other Thanh Nien leaders was with making a revolution rather than with rigorous theorizing, Thanh Nien's ideological orientation is difficult to analyze. Thanh Nien did not appear to have a clearcut ideology; rather, it offered a grab bag of concepts. In its various pamphlets and periodicals, especially the weekly *Thanh nien,* there were elements of both traditional anticolonial patriotism and bolshevism. Nationalist appeals were mixed with antinationalist, internationalist sentiments; calls for national unity appeared beside those for class struggle, and examples from Leninist teachings were juxtaposed with Confucian sayings. The merits of bolshevism and the accomplishments of the October Revolution, for example, featured prominently in the early issues of *Thanh nien.* An article entitled "Ah, Bolshevism!" in the 12 September 1925 issue enthused:

> The Bolsheviks aid the oppressed peoples to regain their liberty and do not cease to repeat to them: educate yourself, don't let yourself

68. As we shall see, the fact that all these "Communists" were selected from Thanh Nien leaders living in southern China and that they did little to promote the establishment of a Communist party for Indochina was an important cause of the subsequent schism within Thanh Nien in 1928–1929. See Tran Huy Lieu, *Lich su tam muoi nam,* 2:21.

be seduced by the honey-worded and self-interested speeches of the imperialists. You are their equal, although belonging to different races.

That is why we must cherish the Bolsheviks and detest their adversaries, the imperialists.[69]

Next to such celebrations of Leninism were commendations of the wisdom of Confucius, whose sayings were often used to encourage Vietnamese revolutionaries. The anniversary of Confucius's birthday in 1927, for example, was occasion for a commemorative article that said in part:

The monarchs venerated Confucius not only because he was not revolutionary, but also because he conducted intensive propaganda in their favor. . . . If Confucius lived in our days, and if he persisted in those views, he would be a counterrevolutionary. It is possible that this superman would rather yield to the circumstances and quickly become a worthy follower of Lenin.

As far as we Vietnamese are concerned, let us perfect ourselves intellectually by reading the works of Confucius and revolutionarily by reading the works of Lenin.[70]

Apparently no one in Thanh Nien at the time saw the irony of an attempt to combine the ideas of the ancestor of Asian conservatism with those of the European archrevolutionary. Patriotism indeed explains many things.

Many of the exhortations in Thanh Nien's publications were in the tradition of patriotic propaganda of earlier organizations, especially the themes of the literati-led movements. There was the fear of "ethnocide" *(diet chung)* "if the Vietnamese people continued in their deep slumber."[71] There was also the call to Vietnamese to "wake up" *(thuc tinh)* and "rise up" *(vung day)* to fight the French and to "save the race" *(cuu giong noi)*. There was an appeal for

69. In Gouvernement général, *Contribution*, 4:17, Louis Marty erroneously asserted that Nguyen Ai Quoc used the first sixty issues of *Thanh nien* to prepare his readers before revealing Thanh Nien's procommunist tendencies. Students of Vietnamese history have generally accepted this error as fact. See I. Milton Sacks, "Marxism in Vietnam," in *Marxism in Southeast Asia: A Study of Four Countries*, ed. Frank N. Trager (Stanford, 1959), p. 117.

70. *Thanh nien*, 20 February 1927. For a stimulating analysis of the fusion of Confucianism and Marxism in Vietnamese society, see Nguyen Khac Vien, "Confucianisme et Marxisme au Vietnam," in *Tradition et révolution au Vietnam*, ed. Jean Chesneaux, Georges Boudarel, and Daniel Hémery (Paris, 1971), pp. 21–57.

71. *Thanh nien*, 5 September 1925.

"unity of forces" *(dong tam hiep luc)* among Vietnamese of all sexes, classes, creeds, ages, at home or abroad, for a struggle for national liberation. This link between Thanh Nien's ideological position and traditional patriotism was best illustrated in the weekly serialization in *Thanh nien* of Phan Boi Chau's *Hai ngoai huyet thu* [Letter from overseas written in blood], which reflected the contemporary concerns of anticolonial Vietnamese.

In addition to sentiments that were readily identifiable with traditional Vietnamese anticolonialism, however, there was an attempt to redefine the nature of patriotism. Until the foundation of Thanh Nien, the Vietnamese definition of patriotism had involved such traditional elements as attachment to the "sacred land" of ancestors, identification with the traditional culture, and protective sentiments toward one's fellow nationals. Patriotism, in other words, had been defined in terms of "fatherland," national culture, and compatriotism. Thanh Nien, however, considered this traditional definition a "crude error," and in offering a Marxist definition virtually rejected the earlier one. At times *Thanh nien* went so far as to label patriotism a dangerous thing, because it could make people dupes of the propertied classes.

> The word fatherland *(to quoc)* was created by the politicians to make the people conform to their laws and to constrain the proletariat to take arms to defend the properties of the landowners and the interests of the capitalists.
> In reality, there is neither fatherland nor frontiers. All revolutionaries who devote their forces to improve the quality of human life are friends and the earth is their only country. What this proves is that our French comrades would fight on our side against their imperialist compatriots who have seized our country.[72]

Probably Thanh Nien's most significant contribution to Vietnamese political thought was its redefinition of the concept *cach menh* (revolution), which the anticolonial literati had introduced into the Vietnamese political vocabulary during the first decade of the century. In this earlier conceptualization, *cach menh* (to take away the mandate) had been presumed to be complementary to the concept *thien menh* (heavenly mandate), which postulated that the legitimate right to rule was based on a mandate from heaven. In practice, however, the term *cach menh* had been used

72. *Thanh nien,* 20 December 1926.

loosely to identify any rebellion against existing political authority. In the Vietnamese anticolonial struggle, every leader or group rising against the French colonial rule was usually referred to as *cach menh*. This understanding of revolution was best expressed in a pamphlet entitled *Cach menh*, prepared in 1925 by Nguyen Thuong Huyen and sent to Nguyen Ai Quoc for comments and criticism.[73] The author explored Chinese and Vietnamese history extensively to find examples of *cach menh*; for the modern period, he chose to include Gandhi's civil disobedience movement and the movements for independence in the Philippines and Egypt.

As used by Thanh Nien, however, the concept *cach menh* assumed the Western connotation of revolution and signified more than just the removal of the right to rule. In Western political theory, the word *revolution* retains the meaning that Copernicus used in his astronomical studies. It refers to a complete circular movement that leads to the replacement of one social and political system by another. In this perspective, revolution is distinct from rebellion. A rebellion is perceived as a negative process, limited in scope and incoherent in its demands. As an act of defiance, it necessarily establishes limits to the conditions considered intolerable. In the words of Albert Camus, a rebel is "a man who says no, but whose refusal does not imply a renunciation."[74] In other words, the rebel can at best be a political reformist who proposes limits to power and demands liberalization. Revolution, on the other hand, originating in the realm of ideas, represents fundamental changes in the historical process. It calls for a basic transformation of the structure and process of rule. Thus, a rebellion reacts to facts, whereas a revolution involves principles. In this sense, a revolutionary is not only a rebel who destroys, but also a builder

73. Nguyen Thuong Huyen's *Cach menh* was dated "the nineteenth of the twelfth month, the Year of Giap Ti (3 January 1925)." Nguyen Ai Quoc's critique [signed "L. T.," for "Ly Thuy"] was dated 9 April 1925; SLOTFOM, vol. 5, carton 45. For an analysis of this traditional understanding of "revolution," see John T. McAlister, Jr., and Paul Mus, *The Vietnamese and Their Revolution* (New York, 1970), pp. 55–77. The extent to which this conception reflects the Vietnamese understanding of revolution as of 1945 is, however, questionable.

74. Albert Camus, *The Rebel*, trans. A. Bower (New York, 1961), pp. 13, 106. For representative works on the Western conception of revolution, see Hannah Arendt, *On Revolution* (New York, 1963); Chalmers Johnson, *Revolutionary Change* (Boston, 1966); and Jack Woddis, *New Theories of Revolution* (New York, 1972).

who constructs a new society. This, too, was Thanh Nien's conception of *cach menh.*

Nguyen Ai Quoc's writings during this period made this concept clear. In his critique of Nguyen Thuong Huyen's pamphlet, in *Duong kach menh,* and in the pages of *Thanh nien,* Nguyen Ai Quoc repeatedly pointed out that the myriad violent changes of monarchical regimes in Chinese and Vietnamese history and the numerous violent acts in opposition to French rule—such as the Tax Protest Movement of 1908, the attempt to poison French troops in Hanoi, and the mutiny at Thai Nguyen—were not *cach menh.* They were only rebellious acts, and even if they had been successful in their objectives they would have effected no fundamental change. In Nguyen Ai Quoc's definition, *cach menh* includes both destruction of the ancien regime and construction of something new in its place. *Cach menh,* in other words, involves a total transformation of the political, economic, and social order. The *Thanh nien* issue of 28 June 1925 put it thus:

> Revolution is the change from bad to good; it is the entirety of all the acts by which an oppressed people becomes strong. The history of all societies has taught us that it was always by revolution that it was possible to give a better form to government, education, industry, organization of the society, etc.

Cach menh, however, was not equivalent to reforms. In Nguyen Ai Quoc's critique of Nguyen Thuong Huyen's pamphlet, he said:

> In the French language, there are the terms "reforms," "evolution," and "revolution." Evolution is a series of successive and peaceful transformations. Reforms are more or less numerous changes brought about in the institutions of a country, changes which may or may not be accompanied by violence. Even after the reforms, there would always remain something of the original form. Revolution entirely replaces the old regime with a new one.[75]

This critique presented Gandhi as a reformer but not as a revolutionary. Gandhi, in this view, never mobilized the Indian popular masses to fight for their national independence; although he demanded reforms, "he never demanded that the English bring about complete changes in the Government of India."

In the *Thanh nien* issue of 28 June 1925, Nguyen Ai Quoc

75. Nguyen Thuong Huyen, *Cach menh,* AOM, SLOTFOM, vol. 5, carton 45.

specified the two periods of the revolution: "the period of destruction" and "the period of reconstruction."

> The goal of the first period is the overthrow of the despotic government. In Vietnam, where the people have been bestialized, dehumanized, exploited, and subjugated, it is necessary to employ skillful propaganda to wake up the proletarians of the two sexes, inculcate in them the shame of slavery and the love of solidarity, unite them in one powerful bloc, raise them against their tyrants, and lead them to the reconquest of their rights.
>
> The goal of the second period is the intensive exploitation of the triumph of the revolution. Thus, after having kicked the French out of our borders, we must destroy the counterrevolutionary elements, build roads for transportation and communication, develop commerce and industry, educate the people, and provide them with peace and happiness.

An important part of Nguyen Ai Quoc's concept of revolution was his emphasis on the role of the masses. Although he ascribed great importance to ideas and leadership, he did not believe that ideas or leaders alone could make history. Indeed, with Thanh Nien, the making of history ceased to be the private preserve of the elite. The crux of revolution for Nguyen Ai Quoc was the translation of ideas into power, and the instrument of this translation was to be the masses. Political consciousness by itself is powerless; such consciousness will turn into power only when the masses possess it.

Thanh Nien's emphasis on "the social question," on the important role of the masses in politics, was thus a significant departure from the Vietnamese political tradition. Perceiving anticolonial politics in terms of a conspiracy among the elite, none of the earlier anticolonial organizations had understood the need for a political base. According to Thanh Nien, this failure to recognize and establish a mass base had been the basic cause of their defeat. For Thanh Nien, the masses must be the subject, object, and instrument of the revolution. To be successful, a revolution must recognize the strength of the masses and depend on them as its main force. In phrases reminiscent of the *Communist Manifesto, Duong kach menh* stated this proposition bluntly, as follows:

> Oppression gives birth to revolution; for that reason the more a person is oppressed, the more lasting his revolutionary spirit, the more determined his revolutionary intention. Formerly, when

capitalism was oppressed by feudalism it became revolutionary. Presently capitalism is oppressing the workers and peasants; therefore, workers and peasants are the bosses of the revolution: (1) because the workers and peasants are the most oppressed; (2) because the workers and peasants are the largest group, therefore the strongest group; (3) because the workers and peasants own nothing; if they lose, they lose only a miserable fate; if they win, they win the whole world; that is why they are very courageous.[76]

This was a new analysis of the political conflict in Vietnam. Until Thanh Nien, the fundamental conflict within colonized Vietnam had been thought of in "national" terms, or rather, in terms of an opposition between two forces: "we" (the entire Vietnamese nation) versus "they" (the French colonialists). The general, naive assumption of the anticolonial literati had been that whoever was Vietnamese was *ipso facto* anticolonialist, including those who were actively collaborating with the French. According to Thanh Nien's new political analysis (although it was not yet a class analysis), three basic forces were at work. While the "they" remained essentially the same, the "we" was perceived to contain two separate forces: the revolutionary forces, or the workers and peasants, and the friends and allies of the revolution. Thanh Nien viewed the conflict in colonized Vietnam as one between the French colonialists and the "most oppressed elements" (the peasants and workers); the other social groups were considered "intermediary elements" who could at best be "friends," "allies," or "fellow travelers" *(ban cung duong)* of the revolutionary peasants and workers. As expressed in *Duong kach menh,* "the workers and peasants are the roots of the revolution. The students, small merchants, and small landowners are also oppressed, but not as miserable as the workers and peasants. Those three groups are only the friends of the workers and peasants."[77]

Another important feature of Thanh Nien's orientation was its insistence on the primacy of "a revolution of national liberation" and not a class revolution. In Leninist terminology, given the political environment of Vietnam at the time, "the national question" was to take precedence over "the social question." Nguyen Ai Quoc emphasized this point repeatedly throughout the prepower

76. Vu bien soan, *Van kien Dang,* 1:14–15.
77. Ibid., p. 15.

period of Vietnamese communism.[78] After the Sixth World Congress of the Comintern (1928) the policy of promoting the internationalist aspect of communism stifled this position and it became the cause of dissension within the Vietnamese Communist movement, leading to the disintegration of Thanh Nien and the eclipse of Nguyen Ai Quoc's authority.

At this initial stage, however, Thanh Nien considered national liberation the principal objective of the Vietnamese revolution. According to *Thanh nien* of 24 October 1927, it would be useless, if not outright harmful, "to preach the revolution in the name of democratic or Communist principles, for the Vietnamese people have not yet received any political education," and Vietnamese society did "not yet possess a true capitalist class." If anything, Vietnamese society was "made up of heterogeneous classes [all of whom were] deprived by the French administration of their rights and revenues." To be effective, a political strategy had to take this fact into account and attempt to forge the resentment of all the social classes into an instrument of revolution.[79] According to the same issue of *Thanh nien,* Vietnam was not yet ready for a class revolution, for

> the actual circumstances oblige the Vietnamese people to foster the national revolution and not a class revolution. That is why it is a duty of the rich, the poor, the mandarins, and the members of the public to unite with one another in order to assure the triumph [of the national revolution].

Thanh Nien also adopted a relatively magnanimous position toward the collaborators. The "Reply to Our Friend Student X" in the *Thanh nien* of 27 September 1925 contained this noteworthy analysis.

> The kings, mandarins, clerks, and interpreters are, according to you, the counterrevolutionaries. You are wrong, friend. For a king is capable of reflection and he knows how to share the unheard-of misfortunes which strike his people. It would thus be preferable for

78. A minority of Comintern leaders, including Lenin, had supported a similar position. For Lenin's position on the "national question," see Joseph Petrus, "Marxism, Marxists, and the National Question" (Ph.D. diss., U. of Texas, 1966).

79. For a concise discussion of the basic issues in the relationship between international communism and the national bourgeoisie of "the East," read Maxine Rodinson, *Marxisme et monde musulman* (Paris, 1972), especially "Marxisme et le tiers monde," pp. 297–310 and 317–318.

him to live the life of a simple citizen rather than to reign over an enslaved people.[80] It is up to us to give lessons to the kings and show them that it is in their interest to make the revolution rather than to live in the clutches of the foreign country.

As to the mandarins, clerks, and interpreters, they serve the French under constraint. Plunged into the darkness of obscurantism since their youth, . . . they do not know why men are happy and slaves are miserable. They resemble the limping hens who feed around the rice mills. They make no effort and are content with the feed that people give to them. It is thus our duty to initiate them to revolutionary theories.

Thanh Nien's position at this stage was clearcut: a national revolution was to occur first, then a world revolution. In fact, the motto of Thanh Nien, which stood at the beginning of its *Regulations* (1926), stated: "First make a national revolution; then make a world revolution."[81] The sixth issue of *Thanh nien* (26 July 1925) elaborated this position; there were "different kinds of revolution: political revolution, social revolution, and world revolution." A political revolution takes place when "the inhabitants of a country, having been oppressed by a despotic government, revolt to regain their liberty and become independent." A social revolution takes place when "the peasants and workers are denied their salaries by their masters" and decide to make a revolution "to repair this injustice and distribute the revenues between capitalists and proletariat in a more equitable manner."

After the political and social revolution, there will still remain oppressed peoples. There will still be differences between nations. It is

80. In his abdication speech in August 1945, Emperor Bao Dai was to use a ringing sentence, *"Tha lam dan mot nuoc doc lap, con hon lam Vua mot nuoc no le"* (I would rather be a simple citizen in an independent country than king of an enslaved nation). This sentence was to haunt him throughout 1949–1954, when he became chief of state of the French-sponsored State of Vietnam. Wherever Bao Dai went, at least in Bac Ky where this author was, he would encounter his portrait in schoolrooms and government offices, emblazoned with his own immortal motto. It was later revealed that Bao Dai's abdication pronouncement had been ghost-written by some members of the Viet Minh Front.

81. This motto was elaborated in the regulations' objectives as follows: "Sacrifice opinions, interests, and life to promote the national revolution (destruction of French power and reconquest of the country) and then a world revolution (the overthrow of imperialism and realization of communism)"; Gouvernement général, *Contribution,* vol. 4, supp. 1, p. 49. It is worth noting that the other friendly rivals of Thanh Nien borrowed this motto and adopted it as their own. See Tran Huy Lieu et al., *TLTK,* 5:15 (for Tan Viet) and 31–32 and 41, n. 1 (for the VNQDD).

then necessary to have a world revolution. After that the peoples of the four corners of the earth will befriend one another. It will be the age of world fraternity.

Vietnam, recommended *Thanh nien,* "ought to begin with a political revolution." This stand, however, did not negate the important connection between the revolution in Vietnam and the world revolution, as *Duong Kach Menh* stated clearly: "The revolution in Vietnam is part of the revolution in the world. Whoever makes a revolution in the world is a comrade of the Vietnamese people."[82] For that reason, although the immediate task of the Vietnamese revolutionaries was to make a "national revolution" *(dan toc kach menh),* they would still be responsible for making a "world revolution" *(the gioi kach menh)* later.

The most eventful phase of Thanh Nien was terminated around the end of 1927, when the organization fell victim to the dispute between Chinese Nationalists and Communists. As the capital of Sun Yat-sen's revolutionary government, Canton had been an active center of revolutionary agitation throughout the years 1924–1927. During this period, the Chinese revolutionary movement developed depth and breadth based on an antiimperialist united front betwen the KMT and CCP. After the death of Sun Yat-sen, however, the right-wing Kuomintang dismantled the alliance and turned against the Communists. Acting on a tip, Nguyen Ai Quoc fled to Moscow around the end of April.[83] In response to KMT persecution, the CCP waged a popular campaign against the former, and on 11 December 1927 the workers and soldiers of Canton launched an insurrection. They established a "Worker-Peasant-Soldier Soviet," but this was soon suppressed by the KMT forces. Because Thanh Nien members were actively involved in the melee on the CCP side, they were arrested in the aftermath of the Canton

82. Vu bien soan, *Van kien Dang,* 1:14.

83. T. Lan [Ho Chi Minh], *Vua di duong vua ke chuyen* [Anecdotes on the road] (Hanoi, 1963), p. 33. This booklet is allegedly a collection of anecdotes on Nguyen Ai Quoc/Ho Chi Minh's revolutionary career as told to the author by Ho Chi Minh in 1951. The author, supposed to be a journalist, cautions against possible inaccuracy due to the retrospective nature of the work. In fact it is well known that this slim volume is an autobiography of Ho Chi Minh himself, the only one he wrote about his early revolutionary career.

Commune.[84] Thanh Nien activities in China came to an abrupt halt. Although on paper Thanh Nien continued to exist until mid-1929, most of its revolutionary activities were carried out by Thanh Nien members in Vietnam without the close supervision of the central bureau in China.

The destruction of Thanh Nien's Canton headquarters notwithstanding, Vietnamese revolutionary patriotism had taken a giant step. Within two years what had begun as a youth movement in search of ideas and techniques for the liberation of Vietnam, without any clear ideological direction, had become part of an international revolutionary movement against capitalist imperialism. In 1925 Phan Boi Chau and Phan Chu Trinh were venerated as national heroes; by the end of 1927, their names were still referred to respectfully, but only as symbols of heroic but futile efforts. In 1925 anyone who spoke up for Vietnamese interests, including the Constitutionalists, was looked up to as a leader; by the end of 1927 reformism alone was no longer considered adequate. In 1925 Marxism-Leninism was only one of many political theories, including those of Gandhi, Sun Yat-sen, and Piłsudski, introduced to Vietnam; by the end of 1927 it had become a leading ideology with an organizational home. From that time on, communism remained an integral part of Vietnamese nationalism.

84. For a recent account of Vietnamese activities in southern China relating to the Canton Commune, see "Cong xa Quang chau voi cach mang Viet Nam" [The Canton Commune and the Vietnamese revolution], *Nhan dan,* 11 December 1977.

CHAPTER TWO

A PARTY OF
THE NEW TYPE

> *The Young Comrade:* The individual has two; the
> Party has a thousand eyes. The Party sees seven
> states. The Party has many hours. The Party cannot
> be destroyed for it fights with the methods of the
> classics, which are drawn from the knowledge of re-
> ality and are destined to be changed in that the
> teachings spread through the masses. Who, how-
> ever, is the Party? Is it sitting in a house with tele-
> phone? Are its thoughts secret, its revolutions un-
> known? Who is it? It is all of us. We are the Party.
> You and I and all of you—all of us. In your suit it is,
> Comrade, and in your head it thinks; wherever I
> live there is its home and where you are attacked,
> there it fights.
>
>> Bertolt Brecht,
>> *The Measures Taken.* Reprinted by per-
>> mission of Grove Press, Inc. Translated
>> from the German by Eric Bentley. Copy-
>> right © 1965 by Eric Bentley.

During the years 1928–1930 there was a second major disaggregation in Vietnamese politics. The first, discussed in the previous
chapter, had occurred in the mid-1920s as a new generation assumed leadership of the anticolonial movement and attempted to

fuse Marxism-Leninism with Vietnamese patriotism. These events led to a division between those who opted for Franco-Vietnamese collaboration and advocates of national liberation and social revolution. These revolutionary patriots had formed numerous organizations, including Thanh Nien, Tan Viet, and the VNQDD, and by the late 1920s a fragmentation had occurred within the Vietnamese revolutionary patriotic movement. While the VNQDD persisted in its emphasis on the primacy of national liberation, important segments of Thanh Nien and Tan Viet were "proletarianizing" and "radicalizing" these parties, pitting advocates of "patriotism in general" *(chu nghia yeu nuoc chung chung)* against social revolutionaries. Like the earlier division, this disaggregation was to have long-term effects on Vietnamese political development. With the destruction of the VNQDD in February 1930, the conversion in the same month of Thanh Nien and Tan Viet into a unified Vietnamese Communist Party (VCP), and the subsequent transformation of this organization into the ICP, the way was open to the dominance of the Vietnamese anticolonial movement by advocates of proletarian internationalism. This victory, however, proved temporary, and the residual conflict between revolutionary patriots and proletarian internationalists characterized Vietnamese communism for several decades.

THE DEFEAT OF REVOLUTIONARY PATRIOTISM

The vicissitudes and ultimate defeat of revolutionary patriotism played an important part in the evolution of Vietnamese communism in the late 1920s. These developments were symbolized in the events that led to the destruction of the Vietnamese Nationalist party (VNQDD).[1] This party, like the other Viet-

1. For comprehensive and detailed histories of the VNQDD, see Nhuong Tong, *Nguyen Thai Hoc, 1902–1930* (Saigon, 1949); Tran Huy Lieu et al., *TLTK,* 5: 27–126; and Hoang van Dao, *Viet-Nam Quoc-Dan Dang* (Saigon, 1970). These authors were active leaders of the VNQDD prior to 1930. Nhuong Tong was one of the founders of the VNQDD; Tran Huy Lieu was chairman of the party's Nam Ky Regional Section; Hoang van Dao, sometime head of the Assassination Committee, was founder of the "Vietnam Hotel," which served both as a meeting place for the VNQDD leadership and as a money-making enterprise to finance party activities.

namese radical groups, had emerged in the political and intellectual ferment of 1925–1927. Its origins are traceable to the Nam Dong Publishing House, founded in Hanoi around the end of 1925 by three young men: a schoolteacher, Pham Tuan Tai, and two journalists, Hoang Pham Tran (alias Nhuong Tong) and Pham Tuan Lam. Specializing in the publication of patriotic propaganda and translations of foreign titles such as *The Chinese Revolution, Biography of Sun Yat-sen, The World Revolution,* and *The Three Principles of the People,* it became a meeting place for young anticolonialists. Many of these, including Nguyen Thai Hoc, Pho Duc Chinh, Ho van Mich, Luu van Phung, and Vu Hien, became leaders of the VNQDD, founded on Christmas Eve 1927.

During its brief existence (1927–1930) the VNQDD embodied the spirit of Vietnamese revolutionary patriotism of the 1920s. Although it had no international connections, the party had many things in common with Thanh Nien: it recruited chiefly among students and young *petits-intellectuels,* such as schoolteachers, clerks, and journalists, and it advocated both national liberation and a social revolution. The party's official motto was also the same as Thanh Nien's: "First make a national revolution; then make a world revolution" *(Truoc lam dan toc cach mang, sau lam the gioi cach mang).*[2] In practice, the party's ideological orientation was as confused as Thanh Nien's. Although the founders and many leaders considered themselves disciples of Sun Yat-sen, most party cadres and members did not seem to have a clear idea about party strategy or political program. All agreed on the fundamental objectives "beat the French" *(danh Tay)* and "save the

2. In Tran Huy Lieu et. al, *TLTK,* 5: 31. Lieu noted that all three major revolutionary patriotic parties–Thanh Nien, Tan Viet, and VNQDD–had had this motto and suspected that it had come from a common source (p. 31, no. 1). Nhuong Tong also noted the similarities between the regulations and action programs of Tan Viet and the VNQDD. Like Tan Viet, the VNQDD projected its revolutionary program in three phases: "embryonic phase" (clandestine activities), "preparatory phase" (clandestine activities) and "destructive phase" (insurrectional activities). Nhuong Tong believed that the VNQDD regulations and action program had borrowed heavily from Tan Viet with the help of Ton Quang Phiet, a Tan Viet leader (Nhuong Tong, *Nguyen Thai Hoc,* pp. 25–26). Because Tan Viet's own regulations and programs had originated with Thanh Nien's, it is permissible to conclude that the governing strategies of these three parties had one and the same source, namely, Nguyen Ai Quoc.

country" *(cuu quoc);* when it came to specific ideology, however, they went separate ways. Most emphasized the primacy of national liberation, but many others insisted that social revolution was the primary objective. Whatever their internal differences, however, the VNQDD was not an anticommunist party.[3] Indeed, according to Tran Huy Lieu, then chairman of the party's Nam Ky Regional Section, potential members in Nam Ky, were selected on the basis of their "internationalist" and "antinationalist" spirit.[4] Party members in Nam Ky included student activists who had been previously trained in Moscow, and VNQDD manuals for political training included such basic Communist works as *ABC of Communism* by N. I. Bukharin and E. A. Preobrazhenskii, and Karl Marx's *The Paris Commune.*[5] Indeed, so similar were the VNQDD and Thanh Nien that in 1928 the former initiated several unsuccessful attempts to merge the two parties.[6]

These similarities notwithstanding, the VNQDD was traditional in its orientation. Indeed, in some ways the party represented the vestige of Vietnamese elite nationalism, in the tradition of the anti-colonial Confucian literati. Inspired by such militant Confucian patriots as Phan Boi Chau, the VNQDD tended to assume that all Vietnamese were patriots, and its heteogeneous membership reflected this assumption. In addition to the urban petit-bourgeois elements, the VNQDD had members from all social strata—young students and seventy-year-old literati, rural notables and landlords, interpreters, government office clerks, and military men. Furthermore, unlike Thanh Nien, which advocated methodical long-term preparation of party members and the masses prior to political action, the VNQDD retained the tactics of militancy and violence

3. Ideological disputes occurred between imprisoned VNQDD and ICP members early in the 1930s, after the destruction of the VNQDD in February 1930. This, however, appeared to be an effect of the Kuomintang-CCP dispute in China and of the sectarian tendency of the ICP at the time. It is obvious from various revolutionary memoirs that many VNQDD activists had wanted to organize joint actions with the ICP before 1930 and while in prison. They were, however, repeatedly rebuffed. See, for example, Nguyen Hai Ham, *Tu Yen-Bay den Con-Lon (1930–1945)* [From Yen Bay to Con Lon (1930–1945)] (Saigon, 1970), pp. 157–163; 171–178.

4. *TLTK*, 5: 40.

5. Ibid., pp. 40–41.

6. Nhuong Tong, *Nguyen Thai Hoc,* pp. 41–43; Hoang van Dao, *Viet-Nam Quoc-Dan Dang,* pp. 40–43.

popular with the anti-French Confucian literati of the first decade of the century. An important part of the party's action program involved military preparations for taking power. To this end, the VNQDD recruited heavily among the Vietnamese troops in the Indochina army; in fact, compared with the other revolutionary patriotic groups the party had a virtual monopoly of recruitment among the military. It manufactured hand grenades and bombs of World War I vintage, and had a special assassination squad supervised directly by its Central Committee. Throughout 1928 and 1929, before the mutiny at Yen Bay, which brought about the destruction of the VNQDD, this squad succeeded in eliminating several spies for the government and those who were condemned as party renegades. In the end, the party's own political violence brought about its demise.

Two events led directly to the destruction of the VNQDD. The first involved the assassination on 9 February 1929 of Bazin, director of the General Office of Indochinese Manpower, which specialized in recruiting coolies for rubber plantations.[7] Bazin's office had recruited coolies by means of deceptive propaganda, kidnapping, druggings, and legal frame-ups. Every year his company and other recruiters supplied approximately eight thousand coolies to the rubber plantations of French Caledonia in the Pacific and forty thousand to those in southern Indochina. Bazin's assassination was an explosive political event. It occurred at a time of heightened political agitation amidst widespread fear and resentment of *me min* (the witch)[8] and other questionable recruitment

7. For Bazin's assassination and the underlying reasons, see *Phu nu tan van*, 2 May 1929; Nhuong Tong, *Nguyen Thai Hoc*, pp. 57–59; Paul Monet, *Les jauniers*, 5th ed. (Paris, 1930), pp. 113–114; Hoang van Dao, *Viet-Nam Quoc-Dan Dang*, pp. 45–50; Truong Ngoc Phu, "Tu vu am sat Bazin nam 1929 den cuoc khoi nghia Yen Bay nam 1930 cua Viet Nam Quoc Dan Dang" [From the assassination of Bazin in 1929 to the Yen Bay insurrection in 1930 of the Vietnamese Nationalist party], in *Su dia* [History and geography] 9, no. 26 (January–March 1974), pp. 98–118.

8. *Me min* (the witch) was a fearful phrase among the rural population of Bac Ky during the latter half of the 1920s. During these years of a rapid expansion of rubber plantations in Nam Ky, Cambodia, and New Caledonia, forcible recruitment practices included druggings and kidnappings of able-bodied men. It was widely believed that hypnosis and witchcraft *(bua me)* were being employed to lure men to their capture. Those who were kidnapped could, however, be ransomed by their families at recruitment centers if they discovered the victims' whereabouts prior to their shipment. For lengthy discussion on the *me min* and other recruitment tricks, see *Argus indochinois*, 2 December 1928, and Monet, *Les jauniers*, pp. 104–122.

strategies. The murder triggered widespread reprisal and led to a continuous cycle of revolutionary violence and repression. In the wave of official retaliation following Bazin's death, several VNQDD sections were destroyed and over one thousand party members arrested, including all members of the Central Committee except Nguyen Thai Hoc and Nguyen Khac Nhu. Throughout the country, according to Tran Huy Lieu, the VNQDD networks were severely dislocated. In some sections "not one person escaped arrest."[9] On 3 July 1929, when 227 VNQDD members were brought to trial, 80 were given prison sentences of from two to twenty years. Meanwhile the VNQDD's political violence continued and brought more arrests and imprisonments.

The final destruction of the VNQDD was the result of an aborted insurrection in February 1930. Typically, this attempt at insurrection stemmed from the VNQDD's advocacy of violence, conspiratorial tendencies, and revolutionary quixotism. After the assassination of Bazin the fortunes of the party had steadily worsened. As more party members were arrested and weapons caches uncovered each month, Nguyen Thai Hoc, chairman of the VNQDD, convoked an emergency conference in January 1930 to decide on a strategy to deal with the new situation. At his recommendation, the conference unanimously resolved to wage a "general insurrection" *(tong khoi nghia)* throughout Bac Ky, recognizing at the same time the probability of failure. The chairman's words at the conference reflected the spirit of the party's leaders: "Even if we fail, we shall go down as martyrs. Why should we hesitate?"[10] On 9–10 February 1930, the VNQDD-sponsored insurrection broke out with a mutiny of Vietnamese troops at the Yen Bay garrison and attacks on the garrison at Hung Hoa and the district headquarters at Lam Thao, Phu Tho province. Throughout Bac Ky, French administrative and military centers became targets

9. Tran Huy Lieu et al., *TLTK,* 5: 49–50.
10. See Nguyen Hai Ham, *Tu Yen-Bay,* p. 53. Nguyen thai Hoc's alleged saying "*Khong thanh cong thi thanh nhan*" (Even if we fail we shall go down as martyrs) is today associated with the quixotic character of the VNQDD. It is derived from a VNQDD slogan, *"Co doc lap phai nhuom bang mau! Hoa tu do phai tuoi bang mau! Khong thanh cong thi thanh nhan"* (Our banner of independence must be dyed with blood! Our flower of freedom must be nurtured with blood! Even if we fail we shall go down as martyrs), cited in Hoang van Dao, *Viet-Nam Quoc-Dan Dang,* p. 24.

of VNQDD attacks. The response of the colonial government, however, was swift and efficient. The revolt at Yen Bay itself was suppressed within one day. Within a fortnight most of the top leaders of the VNQDD were arrested, including Nguyen Thai Hoc, party chairman; Nguyen Khac Nhu, deputy chairman; and Pho Duc Chinh, organizer of the mutiny. Thousands of party members were imprisoned. To terrorize the population, the government used aerial bombardment against villages suspected of VNQDD sympathy. The Criminal Commission of Bac Ky tried 1,086 accused revolutionaries. It acquitted 412 and condemned 80 to death, 383 to exile, 106 to a life sentence of hard labor, and 105 to other prison terms. On 17 June 1930 thirteen of the top VNQDD leaders were taken to Yen Bay, the scene of the mutiny, where they were guillotined.

The events at Yen Bay forced an irreparable split between revolutionary patriots and collaborationist forces. For the Vietnamese population at large, the assassination of Bazin and the mutiny at Yen Bay exemplified heroism to be emulated. The brutal repression appears to have increased the influence of the anticolonial patriots and to have caught the popular imagination throughout the country.[11] While students at Hanoi University organized collections to aid the victims of repression, female secondary school students, pretending to be younger sisters or fiancées of the imprisoned revolutionaries, brought them gifts and acted as their liaison agents. In the villages of Co Am, Hai Duong province and Vong La, Phu Tho province (both of which were bombed by the French in February 1930), VNQDD leaders held conferences in the village *dinh* while the notables acted as sentinels against the government police. In Nam Ky, where press policy was more liberal, *Than chung* [Morning bell], *Phu nu tan van* [Women's news], and other newspapers described the events at Yen Bay, related VNQDD and Thanh Nien activities as glorious events in Vietnamese history, and praised the militants of both parties as *nha cach mang* (respectable revolutionaries) who had sacrificed their lives for the country.[12] In June 1930 the large majority of Vietnamese received

11. See Nhuong Tong, *Nguyen Thai Hoc,* pp. 64–65.
12. After Nguyen Thai Hoc was arrested, *Phu nu tan van* paid him special tribute with a lengthy biographical account, asserting, "Everyone, including women

the news of the execution of Nguyen Thai Hoc and his twelve comrades as a national bereavement. Many vowed to continue the fight.

The events at Yen Bay also revealed the collaborators' true political orientations. AFIMA, for example, affirmed its support of the government's repressive measures; *Nam phong* condemned revolutionary activities and called for violent repression.[13] Reacting to Yen Bay, Pham Quynh wrote that between the "obstinate minority [that] places itself outside the law, using criminal and violent means such as murder, assassination, and rebellion," and the country, there was only a matter of violence. But "since violence is not within our power, we trust that the government will know how to use it for the common good. We believe that the violence of France is always impartial and vigilant: it will strike hard, and also strike at the right place."[14]

The reaction of the Constitutionalists, too, was typical. Profiting by the political tension, they called for dominion status for Indochina and at the same time loudly condemned the revolutionaries. *La tribune indochinoise* and *Duoc nha Nam* [The torch of Viet Nam], their newspapers, protested the French bombing at Co Am and equally denounced the violence perpetrated by the VNQDD, appealing to the young nationalists to exercise "economy of carnage" and "economy of revolution." Perhaps Le Quang Liem encapsulated the political sentiments of the Constitutionalists when, to the delight of Governor-General Pasquier, he told the latter in January 1930, "We are good Frenchmen; all of us rally around you, because you listen to our criticisms and at the same time because we know that with you the real enemies of the coun-

and children, has, for more than a year now, heard of the glorious name of Mr. Nguyen Thai Hoc." The VNQDD leader, according to this account, had spent five years in Canton under the tutelage of the famed Nguyen Ai Quoc. He was alleged to have been Nguyen Ai Quoc's deputy, heading an "interior" division of a revolutionary organization based in southern China. In fact, however, Nguyen Thai Hoc never met Nguyen Ai Quoc, and there were no formal connections between the VNQDD and Nguyen Ai Quoc's Thanh Nien. The press reported the progress of Nguyen Thai Hoc's recovery from the wounds sustained during his arrest as if Hoc had been the national leader. See *Phu nu tan van,* 6 March 1930. It is worth mentioning that the article *nha* is used in Vietnamese to indicate respect; thus, *nha van* (literateur), *nha hoa si* (painter), *nha ai quoc* (patriot).

13. *Nam phong,* no. 146 (January 1930), p. 98.
14. Pham Quynh, *Nouveaux essais franco-annamites* (Hue, 1937), p. 127.

try, that is to say, the sedition mongers, the criminals, will not be able to disorganize Annamese society."[15]

On 6 June 1930, about the time the French were making final preparations to take Nguyen Thai Hoc and his comrades to the guillotine, all the Constitutionalist members of the Nam Ky Colonial Council formed a delegation to meet with Krautheimer, the governor of Nam Ky, to offer their complete support in the fight against the Communists and nationalists. To the horror of the Vietnamese, who knew of only one type of antipersonnel gas—the poison gas used in the First World War—Nguyen Phan Long used this opportunity to propose the use of tear gas and firehoses against strikers and demonstrators.[16] From 1930 on, the French colonials and the Constitutionalists formed what has been designated a "colonial bloc" within Vietnamese society.[17]

For Vietnamese communism the VNQDD debacle had a special significance. The destruction of this nationalist party as an effective political force was a defeat for Vietnamese revolutionary patriotism. From this point on, there was no ideological alternative to international communism as the leading force in the Vietnamese revolution. Revolutionary patriots who survived the French repression came increasingly under the influence of proletarian internationalism. With Thanh Nien and Tan Viet transformed into a national section of the Communist International in the early 1930s, several leading members of the VNQDD became converts to communism while in prison. These included Pham Tuan Tai, one of the party founders; Tran Huy Lieu, chairman of the Nam Ky Regional Section; and To Hieu, a leader of the VNQDD Haiphong branch. Most of those who survived imprisonment eventually left revolutionary politics altogether. Remnants of the

15. Quoted in a letter from the governor-general to the minister of colonies, 29 January 1930; AOM 2431.

16. After this meeting Nguyen Phan Long did his best to explain the existing varieties of antipersonnel gas and the harmlessness of the tear gas that he had proposed (*Duoc nha nam,* 17 June 1930). In his response to Long's suggestion Krautheimer reported that the police did try to bring firehoses to disperse demonstrators at Duc-hoa, Cholon province, but when the fire engines arrived, they discovered that there were no water mains there. As to tear gas, there was none in Indochina and it would take some time to import it from France. As a result of this incident Long earned the nickname "Long-les-gaz."

17. Daniel Hémery, *Révolutionnaires vietnamiens et pouvoir colonial en Indochine* (Paris, 1975), pp. 23–24.

VNQDD and those who assumed that label continued to be active in Vietnamese politics for several decades, in collaboration with the Kuomintang in the 1940s and with the United States in the 1960s. The activities of these latter-day VNQDD politicians, however, did little credit to the memory of the Yen Bay martyrs. Meanwhile, after February 1930 the way was open to Vietnamese Communist domination of the Vietnamese anticolonial movement.

PROLETARIAN INTERNATIONALISM
AND THE VIETNAMESE REVOLUTION

The defeat of Vietnamese revolutionary patriotism in the late 1920s was also a result of its own internationalization. This process had begun in the mid-1920s with the introduction of communism into Vietnam by Nguyen Ai Quoc and specifically with the creation of Thanh Nien. As a result of this process, Vietnamese revolutionary politics became tied to the international context. Communism was to evolve a dual character in Vietnam, being both a national liberation movement, governed by traditional Vietnamese patriotism, and an affiliate of the international Communist movement, profoundly affected by the vicissitudes of the Comintern. Depending on international and local circumstances, sometimes the Vietnamese Communist movement would be directed by revolutionary patriots, who insisted on the primacy of national liberation, and at other times by proletarian internationalists, who tended to be well disposed to sacrifice the cause of Vietnamese independence to the common international revolutionary line determined by the Comintern. The temporary defeat of revolutionary patriotism within the Vietnamese Communist movement was a case in point.

The importance of the international dimension of Vietnamese communism cannot be exaggerated. This was the feature that distinguished the Communist movement from all noncommunist movements in Vietnam and enabled it to survive the ferocious repression of the colonial authorities. Thanks to its international connections, the Vietnamese Communists adopted the Comintern's "scientific" methods of revolution (strategic theories, techniques of organization, cadre training, propaganda, and agitation). They also inherited the cumulative experience of older Communist parties. Moreover, Vietnamese cadres were trained and held in reserve at sanctuaries outside the reach of the French colonial regime (in Moscow, southern China, and northeastern Siam), whence they could return to lead the Communist movement, replenish it with new members, or reconstruct it each time French reprisals destroyed the Party's apparatus. This reconstruction occurred at least twice during the colonial period: after the debacle of the Nghe Tinh Soviet Movement (1930–1931) and after the defeat of the Nam Ky Insurrection (1940). None of the noncommunist anticolonial movements, the VNQDD included, ever enjoyed such effective international support.

Practical advantages aside, international communism offered the Vietnamese revolutionaries two important but less tangible tools, one intellectual, the other psychological. Intellectually, international communism offered both a self-contained ideology and a postindependence program for social change; both a strategy to overthrow French imperialism and an ideological replacement for the outdated Confucian value system. Marxism-Leninism was a new faith for Vietnamese petit-bourgeois intellectuals of the late 1920s and 1930s, as it was for many intellectuals of the West. As a secular faith replacing outdated supernatural religion, it explained the course of world history and it gave hope for the future. The Russian Revolution, the transformation of Europe and Asia, the scramble for colonies, and the crisis of world capitalism appeared to confirm what Marx and Lenin had predicted. At the same time, the universal Marxian indictment of capitalism seemed applicable to the conditions of Vietnam, where the profit, luxury, and comfort of the few were paid for by the loss, misery, and need of many others. In his interview by the French government's 1931 commission of inquiry into the events of northern Trung Ky, Thai van Giai, a member of the ICP's regional committee of Trung Ky, summarized a feeling widely shared by early Vietnamese Communists and offered a succinct explanation for the appeal of the Communist ideology to Vietnamese anticolonialists:

Q. How did you become Communist? . . . Who gave you these [revolutionary] ideas?

A. Nobody! The entire Vietnamese people is nationalist and dreams of independence. Furthermore, there is not a single people on earth who is not nationalist. Patriotism is inborn.

Q. Who leads you to become an adherent of communism?

A. The reading of *ABC of Communism.* . . . *ABC* deals with capitalism and the inequality of classes. Against the contradictions of
the actual society, it shows the harmony of the Communist society, which alone can realize the equality among the classes and
put an end to the oppression of one class by another.

Q. Have you thought about what you have read in this work?

A. Yes, and the reality has been apparent to me. At the factory the
boss exploits the worker, and in the country, the landowner exploits the share-croppers. All that has been said in *ABC.* . . .
[The workers] work a great deal for the lowest salary possible.
At the Timber Company, 12-year-old children work from morning till evening in order to earn 8 to 10 cents. I would have to tell
you a great deal about the horrible manner by which the share-
croppers are exploited. . . . Reading *ABC of Communism* has
made me understand that the Vietnamese could never reconquer
their independence if they were left to themselves and that they
had to have a support that only communism could offer to
them.[18]

The psychological effects of belonging to an international movement were also important. Being Communist was a psychologically
fortifying experience, unobtainable in any other Vietnamese anticolonial organization. The universal anticapitalist ideology not
only helped a communist activist organize his political grievances,
but also fulfilled his idealized self-perception as a fighter for human emancipation, not only in Vietnam but elsewhere in the world.
In Hall No. 2 in the Poulo Condore penal islands, ICP prisoners
followed the progress of the Spanish Civil War or the French Popular Front under the watchful portraits of Marx, Lenin, Stalin, Bar-
busse, Rolland, and Dimitrov.[19] Being Communist also eliminated

18. Commission d'enquête sur les èvénements du Nord-Annam, Vinh, Séance
du 28 juin 1931, "Déclaration de Thai van Giai," AOM, Nouveaux Fonds, dossier
2686.

19. Under the guidance of "professors" Bui Cong Trung, Pham van Dong,
Nguyen van Cu, Ha Huy Giap, and Le Duan, political prisoners at Poulo Condore
could follow events in Europe, Asia, and the USSR. For reading they had French
periodicals and newspapers—*Les nouvelles littéraires, Je suis partout, Vu, Lu, La
flèche,* and even leftist periodicals such as *Défense* and *Le canard enchainé.* For
ideological training, they had all the principal works by Marx, Engels, Lenin, and
Plekhanov, smuggled in by French sailors. The walls of Hall No. 2 were decorated
with hand-drawn maps of Europe, Indochina, China, the USSR (a large number),
and portraits of Marx, Lenin, Stalin, Dimitrov, and others. See Jean-Claude Demariaux, *Les secrets des îles Poulo Condore, le grand bagne indochinois* (Paris,
1956), pp. 158–173; also Hoang Quoc Viet, "Our People, a Very Heroic People," in
Hoang Quoc Viet et al., *A Heroic People: Memoirs from the Revolution* (Hanoi,
1965), pp. 169–174.

the sense of isolation and inferiority in relation to the colonial regime. The Vietnamese Communists took to heart the idea that the proletariat around the world was on their side and that they were not alone in the fight against imperialism. A Party member with the pseudonym "Binh" told Jean Dorsenne of his emotions when, as a colonial subject used to second-class treatment in Vietnam, he stood in Moscow's opera house surrounded by thousands of Communist fighters from around the globe, singing the "Internationale" in unison and feeling certain of the inevitable success of the Vietnamese revolution.[20] International solidarity was also a great source of support. The concerted protests in the world leftist press, the thousands of protest meetings or demonstrations in the cities of France, the harangues of Socialists or Communists in the halls of the French Chamber of Deputies—all these expressions of solidarity emboldened the Vietnamese Communists to continue the fight against colonialism.

One further advantage that international communism offered to the Vietnamese revolutionaries was the ideological appeal with which to rouse the rural masses to action. The character of the appeal, in this case, differed qualitatively from the Marxist appeal to intellectuals. For the intellectuals, communism represented possibilities of political liberation and social renaissance; for the peasants, communism symbolized delivery from misery, oppression, and exploitation, which might or might not be related to conditions fostered by colonialism. The anticolonial intellectuals may be accused of romantic naiveté: of having been witting or unwitting victims of that "opiate of intellectuals," Marxism. They may be accused also of expediency or even opportunism: of having been mere ideological hitchhikers who cared mostly about Vietnam's independence and power and not necessarily about ideological purity.[21] In other words, they may be accused of having arranged a marriage of convenience between Vietnamese patriotism and international communism in a bid to exploit its ready-made organizational and operational techniques and international solidarity, while they were making the Vietnamese revolution largely in their own fashion.

20. See Jean Dorsenne, "Le péril rouge en Indochine," *Revue des deux mondes,* 1 April 1932, p. 534.
21. See, for example, William MacMahon Ball, *Nationalism and Communism in East Asia* (Carlton, Australia, 1956), pp. 81–82.

The Vietnamese peasants' response to communism, however, embodied none of these elements. Their response was not a result of moral outrage: they were the living embodiment of such outrage. The rural poor who had known hunger and starvation and had for centuries suffered petty harassments and exploitation at the hands of village notables, whatever dynasty reigned in Hanoi or Hue, viewed the Communist-led revolution not in the abstract terms of national freedom, independence, or sovereignty, but in terms of a chance to live in dignity with enough to eat. For them, communism was appealing not because of its Bolshevik revolutionary techniques, but because of its millennarian message,[22] as interpreted by the anticolonial intellectuals. Gleaned from the pages of such periodicals as *Thanh nien* [Youth], *Bao cong nong* [Worker-peasant journal], *Linh kach menh* [Revolutionary soldier], and *Lao nong* [Toiling peasants] of the late 1920s, the Vietnamese version of the Marxist ideological message emerged as follows:

> You are poor and miserable; but you do not have to be poor any longer. You are poor not because of any thing you did or failed to do, not because of Fate or bad luck. You are poor and you are exploited, and you are going to be poor and be exploited, because of the existing economic and political conditions; because of the French, the notables, and the landlords.
>
> You do not have to be poor. The conditions that make you poor can be changed. They are going to be changed and you are going to help change them. Whether you are aware of it or not, what will happen is that you are going to make a revolution. Those who rule over you and keep you poor and miserable will be overthrown. By the revolution you can eliminate once and for all the exploitation of man by man; you can enter into a socialist society, in which you can be your own master.

The message was well received. For the Vietnamese peasants, the term *cong san* (communism) had none of the visionary significance that intellectuals assigned it; it meant simply common property, or rather, putting all properties together and dividing them equally among everyone. This definition of *cong san* recurred in numerous revolutionary memoirs, as Vietnamese leaders recounted their early days in the revolutionary movement and their initial understanding of communism. In a moving memoir written

---

22. The Marxian ideological message is best summarized in C. Wright Mills, *The Marxists* (New York, 1962), p. 32. I have used part of Mills's summary in my own summary below.

in the style of a father-to-son reminiscence, Chanh Thi, a high-level official of Vietnam, recounted how hunger drove him out of his village at age fifteen and how in the next few years, in his quest for survival, having only heard of the term *cong san,* he decided to form a group to *lam cong san* (*lam* means "to be, do work, make, earn a living").[23] *Lam cong san* may be translated "to be a communist," "to work as a communist." He told of a naive fellow who asked, "If we *lam cong san,* could we make three piasters a month?" "Of course, not," the author replied. "*Lam cong san* is for us to get together and cut off the heads of the French, of the landlords, and take their properties and divide them among the poor, like ourselves." Communism symbolized hope. Its influence was strongest initially in the poorer provinces of Bac Ky (Thai Binh, Nam Dinh, Ninh Binh) and Trung Ky (Thanh Hoa, Nghe An, Ha Tinh, Quang Binh, Quang Tri, Quang Nam, Quang Ngai, Quang Tin) but not in the relatively well-off provinces of southern Trung Ky or prosperous Nam Ky. These poorer regions happen also to be the locales where other imported faiths, Catholicism and Protestantism, have had the greatest following.

Yet, however important it might have been for the Vietnamese revolution, affiliation with the international Communist movement was not always advantageous for the Vietnamese Communists. International solidarity and concrete assistance notwithstanding, adherence to the Comintern often entailed following political lines that were not always suitable to the conditions of colonized Vietnam or that sometimes proved harmful to the development of communism in Vietnam. Until 1945 the relationship between Vietnamese Communists and the international movement was one of less than wholehearted support and often unwanted meddling. Although the latter resulted from the ardent appeals of those Vietnamese Communists who desired international advice, guidance, and approval, responsibility for international intervention rested squarely with Moscow. In those days of ideological monocentrism, when, to paraphrase Khrushchev, Communist revolutionary movements throughout the world had to synchronize their clocks with Moscow, there could be no talk of a "creative adaptation of Marxism-Leninism to the conditions of Vietnam" (a

23. Chanh Thi, "Roi Ba duoc vao Dang" [And then Father was admitted into the Party], in Bui Cong Trung, et al., *Len duong thang loi* [Onward to victory] (Hanoi, 1960), pp. 7–18.

phrase that has become popular since the late 1950s). As it turned out, ideological disorientation and organizational disarray were part of the price the Communists of Vietnam had to pay for their subservience to an international organization.

THE PROLETKULT

Vietnamese Communist submission to the Comintern and the consequences thereof were most pronounced during the late 1920s and early 1930s. During this period the official policies of the Vietnamese Communist movement existed in the shadow of the Comintern's revolutionary line adopted at the Sixth World Congress of the Communist International (July–September 1928), which was to become a watershed for both the international Communist movement in general and the youthful Communist movement of Vietnam in particular.[24] This congress marked the final defeat of Trotsky and his colleagues in the Comintern and the rise of Stalin. Its lengthy political program was later considered by one specialist on international communism as "no less than . . . a new *Communist Manifesto* geared to the twentieth century."[25] Drafted by Bukharin, this was more than a program of action; it was also the Comintern's first attempt to define precisely both the character and direction of the world revolution and a grand strategy for its future course. The importance of the new line contained in this "Program of the International" consisted not only in its classic Marxist assessment of the progress of the world revolution and the inevitable collapse of capitalism, despite evidence of momentary stabilization; but also in its articulation, for the first time in the history of the Comintern, of the inextricable relation of colonial revolutionary movements to the world revolution.

With regard to the world revolution, the program stated that the fundamental conflict between world capitalism and the world revolutionary forces would reach a new stage. In the so-called Third

24. For a firsthand account of the Sixth World Congress of the Comintern, read Chang Kuo-t'ao's autobiography, *The Rise of the Chinese Communist Party, 1928–1938*, vol. 2 (Lawrence, Kans., 1972), pp. 106–138.

25. Charles B. McLane, *Soviet Strategies in Southeast Asia* (Princeton, 1966), p. 67. For documents of the Sixth Congress of the Comintern, see Jane Degras, ed., *The Communist International, 1919–1943: Documents*, 6 vols. (New York, 1956–60), 2: 572–580. For extracts of various debates at the Sixth Congress on the colonial question, see Carrère d'Encausse and Schram, *Marxism and Asia*, pp. 232–247.

Period, expected to begin in 1928,[26] the temporary stabilization of world capitalism achieved during the Second Period would inevitably deteriorate into a new round of wars and revolutions. During this period an epic struggle would occur between the forces of "fascization" and those of "radicalization," the former represented by the "exploiting" capitalists, the latter by the "exploited" segments of society. The Comintern called for a new "revolutionary purity" involving a "proletarianization" of Communist parties and an adoption of "class-against-class" tactics vis-à-vis the bourgeoisie. For the proletariat to fulfill its historical mission, it must assume its rightful place at the leadership of the "vanguard Party." Petit-bourgeois intellectuals were to be distrusted, however ardent they might have been in the revolutionary cause.

This ultra-leftist revolutionary line was accompanied by a new perception of the role of revolutionary movements in the colonies. In a radical departure from the previous Eurocentrism and inattention to the colonies, the Sixth World Congress assigned the colonies an important place in the world revolutionary movement. Revolutionary efforts in the colonies were now considered an integral part of the proletarian movement of the advanced, capitalist countries. In an analogy that is particularly interesting in the light of Lin Piao's conception of the world revolutionary movement in the 1960s, the Sixth Congress program defined the relation between the colonies and the advanced countries as an economic one, between the "villages of the world" and the "cities of the world."

> The colonies and semi-colonies are important also because they represent the villages of the world, in contrast to the industrial coun-

26. As outlined by Bukharin at the Sixth Congress, the three periods in the world Communist movement coincided with the three periods in the postwar development of capitalism "in the imperialist era." The First Period, characterized by a crisis of world capitalism, with recession, unemployment, and other economic problems, and a rapid development of revolutionary strength, ended in the final months of 1923 with the defeat of the German proletarian uprising. The Second Period, 1924–1928, or the years between the Fifth and Sixth Congresses of the Comintern, was seen as a phase of temporary, partial stabilization of world capitalism, during which the world proletariat stood on the defensive. During the Third Period, beginning in 1928, the Comintern expected the capitalist world again to disintegrate and conflicts to emerge among the imperialist powers. For a discussion of the Comintern's concept of the Third Period, see Kermit McKenzie, *Comintern and the World Revolution, 1928–1943* (New York, 1964), pp. 114–130. See also McLane, *Soviet Strategies,* pp. 64–70.

tries, which play the role of the cities of the world in the international economy. . . . The establishment of a fraternal fighting alliance with the toiling masses of the colonies is therefore one of the chief tasks of the world industrial proletariat, in its capacity of leader who exercises hegemony in the struggle against imperialism.[27]

The importance of the colonies in the world revolutionary scheme received further emphasis in the "Theses on the Revolutionary Movement in the Colonies and Semi-Colonies," read at the Congress by Otto Kuusinen.[28] The liberation struggle in the colonies, according to the "Theses," was the focal point of the worldwide struggle between communism and imperialism, because "the colonial countries at the present time constitute for world imperialism the most dangerous sector of their front." For that reason, it was the duty of the proletariat of the world to give effective aid to the struggle of the colonial peoples. The "Theses" specified the necessity of having a Communist party in each of the colonies, and where none existed, it was the task of all Comintern sections to help create one.

Of equal importance was the Comintern's recommendation of a two-stage revolutionary strategy for the colonial and semicolonial countries. A lengthy resolution defined the "bourgeois-democratic revolutions" in colonial and semicolonial countries as the first stage in a socialist revolution. Communists of these countries were instructed to help overthrow foreign imperialist domination and establish independent republics in preparation for the second stage: a socialist revolution that would establish the dictatorship of the proletariat.[29]

By offering more attention and more promise of support than before to the revolutionary movements in the colonies, however, the Comintern also set the stage for disunity and conflicts within these movements. The strategy favored by both Lenin and Nguyen Ai Quoc had emphasized the coalition of republican forces to create "a democratic dictatorship of the proletariat and peasantry"

27. "Program of the International," in Carrère d'Encausse and Schram, *Marxism and Asia*, p. 237.
28. Unless otherwise noted, all quotations of the Kuusinen "Theses" are from Carrère d'Encausse and Schram, *Marxism and Asia*, pp. 237–239.
29. The importance of this policy is observable in various Communist movements in Asia. This resolution remained effectively the basic strategy of the various Communist parties in Asia long after the dissolution of the Comintern.

that would permit the proletariat eventually to emerge as the dominant power, and the support of the most radical elements in the
bourgeois nationalist parties in the backward nations. In a reversal
of this strategy, the "Theses" cautioned extreme wariness in dealing with these classes and organizations. The peasantry, for example, "a driving force of the revolution," could now be considered
only an ally of the proletariat, not a part of a joint workers' and
peasants' party, because "the Communist party can never build its
organization on the basis of a fusion of two classes." Communists
were also advised to be especially wary in their relations with the
"petit-bourgeois intelligentsia." According to the Comintern, although these elements had played a considerable role in the historical struggle against imperialism, they could escape their class
background only with difficulty and consequently tended to waver
during critical periods. For this reason, few could achieve an
understanding of the tasks of the class struggle of the proletariat.
The "Theses" cautioned:

> It is absolutely essential that the communist parties in these
> [colonial] countries should from the very beginning demarcate them-
> selves in the most clearcut fashion, both politically and organiza-
> tionally, from all the petit-bourgeois groups and parties. . . . In every
> such cooperation, however, it is essential to take the most careful
> precautions so that this cooperation does not degenerate into a fu-
> sion of the Communist movement with the bourgeois-revolutionary
> movement.

The radicalization of the Communist International in the Third
Period was most evident in its cult of the proletariat, or *Proletkult*,
in the Comintern parlance of the time. In a reversal of Lenin's
advocacy of "the educated representatives of the propertied
classes, the intellectuals" as the driving force and guardians of
proletarian interests in Communist parties, the tendency now was
to replace the intellectuals by Party militants of working-class origins whenever possible.[30] In October 1928, one month after the

30. Arthur Koestler was to complain later about this new *Proletkult* in *The God
That Failed,* ed. Richard Crossman (New York, 1959), pp. 48–49: "We
[intellectuals] were in the movement on suffrance, not by right; this was rubbed into
our consciousness night and day. We had to be tolerated, because Lenin had said
so, and because Russia could not do without the doctors, engineers and scientists of
the pre-revolutionary intelligentsia, and without the hated foreign specialists. But
we were no more trusted or respected than the category of 'Useful Jews' in the
Third Reich. . . ." See also Ignazio Silone's essay in the same collection on the
experience of intellectuals in the Communist movement during the 1930s.

Sixth World Congress, "Comrade Ercoli" (Palmiro Togliatti) minced no words in defending the new *Proletkult* and in reminding intellectuals of their place in the Communist movement:

> The intellectuals are not the same as workers. They are easily influenced by the petit-bourgeois milieus from which they come. For that reason they waver easily, especially when difficult decisions must be made. In our movement the intellectuals cannot be allowed to oppose the workers and their leaders. . . . The intellectuals should not be cast aside, but they should understand what their role is. They should adapt themselves to the working class, they should yield to it, but they should not lead the working class and allow the influence of the other classes to permeate its ranks.[31]

The proletarianization movement took a heavy toll of intellectuals and led to a correspondingly sharp increase in the number of workers in leadership positions. At the Tours congress of the PCF (December 1920), for example, only four of thirty-two members of the Central Committee were workers; the rest were intellectuals. In 1929, forty-eight out of sixty-nine were workers, and in 1932 the proportion was forty-nine out of sixty-four. In 1919, the Central Committee of the American Communist party was composed of seven workers out of twenty-two members; in 1935, twenty-five out of thirty-five were workers. In the first *Zentrale* of the German Communist party of 1919, ten out of twelve members were intellectuals, six of them with doctorates in law or philosophy. The only political survivor of the original leadership after the Party's defeat in 1933 was Wilhelm Pieck, a worker. The same transformation occurred in virtually every other Communist party—Italian, Japanese, Chinese, Yugoslav, and so on.[32]

The proletarianization of Thanh Nien began sometime early in 1928, when several members voluntarily left their jobs in urban areas to find work in the mines and factories of Bac Ky. This policy was later formally adopted at the All–Bac Ky Regional Committee Conference of 18–29 September 1928, after the Sixth World Congress.[33] Observing that despite the rapid growth of Thanh Nien in

31. Quoted in Milorad M. Drachkovitch and Branko Lazitch, "The Communist International," in *The Revolutionary Internationals, 1864–1943*, ed. Milorad M. Drachkovitch (Stanford, 1966), p. 187.

32. Ibid., pp. 187–188.

33. See Nguyen van Hoan, "Phong trao 'vo san hoa' nam 1930" [The "proletarianization" movement in 1930], *NCLS*, no. 134 (September–October 1970), p. 11.

the urban areas the number of workers in the organization was minimal, the conference resolved that Thanh Nien members should infiltrate the working class and the peasantry to involve the masses in the revolutionary struggle. The resolutions of the conference read in part:

> In the development of revolutionary bases, we must focus on the workers and peasants, fortify the mobilization of workers and peasants, send cadres to be "proletarianized" as workers in the mines, factories, and plantations, which are the economic trachea [i.e., danger spot] of French colonialism, have appropriate means to make propaganda and educate the masses, and build revolutionary organizations among the workers.[34]

Ngo Gia Tu[35] and Nguyen Duc Canh,[36] the organizers of the conference, assumed the task of encouraging Thanh Nien members to be "proletarianized" and at the same time led a campaign to criticize "petit-bourgeois thinking." Subsequently, in the aftermath of the Comintern's Sixth World Congress, proletarianization became an official Thanh Nien policy. Throughout the country Thanh Nien members left their desk jobs and university benches to go into factories, mines, rural areas, and plantations to share the lives of workers and peasants, bring them the messages of the Marxian classics, and organize them into workers' associations and peasants' associations.

Proletarianization, however, was not intended to be a one-way

34. *Nhung nguoi cong san* [The Communists] (Hanoi, 1977), p. 28.
35. Ngo Gia Tu, alias Ngo Si Quyet, was born 3 December 1908 at Tu Son, Bac Ninh province, to a well-to-do landowning family. In 1925 he was expelled from the exclusive Buoi School in Hanoi following his participation in the student movement to demand amnesty for Phan Boi Chau. He became a member of Thanh Nien in 1926 and led its radical wing to establish the first version of the Indochinese Communist party in June 1929. Some older ICP members insist that Ngo Gia Tu, and not Tran Phu, was the earliest secretary-general of the Party. Arrested in 1930, he was exiled to Poulo Condore in 1933. He disappeared in the sea in 1935 while attempting to escape.
36. Nguyen Duc Canh provided another example of ideological flexibility among revolutionary patriots of the late 1920s. Born 2 February 1908 in Thuy Ha, Thai Binh province, he became a VNQDD member in 1927. Sent by his party to Canton to negotiate a merger with Nguyen Ai Quoc's Thanh Nien, he instead became a convert to communism and a member of Thanh Nien. By 1929 he had become a leader of the radical wing of Thanh Nien and among the founders of the first version of the ICP. An organizer of the Nghe Tinh Soviet Movement, he was arrested late in April 1931. He was executed on 31 July 1932 in Haiphong in connection with his revolutionary activities.

street. Although it was a means of arousing class consciousness in peasants and workers, it was also a deliberate tactic to educate Thanh Nien members politically. Despite the fact that this political organization was supposed to represent the interests of the working class, 90 percent of its members in 1929 were reported to be petit-bourgeois intellectuals,[37] many of them apparently bandwagon followers, not dedicated revolutionaries. As *Thanh nien* put it in January 1929, the Vietnamese revolutionary struggle until 1928 had been merely "Platonic" and had "made no dent," largely because its petit-bourgeois intellectual members were renegades who betrayed the interests of the working class, "held the proletariat in contempt," "abandoned themselves to dissolute living," and "turned up their noses at the orders of the Party,"[38] One objective of the proletarianization campaign was to expose the members themselves to the hardship, humiliation, and oppression of working-class life, in the hope that in the vast school that was the daily life of the proletariat, the intellectuals would learn to remake themselves and gain new political consciousness. As *Thanh nien* stated:

> The comrades must penetrate the masses, carry the good word to the countryside, the factories, the schools, and the barracks. They must abandon their rich clothes and don the rags of the proletarians, become workers, peasants, and men of the people. . . . Only by living in such a manner can our comrades inspire audacity and power in the amorphous or sleepy people's cells in the country. Once the comrades and the proletarians form one united body and soul, the Party will be indestructible and the triumph of the revolution imminent.[39]

In its purpose of bringing the Communist message to Vietnamese workers and peasants, the proletarianization campaign was an unqualified success. Until this time Thanh Nien had not taken concrete action to involve the masses politically. With this campaign, Thanh Nien put into practice its policies of "worker mobilization" and "peasant mobilization." In 1928 the first workers' unions appeared in Vietnam, with 250 workers joining various

37. Letter from the "Vietnamese Communists" to the Comintern received 20 October 1929, cited in Vu Tho, "Qua trinh thanh lap dang vo san," p. 18.
38. *Thanh nien,* 10 January 1929.
39. Ibid.

Communist-sponsored workers' associations.[40] Workers' strikes, too, became more frequent. Hong The Cong's 1933 study on the Vietnamese Communist movement gave the following statistics:[41]

YEAR	NUMBER OF STRIKES	NUMBER OF PARTICIPANTS
1927	7	350
1928	9	1,900
1929	24	6,000
1930	98	31,680

The first Thanh Nien–sponsored peasants' associations were organized in 1929, with 150 peasant members. The effectiveness of these organizations was evident in the peasants' political activities, beginning in 1930. Hong The Cong pointed out that in contrast to 10 peasant demonstrations between 1923 and February 1930, from April to October 1930 there were 400 peasant demonstrations, with 310,413 participants recorded.[42] From May 1930 until late in the summer of 1931 the peasant associations of Trung Ky created a virtual autonomous Communist zone in the Nghe Tinh region.

The proletarianization campaign also helped reveal and correct a fundamental weakness within the revolutionary organization. As an effective measure of the degree of revolutionary commitment, it revealed the failure of many to live up to their verbal dedication. As Tran van Cung later observed in his memoirs:

> The higher the level of the mass movement, the clearer the division within the ranks of Thanh Nien. Several brothers enthusiastically rose with the movement and became its leaders; the passive ones backtracked and dropped off; the wavering elements decreased progressively, for faced with the rising movement, either they had to keep up with the movement or else they were swept aside.[43]

40. Hong The Cong, *Essai d'histoire du mouvement communiste en Indochine* (1933), reprinted in Ban Nghien cuu Lich su Dang (Commission for the Study of the History of the Party), *Buoc ngoat vi dai cua lich su cach mang Viet Nam* [The great turning point in the history of the Vietnamese Revolution] (Hanoi, 1961), p. 92.

41. Ibid.

42. Ibid., p. 100.

43. Tran van Cung,"Chi bo cong san dau tien va Dong Duong Cong San Dang" [The first Communist section and the Indochinese Communist party], in Ban nghien cuu, *Buoc ngoat vi dai,* p. 112. Tran van Cung, alias Quoc Anh, was born in Nghe An province on 5 May 1906. One of the earliest members of Thanh Nien, he

THE DISSOLUTION OF THANH NIEN

Whatever the advantages of *Proletkult* for the expansion of Communist influence in Vietnam, the proletarianization campaign and the Comintern's requirement of a Communist party for each colony created many difficulties for Thanh Nien. Proletarianization exposed the heterogeneous character of Thanh Nien membership and confirmed the necessity of a "general staff [of the revolution] armed with Marxist-Leninist theories to lead the struggle in a correct mannner."[44] These deficiencies became increasingly apparent as the mass movement became more widespread. As Tran van Cung put it:

> There were places where the mass movement arose to a high level, but the cadres were not resolute in their leadership; because within "Thanh Nien" there were those who were enthusiastic and assertive, and others lukewarm and irresolute. In terms of doctrines, with the motto, "First make a national revolution and then make a world revolution," the brothers were united in their patriotism and determination to fight the French and the monarchy-mandarinate, but in actions, there were not united in viewpoints: some leaned heavily on the side of the class struggle, others on the side of the nation; many orientated themselves to communism, while others did not have such an orientation.[45]

As the more radical members of Thanh Nien, encouraged by the colonial "Theses" of the Sixth World Congress (which arrived in Vietnam around the end of 1928), immersed themselves in worker mobilization, they increasingly felt the ideological inadequacy of Thanh Nien and its approach to revolution. In the end, the proletarianization campaign played an important role in creating the schism that led to the dissolution of Thanh Nien in 1929.

Two aspects of the schism led to Thanh Nien's disintegration, one practical, the other ideological. The practical aspect was relatively simple. Until sometime in 1928, Thanh Nien members unquestioningly accepted instructions from the Central Committee in south-

---

became secretary of the Bac Ky Regional Committee and one of the seven members of its secret cell, working to transform the organization into a Communist party. Following the August Revolution he became secretary of the Nghe An–Ha Tinh Joint Province, and then member of the Standing Committee of the National Assembly. He died 31 October 1977 in Hanoi.

44. Ibid.

45. Ibid., p. 111.

ern China. The changing circumstances in both China and Vietnam during the years 1927–1929, however, brought into the open the entire range of fundamental issues concerning the Party organization and leadership. Nguyen Ai Quoc had left Canton in early May 1927, and no one seemed to know his whereabouts. Thanh Nien headquarters had to be moved from place to place (first to Wuchou and then to Hong Kong) to avoid Kuomintang repression. These were also the years during which the proletarianized Thanh Nien members had taken the worker strike movement to an unprecedented level of activism. Two questions arose. First, could a mobile leadership, trying to protect its own survival, direct a movement of which it had little control or understanding? Second, could such a leadership, based abroad, understand the complex situation of the movement at home? In short, could a revolutionary organization effectively direct a movement from a "privileged sanctuary" abroad?

The ideological aspect of the dispute, which was much more serious, concerned the suitability of Thanh Nien as an agent of the Vietnamese revolution. In the view of the more radical members, Thanh Nien remained a patriotic but not a "revolutionary" organization, despite its inclination toward Marxism-Leninism and its borrowing of Bolshevik agitprop techniques. This ideological inadequacy became most acute as Thanh Nien members became proletarianized and "went to the masses." In 1928, when extreme flooding destroyed tens of thousands of hectares of rice fields in Bac Ky and famine threatened, Thanh Nien's standard propaganda line of "patriotism in general" clearly was inappropriate, if not useless, as a slogan to mobilize the masses. As Tran van Cung (alias Quoc Anh) observed in his memoirs:

> The workers and peasants were suffering from hunger and cold. Propaganda would bring no results if it only emphasized "patriotism" and "beat the French" in general. The Vietnamese Nationalists, too, had talked a great deal about "Vietnam belonging to the Vietnamese," but they had no substantial following among the peasants and workers. The masses were demanding their down-to-earth interests.[46]

46. Ibid., p. 110–111. The Vietnamese Nationalists referred to here are the members of the VNQDD.

On the surface it is possible to argue that the radicals' criticism of Thanh Nien leadership reflected both a difference between generations and foreign influences.[47] The generation of Ho Tung Mau and Le Hong Son, who were born in the 1890s, brought up in the Confucian tradition, and willing to follow any political leadership so long as it would lead to Vietnamese national liberation, was now challenged by a younger generation of activists such as Ngo Gia Tu, Nguyen Phong Sac, and Trinh Dinh Cuu, who were born during the first decade of this century, Western-educated, and more selective in their ideology. The older generation's exposure to revolutionary politics had occurred in southern China under the aegis of both the Chinese Kuomintang and the CCP, whereas the younger Thanh Nien members who were active in Vietnam came increasingly under the influence of the Western European working-class movement. This was especially true from 1928 on, after the disappearance of Nguyen Ai Quoc and the destruction of Thanh Nien headquarters in Canton. Classics of Marxism-Leninism—the *Communist Manifesto; The Two Tactics of the Social Democratic Party in the Democratic Revolution; Imperialism, the Highest Stage of Capitalism; What is to Be Done?; One Step Forward, Two Steps Back; The State and Revolution; ABC of Communism*—in French and in Vietnamese now replaced Nguyen Ai Quoc's *Duong kach menh* as theoretical catechism; while periodicals such as *Inprecorr,* a weekly published by the Comintern; *L'humanité,* the PCF daily; and *La vie ouvrière,* the daily of the French Confederation of Labor, took precedence over *Thanh nien.*

The difference between the radicals in Vietnam and the older Thanh Nien leaders in Canton, however, went beyond generational conflict. It reflected a profound schism in the Vietnamese Com-

---

47. Certain habits reflected leaders' cultural inclinations. Whereas Nguyen Ai Quoc and Ho Tung Mau during this period made notations in their letters in Chinese characters, Ngo Gia Tu, Trinh Dinh Cuu, Nguyen Phong Sac, and other members of the younger, radical group made their notations in French. Later on, while in the Poulo Condore prison islands, the young Communists entertained themselves by putting on plays by French writers. Hoang Quoc Viet reported, "We staged some comedies by Molière. Shoemakers and tailors prepared clothes from jute bags and dyed them with charcoal and brick, making them look like clothes of the time of Louis XIV. Even wigs were made for the actors to appear in the exact fashion of the French of old days. Comrade Cuong acted perfectly the part of the countess in the play *Le bourgeois gentilhomme;* Hoang Quoc Viet, "Our People," p. 173.

munist movement between those who emphasized "the national question" (national liberation) and those who stressed the importance of "the social question" (social revolution). This schism was inherent in the nature of Vietnamese communism. As a patriotic movement working for Vietnamese independence, it would always contain an important faction that considered national liberation the primary objective. At the same time, as a Marxist-Leninist movement dedicated to a social revolution, it would include an equally important faction that stressed the proletarian revolution. Until 1928, Nguyen Ai Quoc's political strategy, which emphasized the "national liberation revolution" while advocating a postponement of the social revolution, had been congenial to the leading members of Thanh Nien. In the aftermath of the Sixth World Congress, however, this nationalist line of "patriotism in general" was no longer acceptable to a radicalized generation of revolutionaries. Tension and conflict soon emerged within the movement: between an "Indochinese" faction, which stressed a class struggle and subservience to Moscow, and a "Vietnamese" faction, which emphasized the primacy of national independence and a creative adaptation of communism to the conditions of Vietnam. At least until the August Revolution of 1945, the grafting of proletarian internationalism onto Vietnamese patriotism, or rather, the fusing of the interests of *giai-cap* (class) and those of *dan toc* (nation), continued to be a thorny issue.

The open rift within Thanh Nien was precipitated by the decision of its Central Committee to convene the First National Congress in May 1929. In the committee's view, the Vietnamese revolution had entered a new phase after the Sixth World Congress and the defeat of the Chinese Communist movement, and there was an urgent need to determine new revolutionary strategy and tactics appropriate to the new situation. Faced with this decision, several leading Thanh Nien cadres in Bac Ky decided to organize a Communist party. Thanh Nien existed in a limbo, they argued, because it was outdated organizationally and could not be justified ideologically. It was neither a *hoi* (association) in the sense of a "mass organization" nor a *dang* (party) in the sense of a "party of the new type," like the Communist party. These leaders argued that, given the growing political maturity of the Vietnamese working class, the necessity of having a Communist party was more urgent than ever.

Sometime early in 1929 the first Vietnamese Communist cell was organized at a meeting in a house at 5-D Ham Long Street in Hanoi.[48] Composed of seven members (Ngo Gia Tu, alias Ngo Si Quyet; Tran van Cung, alias Quoc Anh; Nguyen Duc Canh; Do Ngoc Du, alias Phiem Chu; Trinh Dinh Cuu; Duong Hac Dinh, alias Hac; and Nguyen Tuan, alias Kim Ton),[49] this cell worked secretly to transform Thanh Nien into a Communist party while arranging for its members to represent the Bac Ky Regional Committee of Thanh Nien at the prospective national congress. On 28–29 March 1929 the conference of the Bac Ky Regional Committee met. It supported founding a Communist party and sending four members of the original Communist cell to represent Bac Ky at the national congress.

The First (and last) National Party Congress of Thanh Nien was held 1–9 May 1929. According to the French Sûreté, the composition of this Congress was as follows:[50]

Nam Ky	Pham van Dong, alias Nam
	Nguyen van Dai, alias Liem
	Quan (Phan trong Binh?)
Trung Ky	Vu Mai, alias Quoc Hoa
	Nguyen Thieu, alias Nghia
	Nguyen Dinh Tu, alias Nguyen van Cam
	Nguyen Tuong Loan, alias Mac Chan A
Bac Ky	Duong Hac Dinh, alias Hac
	Nguyen Tuan, alias Kim Ton
	Ngo Gia Tu, alias Quyet
	Tran van Cung, alias Quoc Anh
Hong Kong	Le Hong Son, alias Do
	Nguyen Cong Vien, alias Lam Duc Thu

---

48. *Hoi va Dap ve lich su Dang* [Catechism on the Party's history] (Hanoi, 1977), p. 27.

49. According to French Sûreté sources, by the time this Communist cell was formed, Duong Hac Dinh had already become an active police informer. Nguyen Tuan (alias Kim Ton) submitted to the French sometime in June 1929 after his return from the ill-fated Thanh Nien congress and betrayed Party secrets. His comrades killed him sometime in 1930.

50. Les associations anti-françaises en Indochine et la propagande communiste: Historique I; SLOTFOM, vol. 3, carton 48. Cited hereafter as NPM [Note périodique mensuelle], following the system of monthly reports by the French Sûreté.

	Le Duy Diem, alias Le Loi
	Ly Phuong Duc.
Siam	Luu Khai Hong, alias Sau
	Dang Canh Tan

From the first session it became obvious that the China-based leaders had lost much of their influence over their subordinates in the interior. The Bac Ky representatives demanded that the issue of creating a Communist party to replace Thanh Nien be part of the agenda. The Central Committee, with the support of representatives from Nam Ky and Siam, rejected the demand. Faced with the insistence of the northerners, Lam Duc Thu reportedly made maximum use of his chairmanship: "As chairman of the congress, I rule a suspension of all discussion on the question of founding a Communist party. Whoever wishes to form such an organization may leave and discuss it somewhere else."[51] Tran van Cung, Ngo Gia Tu, and Nguyen Tuan rose and walked out of the congress. Duong Hac Dinh, whom the French Sûreté later identified as "our proven agent,"[52] was the only northern representative to remain.

The national congress of Thanh Nien continued to function despite the departure of the schismatic delegates. When the congress ended on 9 May 1929, it published resolutions expressing the opinions of the majority. The congress preduced a "Manifesto" proclaiming the program of action for the party and made an appeal to the Comintern, requesting formal recognition of Thanh Nien as a national affiliate. Though recognizing the necessity of a Communist party for Vietnam, the congress declared, "Considering that the proletarians are still weak and incompletely conscious, and that the revolutionaries are still insufficiently imbued with Communist doctrines and theories, the conditions for creating a truly Bolshevik party are still unfavorable."[53]

The congress also had a few unkind words to say about the schismatic delegates of the northern bureau.

> Quoc Anh, Quyet, and Kim Ton (representing Bac Ky), having quit the Congress before the congressmen could examine their incoher-

51. Tran van Cung, "Chi bo cong san dau tien," p. 117.
52. NPM, March–April 1930.
53. "Décision au sujet de la proposition de création d'un parti communiste," in "Demandes minimales et programme de combat du parti Viet Nam Cach Menh Thanh Nien," in Gouvernement général, *Contribution*, vol. 4, supp. 2, p. 59.

On 17 June 1929 more than twenty delegates from various recently organized Communist cells in Bac Ky held a conference at 312 Kham Thien Street, Hanoi. The conference declared the dissolution of Thanh Nien and the establishment of the Dong Duong Cong San Dang (DDCSD) (Indochinese Communist Party). The new party published a manifesto formally announcing its inauguration. It also published statutes and regulations of the Party, based on the Comintern's ready-made "Model Statutes for a Communist Party" and the Comintern's *Program* (1928). The new Party immediately published three revolutionary periodicals for propaganda purposes: *Co do* [Red flag], *Bua liem* [Hammer and sickle], and *Cong hoi do* [Red trade union]. The first two were intended for general theoretical preparation of Party members; *Cong hoi do* was intended specifically for workers. Within a few months the Party succeeded in absorbing virtually all former Thanh Nien party members in Bac Ky and began to establish Party branches in Trung Ky and Nam Ky. Its prestige was so great that wherever its propaganda leaflets and manifesto appeared, Thanh Nien ranks disintegrated and the most active Thanh Nien members applied for membership in the new organization.[56] The new Party was much more active than Thanh Nien had been in political agitation, in making propaganda, and in "worker mobilization" *(cong van)*. DDCSD activities led to workers' strikes and work stoppages in Hanoi, Haiphong, Nam Dinh, Hongay, Vinh, Danang, and Saigon.

The second self-styled Communist party appeared in the autumn of 1929. This faction was little more than a new name for what was left of Thanh Nien in Nam Ky. By August 1929, DDCSD propaganda had destroyed Thanh Nien influence and organization in Bac Ky and Trung Ky and had begun to make inroads into Thanh Nien party branches in Nam Ky. Faced with this difficult situation, the remaining Thanh Nien leaders in the South decided to negotiate a possible fusion with DDCSD, but the latter rejected their overture. With encouragement from the overseas leaders of Thanh Nien in Hong Kong, the southerners decided to dissolve Thanh Nien and transform it into a Communist party, calling it Annamese Communism.[57] The remnants of Thanh Nien rapidly assumed the new

56. Vu Tho, "Qua trinh thanh lap dang," p. 20.
57. All the Vietnamese sources, including the memoirs of Nguyen Nghia (alias Thieu), one of the leaders of this faction, referred to the group as An Nam Cong San (Annamese Communism). Sûreté reports referred to it as the Viet Nam Cong San

Party label. The new Communist group, inheriting from Thanh
Nien approximately twelve hundred members (four hundred regular and eight hundred probationary),[58] published a manifesto
criticizing DDCSD and made public its own political program and
regulations. It published two periodicals: *Do* [Red], a propaganda
organ, and *Bon-se-vich* [Bolshevik], its internal theoretical organ.

A struggle for influence then commenced between the two Communist factions. The aggressive DDCSD drive to take control of
the entire Communist movement in Vietnam was now thwarted by
the new organization, the former southern section of Thanh Nien
that had been well known for its lethargy. Up to this time, the
problems of expansion had been relatively simple for DDCSD. By
simply denouncing Thanh Nien leaders as "petit-bourgeois opportunists," "antiworkers," and "false revolutionaries" they had been
able to subvert the old Thanh Nien organization.[59] But the problems of identification now became more complex for both leaders
and followers. Both groups were composed of people who not long
before had considered themselves ardent members of Thanh Nien.
All now called themselves "Communists," "true representatives of
the working class," and "true revolutionaries" while denouncing
their opponents as "false revolutionaries" and "opportunists."[60] It
subsequently became quite difficult to distinguish between "true"
and "false" revolutionaries. For the DDCSD, the organizers of
the Annamese Communist group were "vacillating opportunists."[61]

> Only yesterday they were still interested in preserving Thanh Nien,
> refusing even to discuss the question of forming a Communist party.
> As soon as they saw that other people had organized a Communist
> party and that the two words *cong san* (Communist) could attract
> the masses, they hastened to organize a Communist party. In fact,
> these were false Communists, using the two words *cong san* to serve
> their self-interests.[62]

Dang. See AOM, SLOTFOM, vol. 3, carton 34, *NPM*, March–April 1930. See also
Nguyen Nghia, "Gop them mot it tai lieu ve cong cuoc hop nhat cac to chuc cong
san dau tien o Viet-Nam va vai tro cua dong chi Nguyen-ai-Quoc" [Some new
materials on the unification of the first Communist organizations in Vietnam and the
role of Comrade Nguyen Ai Quoc], *NCLS*, no. 59 (February 1964), pp. 3–8.
58. NPM, December 1929.
59. Nguyen Nghia, "Cong cuoc hop nhat," p. 3.
60. Tran Huy Lieu, *Lich su tam muoi nam*, 2: 25.
61. Nguyen Nghia, "Cong cuoc hop nhat," p. 4.
62. Ibid.

Similarly, according to the Annam group, DDCSD was not a true revolutionary organization. It was only an "unprincipled," "leftist deviationist," "infantile" Bolshevik group resembling true Communists as much as "chickens donning peacock feathers."[63] The competition between the two factions to prove that each alone was the "true" revolutionary force led to a wave of anticolonial strikes and work stoppages.

TAN VIET AND THE LEAGUE OF INDOCHINESE COMMUNISTS

While the two Thanh Nien–derived Communist factions were engaged in an internecine ideological conflict and organizational rivalry for the leadership of the Vietnamese revolutionary movement, a third Communist faction, unconnected with Thanh Nien, emerged around the beginning of 1930. This faction, called the Dong Duong Cong San Lien Doan (League of Indochinese Communists), was the successor of Tan Viet Cach Menh Dang (New Vietnam Revolutionary Party), or Tan Viet, a political organization based in Trung Ky. Founded in 1926 by Tran Mong Bach and other anticolonial literati leaders who had been released from Poulo Condore, this Party had borrowed so heavily from Thanh Nien's ideology and organizational techniques that there had been scarcely any difference between the two organizations. Tan Viet leaders, however, had nourished resentment toward Thanh Nien after the defection of several of its best members to join the latter party. Three times Tan Viet had sent leaders to Canton to propose a merger with Thanh Nien, only to see its proposal rejected and its emissaries return to Trung Ky as ardent Thanh Nien supporters arguing Thanh Nien's case.[64]

63. Tran Huy Lieu, *Lich su tam muoi nam*, 2: 25.
64. The most prominent cases involved Le Duy Diem and Tran Phu, who left Tan Viet and became leading members of Thanh Nien. Tran Phu, alias Likwe, was to become an important figure in the evolution of Vietnamese communism. Born 1 May 1904 in Duc Pho, Quang Ngai province to the family of a district mandarin, he studied at the prestigious Quoc Hoc School in Hue and became a schoolteacher in Vinh in 1922. A member of Tan Viet by 1925, he was sent in 1926 to Canton to negotiate a merger with Thanh Nien. Instead, he became a member of Thanh Nien and a convert to communism. In 1927 Nguyen Ai Quoc sent him to Moscow to study at the KUTV. Appointed by the Comintern to the central committee of the ICP, he returned to Hanoi in April 1930. Although according to official sources Tran Phu was the earliest secretary-general of the Party, there is no confirmation as to the circumstances and approximate date of his selection as Party leader. Indeed, there exists doubt as to whether Tran Phu was secretary-general at all. In any case,

Following the dissolution of Thanh Nien in May 1929 and the creation of the DDCSD in June 1929, Tan Viet approached the new Communist group about the possibility of a merger. DDSCD, however, specified the same condition that Thanh Nien had recommended earlier: that Tan Viet be dissolved so that its members could be admitted to Communist membership on an individual basis. Frustrated at being repeatedly rebuffed and considered second-class revolutionaries, several leading Tan Viet members decided to create a Communist group of their own. On 1 January 1930 a conference formally transformed Tan Viet into the League of Indochinese Communists. Like the other two existing Communist factions, the league had its own mass organizations: workers' association, student association, women's association, and so on. Thus, by the beginning of 1930 three Communist organizations had emerged in Vietnam, each calling itself the legitimate representative of the Vietnamese working class, competing with the others in propagating Marxism-Leninism and organizing working people into Communist cells. All three factions sought formal recognition from the Communist International.

THE UNIFICATION CONFERENCE

Several attempts were made to reunify the deeply divided Vietnamese Communist movement. Confronted with the existence of three rival Communist organizations in Vietnam, the Comintern issued a directive, dated 27 October 1929, entitled "On the Formation of a Communist Party in Indochina."[65] The Comintern judged that Indochina already had an independent workers' movement. The existence of the various Communist groups was seen as a clear indication that conditions were ripe for forming a Communist party:

> The maturity of the revolutionary movement in Indochina, the hatred of the vast popular masses against French imperialism, and especially the development of an independent workers' movement

---

he was reported to have prepared the ICP's *Political Theses* (1930), which were adopted as the Party's political program. Arrested 19 April 1931 in Saigon, he died 6 September 1931 in a prison hospital.

65. "Ve viec thanh lap mot dang Cong-san o Dong-duong," *Hoc tap*, no. 48 (1960), pp. 9–12.

and the existence of various Communist groups are creating the necessary conditions and the urgent necessity for the formation of an Indochinese Communist party.

The directive emphasized further:

The most important and absolutely most urgent task at the moment is for all the Indochinese Communists to establish a revolutionary party for the proletarian class, that is, a Communist party having a mass character. That party must be the only party, and Indochina may have only that party as the unique Communist organization.

Finally, the directive issued criticism:

All the hesitations and indecisions on the part of some groups vis-à-vis the question of the immediate creation of a Communist party are erroneous. [Also, they are] a great danger for the immediate future of revolution in Indochina.

The first concrete attempt to reconcile the Communist factions occurred around the end of 1929. Ho Tung Mau, one of Thanh Nien's earliest and most respected leaders, had asked the two major factions, the DDCSD and Annamese Communists, to send their representatives to Hong Kong for a special meeting. When the representatives met, however, it was clear from the outset that no success could be expected. Having repeated all the anti-Annamese arguments, the DDCSD representative, Phiem Chu, made it clear that he saw little ground on which the two parties could be fused on an equal basis. Annamese Communism, alleged the DDCSD, being only a new name for the former Thanh Nien, no doubt contained within itself "heterogeneous elements" *(phan-tu phuc-tap)*, whereas DDCSD, being a rigorously organized Party, had restricted its membership to militants who had demonstrated their commitment, ability, and loyalty to the revolutionary cause. Furthermore, the Annamese faction, being the younger organization, enjoyed only limited influence confined to Nam Ky, whereas DDCSD, being a Communist organization from the beginning, had established stronger and more extensive mass bases throughout Vietnamese territory. In Phiem Chu's view, therefore, the only way to form a unified Vietnamese Communist movement was for the Annamese group to dissolve itself; those who wished to become DDCSD members would then be selected on individual merit. Except for a clearer understanding of the position of the other side, the representatives accomplished little and returned to their respective organizations empty-handed.

It was in a meeting in Hong Kong on 3–7 February 1930 that the two rival Communist factions finally formed one comprehensive organization.[66] This meeting, now called the Unification Conference, was convoked by Nguyen Ai Quoc in the name of the Communist International. In addition to those already present in Hong Kong (Ho Tung Mau, Le Hong Son, and Le Tan Anh), two representatives from each of the first two Communist factions were present: Nguyen Duc Canh and Trinh Dinh Cuu represented the DDCSD, Chau van Liem and Nguyen Thieu the Annamese Communists. The delegates were unaware until after the conference that Tan Viet had transformed itself into the League of Indochinese Communists. After a few days of exchanging invective, recriminations, and mutual accusations, the two groups agreed to unite. With some reluctance, they also agreed to dissolve their own groups and to establish a unified Communist party, to be called Dang Cong San Viet Nam, or the Vietnamese Communist Party.[67] The VCP was founded in accordance with the Comintern's revolutionary line and the theses on the colonial question adopted at the Sixth World Congress. It made provisional arrangements for the formation of a Central Committee, called for an end to factional dispute, and accepted all Communist-oriented revolutionaries living in Vietnam, including the Tan Viet and overseas CCP members, for Party membership.

In addition to deciding organizational matters, the new Party also published two documents, the "Sach luoc van tat cua Dang" [Party's strategies in summary] and "Loi keu goi" [Appeal], aimed at workers, peasants, soldiers, young people, students, and ex-

66. Today 3 February 1930 is commemorated as the birthday of the Vietnamese Communist party. Until the Third Congress of the Vietnam Workers' party in September 1960, however, the Party celebrated its founding on 6 January, mistaking the date in the lunar calendar for the date on the Gregorian calendar. Due to this error, the first national elections under the Viet Minh government were held on 6 January 1946.

67. It is worth noting that from this time on, Vietnamese syntax characterized Party names. Before this, all Communist and noncommunist anticolonial groups had used Chinese syntax, e.g., Viet Nam Quoc Dan Dang, Dong Duong Cong San Dang. The new name was emphatically Vietnamese, though its terms were of Chinese origin: Dang Cong-san Viet Nam. The same name, with Chinese syntax, would be Viet Nam Cong San Dang.

ploited people. The summary of Party strategies,[68] though committing the Party to be the "vanguard of the proletariat," nevertheless contained elements that the Comintern and radicals within the Party found objectionable. The fourth clause stated:

> The Party must do its best to maintain relationships with the petit-bourgeois, intellectual, and middle peasant groups such as Thanh Nien, Tan Viet, Nguyen An Ninh faction, etc., to attract them to follow the proletariat. As concerns the rich peasants, medium and small landowners, and Vietnamese capitalists who have not shown themselves to be clearly counterrevolutionary, we must make use of them, or at least neutralize them. Whichever organization has demonstrated its counterrevolutionary character (such as the Constitutionalist party, etc.) must be overthrown.

The fifth clause specified:

> While making propaganda for the slogan "an independent Vietnam," we must make propaganda for and establish contacts with the oppressed peoples and the world proletariat, especially the French proletariat.

These clauses constituted the nexus of the continuing ideological conflict within the Vietnamese Communist movement.

THE INDOCHINESE COMMUNIST PARTY (ICP)

The arrangements made at the Unification Conference proved transitory. In less than a year they were abandoned, having been denounced by the Comintern as "unprincipled" and violating the spirit and letter of its directives. Acceding to Comintern orders, the VCP organized a conference, now referred to as the First Plenum of the Party's Central Committee, in Hong Kong in October 1930 to rectify the situation.[69]

68. For the text see Ho Chi Minh, *Ket hop chat che long yeu nuoc voi tinh than quoc te vo san* [Fusing intimately patriotism with proletarian internationalism] (Hanoi, 1976), pp. 74–75.

69. The following leaders participated in the Plenum: Nguyen Ai Quoc, representing the Comintern; Tran Phu, secretary-general designate; Le Mao, representing the Trung Ky Regional Committee; Nguyen Trong Nha, representing the Nam Ky Regional Committee; Ngo Duc Tri, representing the Nam Ky Regional Committee; and A Lau, representing the special committee for Chinese CCP members residing in Indochina. T. C., "Nhin lai cac co so bi mat cua co quan lanh dao Dang Cong san Dong duong (tu 1930 den 1935)" [Retrospective view on the secret bases of the leadership organs of the Indochinese Communist party from 1930 to 1935], *NCLS*, no. 37 (April 1962), pp. 20–26.

Reviewing past activity, the Conference ascertained that the Party had committed serious errors, which caused a slackening in the progress of Party development. Many of the erroneous policies were traceable to the Unification Conference, which disregarded the Comintern's instructions with regard to the Party's organization, strategy, and appellation. Violating the spirit of "revolutionary purity" of the Sixth World Congress, the VCP had failed to purge the movement of "heterogeneous elements" and to reform its constituent factions of their "sectarian" approach to politics. The "Resolution" of the First Plenum stated:

> The "Unification Conference" stressed only the unification of existing organizations, paying little attention to the elimination of their sectarian thoughts and activities. For that reason, the Party, though unified, allows its constituent groups to retain their former thoughts and habits. . . . There is little coherence in the day-to-day activities of the different echelons of the Party.[70]

The second, more serious problem concerned the "erroneous and dangerous" political line of the VCP expressed in its summary of strategies. In calling for serious attempts to "maintain relationships" with the petit-bourgeoisie, intellectuals, and middle peasants, the VCP had allegedly violated the class principle of communism.

> The landlords are a class which does not participate in the cultivation of the land, nor does it live like peasants. They use their land in order to get their share of the crops, that is, they oppress and exploit the peasants. Although it is true that some of them may have a few hundred hectares while others five to seven thousand hectares, all of them belong to the landlord class, the enemy of the peasants. They must be overthrown, and their land confiscated.[71]

It was also a serious error to think that the Party could make use of those bourgeois elements who had not proved themselves to be counterrevolutionaries.

> While it is true that there exists such a group, they cannot be on our side, nor can we make use of them. . . . The Party must do its best to

70. "An nghi quyet cua Trung uong toan the hoi nghi noi ve tinh hinh hien tai o Dong-duong va nhiem vu can kip cua Dang" [Resolutions of the Plenum of the Central Committee on the present situation in Indochina and the urgent tasks of the Party], in Vu bien soan, *Van kien Dang,* 1:58.
71. Ibid., p. 59.

destroy their influence among the masses. (We have to unmask them, exposing their wishy-washy attitude with regard to the imperialists and landlords and with regard to the workers and peasants.) To say that the Party at least ought to neutralize them is to tell the Party not to advocate the struggle of the workers and peasants against the native bourgeoisie. The Party cannot have such a policy.[72]

Finally, the Party's appellation, Vietnamese Communist Party, itself reflected a dangerous ideological deviation. In emphasizing the antiimperialist struggle and the slogan of "an independent Vietnam" the VCP was said to have promoted narrow national chauvinism while downplaying the importance of proletarian internationalism.

> Calling the Party the "Vietnamese Communist Party" would exclude Cambodia and Laos. At the same time, it is wrong to leave the working class of those two countries outside the framework of the Party, for although the Vietnamese, Cambodian, and Laotian proletarians differ in their linguistic, customary, and ethnic background, in political and economic aspects they must maintain intimate relationships.[73]

The Conference thus decided to renounce the Party's existing name in favor of a new one: the Indochinese Communist Party (Dang Cong san Dong duong) or ICP. *Cong nong binh* [Worker, peasant, and soldier], a Party periodical, later explained this important decision in the following terms:

> Although the three countries are made up of three different races, with different languages, different traditions, different behavior patterns, in reality they form only one country. . . . It is . . . not possible to make a revolution separately for Vietnam, Cambodia, and Laos. In order to oppose the enemy of the revolution which has a united concentration of force in the entire Indochina, the Communist party will have to concentrate the forces of the Indochinese proletariat in a united front, under the leadership of the Indochinese proletariat. . . . Although the Party's name is only a form, since the form is important for the revolution, the change has to be made.[74]

Not all in the movement, however, readily accepted the new name. Many, especially the leaders of the Trung Ky Regional Com-

72. Ibid.
73. Ibid., p. 60.
74. *Cong nong binh* [Worker, peasant, and soldier], 6 February 1931, quoted in Tran Huy Lieu, *Lich su tam muoi nam*, 2:36.

mittee, preferred to keep the name Vietnamese Communist party, arguing that it reflected the indomitable will of the Vietnamese nation for independence and that Cambodia and Laos would have to form their own Communist parties before they could join with Vietnam in founding an Indochinese party.[75] In those days of Bolshevization, the believers in internationalism easily overruled this "nationalist" and "narrow-minded chauvinist" view. Significantly, this was the first Vietnamese debate on the Communist concept of an Indochinese federation. In any case, the new name remained the official one until the ICP was dissolved *pro forma* in November 1945.[76]

THE POLITICAL THESES

Another significant decision of the First Plenum was its adoption of the *Political Theses of the Indochinese Communist Party,* drafted by Tran Phu,[77] as the fundamental guideline of the Party. This document, which borrowed heavily from the Comintern's "Program of the International" and "Theses" on the colonial question adopted at the Sixth World Congress, was an attempt to adapt the new Comintern line to the specific situation of Indochina. The ICP's *Political Theses* is composed of three parts. The first part, dealing with the world situation, distinguished the three periods of world economic and political development since the end of the

75. Nguyen Ai Quoc to the ICP Central Committee, 21 April 1931, reprinted in Gouvernement général, *Contribution,* vol. 4, supp. 12, p. 114.

76. In 1951, when the Party reemerged as a "Party in power," it adopted the name Dang Lao dong Viet Nam (Vietnam Workers' Party). At the Fourth Congress of the Party, held in Hanoi in December 1976, the cycle became complete: the Party reverted to the name originally given it by Nguyen Ai Quoc in February 1930: Dang Cong san Viet Nam (Vietnamese Communist Party).

77. The *Luan cuong chinh tri cua Dang Cong-san Dong-duong* [Political theses of the Indochinese Communist Party], usually abbreviated as *Luan cuong chinh tri* [Political theses], is reprinted in full in Ban Nghien cuu, *Buoc ngoat vi dai,* pp. 78–89. In 1932 the Provisional Central Executive Committee of the Indochinese Communist party (Trung Uong lam thoi chap uy cua Dang Cong san Dong duong) published another important document, *Chuong trinh hanh dong cua Dang Cong san Dong duong* [Program of action of the Indochinese Communist party]. This document, however, was only an elaboration of the *Political Theses* and had little effect on a Party that was in total disarray. Although the *Political Theses* was significantly modified by the "Resolutions" of the Eighth Plenum of the Party in May 1941, its strategy of a double, or parallel, revolution remained fundamental throughout the Party's first five decades. All quotations of the *Political Theses* cited in this section are from the original version reprinted in *Buoc ngoat vi dai.*

First World War and predicted the crisis of world capitalism. The second part, entitled "The Characteristics of the Situation in Indochina," noted the increasing internal contradictions within Indochina, accompanied by radicalization of the Vietnamese anticolonial struggle. The Party contended that from a purely national liberation phenomenon, the struggle had become increasingly a class-oriented movement.

> The Indochinese proletariat is not yet numerous, but the number of workers, especially plantation workers, is on the increase. They fight ever more actively. The peasants have also awakened and fiercely opposed the imperialists and feudalists. The strikes in 1928, 1929, and the violent outbursts of workers and peasants this year [1930] have clearly proved that the class struggle in Indochina is gaining momentum. The most outstanding and important feature in the revolutionary movement in Indochina is that the struggle of the worker-peasant masses has taken on a very clearly independent character and is no longer influenced by nationalism as it used to be.

The third part, "The Characteristics and Tasks of the Indochinese Revolution," was to become the basic strategy for the Vietnamese Communist movement for several years to come. Following the Comintern's colonial strategy, the *Political Theses* considered the Indochinese revolution at this stage the "bourgeois-democratic revolution" *(cach mang tu san dan quyen),* a stepping-stone toward the second stage, the socialist and proletarian revolution, bypassing the stage of capitalist development of the economy.

> The bourgeois-democratic revolution is a preparatory period leading to socialist revolution. Once it has won victory, and a worker-peasant government has been established, industry within the country will develop, proletarian organizations will be reinforced, the leadership of the proletariat will be consolidated, and the balance of class forces will be altered to the advantage of the proletariat. The struggle will develop in depth and breadth and the bourgeois democratic revolution will advance toward the proletarian revolution.

Specifically, the *Political Theses* considered the essential objective of the Indochinese revolution to be a double, or parallel, revolution.[78] Indochinese society, according to this analysis, con-

---

78. For authoritative discussions of the strategic lines of the Vietnamese revolution, read Truong Chinh, "Les principes stratégiques directeurs de notre parti," in *En avant sous le drapeau du parti* (Hanoi, 1965), pp. 71–93; and Le Duan, "Mot vai dac diem cua cach mang Viet Nam" [Some special characteristics of the Vietnamese revolution], in *Lien minh cong nong,* pp. 9–48.

fronted two fundamental contradictions: that between Indochinese society and foreign imperialism, and that between the popular masses and the feudal landowning classes. From this perspective, foreign imperialism and the native feudal class had entered into a collusive relationship. The French colonialists, in this view, could effectively control, exploit, and oppress the Indochinese people only with the cooperation and support of the "class of feudal landowners, especially the great landlords." The king, mandarins, and local notables, on the other hand, relied on the French and became their agents in order to preserve the interests of the landowning class, which they represented.

To resolve these contradictions, the Indochinese revolution faced two simultaneous tasks: "antiimperialism" *(phan de)*, or the destruction of French colonial imperialism; and "antifeudalism" *(bai phong)*, or the elimination of all vestiges of the feudal society, bringing about land reforms and realizing the slogan "land to the tillers" *(nguoi cay co ruong)*. These two tasks were intimately linked. In order to destroy French imperialism, it was necessary to destroy its base of support, the native feudalist class; and in order to destroy the feudal class, it was necessary to destroy its supporting agent, French colonial imperialism. The *Political Theses* stated the goals thus:

> The essential aim of the bourgeois-democratic revolution is, on the one hand, to do away with the feudal vestiges and modes of precapitalist exploitation and to carry out a thorough agrarian revolution; on the other hand, to overthrow French imperialism and achieve complete independence for Indochina. The two faces of the struggle are closely connected, for only by deposing imperialism can we eliminate the landlord class and carry out a successful agrarian revolution; conversely, only by abolishing the feudal regime can we defeat imperialism.

This double revolution remained the fundamental strategic line of Vietnamese communism until the defeat of U.S. imperialism in Vietnam in 1975.

Adoption of the *Political Theses,* however, implied the Vietnamese Communists' acceptance of certain principles fundamental to international communism. The first principle is the *class approach to politics;* that is, the entire policy of Communists, their approach to sociopolitical problems and their appraisal of other parties and trends, is always class based. For Communists, political parties ultimately express the interests of definite classes or social strata. Also, whereas political parties representing bourgeois or petit-bourgeois interests most often conceal their class essence, the Communist party openly proclaims its identification with the interests of the working class.

Second, and connected intrinsically with the class approach, is the principle of *revolutionism*. This amounts to the belief that only through a revolution, a social upheaval that would overthrow capitalism and eliminate all forms of exploitation and oppression, can the interests of the working class be realized. This principle requires that Marxist-Leninists reject "opportunism"[79] and "reformism,"[80] which are tantamount to "class collaboration"; that is, the willingness to work for social change within the capitalist framework.

Finally, the principle of *internationalism* assumes that although each Communist party operates within a definite set of national conditions and must formulate its strategy and tactics in accordance with specific conditions and alignments of political forces,

79. Communists tend to attack as "opportunists" those who seriously deviate from the "correct" revolutionary line of the Party. Lenin emphasized that the class essence of opportunism lies in the fact that its proponents are allies and agents of the bourgeoisie and that political opportunism inevitably leads to renunciation of Marxism-Leninism. In Leninist theory, there are both "right" opportunism and "left" opportunism. The former entails denying revolutionary methods of struggle and seeking compromise with the bourgeoisie and, ultimately, withdrawing from the struggle for socialism. "Left" opportunism involves paying lip service to the most resolute and ultrarevolutionary methods of struggle and verbally rejecting all forms of compromise and reform. Left opportunism leads the movement to revolutionary defeat, for in seeking to accelerate the revolutionary process it fails to take into account the concrete situation, separates the Party from the masses, and discredits its ideals. Both forms of opportunism are considered harmful to the revolutionary process and misleading to the revolutionary masses. Right opportunism leads to "class collaboration" with the bourgeoisie; left opportunism leads to adventurism.

80. "Reformism" is considered a species of opportunism. Its proponents tend to be liberal democrats who seek social reforms to ameliorate the social and economic conditions of the working masses, but at the same time reject revolutionism, or the principle of class struggle and the overthrow of the bourgeoisie. Reformists advocate collaboration of all classes within capitalist society, contending that capitalism can be "improved" and its evils "reformed" while preserving the foundations of the liberal bourgeois society. For Marxist-Leninists, reformism is a dangerous doctrine, perhaps more dangerous than anticommunism, for it helps smooth the rough edges of capitalism, blurs class lines, and "immunizes" the workers from the class struggle. Indeed, it may be seen as bolstering capitalism.

Marxist-Leninist parties are tied with one another by the bonds of international solidarity. This common struggle of all Communists is expressed both in their ideology and in their task of defeating world capitalism.

The adherence of Vietnamese revolutionaries to these Communist principles during the ultra-leftist orientation of the Comintern led to a type of "left opportunism" characteristic of revolutionary infantilism. The political line of the ICP's *Political Theses,* though conforming with the Comintern's revolutionary line, showed no understanding of the necessity for creative adaptation of Marxism-Leninism to the specific situation of a colonized society. It denied the reality of Vietnamese patriotism and at the same time rejected the virtues of national unity in the antiimperialist struggle. As a result, the new ICP line became the source of great difficulty for the Party during the next several years.

PARTY ORGANIZATION

Organizational aspects of the Vietnamese Communist movement were another significant feature decided upon at the First Plenum. These organizational features have remained largely unchanged throughout the history of Vietnamese communism despite modifications or complete alterations in the political line of the Party. Although most of the external forms of the Communist organization such as its front organizations, are subject to constant change in response to changing conditions, the internal structure of the ICP, now the VCP, has remained unchanged. Indeed, organization was one of the key weapons in the ICP's seizure and retention of political power. Organization, propaganda, and agitation—these basic operational features of the ICP complemented one another: organize in order to agitate and make propaganda; make propaganda in order to agitate and organize; agitate in order to make propaganda and organize. Three basic functions of the Communist organization worked interdependently to widen the parameters of Communist influence, mobilize the masses, and establish legitimacy for the ICP. As Le Duan, secretary-general of the VCP, said several years later in his theoretical work, *The Vietnamese Revolution: Fundamental Problems, Essential Tasks:*

Before seizure of power and in the pursuit of that aim, the only weapon available to the revolution, to the masses, is organization. The hallmark of the revolutionary movement led by the proletariat is its high organizational standard. All activities aimed at bringing the masses to the point where they will rise up and topple the ruling classes may boil down to this: to organize, organize, organize. The purpose of political propaganda and agitation is indeed to organize the masses; only by organizing them one way or another will conditions be created for educating them and building up the immense strength of the revolution, for once organized, their power will increase one hundredfold. . . . Therefore, propaganda, organization, and struggle must go hand in hand, the common purpose being to form and enlarge the political army of the masses in preparation for the decisive leap.[81]

Although it took the ICP another decade to master the theory and practice of Leninist revolutionary organization, in the years 1929–1931 the fundamental Leninist organizational elements emerged that differentiated the ICP from all previous Vietnamese anticolonial organizations, Thanh Nien included. Like other Bolshevik parties, the ICP claimed to be a "party of the new type,"[82] which conceptually differed from all "bourgeois" political parties in concept, organization, and objectives. In the Communist perspective, "bourgeois" parties are only "auxiliary electoral machines" created for the purpose of gaining power through manipulation of elections. Accepting the existing political structure and processes, these parties could at best be "reformist," never "revolutionary." The Bolshevik party, too, is organized to seize power, but as a "revolutionary" party its ultimate purpose in seizing power is to transform society by restructuring the political system and social relations. When possible, a Bolshevik party will obtain power through electoral routes; when this is not possible, it will use less overt and less legal means.

81. Le Duan, *The Vietnamese Revolution*, p. 51.
82. Lenin first proposed the concept of the "party of the new type" in opposition to "revisionists"—the social democrats—who saw the working-class party, like other political parties, as an electioneering machine. Lenin postulated that the working-class party must have the following five characteristics: the Party is the *organized vanguard* of the working class; the Party is the *supreme organizational expression* of the working class; the Party is an *instrument* of proletarian dictatorship; the Party is a bloc of united determination that does not tolerate sectarianism; and the Party grows in strength by eliminating "opportunist elements." Leninist parties thus call themselves parties "of the new type" in order to distinguish themselves from socialist and other noncommunist political parties.

On paper at least, the ICP developed in accordance with Lenin's conception of a revolutionary party as a "sum of organizations," with the organization of "professional revolutionaries" acting as the intellectual head and the nucleus of a multiplicity of mass organizations of workers, peasants, students, and women, who would serve as the organizational base for the revolution.[83] Thus, the ICP was not one organization, but a system of organizations, composed of two networks: a vertical network—the ICP itself—and a horizontal network of "mass organizations" *(to chuc quan chung)* to achieve mass mobilization.

The ICP's vertical network was a militant, centralized, hierarchical organization constructed on the basis of a specific body of doctrine, developed precisely in theory, and then applied in practice. As such, it was a political warfare organization, or in Lenin's words, the "general staff of the revolution," whose ultimate objective was to seize political power in the name of the movement or the nation, and, once it became a party in power, to assume the management of society single-handedly, regardless of the extent to which it appears to constitute a national front.[84] This vertical network was the base of what Lenin called "the professional revolutionaries," who, like secular monks, vowed total and unconditional obedience to the supreme leadership of the party, had no other vocation but to make a revolution, and depended on the organization for material sustenance. Cutting themselves off from normal social ties, the professional revolutionaries were wedded to the organization; the party became their family, and their comrades relatives. Thus, just as the party was a state within a state—with its own administration, police, army, and judiciary—it was also a society within a society.

In the early 1930s the ICP's vertical network was linked with the

83. In *One Step Forward, Two Steps Back* (1904), Lenin stated: "I . . . warned in my speech [at the Second Congress that] it should not be imagined that Party organizations must consist only of professional revolutionaries; we need the most variegated organizations of all types, ranks and shades, beginning with very narrow and secret and conspiratorial and ending with very broad, free *lose Organizationen"* *(Selected Works,* 1:308).

84. For a discussion of the Leninist concept of organization, see Abdurakhman Avtorkhanov, *The Communist Party Apparatus* (New York, 1966), pp. 1–18; Robert C. Tucker, *The Soviet Political Mind: Stalinism and Post-Stalin Change,* rev. ed. (New York, 1971), pp. 7–13; Alfred G. Meyer, *Leninism* (New York, 1962), pp. 37–56.

Communist International headquarters in Moscow via both the CCP and PCF. Through these foreign Communist parties, the ICP received financial subsidies (approximately five thousand francs monthly in 1930 and 1931),[85] instructions, directives, theoretical assistance in terms of publications, and sometimes some handguns.[86]

Within Vietnam the ICP was organized on a strictly hierarchical principle: the nucleus of each superior organization was the directing organ for the next lower one, and the entire network was under the supreme authority of the Central Committee, which was at once legislative, executive, and judicial. Thus, the ICP had a complicated organizational structure, with theoretical responsibility for Party organization of Indochina as a whole (in practice only Vietnam had Party organizations; not until 1934 did Laos have Party locals) and for each of the three regions of Vietnam down to the district and local branches. The overall Party organization was divided into six levels:[87]

The Central Committee (Trung uong Dang bo), responsible for the operation of the entire Party within Indochina and serving as a liaison with the Communist International, its regional sections in East and Southeast Asia, and the PCF (see Appendix, Chart 2).

Three regional committees *(xu bo)* responsible for each of the regions of Vietnam: the Xu bo Bac Ky, Xu bo Trung Ky, and Xu bo Nam Ky. (There were also established two "Special Bureaus," equivalent in hierarchical rank to the *xu bo,* for Vietnamese residents in Laos and Siam.) The regional committees were responsi-

---

85. Gouvernement général, *Contribution,* 4:29.

86. Hoang Quoc Viet, for example, was the liaison between the Vietnamese Communists and the PCF in 1929. As a sailor on the S.S. *Chantilly,* plying between Saigon and Marseille, he brought back to Vietnam on one occasion "a few suitcases full of Communist books and a few revolvers for self-defense" as presents of the PCF to the Vietnamese. Nguyen Trong Con, "Nhung hinh thuc to chuc va dau tranh cua thuy thu Viet Nam tu nam 1929 den 1935" [The forms of organization and struggle of the Vietnamese sailors from 1929 until 1935], *NCLS,* no. 151 (July–August 1973), p. 27.

87. The organizational structure summarized here is based on the ICP's regulations; see "Statuts définitifs du parti communiste indochinois et de ses organisations annexes," in Gouvernement général, *Contribution,* vol. 4, supp. 6, pp. 77–95. Other documents on Party reorganization as a result of the Unification Conference and the First Plenum are found in AOM, SLOTFOM, vol. 3, carton 149, NPM, March–April 1930, May–June 1930, December 1930–January 1931, March–April 1931.

ble to the Central Committee for all Party affairs in their regions (see Appendix, Chart 3, for structure of Bac Ky Regional Committee).

Provincial committees *(tinh bo),* responsible for all Party affairs in each province.

Municipal committees *(thi bo),* responsible for the Party affairs in given cities.

Prefectural, or district committees *(huyen bo)* for each district.

Party locals *(chi bo).*

The *chi bo* was considered the fundamental organization of the Party. This was theoretically "the professional cell" the members of which (mechanics, miners, coolies, railroad workers, soldiers, and students) worked in the same establishment.[88] Three members could form a *chi bo;* once the *chi bo* had gained an "excessive number of adherents" (more than ten) they were to be subdivided into small cells [*tieu to*], or "fractions," whose membership should never exceed five.

THE UNITED FRONT

In addition to its vertical network, the ICP had, at least on paper, a horizontal network of "mass organizations." These represented ICP implementation of the United Front tactic, an ingenious Leninist organizational instrument that VCP leaders today have repeatedly credited as an important factor in the Communist success in Vietnam.[89] Essentially, the United Front tactic attempts to provide links between the Party and noncommunist elements. It was motivated by the desire to establish political bases among the "amorphous masses" in order to mobilize the "intermediary elements" (intermediary between the Party and "the enemy"), to prevent the isolation of revolutionaries from society, and to allow the Party to sink "deep roots" in the masses.[90] Thanks to its system of

88. Gouvernement général, *Contribution,* vol. 4, supp. 6, p. 79.

89. See, for example, Truong Chinh, *En avant,* pp. 44–45; and Vo Nguyen Giap, *Guerre du peuple, armée du peuple* (Paris, 1966), pp. 30–31, 34.

90. Commenting on the utility of mass organizations, Lenin stated in *What Is to Be Done?* (1902), "Our movement cannot be unearthed, for the very reason that it has countless thousands of roots deep down among the masses. . . . As far as 'deep roots' are concerned, we cannot be 'unearthed' even now, despite our amateurism" (*Selected Works,* 1:199).

mass organizations, over the years the ICP was able to penetrate deep into the social systems of Indochina—among lowland Vietnamese as well as the ethnic minorities of the mountains, among petit-bourgeois intellectuals as well as workers and peasants, among Vietnamese abroad as well as those at home. Indeed, the ICP's United Front policy may well be the principal reason for the Party's survival despite repeated, thorough, and brutal repression by the colonial government. Its "deep roots" in the masses, which could not be all "unearthed," accounted in large part for its reemergence after each wave of repression and thus its eventual successful seizure of power in the autumn of 1945.

The increasingly sophisticated adaptation of the United Front policy in Vietnam had its origins in Nguyen Ai Quoc's attempts to organize workers, peasants, students, and soldiers in the early days of Thanh Nien. In formally defined terms, however, the United Front policy was put into practice only as a result of the proletarianization campaign. Conceived of as the organizational front of the Communist party, the United Front was supposed to be its architectural facade, composed of social and functional organizations whose dual function was to shield the Party from unfriendly forces and at the same time promote the Party's ideological values and policies as widely as possible.[91]

Conceptually, then, the Leninist party is the nucleus of a system of political organizations. The nuclear organization contains the professional revolutionaries, whereas the mass organizations are the bases of "fellow travelers" *(ban cung duong)*, those who agree with the Party's objectives but prefer not to march under its banners.[92] In practice, this type of organizational front may consist of either a single organization or a series of onionlike, concentric

91. For Lenin's discussion of the organizational front, see "The Reorganization of the Party," in *Selected Works,* 1:567–574. For a detailed discussion of the concept and practice of the United Front see Philip Selznick, *The Organizational Weapon* (Glencoe, Ill., 1960), pp. 113–170. Shortly prior to the formation of the National Front of Liberation of South Vietnam (NFL), the theoreticians in the Vietnam Workers' party debated the meaning of the concepts "front," "movement front," "organization front," etc. See Van Tao, "Tim hieu qua trinh hinh thanh va phat trien cua Mat Tran Dan toc Thong Nhat Viet Nam" [Understanding the history of the formation and development of the national united front in Vietnam], *NCLS,* no. 1 (1959), pp. 27–41. See also Hoang Ho, "Ban them ve bai," pp. 47–62.

92. For a literate discussion on the nature of Communist-inspired mass organizations, read David Caute, *The Fellow Travellers* (London, 1973).

layers of organizations, with the revolutionary party as the center of all the layers. The principal advantage of this organizational tactic is its flexibility. There are no limits to the number of mass organizations in a front. Any social category may be used as the basis for a mass organization: age, education, sex, profession, or religion. Nor are there limits to the number of members in a Party-affiliated mass organization: three to five people can form one. In its primitive form, the organizational front proposed by the First Plenum in October 1930, the ICP was to be surrounded by seven specific mass organizations: the Communist Youth Corps (Thanh Nien Cong san Doan), the General Association of Peasants (Tong Nong Hoi), Indochina's General Association of Workers (Tong Cong Hoi Dong Duong), The League of Indochinese Women (Dong Duong Phu Nu Lien Hiep Hoi), the Indochinese Red Aid Society (Hoi Cuu Te Do Dong Duong), the Self-Defense Militia (Doi Tu ve), and the Indochinese Antiimperialist Alliance (Hoi Phan De Dong Minh Dong Duong) (see Figure 1).[93]

In addition to the organizational front, the Party also sought a temporary alliance with existing Vietnamese parties, regardless of their political tendencies. With this purpose, it proposed to other parties an Indochinese Antiimperialist Alliance (Hoi Phan De Dong Minh Dong Duong). This front, unlike the organizational one, was to be entirely expedient in nature: the existing political parties would form a coalition for a specific objective. In Communist parlance, this is a "united front from above" or a "movement front," and the term *front* has military implications. Like a military battle formation against a common enemy, the "united front from above" is only temporary; it ceases to exist the moment the common objective is achieved.

In the months following the First Plenum, the ICP made several attempts to invite other political parties to join the Indochinese Antiimperialist Alliance, but its success was minimal. Curiously, the Party courted not only the VNQDD but also the Constitutionalist party. In its appeal the ICP said:

> The revolutionary parties in Indochina are: the VNQDD, the Constitutionalist party, the Tan Viet party, the Thanh Nien party, the Indochinese Communist party.

93. See Tran Huy Lieu, *Lich su tam muoi nam*, 2:38–39.

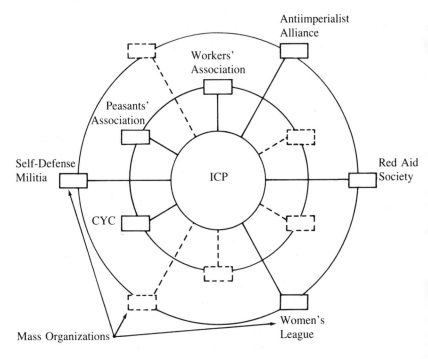

Legend: Solid lines (and boxes) indicate existing mass organizations as of December 1930.

Broken lines (and boxes) indicate potential mass organizations.

Figure 1. The ICP and its front networks

We cannot say which of these parties is truly capable of guiding the workers and peasants in their struggle for emancipation, which tends to become counterrevolutionary. Whatever the case may be, all have leaders capable of promoting the revolution. But if they do not have slogans summarizing the aspirations of the people, it would be impossible for them to bring all the revolutionary forces together in a united front of combat, and these forces risk the possibility of dividing among themselves and destroying themselves for the benefit of the French imperialists.[94]

The Indochinese Antiimperialist Alliance never acquired a significant membership. By the time the ICP published its appeal, Tan Viet and Thanh Nien were no longer in existence, the Nguyen An Ninh group had been destroyed; and so had the national framework of the VNQDD. The possibility of forming an anti-imperialist front with the pro-French Constitutionalist party was beyond hope. Only in Nam Ky were there some relations between ICP members and certain left-wing VNQDD members under the aegis of the antiimperialist alliance.[95]

The year 1930 was to be commemorated as a turning point in Vietnamese history. The Yen Bay Mutiny is today remembered for the martyrdom of the insurrectionists but also as the cause of the VNQDD's demise. The Unification Conference, on the other hand, is celebrated as the official beginning of Vietnamese communism. The destruction of the VNQDD and the conversion of Thanh Nien and Tan Viet into a unified Communist party marked a new phase in the development of the Vietnamese revolutionary movement. Revolutionary patriotism, that peculiar blend of traditional Vietnamese patriotism and imported revolutionism which had fired the imagination of many Vietnamese throughout the second half of the 1920s, suffered a serious setback. The nationalist-oriented slogan of Thanh Nien, "First make a national revolution, then make a world revolution," which had moved anticolonial Vietnamese of all social strata and ideological orientations, had now been discarded as old-fashioned and inappropriate. In its place were all the slogans and jargon of the Comintern's Third Period—"proletarianization," "Bolshevization," and "class-against-class" tactics. This subordination of Vietnamese patriotism to left-wing Communist sectarianism almost caused a fatal collapse of the ICP.

94. *Thanh nien,* May 1930.
95. Tran Huy Lieu, *Lich su tam muoi nam,* 2:40–41.

CHAPTER THREE

THE CRISIS OF INFANTILE COMMUNISM

> *Judge:* What is your profession?
>
> *D. v. Khoi:* I used to be a typist, but my profession now is to make a revolution.
>
> *Judge:* You declared that you have been a member of the Communist Party since 1930 in order to defeat French imperialism.
>
> *D. v. Khoi:* My intention is to overthrow all imperialisms in our times, and not just French imperialism.
>
> > Interrogation of Dang van Khoi, alias Van Son, age eighteen, Proceedings of the Hanoi Criminal Commission (May 1931)

For students of Vietnamese communism, the early 1930s present a paradox. By the yardstick of the late 1920s, this should have been an opportune time for the rapid expansion of Communist influence in Vietnam. Communism had made great strides in 1928–1930 despite competition from Vietnamese revolutionary patriotism and unbridled repression by a colonial regime. By the spring of 1930, revolutionary patriotism had been defeated—the VNQDD had been destroyed, and Thanh Nien and Tan Viet had become a unified Communist party. By late 1930, the colonial regime faced an unprecedented crisis, brought about by the Great Depression and heightened anticolonial feeling in France. Yet the first half of the 1930s was one of the ICP's bleakest periods. Favorable circumstances alone were no guarantee of revolutionary progress. Plagued with internal factionalism while trying to follow the tortuous course set by directives from outside the country, the ICP experienced one of its most serious crises. By 1932, only two years after its founding, the Party lay prostrated, with virtually all its leaders killed or imprisoned and its organizational apparatus totally shattered. Meanwhile, as the prevailing Communist trend emphasized class struggle and downgraded "bourgeois nationalism," communism itself, which had been exalted by many in Vietnam only a few years before, suffered eclipse. The ICP's misfortunes can be understood only in the general context of contemporary Vietnamese politics and the Party's internal situation, especially its relationship with the international Communist movement.

FRENCH COLONIALISM AT THE CROSSROADS

As the decade began, the general political situation of Vietnam seemed to favor a rapid expansion of Communist influence. The French were involved in an unprecedented economic and political crisis. As a consequence of the Great Depression, the previously uninterrupted prosperity of Indochina came to an end. Industrial stagnation, widespread unemployment and misery—conditions that created an ideal breeding ground for communism—were endemic. Such economic and social problems were unexceptional for the early 1930s, but the political difficulties of the French in Vietnam were not. For the first time cracks appeared in the solidarity of the European community in Indochina; meanwhile, in France anticolonial sentiments had reached a high point, threatening the de facto autonomy of the colonial regime. In retrospect, it is clear that these political difficulties were the beginning of an erosion of colonial authority that continued unabated until the end of French rule in Vietnam. When they were overthrown by a Japanese coup d'état in March 1945, the French still had not recovered the economic prosperity or political authority they had enjoyed up to 1930.

The crisis of French Indochina was largely economic. As a direct consequence of sharing in the worldwide economic boom of the 1920s, Indochina was enormously affected by the Great Depression.[1] The economic crisis hit Indochina around the second half of 1930, and from then until the end of 1933 the Indochinese economy was in great difficulty; industrial production came close to a standstill, and both the commercial and agricultural sectors experienced great losses. In 1929 the total value of Indochina exports stood at 228 million piasters. By 1932 this figure was at 102 million. During the same period, imports dwindled from 227 million to 94 million piasters. As elsewhere in the world, the effects of the Great Depression were manifested in a high rate of unemployment, business failures, bankruptcies, and widespread suffering. Only by 1935 did the effects begin to wane, and only in 1937 could it be said that Indochina was on its way to economic recovery.

Although there are as yet no comprehensive statistics on the social effects of the economic crisis, they can be seen in newspaper reports of retrenchment, of suicides due to loss of jobs, and of emigrant Chinese being sent back to China for lack of employment. One author estimates that "approximately more than one-third of the working class was completely unemployed during the years of the economic depression."[2] Although the accuracy of this estimate cannot be independently verified, it was a fact that many of those who were employed were either semiemployed or working extended hours at drastically reduced wages. Meanwhile, for lack of employment, during the first six months of 1931 alone, fourteen hundred Chinese were forced to return to China.[3] Civil servants

1. The most comprehensive and detailed study of the effects of the Great Depression on the Indochinese economy is André Touzet, *L'économie indochinoise et la grande crise* (Paris, 1934). For a thorough discussion of the fundamental economic problems of French Indochina, see Paul Bernard, *Le problème économique indochinois* (Paris, 1934) and *Nouveaux aspects du problème économique indochinois* (Paris, 1937). My discussion in this section generally follows the materials presented in these works.
2. Tran van Giau, *Giai cap cong nhan,* 1: 35. For the material conditions of Vietnamese workers during the depression years, see ibid., pp. 33–61.
3. *Phu nu tan van,* 23 July 1931.

fared no better than those in the private sector. In October 1931, for example, the government laid off one-seventh of all functionaries, reduced by 25 percent the wages of those who were employed, and compelled numerous older workers to retire. Another massive retrenchment and reduction of wages occurred in October 1932. Those who remained on the government payroll after this date suffered a cut of 30 percent in their already diminished salaries.[4]

The Great Depression also shattered the solidarity of the European community in the colony. By the logic peculiar to the market system, instead of much-needed unity, a Hobbesian situation prevailed in the community of European planters and businessmen as they faced the common crisis. Capitalists pitilessly seized the properties of their less fortunate fellows, and *colons,* sometimes instigated by Communist Vietnamese, marched in the streets against their compatriots. A fairly well-defined division developed among the colonial capitalists during these years. On one side stood the all-powerful Bank of Indochina, representing the great corporations of the mother country and supported by the colonial government. On the other side stood a coalition of local French and Vietnamese landed and business interests. Toward debtors who were unable to pay accumulated interests, the bank showed no leniency. Favored by the crisis, it maintained a high interest rate and mercilessly executed a policy of "cleansing" and "rationalization of colonial production." In practice, this meant seizure of real estate and other forms of collateral upon defaulted debts.[5] In these circumstances functionaries, landowners, rice planters, small- and medium-scale rubber planters, and businessmen, who had become indebted to the bank during the prosperity of the 1920s, now faced the distinct possibility of financial ruin.[6]

---

4. *L'Asie française* 33 (April 1933): 143–144.

5. An outrageous instance of the reckoning of accounts by the Bank of Indochina was the auctioning of the de la Souchère plantation on 28 September 1933. Valued at $2 million, it was awarded $100,000 by the bank.

6. An official French government report made at the conclusion of the Reynaud visit to Indochina aptly summarized the root cause of the internal contradictions of Indochinese colonial capitalism: "While the debtor cried: pity, ruin, delay; the Bank replied: law, liabilities, Civil Code, foreclosure." Gaston Joseph, "Conclusions sur le voyage de P. Reynaud en Indochine," 28 December 1931, AOM 635.

The internal contradictions of Indochinese colonial capitalism centered on the issue of the "stabilization" of the piaster.[7] This involved the government's decision to peg the piaster to the gold standard instead of the usual silver standard. The decision led, ironically, to a destabilization of the Indochinese European community. In a curious political turnabout, European planters and businessmen affected by this measure blamed the Bank of Indochina and the government as the source of their economic woes and threatened to take direct action against "the culprits." From January 1932 until late in 1934 Saigon was a turbulent center of political agitation not only for young Vietnamese radicals, but also for European *colons*. While the colonial press gave free vent to its dissatisfaction with the bank,[8] the Europeans staged protest meetings, marches, and business shutdowns to demand restrictions on the power of the bank and removal of Pierre Pasquier, the governor-general. In 1933 alone there were eight European demonstrations and rallies, involving thousands of *colons* and supported by southern Vietnamese landowners.[9] White planters and busi-

7. For a thorough discussion of the problems of the "stabilization" of the piaster in the 1930s, see Gaetan Pirou, "La piastre et le franc," *La revue indochinoise juridique et économique*, no. 5 (1938), pp. 5–28. See also Guy Lacam, chapter 4, "Capital and Its Circulation," in Charles Robequain, *The Economic Development of French Indochina* (London, 1944), especially pp. 137–149. By the French governmental decree of 18 July 1895, the piaster was tied to the French franc and was pegged to a twenty-seven-gram coin of 0.9 standard silver. As such, the piaster's value varied according to two factors: the value of silver and the value of the franc. Because of these fundamental connections, the value of the piaster fluctuated widely until "stabilization." On 1 August 1914, for example, the piaster was worth 2.50F. By February 1920 it had reached a high of 16.50F. By May 1920, however, it had fallen to 8.00F and reached a low of 6.71F in February 1931. The piaster then regained a high of 10.07F by the beginning of 1924, reaching a maximum of 27.50 in July 1926. From 1927 until 1930 it fluctuated between 10.00 and 13.00F. See Pirou, "La piastre et le franc," p. 7–8.

8. The headlines of three articles on the front page of *La presse indochinoise*, 19 March 1933, are illustrative: "Customs autonomy: Indochina will perish if its fate is tied with that of the mother country"; "One must take into account the fact that Indochina is sixteen thousand kilometers from France"; "What do we demand? Simple. We have a privileged bank, and we want a minting institute."

9. The rally on 27 October 1933, for example, brought out over three thousand Europeans; fifteen hundred Europeans marched in Saigon on 2 April 1934. At the peak of this wave of protest, fifteen thousand *colons*, civil servants, and businessmen marched on Rue Catinat, shouting "Long live the silver piaster! Down with the Bank of Indochina" (Hémery, *Révolutionnaires vietnamiens*, pp. 28–29). For a chronology of the European protests, see Hémery, pp. 60–61, n. 70.

nessmen, often the very ones who a year or two earlier had insisted
on the gallows for Vietnamese nationalists and Communists, were
now listening attentively to and even applauding Vietnamese Communist speakers who denounced the evils of capitalism. Nguyen
van Tao and Tran van Thach, the two leading Marxist radicals who
had been forcibly repatriated for anticolonial agitation in France,
found themselves sought-after speakers at European protest rallies.[10] When, at a rally on 27 October 1933, Tran van Thach urged
his European listeners to stage a protest march, he was wildly
acclaimed.[11] In August 1933, when Paul-Vaillant Couturier,
Nguyen Ai Quoc's comrade and a PCF central committee member,
visited Saigon as leader of an antiwar delegation, he was warmly
welcomed by the colonial press and was received as an official
guest of the Saigon municipality.[12]

ANTICOLONIALISM IN FRANCE

While the colonial regime in Indochina was buffeted by a
paralyzing economic crisis and debilitating internal tensions, it had
to confront, in France, a nation that was shocked and dismayed by
reported colonial abuses, continuous Vietnamese anticolonial activities, and brutality in quelling native rebellion. In the aftermath
of the Yen Bay Mutiny, many Frenchmen openly questioned the
ability of the colonial administrators to govern Indochina. In the
press, at mass rallies, and in the Chamber of Deputies Socialists
were joining Communists in denouncing the "native policy" *(la
politique indigène)* of the Indochinese regime. Many, including
those who had worked in Indochina, even discussed an eventual
French evacuation of the colony.[13] These denunciations, however,

10. Ibid., p. 61.
11. Ibid.
12. Ibid., pp. 61–62.
13. The reaction of Béziat, a Socialist and former mayor of Saigon, provides an
example. Yen Bay, for him, had been a "peal of thunder": "How could we Frenchmen get there after sixty years' stay in Indochina? . . . What have they done? They
have tried to maintain this people under slavery; they have humiliated it, despised
it. . . . They have wanted to explain Yen Bay away with communism. That is a
myth. . . . The abuses of our policy explain and perhaps justify the events at Yen
Bay. . . . If we had to recommence the policy of slaughtering and shooting, it would
be better for us to leave Indochina" (*Le courrier de Saigon,* 7 July 1931).

were not momentary reactions to a particular colonial policy; rather, they were part of a French political tradition.

Colonial imperialism in general and colonial rule in Indochina in particular had never been in high esteem among Frenchmen at home. The issue of overseas dominion had always been a divisive one. It had been the point of confrontation between the "two Frances": *la France continentale* and *la France maritime.*[14] Continental France was firmly planted on its own European soil and ever concerned with the threat of its powerful neighbor, Germany. Maritime France, the nation of colonial expansion, belonged to the Church, the military caste, and the circles of high finance—the France with which ordinary citizens had little contact. It was maritime France that cast its eyes over the horizons and dreamed of adventure. Its traditional adversary, unlike that of continental France, was Great Britain, not Germany. Within the home country, maritime France was represented by an unpopular colonial lobby, the *parti colonial,*[15] composed of members of the military establishment, the church, and the banking and industrial enterprises. Thus, over the centuries, the history of domestic France and that of the French colonial empire seldom converged; the two Frances were impelled by different forces and went separate ways. Whatever colonies maritime France established overseas were eventually sacrificed by continental France, often without regrets: Canada, Louisiana, India, St. Dominique, Suez, Panama, and more recently, Indochina and North Africa.

Indochina was the source of division within France from the earliest years of colonization. The Tonkin campaign of the 1880s, for example, had been the occasion of bitter controversy.[16] Long after the conquest of all Indochina, the French nation continued to show little interest in the acquisition. Just before the First World

14. Auguste Thomazi briefly discussed the concept of the "two Frances" in the preface of his book on French colonization of Indochina. The phrases "la France continentale" and "la France maritime" belong to him; *La conquête de l'Indochine* (Paris, 1934), pp. 7–8. For a brilliant analysis of the conflict of the "two Frances," see Herbert Luethy, *France against Herself* (New York, 1968). On French colonialism, read part 2, "Overseas France," pp. 203–282.

15. For a history of the *parti colonial,* see Henri Brunschwig, *French Colonialism, 1871–1914: Myths and Realities* (London, 1966), pp. 105–134; see also Xavier Yacono, *Histoire de la colonisation française* (Paris, 1969), pp. 46–48.

16. While the government of Premier Jules Ferry persisted in the campaign, viewing Indochina as a long-term investment, a hostile public considered the enterprise an affair of covetous adventurers and a waste of public funds. After several months of debate, the French Chamber of Deputies finally approved in December

War there were French writers who suggested exchanging Indochina for Alsace-Lorraine, and after the war, giving it to the United States to discharge the war debt.[17] The French at home were prepared to think the worst of the *colons* in Indochina. The possession was generally viewed as an exotic country of noble savage-natives with an ancient civilization, which the parochial brutes of the French provinces were destroying. Parisian writers caricatured the *colons* as hicks living in dissolute, luxurious idleness with little to do but oppress and exploit the natives, roam the streets in their pajamas, and shame the French nation by their petty disputes and wife swapping.[18]

A corollary of this latent anticolonialism and the romantic admiration for the exotic native culture was a ready support for all colonial causes, provided they criticized the government. Every time a colonial scandal came to light, each time an attempted insurrection exploded in Vietnam, the *parti colonial* scurried to cover it up while denunciations of colonialism blossomed. After the First World War this basic anticolonial prejudice and indigenophilia were strengthened by a sincere gratitude and appreciation for the role played by the Vietnamese during the war. Thus, despite the resentment of the *colons* in Vietnam, Vietnamese anticolonialists normally evoked sympathetic interest among the French people. Paris, Marseille, Aix-en-Provence, and Toulouse became their friendliest havens and forums, where French audiences applauded their strictures against French colonialism. During the first quarter of the century, Phan van Truong, Phan Chu Trinh, Nguyen Ai

---

1885 the necessary military credits for the Tonkin expedition. There were 274 votes for the expedition, and 270 against. See Thomazi, *Conquête de l'Indochine*, pp. 278–282.

17. Virginia Thompson, *French Indochina* (New York, 1968), p. 405.

18. Popular writings on Indochina during the first decades of the century, such as Claude Farrère's *Les civilisés*, Léon Werth's *Cochinchine*, Roland Dorgelès's *Sur la route mandarine*, and Luc Durtain's *Dieux blancs, hommes jaunes*, painted an ugly portrait of the *colon* society of Indochina. The colonial entrepreneurs were alleged to be dregs of the European failures, who tried to subjugate the more civilized natives. Jean Dorsenne, for example, reported the indignation of Cambodian women when a Frenchman, out of malice toward the well-known Cambodian modesty, urinated in front of them at a public market, *Faudra-t-il évacuer l'Indochine?* (Paris, 1932), p. 42. Not all French people in Indochina, however, behaved in such a manner. The French society of Indochina was deeply divided by hierarchy and social class; yet at the same time it was united by racial and national origins and the need for mutual protection. Along with the crude and the brutal, there were those who sincerely admired the old Vietnamese culture and attempted to cement the two races.

Quoc, Nguyen An Ninh, and Nguyen The Truyen, among Vietnam's celebrated patriots, found Paris the best refuge and political base from which to launch attacks on French colonialism in Vietnam. Throughout the second half of the 1920s, France was also one of the regions outside Vietnam that nurtured young Vietnamese Marxist revolutionaries (Nguyen van Tao, Ta Thu Thau, Phan van Hum, Tran van Giau, Tran van Thach, to name a few), preparing them for the grafting of Marxism-Leninism onto Vietnamese patriotism.

Not surprisingly, the explosive events of 1929–1931 in Vietnam were accompanied by a French cacophony of political analyses, denunciations, and demands for political reforms. Each successive event in the colony increased the emotional tension, already high. The assassination of Bazin, the numerous worker strikes and peasant demonstrations, and particularly the mutiny at Yen Bay were the subjects of daily reports and feature articles in Parisian newspapers of all ideological persuasions. Although the *parti colonial* did its best to minimize the importance of these events and even attempted to mount a propaganda campaign of its own to advertise the accomplishments of the *colons* in Indochina, it faced increasing criticism in the press. Newspapers of such varied political tendencies as *Le temps, Le populaire, Le petit parisien, Le matin, Le journal,* and *L'humanité* gave full coverage to the events in Vietnam. Whatever their ideological stance, they shared the enjoyment of administering daily verbal floggings to the colonialists in Indochina.

Ultimately, however, it was the French government that decided the fate of French colonialism in Indochina. The French Chamber had long considered Indochina an enfant terrible. The abuses by the *colons* in Indochina had repeatedly been the subject of parliamentary investigations. In his budget report of 1910, for example. Deputy Messimy drew widespread attention to the multiple abuses of the colonial regime. In 1911 the Violette budget report again brought Indochina into the limelight. This report, the most violent official attack on the Indochinese *colons* ever issued, cataloged abuses that made the *colons* appear to have destroyed virtually everything in the colony without contributing anything, except possibly inducing native consumption of officially approved alcohol and state-controlled opium.[19] Partly as a result of this re-

19. Rapport Violette, *Journal officiel,* 12 July 1911.

port, procolonial and anticolonial forces within the Chamber of Deputies coalesced into opposing blocs. The Métin report of 1912 was much more balanced but no less critical of the colonial government of Indochina.[20] The 1918 report by Marius Moutet was in no way kinder to the *colons;* nor were the other official reports that followed.

In the critical years of the early 1930s, however, it became obvious to all concerned that the French government at home was no longer confident that the colonial regime could govern Indochina effectively without increased supervision from Paris. Indochina was the principal topic of debate in the Chamber from 28 January until 1 February 1930, when the colonial budget was tabled. This was before Yen Bay. When, during the sessions of 25 and 26 March, six weeks after the Yen Bay Mutiny, the Senate discussed the colonial budget, Indochina was singled out for special attention. As the violence in Vietnam continued, the Chamber devoted four special sessions to interpellations on Yen Bay and other Indochinese events. It concluded that it was necessary to impose restraints on the colonial government. Édouard Daladier, who was to be premier in the waning days of the Popular Front, proposed the creation of a "parliamentary commission for information and study" on Indochina and recommended the establishment of a "Permanent State Under-Secretariat for Indochina," which would govern Indochina more or less directly from Paris.[21] On 29 October 1930 the Summit Colonial Council, composed of all former ministers of colonies and former governors-general, met on Indochina. Governor-General Pasquier of Indochina was recalled to report to one of its sessions in December. In the autumn of 1931, for the first time ever, the French government dispatched its minister of colonies, Paul Reynaud, to Indochina for an on-site study mission, and the days in which a colonial administration could rule Indochina unchecked came effectively to an end.

THE NGHE TINH SOVIET MOVEMENT

The crisis of European colonial capitalism, the appalling living conditions of most Vietnamese, and the determination of

---

20. Albert Métin, *L'Indochine et l'opinion* (Paris, 1916).
21. *L'Asie française* 30 (August–September 1930): 277.

French anticolonialists to curb the Indochinese colonial regime—these circumstances should have been ideal for the rapid growth of communism in Vietnam. Favorable political conditions notwithstanding, the early 1930s were a time of crisis for Vietnamese communism. The intense radicalization of the ICP leadership that had begun in 1928–1929 had created severe factionalism between revolutionary patriots and the proletarian internationalists and led to the defeat of the Nguyen Ai Quoc strategy. Meanwhile, as the youthful ICP eagerly accepted foreign directives that demonstrated little understanding of local conditions, the years 1930–1931 brought a "revolutionary upsurge" with all the earmarks of the current Comintern policies for East Asia. A coordinated nationwide peasant-worker movement took the country to the brink of political upheaval with widespread worker strikes, peasant demonstrations, and market boycotts, culminating in the establishment of several "Red villages" (or "Soviets") in the Nghe Tinh region. Yet after two years of violent struggle, the Communist movement came close to a fatal collapse under the terrorist reprisals of the colonial government. So devastated was the ICP in the aftermath of the soviet movement that it was more than a decade before the Party could launch another nationwide mass movement, which this time took the Communists to power.

The ICP's own activities precipitated the crisis, the aftermath of a Communist-instigated nationwide unrest, unprecedented in scale and scope. The "revolutionary upsurge" started with strikes by three thousand workers at the Phu Rieng rubber plantation in Nam Ky (February 1930), four thousand workers at the Nam Dinh Textile Mill in Bac Ky (March 1930), and four hundred at the match factory and sawmill at Ben Thuy in Trung Ky (April 1930). The movement increased in momentum after Labor Day (May First) 1930, when workers' activities spread from the industrial firms in Hanoi, Haiphong, Nam Dinh, Hon Gay, Cam Pha, Vinh, Ben Thuy, Saigon, and Cholon to rural areas such as Thai Binh and Ha Nam in Bac Ky; Nghe An, Ha Tinh, and Quang Ngai in Trung Ky; and Gia Dinh, Vinh Long, Sa Dec, Ben Tre, Can Tho, Long Xuyen, Tra Vinh, Thu Dau Mot, and My Tho in Nam Ky. From 1 May 1930 until the summer of 1931 there were few days without some sort of political agitation—worker strikes, peasant demonstrations, sabotage, assassinations of government officials, and dissemination of Communist leaflets.

Indeed, not since the Can Vuong (Support the King) Movement of the nineteenth century had there been such intense, widespread, and sustained political agitation. The Tax Protest Movement of 1908, for example, had involved only a few provinces of Trung Ky; the VNQDD–organized insurrection in February 1930, only a few isolated areas in Bac Ky. Neither movement had lasted more than two months. The Communist-led agitation, however, persisted for more than a year and involved twenty-five provinces in the three regions of Vietnam. In Nam Ky alone, the movement extended to thirteen out of thirty provinces. An unofficial tabulation appearing in Saigon newspapers at the time listed 124 peasant demonstrations.[22] According to an official Communist report, a total of 95 worker strikes occurred.[23] Saigon itself witnessed several mass demonstrations—6 in 1930, 3 in 1931—some of which involved violence. For example, a French policemen, Legrand, was killed by a Communist "self-defense unit" on 9 February 1931 when he interrupted a mass rally at the football stadium. In Bac Ky, where police vigilance remained strong after the fearful repression following the Yen Bay Mutiny, the agitation movement was not so widespread. Yet despite these circumstances, worker strikes took place in Haiphong and Nam Dinh and peasant demonstrations occurred in Thai Binh.

It was in Trung Ky, however, that the movement reached its apex. Starting with a joint worker-peasant action (a worker strike coordinated with a peasant demonstration) in the Vinh–Ben Thuy area on 1 May 1930, unrest quickly spread to outlying rural areas of the Nghe Tinh region. In the early days of the movement, unarmed peasant demonstrators marched to the district government offices to present petitions demanding abolition of certain taxes, postponement of tax collection, raising the official buying price of salt (the government then held the monopoly). Before long these peaceful demonstrations became armed struggles. Armed "self-defense militia" emerged for the first time in the summer of 1930, equipped with farm utensils and other instruments. Violence soon erupted. Provoked by the colonial regime's terrorism, the peasants

22. Hémery, *Révolutionnaires vietnamiens,* p. 22, n. 1.
23. Propaganda Section, Central Committee of the Vietnam Workers' Party and Commission for the Study of the History of the Party, *Trente ans du Parti de la classe ouvrière vietnamienne* (Hanoi, 1960), p. 33.

stormed and ransacked government buildings and sometimes murdered officials. A general disintegration of the administrative machinery followed, and by August 1930 several village and district
officials had sided with the peasant rebels, while others submitted
their seals of office and official documents to local Red Peasant
Associations. Many others escaped for their lives. The situation
was most acute in the provinces of Nghe An and Ha Tinh: while
the government continued to function at the provincial seats, the
rural districts gradually fell into the hands of Communist-led peasants.

In early September 1930, "Red villages" *(lang do)*, sometimes
called "soviets" *(xo-viet)*, were established in several rural districts
of Nghe An. (These were terms used officially by the ICP to designate villages that had come under the control of the Communist-
created Red Peasant Associations.) According to one Communist
author, seventeen soviets were established in Nghe An alone between September and December 1930, and fourteen others in Ha
Tinh in January–February 1931.[24] There were attempts to create
similar soviets in other areas of Trung Ky such as Quang Tri, Dong
Hoi, and Quang Ngai, but they were unsuccessful. Within each
soviet, the local Red Peasant Association performed governmental
functions under the direction of the ICP Provincial Committee of
Nghe An. Each soviet was governed by an Executive Committee,
which was essentially the village section of the Red Peasant Association. According to an ICP directive on the limits of power of the
village's executive committee, the committee was to be "elected
by the representatives of an all-village conference."[25] Furthermore, the executive committee

> is responsible to the entire village and to the District Committee. It
> has a tenure of office of three months. During its term of office, the
> Executive Committee has to assume all responsibility for affairs in
> the village, such as propaganda and mobilization of the people to
> cope with all difficulties.[26]

24. Tran van Giau, *Giai cap cong nhan*, 1: 124–125.
25. "Quyen han cua Ban chap-hanh xa-bo" [The limits of power of the executive
committee of the village section], quoted in Trung Chinh, "Tinh chat doc dao cua
Xo-viet Nghe Tinh" [The originality of the Nghe Tinh soviets], *NCLS*, no. 32
(November 1961), p. 12.
26. Ibid.

According to the same directive, each village executive committee was to be composed of eight subcommittees: secretariat, communications, organization, finance, control, training, investigation, and struggle.

In practice, under the rule of the Red Peasant Association, life in the soviets was reorganized and, to some extent, "revolutionized." Despite the fact that the colonial and royal governments retained actual control of the provincial seats and government raids were frequent in the Red areas, significant political, social, and economic reforms were instituted. An intense political life pervaded the Red villages. Mass demonstrations took place virtually daily. Sometimes these demonstrations took on a violent character: countless pagodas were burned; houses of "reactionary landlords" were sacked. The peasant masses, often encouraged by inexperienced Communist cadre members and led by workers from Vinh or Nghe An, seemed intoxicated with their newly found power. Along side these mass actions came radical political, social, and economic reforms. Political life assumed a collective and Red character. Techniques of political struggle and village affairs were freely discussed. The *dinh,* which before had served as a place of competition for priority among village notables, now became a communal center for political discussions. Communist publications such as *Co vo-san* [The proletarian flag], *Tien len* [Forward], and *Do* [Red], which previously had been forbidden for public display, now circulated freely. In the evening, Party members would assemble the village population at the *dinh* to read revolutionary newspapers and discuss social and economic issues.

Among the important reforms implemented by the Red Peasant Association were mutual assistance measures, which had immediate effects, and measures designed to have longer-term influence. Most of the social reforms, however, reflected the puritanical tendencies typical of the early stages of revolution. Expensive traditional observance during ceremonial occasions such as weddings and funerals, for example, was curtailed; alcoholic beverages were formally prohibited and gambling and petty thievery severely punished. In addition to imposing moral strictures, the Red Peasant Association also waged a literacy campaign designed to teach *quoc-ngu* to education-hungry peasants. Economic reforms included abolition of all taxes previously imposed by the colonial and royal governments (such as head tax, salt tax, market tax, and ford tax) and annulment of debts incurred by poor peasants to landlords. Local cadres in several Red villages took it upon themselves to seize all lands, public and private, controlled by notables and landlords, for redistribution to poor peasants. Some of the holdings thus redistributed in several villages in the districts of Thanh Chuong, Nghi Loc, and Hung Nguyen remained in the hands of the peasants until the agrarian reforms of 1953–1956.

The colonial government was determined not to allow this Communist autonomy to go unpunished. In response to the crisis, the government resorted to its usual remedy: more systematic, harsher reprisals. Vietnamese troops patrolling the region were now replaced by the more reliable Yao (Tho) (a non-Vietnamese ethnic minority living in the mountainous regions of Bac Ky and northern Trung Ky) and the much-feared French Foreign Legion troops. Planes unleashed bombs indiscriminately on unarmed demonstrators. Eight thousand peasant demonstrators marching towards Vinh on 12 September 1930 were met with planes and bombs. *L'Asie française,* the periodical of the *parti colonial,* summarized the events:

> The planes, by way of warning, dropped a few bombs ahead of the column. It continued to advance. The three planes then bombed the column itself. The effect was immediate: the rebels fled in disorder, leaving behind the dead and the wounded. A few groups tried to reform, but they were chased by the machine guns of the flyers.
>
> What was the balance sheet of this bloody morning? Sixty-seven dead and 51 wounded were gathered at the spot. But the real figures were probably higher. There were reports, perhaps with some exaggeration, of 200 dead and 800 wounded.[27]

An entirely new system of patrolling and hundreds of military posts were established. In Nghe An, sixty-eight new military posts were created, in Ha Tinh, fifty-four. In the district of Thanh Chuong alone, where the agitation had been strongest, sixteen new posts were established, four of them manned with French Foreign Legion troops whose sadism was to become part of Vietnamese folklore.

The colonial regime officially sanctioned terrorism by the patrolling troops. Troops were explicitly ordered to kill as many as

27. *L'Asie française* 30 (November 1930): 354.

possible and to take few prisoners. Later, in justifying these troops' sadism, the military affairs bureau of the colonial government revealed that the legion had "received from the civilian French and native authorities very tough orders, to kill and to take the fewest prisoners possible. . . . They received . . . orders to kill 9 out of 10 of the Communists, the prisons being too small to incarcerate all the accused."[28] In the districts of Thanh Chuong and Nam Dan, village after village was burned and razed. In his deposition to a commission investigating events in northern Trung Ky, Inspector Petit declared that he himself had "ordered the burning of the two villages [of Yen Tha and Yen Phu], while sparing the pagodas," after discovering the villages to be empty and having waited in vain for their inhabitants to return.[29] Throughout the provinces of Nghe An and Ha Tinh, villagers—old men and young, women, and children—were killed for no other reason than having been caught by government troops.[30] With obvious exaggeration, historian Buttin-

28. "Note sur les incidents de Vinh du 9 mars 1931 et de Nam Dan du 29 mai 1931," 4 October 1933, AOM, Nouveaux Fonds, carton 286, dossier 2639.

29. Commission d'enquête sur les événements du Nord Annam (the Morche Commission), Séance du 27 Juin 1931, "Déclaration du M. Petit, Inspecteur de la garde indigène de Vinh," AOM Carton 333, dossier 2687.

30. Horrible tales were told by the Foreign Legion troops during their trial in Hanoi, 12–14 June 1933. The following excerpts are taken from the stenographic record of the trial, published in *L'ami du peuple indochinois,* 14 and 15 June 1933, and reprinted in Andrée Viollis, *L'Indochine S.O.S.* (Paris, 1949), pp. 186–199.

Attorney General: Would you have killed, had Perrier not been assassinated?

Layon: . . . Everyone killed. The *garde indigène,* the Legion, the Secret Police. . . .

Attorney General: Who gave the orders?

Layon: All the officials: Commander Lambert, the Residents Guilleminot, de Bottini, Governor Robin, the Annamese ministers. To avoid overcrowding, we killed the prisoners every night, often innocent people. . . .

Presiding Judge: Why did you ask Layon to take these prisoners in his truck? In order to throw them into the river or onto the road without firing a bullet into their heads?

Von Bargen: I did not need any subterfuge. We had the orders to kill. We had to kill nine out of ten.

Presiding Judge: You have even found the way to kill eleven out of ten, since you killed a witness.

Von Bargen: That was being done in all the posts. . . .

Layon then declared that he had wanted not only to avenge Perrier but also to imitate his superiors, who amused themselves by cutting off heads, even with a regular knife. During the interrogation of Commander Lambert, the witness stated: "We had very firm orders. . . . We received verbal orders from Governor Robin. The residents gave these orders to the Legion troops: Repress, kill, take the least prisoners possible."

ger cited ten thousand killed and fifty thousand deported.[31] A tabulation by the ministry of colonies for the period February–October
1930 gives an incredibly low figure for the losses suffered by both
sides: six European officers and NCOs lost their lives and six
others were wounded; fewer than forty Vietnamese soldiers and
mandarins or notables were killed or wounded; less than five hundred "rebels" were killed or wounded; and over four hundred arrests were made during the operations in Nghe Tinh.[32] Regardless
of statistical claims, there is no doubt about the ferocity of the
reprisals.

By the spring of 1931 the peasant movement, then under inces-
sant government repression, also took a violent turn. The surviving
political literature of the period is replete with calls for violence
and political "adventures" *(lieu linh)*. The slogan of the day was in
verse form, easy to commit to memory: "Those intellectuals, rich
people, landlords, and notables; / Let us dig them out at the stump,
pull them out at the roots" *(Tri, phu, dia, hao; / dao tan goc, troc
tan re)*.[33] The tone of the article "Let us resolve to overthrow the
opportunists," in *Guong vo san* [The proletarian example], the
organ of the Anh Son ICP District Committee, was representative.
The article said in part:

> The brothers and sisters ought to recognize that most of the obsta-
> cles [to the revolution] have originated with the intellectuals, the
> rich, the landlords, and the notables. They are ever ready with their
> commandeering mentality. When the movement first arose, they
> stood out, promoting the movement, pretending zeal. They did so to
> gain a good reputation and earn the confidence of the masses. But
> when the movement did rise to a high level, affecting their personal
> interests and bringing about vicious imperialist attacks, some of
> these elements were intimidated while others sided with the im-
> perialists and betrayed the workers and peasants. . . . We have to
> solidify our forces quickly. We have to dig out the stump, pull out
> the roots, destroy all the influence of these opportunists."[34]

31. Joseph Buttinger, *Vietnam: A Political History* (New York, 1968), p. 180.
32. "Récapitulation générale (chiffres résultant des télégrammes parvenus d'Indochine entre le 10 février et le 10 octobre 1930)," AOM, Nouveaux Fonds, carton
326, dossier 2636.
33. Tran Huy Lieu, *Lich su tam muoi nam*, 2: 82.
34. "Quyet liet da dao tui hoat dau" [Let us resolve to overthrow the opportun-
ists], *Guong vo san* [The proletarian example], n.d., quoted in Tran Huy Lieu, *Lich
su tam muoi nam*, 2: 81.

Elsewhere, *Guong vo san* repeatedly called for "adventurism." In an editorial appearing late in the summer of 1931, toward the final days of the soviet movement, it stated, "To regain our right to life and freedom, we must struggle; to struggle we have to be adventurous."[35]

With the leadership of the ICP in disarray, the peasants now turned against well-to-do families, educated people, and even surviving ICP members who were suspected of being "wavering" and "indecisive." In addition to ambushing government patrols, "self-defense units" of the Red villages now also attacked landlord households in "rice-borrowing" operations. Leading ICP members were "expelled" from the Party for "wavering attitudes," "rightist deviation," or "exploiting-class" origins. Those so condemned were often people who hesitated to support the advocates of armed violence.

Under all-out repression, the soviet movement came to an end late in the summer of 1931. By this time several of the Red villages had been razed and thousands of people killed or imprisoned; the ICP itself had been demolished. In 1931 and 1932 the government published a newspaper, *Thanh Nghe Tinh tan van* [News of Thanh Hoa, Nghe An, and Ha Tinh] to compete with Communist propaganda. It also established a rump political party, the Ly Nhan Dang (Party of Village People), to assemble people loyal to the government. The government also took advantage of the peasants' hunger by offering rice supplies to those who consented to carry a "certificate of submission." In several Nghe Tinh areas the peasants had by now turned against the Communist cadres. They detained members creating propaganda and turned them over to the government.[36] The ICP's roots in the Nghe Tinh region, however, were never destroyed. When Paul Reynaud visited the region in November 1931, he was greeted with leaflets denouncing French colonialism, including one that said, "Down with Reynaud!"[37]

---

35. Tran Huy Lieu, *Lich su tam muoi nam*, p. 85.

36. See various interviews by the Commission d'enquête sur les événements du Nord Annam, especially interviews with Billet, Sûreté commissioner for Vinh; Thai van Giai, member of the ICP Trung Ky Regional Committee; and Ngo Duc Dien, member of the ICP Vinh Municipal Committee; AOM, Nouveaux Fonds, carton 212, dossier 1597.

37. Gouvernement-général de l'Indochine, *Discours de M. Paul Reynaud, 16 November 1931* [Hanoi?], 1931.

Sporadic Communist propaganda activities persisted throughout the 1930s. During the general insurrection that led to the August Revolution, Nghe Tinh was among the first regions in which the Communists established power.

In retrospect, the Nghe Tinh soviets were an expensive experiment for the ICP. As a consequence of thoroughgoing repression the ICP's organizational apparatus was virtually demolished, from the Central Committee to local section levels. With the assistance of well-placed renegades (including Nghiem Thuong Bien, chairman of the Bac Ky Regional Committee; Duong Hac Dinh, member of the Bac Ky Regional Committee; and Ngo Duc Tri, one of the three members of the Standing Committee of the ICP Central Committee), the French were able to arrest virtually all important Party leaders in April 1931. The entire Standing Committee of the ICP Central Committee (Tran Phu, Ngo Duc Tri, Nguyen Trong Nha) was jailed; so were all six members of the Nam Ky Regional Committee (Ung van Khiem, Nguyen van Gi, Le Hoa Binh, Ha Huy Giap, Nguyen van Tay, and Pham van Dong). The Trung Ky Regional Committee was also incapacitated: Le Mao, Le Viet Thuat, and Nguyen Duc Canh were killed, and Nguyen Phong Sac was imprisoned. Around the same time all members of the Bac Ky Regional Committee were also detained. The Party's international connections were broken not long thereafter. On 5 June 1931 the British arrested Nguyen Ai Quoc and his aides in Hong Kong.

By the end of 1932 there were few signs to indicate that the ICP was still functioning. So shattered was the Party that some surviving cadres in Nam Ky "even wrote to the PCF and the Communist International around the end of 1931 to announce in poignant terms 'the dissolution of the Party during this historic period.'"[38] The colonial government was well aware of the state of the Party and was satisfied with the results of its repressive policies. Speaking to the Government Council on 17 December 1932, Governor-General Pasquier stated, "As a force capable of acting against the public order, communism has disappeared."[39] As if to confirm Pasquier's opinion, Ho Nam [Tran van Giau] wrote in September 1933:

38. *Tap chi Bon-so-vic* [Bolshevik review], no. 8 (December 1934). The subtitle of this review is *"Co quan ly thuyet cua Ban Chi Huy o Ngoai cua Dang C.S.D.D."* [The theoretical organ of the Overseas Leadership Committee of the ICP].
39. Quoted in Isoart, *Phénomène national vietnamien*, p. 291.

"Ninety-nine per cent of our leaders were arrested during 1931 and 1932. Those who are at large are weak in theory and practice, and so few are they that one single person must do all the work which was done in the past by six or seven militants."[40] The destruction of the Party apparatus was so complete that it took the ICP more than a decade to recover. Although by March 1935 the ICP theoretically had a new organizational network, in reality its disorganization persisted at least until the early 1940s when Nguyen Ai Quoc returned to the country and built a new party.

Another significant consequence of the Nghe Tinh soviets was the urban petite-bourgeoisie's disaffection with communism. Throughout the 1920s this stratum had been both the main base of support and source of leadership for all anticolonial movements, the Communists' included. Patriotic, the urban petite-bourgeoisie had fought for Vietnamese national independence, but they had understood the Vietnamese revolution only in political, not social terms. Elitist, they had thought of themselves and others in their social stratum as suitable postindependence leaders. Contemptuous of "rural hicks" (nha que) and "coolies" (that is, the urban proletariat), they could not conceive of an active political role for these people, who constituted more than 90 percent of the Vietnamese population at the time. Their support of the protocommunist movements had been an expression of their anticolonialism but also reflected their ignorance of communism's social mission and emphasis on the important role of the masses in politics. The ICP's politics in 1930–1931 emphasized not patriotism, but "the social question"; the Communist-instigated "revolutionary upsurge," which unleashed the peasants and workers against landowners and petit-bourgeois elements like themselves, revealed to them for the first time what a Communist society might be like. They did not like what they saw. Throughout 1931, the very newspapers—*Than chung* [Morning bell], *Phu nu tan van* [Women's news], and *Tieng dan* [Voice of the people]—that had previously extolled the *nha cach mang* (respectable revolutionaries) of Thanh Nien, Tan Viet, and the VNQDD now referred to the *hoa cong-san* (the Communist menace) and expressed the hope that the government would quickly suppress the Communist movement to bring about peace

40. Ho Nam [Tran van Giau], *Tap chi cong san* (September 1933).

and order in society. Meanwhile, the urban youth showed decreasing interest in politics of any kind. Disillusioned and directionless, they found their mental anesthetics in the romantic novels of the Tu Luc Van Doan (Self-Initiative Literary Group) or in the "healthy entertainment" allowed by the government, available at the dancing halls and opium dens.

A third and equally significant consequence of the soviet experiment was not immediately observable: the developing ideological unity of ICP members who were in prison. The incarceration of approximately ten thousand political activists (most of whom were Communists) in the early 1930s had considerable utility for a resourceful party like the ICP. Prisons throughout Vietnam quickly became centers for ICP recruitment and Marxist education. In 1930–1931, ICP sections were organized among prisoners in the Central Prison of Hanoi (colloquially known as *"Hoa Lo"* [Hell's Hole]), Saigon's *"Kham Lon"* (Big Prison), and the prisons of Haiphong, Vinh, Son La, and elsewhere. The Party section at Poulo Condore was organized in 1932. Supervised by the foremost leaders of the ICP at the time—including Ngo Gia Tu, Tong van Tran, Ta Uyen, Le Duan, Pham van Dong, and Bui Cong Trung—Poulo Condore became the most important of all the "revolutionary universities" of Vietnam. Here and in other prisons ICP leaders gave courses on general education and Marxist theory and systematically reviewed and recapitulated previous experiences in preparation for future combat.[41] Periodicals and books were published and Marxist-Leninist classics were reproduced in large quantities, read, and studied.[42] In June 1932, for example, prison

41. There were two types of Marxist training courses. Long-term courses were for those sentenced to five-year or longer prison terms. This theoretical training, led by Le Duan and Bui Cong Trung, involved a relatively systematic, thorough study of Marxism-Leninism and the policies of the ICP. Short-term courses were for prisoners with short sentences. They studied documents such as Bukharin's *Historical Materialism* and *ABC of Communism*, the ICP's *Political Theses*, and *Secret Operation.* See *Hoi va Dap ve lich su Dang* (Hanoi, 1977), p. 77.

42. *Nhung nguoi cong san*, pp. 58–60. In Poulo Condore, for example, there was a regular monthly periodical entitled *Y kien chung* [Shared opinion]; at the Quang Ngai prison, *Tien len!* [Forward!]; at the Hanoi prison, *Lao tu tap chi* [Prison review]; at Son la, *Sao do* [Red star]. The list of contributors to these periodicals reads almost like today's VCP Politburo membership: Le Duan, Pham van Dong, Truong Chinh, Nguyen van Cu, Xuan Thuy, Bui Cong Trung, Khuat Duy Tien, and so on.

authorities in Hanoi seized several caches containing in all nearly two hundred books and periodicals that had been edited or copied in prison, including copies of issue number 25 of the periodical *Lao tu tap chi* [Prison review].[43] A general search of the Saigon prison on 7 February 1933 also yielded numerous documents, including a Vietnamese version of Bukharin's *ABC of Communism,* the 1932 *Program of Action of the Indochinese Communist Party,* and a *cai luong* (popular theater) piece entitled *A Tragic Episode of the History of the Indochinese Revolution,* dedicated to the revolutionary upsurge of 1930–1931.[44]

Thus, although the ICP was temporarily in organizational disarray and its mass base severely dislocated, the experiences of worker mobilization, the soviet movement, and especially prison life supplied Party members with a discipline, "class consciousness," and theoretical homogeneity the Party had never had before. Sûreté records ruefully noted no perceptible evidence of a reduction in the prisoners' revolutionary commitment. If anything, they appeared to have become more determined and increasingly better organized into cells, with their influence spreading among the VNQDD and common-law prisoners. In a special report on Communist prisoners, the French police concluded:

> Far from reforming the political prisoners, the detention seems to exalt their revolutionary spirit and every one of them makes the best use of his time in prison to refine his own education or to educate the other prisoners, including common-law detainees. All of them have the firm will to resume agitation as soon as they are released, and every day the prisons open their gates to free numerous prisoners whose own experiences have now been reinforced with the techniques learned from the "returnees from Moscow". . . . We ought to dread the months to come, since the new Communist organization will be stronger and better tested.[45]

The police reports proved to be prophetic. In the political development of Vietnam throughout the Popular Front period and the Viet Minh Front, it was the graduates of such revolutionary universities who led the movement.

Several questions arise regarding the origins and character of the

43. AOM, SLOTFOM, series 3, carton 49, NPM, July–August 1932.
44. AOM, SLOTFOM, series 3, carton 49, NPM, first trimester 1933, p. 52.
45. Ibid.

Nghe Tinh Soviet Movement. Was the creation of the soviets one of the Comintern's objectives for Southeast Asia? Were they part of the program of action of the Peasants' International? Or were these soviets the local initiatives of ICP cadres in Trung Ky? In other words, who was responsible for the planning, initiation, and direction of the Nghe Tinh soviets?[46] Unfortunately, while so little documentation is available outside the Communist world, there can be no definite answers to these questions.

It is possible to argue, as some historians have, that the creation of the soviets in the Nghe Tinh region was a local initiative but not a result of an ICP Central Committee decision. The soviets, according to this theory, were a makeshift administration created by local and regional ICP cadres to govern areas that had been abandoned by rural notables fearful of peasant action. The Party's leadership at the central level was, according to this thesis, subsequently forced to support a *fait accompli* by presenting the French with a coordinated nationwide "revolutionary upsurge" to distract the French from concentrating their reprisals on Nghe Tinh.[47] On the surface, the evidence to support this line of argument is overwhelming. The ICP Central Committee, then occupied with the problems of organizational consolidation, was apparently caught by surprise by the establishment of the soviets. Their initial reaction to the news was to publish a directive in September 1930 indicating disapproval.

> The executive committees at Thanh Chuong and Nam Dan [districts in Nghe An Province] by their own initiative have already advocated violence (such as establishing soviets, redistributing land, etc.). Such a policy fails to meet the appropriate situation of our country,

46. These are among the basic questions that Vietnam's scholars are researching today. Soviet scholars at the Institute of Oriental Studies of the Academy of Sciences, USSR, are also conducting a special study on the Nghe Tinh Soviet Movement.

47. This thesis was originally advanced in 1961 by Trung Chinh of the Historical Studies Institute, Hanoi. Since then, some scholars outside Vietnam have adopted the same argument. See Trung Chinh, "Tinh chat tu phat cua Xo-viet Nghe Tinh" [The Spontaneity of the Nghe Tinh soviets], *NCLS*, no. 31 (October 1961), pp. 1–6; William J. Duiker, "The Red Soviets of Nghe Tinh: An Early Communist Rebellion in Vietnam," *Journal of Southeast Asian Studies* 4, no. 2 (September 1973), pp. 186–198; and Ngo Vinh Long, "The Indochinese Communist Party and Peasant Rebellion in Central Vietnam, 1930–1931," *Bulletin of Concerned Asian Scholars* 10, no. 4 (December 1978), pp. 15–34.

because the level of preparation of the Party and the masses in the country is not yet adequate and we do not yet have means for waging armed violence. Political violence in a few separate areas at this time is too early and is a premature action.[48]

While launching a campaign to save the soviets from the expected repression, the ICP Central Committee also attempted to forestall the creation of other soviets elsewhere. In October 1930, for example, the ICP Central Committee issued another directive, this time to all levels of the Party, again denouncing the Nghe Tinh soviets. The directive said in part:

> If it were the masses which acted on their own, then there was little that we could say, and the Party ought to lead them. But in this case, it was the executive committees that decided [on creating soviets], that is very wrong, because: . . .
> b. Although the people in those few villages may be sufficiently conscious and have sufficient vehemence for struggle, they have not been prepared for armed struggle. Because of the situation of the country at this time, the level of preparation of the proletariat and toilers of the cities, of the countryside and of the Party, and the general situation of the enemy, to practice violence separately in a few localities is premature actionism *(manh-dong chu-nghia)* and not a correct policy.[49]

From what we know, however, there are reasons to believe that although the soviet movement was not the work of the ICP Central Committee, it was unlikely to have resulted from local initiatives. With the information now available it is possible to speculate that the soviets were not necessarily temporary local initiatives, but part of a planned program of action, perhaps a planned insurrection with international connections.[50] Among the ICP documents captured by the French, for example, is a "General Plan of Attack" ("Tong Cong Kich Ke Hoach") of unknown origin,[51] a meticulously detailed strategy for the seizure of power. It provided for

48. Quoted in Trung Chinh, "Tinh chat tu phat," p. 5.
49. Ibid.
50. Although providing little evidence for his contention, the late historian Tran Huy Lieu held a similar view. In one of several articles on the soviets of Nghe Tinh he said, "If we go deeply into the documents available, we can see that the creation of the soviets was not a temporary local initiative, but was the result of a planned program reflecting a political line." "Bai hoc lich su ve Xo Viet Nghe Tinh," *Van su dia* [Literature, history, geography], no. 32 (September 1957), p. 4.
51. AOM, SLOTFOM, series 3, carton 3 (December 1930), supp. 9.

winning over and organizing the government's armed personnel; stockpiling supplies; investigating in detail different sectors of society and the economy; preparing organizationally and militarily for the attack; conducting foreign relations; making the attack; and organizing power after taking over the city. Under the category of investigation, for example, the plan called for the following (among others):

> investigation of the French population in the country: how many troops, how many civilian functionaries, how many merchants. . . .
> investigation of the military posts in the country: how many? Which ones were most important and for what reasons? . . .
> investigation of the most important organs: general staffs of the land army and navy; office of general commandant: how many people, what is the necessary material? Wireless sets, post and telegraph systems, what to do to destroy them? . . .
> investigation of the persons who might collaborate with the Party: how many military men, how many civilians?
> investigation of the French war machinery: how many planes, in what areas? How many warships, where? How many attack tanks, armored vehicles, where? How many warehouses, where? How many cannons, where?
> investigation of our own war machinery: how many bombs, knives, revolvers, rifles?

Under the rubric of foreign relations the plan specified:

> Before launching the attack, the Party's central committee must send diplomats to negotiate with foreign nations to obtain their support. In the actual state of the world, it would be good that we have diplomatic relations with China, the United States, Germany, Russia, Siam, and Italy.

After taking over power, the leadership was to proclaim "immediately the regulations on public security," organize "the troops according to the principles already elaborated by the Central Committee," and organize the "Provisional Regional Military Government" *(Lam thoi dia phuong quan chinh-phu)*. The French Sûreté possessed scores of ICP documents showing results of detailed investigations (the Nam Dinh Textile Company, the Haiphong Portland Cement Factory, various mines, French warships) and containing detailed plans of operation.

The authorship of this general plan is perhaps the most baffling issue related to the Nghe Tinh soviets. One possible source, not for

the authorship of the general plan itself, but for the origination of
the "revolutionary upsurge" and the policy of establishing soviets,
is the Comintern itself. Indochina, according to one specialist,
ranked high among the Comintern's Asian interests; only after
China and India, in the aftermath of Yen Bay.[52] In fact, according
to the same author, "During the [Yen Bay] era, coverage of developments in Indochina in Soviet and Comintern publications was
more intense than of any other events in Southeast Asia to date,
including the 1926–1927 uprisings in Indonesia, and it continued so
for some years."[53] In the Comintern's perception, however, the
Communist movement of Indochina was an extension of the Communist movement in China, "the younger sister of the glorious
Chinese Communist Party,"[54] and the policy of establishing
soviets, officially advocated by the Comintern for China, was apparently applied in the case of Vietnam as well. The ICP was
repeatedly told to "struggle for the masses" through strikes, peasant activities, judicious organization, and preparation for the establishment of soviets. A primary tactic outlined in these directives
was for the Communists to win over the peasants, guide them in
the establishment of soviets, and coordinate the rural movement
with the "worker mobilization" *(cong van)* in the cities.

This official Comintern policy of promoting the establishment of
soviets in Vietnam continued for some time after the defeat of the
Nghe Tinh movement. The 1932 *Program of Action of the Indochinese Communist Party (Chuong trinh hanh dong cua Dang Cong
san Dong duong),*[55] published by the Provisional Central Committee of the ICP, clearly with the approval of the Comintern, included this point among the ten fundamental objectives of the
Party: "The establishment of a worker-peasant revolutionary government according to soviet forms and the organization of a revolutionary worker-peasant army."

Ironically, despite the fact that the soviet movement coincided
with official Comintern policy, Nguyen Ai Quoc was to receive the

52. McLane, *Soviet Strategies in Southeast Asia,* p. 153.
53. Ibid.
54. G. Safarov, "Indo-Kitai i frantsuzskii imperialism," quoted in ibid., p. 161.
55. *Chuong trinh hanh dong cua Dang Cong san Dong duong* [Program of
action of the Indochinese Communist party], handwritten and printed by lithog-
raphic stone medium, n.p. 1932.

blame for both the soviet movement and its failure. This, however, is nothing strange to students of world communism. Ever since the days of Lenin the Comintern had adopted a peculiar tactic of dispatching special secret emissaries to foreign countries "with instructions affecting the entire future of individual communist parties—without the knowledge of the local leaders themselves."[56] Should such missions fail, it was usually the emissaries who had to assume responsibility for the failure. The experience of the CCP during the late 1920s and early 1930s demonstrates this pattern.[57] Li Li-san, the CCP leader then, was blamed for "erroneous policies" that had in fact been prepared in Moscow; by the second half of the 1930s he had become a mere cipher in the international Communist movement. Nguyen Ai Quoc's own eclipse is discussed later in this chapter.

There is also strong circumstantial evidence that Nguyen Ai Quoc himself may have played a considerable role in the conceptualization and direction of the soviet movement. In a document prepared late in 1927 for the German Communists' military school in Moscow, "The Party's Military Work among the Peasants,"[58]

56. Drachkovitch and Lazitch, "The Communist International," p. 167. Paul Levy, a figure in the *Zentral* of the German Communist party, wrote shortly before he was expelled from the Party that the Comintern's secret emissaries "never work with the leadership of individual Communist parties, but always behind their backs and often against them. They enjoy the confidence of Moscow, but the local leaders do not. . . . The Executive Committee [of the Comintern] acts as a Chrezvychaika [Cheka, the original Soviet secret police] projected outside Russian borders"; Paul Levy, *Unser Weg wider den Putschismus* (Berlin, 1921), pp. 55–56, quoted in Drachkovitch and Lazitch, "Communist International," p. 167.

57. For the Comintern–CCP relationship during the leadership of Li Li-san, see Robert C. North, *Moscow and the Chinese Communists* (Stanford, 1953), especially pp. 127–37. See also Chang Kuo-t'ao, *Rise of the CCP*, pp. 106–138.

58. Nguyen Ai Quoc, "The Party's Military Work among the Peasants: Revolutionary Guerrilla Methods," in A. Neuberg [Franz Neumann], ed., *Armed Insurrection* (London, 1970), pp. 255–271. This book was originally published in German in 1928. In his 1970 introduction to Nguyen Ai Quoc's essay ("Ho Chi Minh: Peasant Insurrection"), Erich Wollenberg, who was on the technical staff of the Moscow Marx-Engels Institute in 1928, revealed that when he arrived in Moscow in 1924 Nguyen Ai Quoc was already working in the agitprop division of the Comintern. His appointed fields were the colonial and peasant questions. In addition, Nguyen was then vice-president of the Peasants' International. "This organization had links with various peasant parties and associations, e.g., in Poland, in the Balkans, in France and Italy, in South America and in Asia." It was not however, regarded seriously by the Comintern leadership. Wollenberg added, "In Moscow, as earlier in Paris, Ho

Nguyen had presented a strategy of "partial insurrection" containing the same basic conceptual elements present in the Nghe Tinh soviets. Briefly, this strategy recommended that although revolutionaries ought to be prepared to seize total power at an opportune moment where local conditions permitted, they also ought to be prepared to stage a partial insurrection to seize control region by region, which would lead to a general insurrection to take over the entire country. In introducing this work, which was based on the current situation in China and was critical of the CCP's policies then ("It must be clearly stressed that the Communist Party's bad policy on the peasant question was one of the fatal causes of the defeat of the Chinese revolution in 1927"),[59] the author asserted:

> The victory of the proletarian revolution is *impossible* in rural and semi-rural countries *if the revolutionary proletariat is not actively supported* by the mass of the peasant population. This is an incontrovertible truth for both the bourgeois-democratic and the proletarian revolution.[60]

The author then recommended close coordination of the activities of the urban proletariat and the peasantry in a partial uprising in a "specific province or group of provinces."

In a passage that might well have doubled as orders for the ICP's preparations for insurrection in Nghe Tinh, Nguyen Ai Quoc wrote:

> To ensure the greatest possible simultaneity of action between the proletariat and the peasants, the party of the proletariat, above all in rural and semi-rural countries, must devote its attention to political and organizational (including military) work among the peasants. This work must not be left to chance, must not be carried out in an unplanned, uniform manner throughout the country. . . . Uniform political agitation or organizational work, in a country as vast as China, will inevitably lead to the dispersal of manpower and resources. . . . Naturally, revolutionary agitation must be carried out among the peasants everywhere, but its *main weight* must be di-

---

had to struggle against the prejudices of the Comintern parties from industrial countries, who denied the revolutionary role of the peasantry in the proletarian liberation struggle. He laughingly alluded to his activity as that of 'a voice in the wilderness.'" Aside from *Duong kach menh*, this is Nguyen Ai Quoc's only known lengthy work of a theoretical nature. I am grateful to Carlyle Thayer for having made available to me a copy of this valuable essay.

59. Neuberg, *Armed Insurrection*, p. 258.
60. Ibid., p. 255.

rected toward a specific province or group of provinces. This principle derives from the universally recognized truth that in countries
like China, which present an infinite diversity of geographical, economic, and political conditions, the revolution . . . cannot be accomplished as a single act (that is, in the space of a few weeks or
months), but must necessarily fill an entire more or less prolonged
period of revolutionary movements in the various provinces or industrial and political centers.[61]

In this same work, Nguyen Ai Quoc predicted the need to establish
revolutionary political and military control over a specific region,
"which will serve as a base for the subsequent development of the
revolution."[62]

Thus, when the revolutionary party foresees the approach of an
immediate revolutionary situation, it must (while continuing to educate and mobilize the working class) indicate which provinces or
districts are most important from the point of view of agitation
among the peasants, and must fix its attention and concentrate its
resources accordingly upon these provinces. With respect to agitational work among the peasants, the Party must concern itself above
all with the areas surrounding the main industrial and political centers.[63]

In addition to the theory of a partial uprising, there are indications of Nguyen Ai Quoc's direct involvement with the soviet
movement. Bonvincini, a correspondent for *L'opinion,* a Saigon
newspaper, reported having visited the Red villages and meeting
with a Communist leader who resembled Nguyen Ai Quoc and who
was supported by a Chinese cadre.[64] Nguyen Duy Trinh, an activist in the Nghe Tinh Soviet Movement and today Vietnam's deputy
prime minister, noted in his memoirs that participants asked themselves whether Nguyen Ai Quoc had returned to lead the movement.[65] Finally, among the recently published writings of Nguyen
Ai Quoc is a letter to the Peasants' International reporting progress
in the development of the Nghe Tinh soviets and conveying the

61. Ibid., p. 259 (italics in original).
62. Ibid.
63. Ibid.
64. See Nguyen Khanh Toan, *Van de dan toc trong cach mang vo san* [The
national question in the proletarian revolution] (Hanoi, 1962), p. 40.
65. Nguyen Duy Trinh, "Tu kham tu vi thanh nien den truong hoc Xo-Viet
Nghe-Tinh," in Hoang van Tam et al. *Trong kham tu vi thanh nien* [In the juveniles'
prisons] (Hanoi, 1965), p. 34.

general impression that he was in charge of the movement. After a detailed report on various peasant demonstrations and soviets, the letter concluded:

> *In the near future, we are going to organize the First Peasants' Congress. Please give us your opinions and necessary directives, together with a letter boosting the morale of the Congress. Please respond to us through the Communist International, and we also think, if the Peasants' International could urgently aid the victims of terrorism, that would be very good.*[66]

In 1934, when his influence in Vietnamese Communist circles was lowest, Nguyen Ai Quoc was attacked for his "erroneous policies," especially those involving the establishment of the soviets, which "was not part of the Party line."[67]

The origins of the Nghe Tinh Soviet Movement remain largely a mystery. To what extent was the Comintern responsible for the policies leading to the establishment of the soviets, and therefore the debacle of the ICP? To what extent was Nguyen Ai Quoc personally responsible? Was Nguyen Ai Quoc made a scapegoat for this near fatal collapse of the Vietnamese Communist movement? It is to be hoped that one day such questions will be resolved by scholars with access to the Comintern's and ICP's archives.

MOSCOW AND VIETNAMESE INFANTILE COMMUNISM

Two dates in the immediate postsoviet period, 11 April 1931 and 25 July 1935, are important in the history of Vietnamese communism. The first marked the recognition of the ICP as an independent section of the Comintern by the Executive Committee of the Communist International (ECCI) at its Eleventh Plenum. The second was the beginning date of the Seventh World Congress (25 July–25 August 1935) of the Communist International, at which the international body formally recognized the ICP as one of its national sections. These events, occurring while the ICP was virtually nonexistent as an organization, symbolized the full attention of

66. Nguyen Ai Quoc, "Thu gui quoc te nong dan" [Letter to the Peasants' International], 5 November 1930, in *Ket hop*, pp. 77–78 (italics in original).
67. *Tap chi Bon-so-vich*, no. 8 (December 1934).

the international Communist movement to developments in Indochina. Paradoxically, this attention, which the Vietnamese Communists had long desired, was to have a negative effect. The period between these two dates was a low point in the ICP's history—the phase referred to by Party historians as the "revolutionary ebb" *(cach mang thoai trao)*.[68] "Left-wing sectarianism," that disease of infantile communism denounced by Lenin but widespread during the heyday of Stalinism, refused to acknowledge the necessity of fusing patriotism with proletarian internationalism. In March 1935, when the ICP was reconstructed on paper, it became, despite retention of the old name, a new party. Representing a victory of proletarian internationalists, it became a party of Moscow *apparatchiki* (organization men). For a time, the ICP maintained no connection with Vietnamese traditions and no longer resembled the Party that Nguyen Ai Quoc had built. Vietnamese Communist writings today say little about internal Party developments during the "ebb."

The ICP paid a heavy price for its international connections, but during its postsoviet reconstruction there were advantages in belonging to the international Communist movement. International solidarity, orchestrated by the Comintern in support of the Party, was overwhelming. Moral and material support poured into Indochina during this period. In thousands of political rallies and meetings and in the leftist press throughout the world, attention was focused on the plight of the Indochinese people under French colonial rule. Meanwhile, the Comintern and its national affiliates connected with the ICP (the Siamese, French, and Chinese Parties) gave whatever support they could to ensure the survival of the Party. ICP cadres, trained and held in reserve in foreign sanctuaries such as Siam, France, the USSR, and southern China, were now sent home to replace those who had fallen to French repression. Because of such support ICP adherents, despite their misfortunes, could look forward with "revolutionary optimism" to resuming combat. This international support enabled the Party slowly to revive by the mid-1930s.

In the reconstruction of the ICP, the Comintern both intervened directly and coaxed fraternal parties into supportive activity. Direct Comintern action was considerable. By the end of 1931, hav-

68. Tran Huy Lieu, *Lich su tam muoi nam*, 2: 98.

ing received no news from Indochina for over six months and assuming that French reprisals had destroyed the entire ICP apparatus, the ECCI decided to reorganize the Indochinese Party altogether. The Comintern's plan for the ICP reconstruction allegedly involved three general steps: first, the Comintern would dispatch to Indochina a large number of Indochinese "professional revolutionaries" trained at Moscow's KUTV; second, once in Indochina, these Moscow-trained *apparatchiki* would remain in close touch with the ECCI and would receive continued support from the various national sections connected with Indochina, such as the PCF, the CCP, and the Siamese Communist party; third, disregarding the former Party organization, these cadres would reassemble the old ICP to create an entirely new party organization.[69]

Outwardly, the results were impressive. Around the beginning of 1932 the Communist party of Siam (most of whom were then overseas Chinese members of the CCP) cooperated in organizing a Committee for Assistance to Indochina (Dong Duong Vien Tro Bo). Among members of this committee were several Vietnamese Communist militants residing in Siam, including Ngo Tuan, Hoang Luan, and Tran Tho Chan.[70] Northeastern Siam became an ICP "frontier station" where Vietnamese Party members could hold conferences and train new recruits from Vietnam in relative safety. An important conference of the ICP reportedly took place in April 1933 in Ban Mai, Nan province, just across the border from Laos.[71] In 1932 and 1933 the committee reportedly sent two agents, Ngo Tuan and Hoang Luan, to Trung Ky to help rebuild the Party organization there.

The PCF also provided considerable assistance. Beginning in January 1933, the French party sponsored perhaps thousands of protest rallies, meetings, press campaigns, and interpellations in parliament to denounce colonial rule in Indochina and to pressure the government to release ICP prisoners. In 1933 the PCF joined with the Red Aid International (SRI), and several well-known French literary figures (including André Malraux, Léon Werth, and Paul Rivet) and created a Committee of Amnesty and Defense of

69. AOM, SLOTFOM, series 3, carton 55, NPM, second semester, 1935, p. 45.
70. T. C., "Nhin lai," pp. 23–34.
71. AOM, SLOTFOM, series 3, carton 51, NPM, second semester 1932, p. 47.

the Indochinese. When, in May 1933, the colonial government staged a mass trial of 121 top ICP leaders (from the provincial to Central Committee levels), the PCF, through the SRI, arranged for barrister Charles Cancelleri to defend the Vietnamese revolutionaries. In August 1933, Paul Vaillant-Couturier, PCF Central Committee member, while en route to Shanghai to attend an antiwar congress, used a stopover in Saigon to denounce the colonial government and to support Vietnamese revolutionaries at public meetings. Finally, in March 1934 a "workers' delegation of investigation" sent by the PCF, SRI, and the committee for amnesty, went to Indochina to study the situation there. Composed of Gabriel Péri (PCF), Jean Barthel (SRI), and Bruneau (Red Trade Union), the delegation met and talked with hundreds of people in various factories, villages, and towns. Although they were not permitted to visit Bac Ky and Trung Ky, their presence on Vietnamese soil provided additional, welcome evidence of international solidarity.

CCP support for the ICP during this period was much less evident. Although recent Vietnamese Communist publications have given much credit to the "exhortations" and other assistance extended by the CCP, so far there exists no known documentary evidence of the extent or nature of any material aid. In an open letter to ICP members,[72] which one Comintern specialist suspects was prepared by the ECCI rather than by the CCP leadership, the CCP Central Committee warned their Vietnamese comrades to beware of the "rebirth of factional and sectarian tendencies" within the ICP. The letter expressed special concern over the alleged lethargy of the Communist movement in Indochina following the collapse of 1931. It called for a "more combative Party" and urged emulation of the examples of the Soviet Union and China as "a sure and proven path leading to victory. . . . The boundary between Kuomintang China and French Indochina will cease to divide our peoples. Soviet Indochina and Soviet China will unite in the World Federation of Soviet Republics." There is no indication of any other CCP assistance.

In addition to orchestrating international support, the Comintern itself took concrete steps to reconstruct the ICP. It created in 1932 a new ICP Provisional Central Committee of unknown composi-

72. "Lettre ouverte du Comité central du P.C. de Chine aux membres du P.C. de l'Indochine," *Cahiers du bolchévisme* (15 August 1934): 857–868.

tion and sent to Indochina approximately forty ICP members who had been trained at KUTV. Meanwhile, it placed Communist activities in Indochina under two separate jurisdictions: those in southern Indochina (Nam Ky, southern Trung Ky, and Cambodia) were assigned to a special committee, headed by KUTV–trained Tran van Giau (alias Ho Nam), which had to report to the PCF; Communist activities in northern Indochina (Bac Ky, northern Trung Ky, and Laos) were governed by a newly created Overseas Leadership Committee (Ban Chi huy o Ngoai) led by Le Hong Phong (alias Hai An or Chayan), a KUTV-trained special ECCI representative.[73] As part of the organizational restoration, a special conference took place in Macao in June 1934 between this committee and the "delegates from the interior." This was the first time the overseas committee succeeded in establishing contacts with the various surviving ICP sections in the country.

The apparent organizational efficiency, however, had little actual positive influence on the reconstruction of the ICP, largely because of the questionable quality of the "professional revolutionaries" that the Comintern had sent to Vietnam. Most seem to have lacked the dedication and commitment required of revolutionaries; at the same time, their tendency to accept Moscow's instructions literally proved to be no less harmful to the Vietnamese movement. Of the seven KUTV-trained personnel sent to Indochina during 1932, for example, one refused to return to Indochina once he reached France, one (Nguyen Huy Bon, alias Barsky) had to be sent back to the Soviet Union to be disciplined for insubordination, and four either surrendered to the French or were arrested "within a few days" after their arrival in Indochina.[74] Of the thirty-five sent to Indochina between 1932 and 1935, twenty-two voluntarily or involuntarily surrendered to the French police and gave them detailed statements. Thanks to such information, the French Sûreté was able to compile comprehensive, detailed studies on the process of their recruitment and training in Moscow, their methods of travel to and from Moscow, their financial subsidies and other forms of support, the plans of Madame Vassilieva (the Comintern official in charge of Indochinese trainees), and the like.[75] A French

73. AOM, SLOTFOM, series 3, carton 55, NPM, second trimester 1935, p. 47.
74. Ibid., p. 58.
75. Ibid.

Sûreté report noted with satisfaction that "the French Communist Party has not, in effect, had a happy time until now, and the 'returnees from Russia' who refused to go back to Indochina or who, barely repatriated, turned themselves in, constituted an important percentage. The intractable ones constitute only rare exceptions."[76]

The low quality of these *apparatchiki* was ultimately traceable to Stalin's policy of "proletarianization." From 1926 to 1929, most Vietnamese candidates for Moscow's KUTV had been proven revolutionary leaders carefully selected by Nguyen Ai Quoc and the Thanh Nien Central Committee, or else by the PCF among the leading Vietnamese Communists in France. Without exception these were *petits-intellectuels* (mostly schoolteachers) typical of the militants of their generation.[77] After the Sixth World Congress, however, the Comintern ordered the PCF and ICP to select candidates only from among workers, and only when lacking a sufficient number of these, from among "proletarianized" students. The consequence of this policy was felt quickly in Moscow. With the ICP embroiled in a crisis of survival in Indochina, KUTV candidates could now be selected only from among Vietnamese workers in France, most of whom were cooks, domestic servants, and sailors. Though meeting the social class requirements, few of these proletarian trainees demonstrated much "political consciousness" or revolutionary commitment.[78] Mostly illiterate even in their native national language *(quoc ngu),* they were unable, once in Moscow, to follow courses given in Russian, French, or Chinese.[79] Back in France from Moscow, most refused to have anything to do with

76. SLOTFOM, series 3, carton 59, NPM, third trimester 1935, p. 52.
77. Among those sent by Nguyen Ai Quoc to the KUTV during this period were Tran Phu (Likwe), Le Hong Phong (Litvinov), Tran Ngoc Ranh (Blokov), Ha Huy Tap (Sinikine), Ngo Duc Tri (Leman), and Bui Cong Trung (Giao). The names in parentheses are the Russian aliases given the trainees at KUTV.
78. During the 1933/34 academic year, for example, Nguyen Khanh Toan (Minin) was engaged by the ECCI to teach these workers *quoc ngu.* AOM, SLOTFOM, series 3, carton 59, NPM, second trimester 1935. According to Nguyen Khanh Toan himself, while Nguyen Ai Quoc was in Moscow between late 1933 and 1938, the latter was also involved in elementary instruction of these worker-trainees. Nguyen Khanh Toan, "En U.R.S.S. avec l'Oncle Ho," in Nguyen Khanh Toan et al., *Avec l'Oncle Ho* (Hanoi, 1972), pp. 146–149.
79. After the Sixth World Congress the PCF attempted to show its concern with the revolutionary movement in Indochina by employing scores of Vietnamese workers as "revolutionary bureaucrats" in salaried positions in various sections of the PCF in France. Several of the candidates for Moscow were chosen from among

revolutionary politics. Among those who stayed on in France, some cooperated with the French Sûreté, selling whatever information they had on their comrades.[80] A majority of those who returned to Vietnam quickly surrendered to the French police there. The Sûreté report quoted above noted:

> One can foresee in advance the attitude that a returnee from Russia would adopt in front of the judge in case of arrest. If the accused was recruited in France, whether sailor or worker, it is probable that he would rapidly become a source of precious information for the judge. If, on the other hand, he was sent to Moscow by the Central Committee of the ICP, the judge would interrogate him in vain for hours and days.[81]

The repatriation of the KUTV trainees also prompted the ascendancy of the proletarian internationalists over revolutionary patriots within the ICP. Unlike other colonial and semicolonial countries of Asia, such as China, India, and Indonesia, Vietnam never had an effective noncommunist nationalist party during the French colonial period. From its very beginning in 1925 and expecially following the demise of the VNQDD and transformation of Thanh Nien and Tan Viet into a unified Communist party in February 1930, the Communist movement had always dominated Vietnam's anticolonial revolutionary scene. It would, however, be inaccurate to say that there existed no Vietnamese nationalist movement. If anything, it existed within the ICP itself. The Party had always contained two basic segments: a powerful group of revolutionary patriots, who emphasized the political objectives of the Party, that is, the primacy of national liberation;[82] and a much smaller group

---

these "bureaucrats." According to a report of an informer inside the PCF, once selected for the journey, a candidate could not refuse to go except for health reasons. A healthy candidate who refused to make the trip would be expelled from the Party. AOM, SLOTFOM, series 3, carton 55, CAI, no. 198 DX, Marseille, 2 February 1933.

80. One of the most useful agents for the Sûreté in France was Dang Dinh Tho (Lomani). While remaining active in PCF and Vietnamese Communist circles there, he accumulated and provided the French with detailed information on Vietnamese Communists in France. In the French National Archives today, his handwritten notes are kept in two separate cartons: SLOTFOM, series 2, "Agents secrets du Service," "Agent Thomas," cartons 18 and 22.

81. AOM, SLOTFOM, series 3, carton 59, NPM, third trimester 1935, p. 48.

82. As late as 1960 Hoang Tung, editor-in-chief of *Nhan dan* [The people], the central organ of the Vietnam Workers' party, was to complain that most Party members failed to understand the ultimate social mission of the Party. See Hoang Tung, *Dang cua giai cap cong nhan* [The party of the working class] (Hanoi, 1960), pp. 16–17.

of proletarian internationalists, who stressed the Party's social mission, that is, the classic social revolution.

Serious disputes broke out between the two factions in the aftermath of the Nghe Tinh soviets, with the internationalists, who took their cues from the Comintern, having the upper hand. The tendency of the revolutionary patriots had been to opt for a liberal interpretation of Marxism-Leninism and to adapt Comintern directives selectively to the conditions of Vietnam. Proletarian internationalists, on the other hand, tended to stress ideological purity and insisted on complete submission to the revolutionary lines of the Comintern. Emphasizing "a national revolution first, then a world revolution," the revolutionary patriots (condemned by radicals in the Communist movement then as "revolutionary *nationalists*") advocated a moderate strategy—national unity, alliance with the petit-bourgeoisie, neutralization of the landowners and the bourgeoisie. On the other hand, the internationalists, stressing the proletarian revolution, called for a class struggle and rejected the importance of a national struggle. In ICP publications during the 1930–1935 period, for example, the deliberate avoidance of phrases that smacked of "nationalism" or "patriotism" was obvious. If anything, during the ascendancy of the proletarian internationalists, the Party adopted an antinationalist stance. An article in the eleventh issue of *Cung kho* [Commiseration] (1931), stated a typical official ICP position. In answer to its title, "Do We Toilers Have a Fatherland?," the article observed:

> The two words *to quoc* [fatherland] have often been flaunted by the bourgeois, intellectual counterrevolutionaries to exploit us toilers so that they could use us as their shield to enjoy their selfish interests. Fatherland is not necessarily composed of people with the same skin color, or the same language. It is the political power of a class. At present, we toilers in Indochina do not in fact have a fatherland.[83]

Elsewhere, the Party leadership expressed its determination to do away with the "nefarious" influence of "revolutionary nationalism" within the Party. The Overseas Leadership Committee wrote in 1934:

> The Indochinese revolution being a part of the world revolution, the militants of one are the same ones of the other. Yet, some say, "It is necessary to make a national revolution prior to that of the world."

83. Quoted in Tran Huy Lieu, *Lich su tam muoi nam*, 2: 90–91.

They believe in effect that each nation must make its own revolution before uniting with the others to combat world capitalism and realize the world revolution. This gross error, which is infinitely dangerous for the Party, is a vestige of the petit-bourgeois ideology of the intellectual "leaders" and dreamers of the Thanh Nien and Tan Viet parties. As these vestiges still exist among a minority of the comrades, the Party has the duty to persecute it until its disappearance.[84]

THE ECLIPSE OF NGUYEN AI QUOC

Another consequence of direct Comintern intervention and the ascendancy of the proletarian internationalists within the ICP was the sharp decline of Nguyen Ai Quoc's influence within Communist circles. For almost ten years, from the time of his arrest on 5 June 1931 by the Hong Kong police until he chaired the Eighth Plenum of the ICP in May 1941, only the handful of people privy to Party secrets knew his whereabouts. Most had tended to accept the rumors that Nguyen had died of tuberculosis in Hong Kong's Victoria Prison.[85] Memorial services were held in Moscow, Paris, and other Communist centers in August 1932 following news of his death. Communist newspapers and periodicals worldwide carried obituaries lauding his contribution to the world revolution, and in one instance even specified 26 June 1932 as the date of his death.[86] As far as is known, from 1932 to 1939 the name Nguyen Ai Quoc was not mentioned once in connection with the revolutionary movement in Indochina, except for those few instances in 1934 when he was singled out for criticism.

Where was Nguyen Ai Quoc? What happened to him? Why did he not aid in the reconstruction of the Party during these difficult years, when his wide-ranging experience, prestige, and skillful leadership would have been most needed? As an energetic, committed revolutionary, how could he have restrained himself from

84. "Tranh dau tren hai mat tran" [Struggle on two fronts], *Tap chi Bon-so-vich,* no. 4 (September 1934).
85. According to Mrs. Loseby, it was Frank Loseby, Nguyen Ai Quoc's English attorney, who floated the rumor to throw the French secret police off Nguyen's track; interview with Mrs. Frank Loseby in the *New York Times,* 6 September 1969. For an account of the Comintern's memorial service for Nguyen Ai Quoc in Moscow in 1932, see Nguyen Khanh Toan, in Nguyen Khanh Toan et al., *Avec l'Oncle Ho,* pp. 143–144.
86. *Cahiers du bolchévisme* 10 (15 February 1933): 278.

taking part in Vietnamese revolutionary activities for almost a decade? By his own account, following his release from prison Nguyen Ai Quoc went to Moscow late in 1933, with the assistance of Paul Vaillant-Couturier, his comrade in the PCF.[87] He stayed in Moscow until the winter of 1938,[88] when he returned to Vietnam via China.

What did Nguyen Ai Quoc do in Moscow? Was he ordered to remain in Moscow in reserve for future Communist activities, as were the several European Communist leaders (Georgii Dimitrov, Maurice Thorez, Palmiro Togliatti, Klement Gottwald)? Or was he confined to Moscow for self-criticism as a penalty for the "errors" he committed while leading the Indochinese movement? Given the limited information available on the ICP, it is not possible to find definite answers to these questions. Nguyen Ai Quoc himself steadfastly refused to divulge details of his revolutionary career, even to his closest comrades, and there is as yet no access to Comintern archives. Even if they were available, it is doubtful that documents could tell the entire story. It is obvious that Nguyen Ai Quoc had fallen out of favor with the current Comintern leadership. It is on record that, while in Moscow, he attended a six-month "accelerated course" at Lenin University, a higher revolutionary institute "for the training of the leading cadres of the fraternal parties."[89] (Li Li-san of the CCP also went to Moscow "for study" after he had lost power in his Party.) Upon completion of this course, he was assigned to work at the Comintern's Institute for National and Colonial Questions, teaching courses on "organization" and "history of the Party" to the Vietnamese group at the KUTV.

Much of his time was spent teaching *quoc ngu* to illiterate Vietnamese KUTV trainees or composing lessons on Vietnamese history and geography in verse form to facilitate memorization for these revolutionary novices.[90] It was obvious that his service to

87. T. Lan [Ho Chi Minh], *Vua di duong*, pp. 61–68; also (Madame) Marie-Claude Vaillant-Couturier, "Le Président Ho Chi Minh n'oubliait pas ses amis français disparus," in *Notre camarade Ho Chi Minh*, memoirs of several PCF militants, comp. and ed. Leo Figuères and Charles Fourniau (Paris, 1970), pp. 115–116.
88. Nguyen Khanh Toan, *Avec l'Oncle Ho*, p. 150.
89. Ibid., p. 145.
90. Ibid.

the ICP at the time was not otherwise required. Throughout the 1930s Nguyen Ai Quoc held no known official post in either the Comintern or the ICP.[91] At the Seventh World Congress of the Comintern (July–August 1935) Nguyen Ai Quoc, the founder, unifier, and most prominent leader of the Vietnamese Party, did not officially represent the ICP. He attended the congress not as a delegate but, according to a document of the Marxist-Leninist Institute of Moscow, as a "consultant" *(à titre consultatif)* to the ICP delegation led by Le Hong Phong.[92] During this same period the ICP leadership severely criticized his political views and activities in connection with the early development of the Party.

The decline of Nguyen Ai Quoc's authority was a direct consequence of the Comintern's adoption of ultra-left policies at the Sixth World Congress in 1928. Until this congress, Nguyen Ai Quoc had had a great deal of discretionary authority in organizing the Communist movement in Indochina. An influential figure in the Comintern's Bureau of the East, he had been head of the Southern Bureau, in charge of organizing the communist movements not only in Indochina, but also in Siam and British Malaya. As one of the most respected Asian figures within Comintern circles, Nguyen Ai Quoc had been relatively free to interpret mainland Southeast Asian conditions, especially those in Indochina, to the Comintern. A combination of factors had made this independence possible: the relative autonomy allowed to the various national sections by the Comintern before 1928; the ECCI's lack of interest in colonial questions prior to the Sixth World Congress; and a lack of Party

91. It is possible that Nguyen Ai Quoc may have been an OMS officer. The OMS *(Otdelenie mezhdunarodnoi sviazi),* or International Communications Section, was an organization within the Comintern responsible for all the latter's secret activities, including assistance to foreign Communist parties throughout the world. W. G. Krivitsky, a former Comintern intelligence officer, reported later that the OMS was a "world-wide network of permanently stationed agents" who served as liaison officers between Moscow and the supposedly autonomous Communist parties. "Neither the rank and file, nor even the majority of the leaders of the Communist parties, know the identity of the OMS representatives, who is responsible to Moscow and who does not participate directly in party discussions." W. G. Krivitsky, *In Stalin's Secret Service* (New York and London, 1939), p. 52, quoted in Drachkovitch and Lazitch, "The Communist International," p. 197). Krivitsky's description generally appears to fit the situation of both Nguyen Ai Quoc and Le Hong Phong, neither of whom held posts in the ICP, and both of whom were "representatives of the Comintern with the ICP."
92. T. Lan [Ho Chi Minh], *Vua di duong,* p. 53, n. 1.

members from Southeast Asia. After the Sixth Congress the Comintern demanded the total obedience and subservience of "professional revolutionaries" and of the various national sections. It also paid much more attention to the revolutionary movements in the colonies as part of its global strategies. Finally, there was no lack of Vietnamese Communists who, much younger and much less experienced than Nguyen Ai Quoc, were willing to accept Comintern guidance and instructions unquestioningly. These new circumstances led directly to Nguyen Ai Quoc's diminished stature within both the international and Vietnamese Communist movements.

The eclipse of Nguyen Ai Quoc within his own Party had begun as early as 1929. During the factionalism that preceded the formation of a unified Communist party, those who were anxious to abolish Thanh Nien and create a Communist party associated Nguyen Ai Quoc with the "petit-bourgeois, fraudulent revolutionaries" among Thanh Nien leaders. Thus, when the DDCSD faction insisted on selecting members for a newly constituted Communist party on the basis of individual merit, it also contended that all Thanh Nien leaders, Nguyen Ai Quoc included,[93] must go through the same procedures for admission. At the Unification Conference (February 1930), a DDCSD delegate reportedly even demanded that Nguyen Ai Quoc produce his credentials as the genuine "representative of the International."[94] In the aftermath of this conference, the DDCSD faction (now fused within the unified Party) continued to resent the partiality that it felt Nguyen Ai Quoc had shown the old Thanh Nien faction while he chaired the conference. Their vindication came half a year later at the First Plenum of the Party's Central Committee (October 1930), when KUTV-trained *apparatchiki* Tran Phu and Ngo Duc Tri, armed with "instructions from the Comintern," rectified most of the "erroneous" resolutions

93. AOM possesses a collection of over thirty secret letters and documents exchanged between DDCSD and the Thanh Nien headquarters in Hong Kong on the question of dissolving Thanh Nien and founding a Communist party. Originally written in invisible ink, they were exposed, photographed, and translated into French. In the letter to the Central Committee of Thanh Nien dated 9 October 1929, DDCSD rejected any suggestion of reconciliation but promised to consider application for membership by Thanh Nien leaders on an individual basis. The letter then added, "If Vuong [Nguyen Ai Quoc] returns, we shall follow the same procedures toward him as toward you"; AOM, SLOTFOM, series 3, carton 129.

94. Thep Moi, *Thoi dung Dang* [The Party-building period] (Paris, 1976), p. 114.

of the Unification Conference and persuaded those present to adopt positions similar to the ones advocated earlier by the DDCSD faction.

The decline of Nguyen Ai Quoc's influence within the ICP leadership became apparent as a widening rift developed between him and the ICP Central Committee, with the Comintern apparently supporting its younger *apparatchiki*. In the early months of 1931 the ICP Central Committee, in an assertion of its own authority, decided not to forward to Nguyen Ai Quoc reports of local committees, as was usually done. In a letter to him the Central Committee pointedly stated that "it would be illogical and disorderly" to send him these reports.[95] As the breach widened, Nguyen Ai Quoc requested early in 1931 that the Bureau of the East assign him to another post, "for the role of the mailbox can be played by another comrade."[96]

> I transmit [to the Bureau of the East] the letters of the Central Committee as they reach me. My role is determined by the Bureau of the East. That is why, when something happens the Bureau of the East lets me know and if I have some ideas to suggest, such as the recent critique of the work in Bac Ky and Trung Ky, I have the endorsement of the Bureau of the East. That is why if the Party decided to do something or to present certain wishes, it is necessary that I know about them. If I know nothing about them at all, how could I respond to the questions which are asked? If my mission consisted only in transmitting correspondence, if I could not give my opinions to the Bureau of the East and to the Central Committee, my presence here would be of little interest, since the work of transmitting letters could be assumed by another comrade. In brief, the Central Committee will have to resolve the question of the responsibility of Vuong [Nguyen Ai Quoc].[97]

During the next few years, under the guise of "ideological unity" proletarian internationalists in the Party waged a systematic campaign of vilification against most of the theoretical positions, strategies, and tactics that Nguyen Ai Quoc had advocated for the Vietnamese revolution. His devotion to the cause of Vietnamese

95. Quoted in Nguyen Ai Quoc's letter of 23 April 1931 to the ICP Central Committee, translated and reprinted in Gouvernement général, *Contribution*, vol. 4, supp. 13, p. 121.
96. Ibid., p. 120.
97. Ibid., p. 121.

national independence was cited as evidence of his "petit-bourgeois hangover." His *Duong kach menh* [The road to revolution], which for several years had been the handbook for Thanh Nien revolutionaries, was now attacked as "a document which reeks of nationalist stench."[98] His favorite strategy of revolution by three stages, accepted during the days of Thanh Nien, was now attacked as an impediment to the rapid development of communism in Indochina.[99] Finally, his counsel of keeping violence against the counterrevolutionaries minimal and of neutralizing the landowners and bourgeoisie was denounced as "opportunistic." In a particularly virulent attack on Nguyen Ai Quoc ("the rightists"), Hong The Cong, apparently the pseudonym of a high-level ICP leader, stated:

> Starting from this false conception [of revolution by stages] the opportunists of Tonkin stubbornly insist in saying that we have not yet arrived at the phase of struggle and oppose to put into practice the resolutions of the First Plenum of the Central Committee of the Indochinese Communist Party and the directives of the Communist International. They see everywhere in the decisions of the ICP and the Communist International tactics "of the Left," of putschism, leading the Indochinese revolution to inevitable defeat. But in reality they are only the rightists, denying the principles and the most elementary tactics of Bolshevism whose defenders they claim to be. . . .
> *The opportunists counseled the Party not to use violence against the counterrevolutionaries,* but what violence is it? Certainly, the Communist party does not recognize individual violence or individual terrorism as a tactic of class struggle, but it advocates the necessity of violence of the masses against the enemies of the proletariat and of the peasantry.[100]

Criticism of Nguyen Ai Quoc reached a peak in 1934 and apparently had the approval of the Comintern. The Overseas Leadership Committee, the Comintern's arm for reconstructing the ICP, issued the majority of the repeated public criticisms of Nguyen Ai Quoc, sometimes singling him out by name. Meanwhile, Nguyen Ai Quoc's revolutionary concepts and strategies were ridiculed as

98. Hong The Cong, *Essai d'histoire du mouvement communiste en Indochine* (1933), quoted in Vu Tho, "Tu 'Duong Cach Menh' den 'Luan cuong chinh tri cua Dang Cong San Dong Duong'" [From "The Road to Revolution" to the "Political Theses of the Indochinese Communist Party"], *NCLS,* no. 72 (March 1965), p. 15.

99. Hong The Cong, "Le travail du parti communiste indochinois," *Cahiers du bolchèvisme* 7 (1 February 1932): 178.

100. Ibid. (italics in original).

showing little understanding of communism and having harmful effects on the Vietnamese revolution. In an article reviewing the history and accomplishments of the ICP during its first five years of existence, *Tap chi Bon-so-vic* [Bolshevik review], the theoretical organ of the Overseas Leadership Committee, reminded readers of the harmful influence of Nguyen Ai Quoc in the Vietnamese Communist movement.

> The services that Nguyen Ai Quoc has rendered to our Party is great, but our comrades nevertheless ought not to forget the nationalist vestiges of Nguyen Ai Quoc and his erroneous instructions on the fundamental questions of the bourgeois-democratic revolutionary movement and his opportunistic theories, which are still rooted in the minds of most of our comrades, just as the bourgeois vestiges have survived in the minds of the adherents of Thanh Nien, Tan Viet, and Vung Hong.[101]
>
> Nguyen Ai Quoc did not understand the directives of the Communist International; he did not fuse the three communist organizations of Indochina from top to bottom. . . . The pamphlet "Political Principles" ["Party's Strategies in Summary"] and the statutes of the unified party did not follow exactly the instructions of the Communist International. Nguyen Ai Quoc otherwise advocated a reformist and collaborationist tactic: "neutrality toward the bourgeoisie and the rich peasantry," "alliance with medium and small landowners," etc. It is because of these errors that from January to October 1930 the ICP followed a strategy opposed on several points to the instructions of the Communist International, despite the fact that it led the masses energetically to the revolutionary struggle. Equally it is because of such errors that the policy followed by the soviets of Nghe An was not in the line of the Party.[102]

For approximately ten years after the defeat in Nghe Tinh, while Moscow-trained *apparatchiki* dominated the ICP and the Party floundered in organizational disarray without a universally accepted leader, Nguyen Ai Quoc played no role in the development

101. The Vung Hong (Aurora) group, whose name evoked early Leninism, was one of several splinter Communist groups emerging in Nam Ky around the beginning of 1931. Officially named Lien Minh Cong San (Communist League), it was organized by Dao van Long, a signboard painter who had been a member of Thanh Nien. With an active membership of approximately fifty, this group denounced the ICP for its alleged neglect of workers' mobilization. The group published a clandestine periodical, *Vung hong,* from which it derived its informal name. In mid-1931, having established contact with Ho Huu Tuong, a "returnee from France," the group veered toward Trotskyism; "Note de la Sûreté du 20 novembre 1932," AOM, SLOTFOM, series 3, carton 131.

102. *Tap chi Bon-so-vic,* no. 8 (December 1934); AOM, SLOTFOM, vol. 3, carton 48, supplement to NPM, first trimester 1935.

of Vietnamese communism. Only in 1938, when the colonial question occupied much less of Stalin's attention and after the Comintern had adopted the "reformist" and "class collaborationist" policies of Georgii Dimitrov, which were similar to the flexible tactics advocated by Nguyen Ai Quoc a decade earlier, was Nguyen Ai Quoc received into Comintern favor once again. The first documentary evidence of his rehabilitation appeared in July 1939, when he submitted a report to the Comintern on the ICP's policies during the Popular Front period.[103]

THE MACAO CONGRESS

The obscurity of Nguyen Ai Quoc, the destruction of the Party he had helped build since 1925, and the dominance of the Stalinist faction were most evident at the First National Party Congress of the ICP. Meeting 27–31 March 1935 in Portuguese Macao, this congress marked the completion of organizational reconstruction. In a formal sense only, this event can be considered a turning point in the history of the Party. According to Party regulations, the national party congress is the highest decision-making authority of the Party. Each time a national congress meets, it is supposed to determine the strategic guidelines for the entire Party during the next historical phase. There have been only four such congresses during the half century of existence of the Vietnamese Communist party.[104] On each occasion, the Party reviewed past performance, inaugurated a new party line, and defined the nature and tasks of the movement during the next period.

In reality, the Macao congress was of little significance. Aside from symbolizing the reemergence of the ICP and revealing the current relationship between the Vietnamese Communists and the

103. For the text see Ho Chi Minh, "Y kien ve duong loi, chu truong cua Dang trong thoi ky Mat tran dan chu" [My opinions on the line and policies of the Party during the Democratic Front period], in "Bao Cao" [Report]; lengthy excerpts are reprinted in Ho Chi Minh, *Ket hop*, pp. 79–81.

104. At the second congress, held in the Viet Bac region in March 1951, the self-dissolved ICP was reconstituted as the Vietnam Workers' Party (Dang Lao dong Viet Nam). This congress, which also reemphasized the national mission of the Party, marked the formal transition of the Communist party from an illegal, clandestine organization to a "party in power." The third congress, held in Hanoi in September 1960, officially hailed the completion of the first, national democratic (bourgeois-democratic) stage of the two-stage revolution and the beginning of "socialist reconstruction" in North Vietnam. The Fourth National Party Congress,

Comintern, the congress accomplished virtually nothing. The sorry state of the Party was reflected in the composition of the congress itself. The following people attended: Ha Huy Tap (alias Nho), Overseas Leadership Committee; Phung Chi Kien (alias Ly), Overseas Leadership Committee; Hoang Dinh Rong (alias Van Tu), Bac Ky; "Female Comrade" Luong, Bac Ky; Ngo Tuan (alias Ba Doc), Trung Ky; Vo Nguyen Hien (alias Chat Ke), Trung Ky; Vo van Ngan (alias Xu), Nam Ky; Nguyen Chanh Nhi, Nam Ky; Xo, Laos; Tran To Chan, Committee for Assistance to Indochina, Siamese CP; one CCP representative; two Siamese CP representatives.[105]

None of the known leaders of Vietnamese communism was present. Nguyen Ai Quoc was in disgrace. Le Hong Phong, chairman of the Overseas Leadership Committee, was en route to Moscow to attend the Seventh World Congress. Ho Tung Mau, Le Hong Son, Ngo Gia Tu, Nguyen Duc Canh, Tran van Cung, and other leaders of 1925–1931 were either dead or in prison. Neither Tran van Giau, chairman of the Provisional Committee for Nam Ky, nor Nguyen van Dut, the official liaison between Nam Ky and the overseas committee, was present. Those who attended, with the possible exception of Ha Huy Tap, were new names and new faces to one another. Of the delegates, only three (Ha Huy Tap, Phung Chi Kien, and Hoang Dinh Rong) would play leading roles in the Party after the congress.

Nor did the revolutionary line adopted at the Macao congress affect the long-term course of the Party. Indeed, as the ICP delegates labored over the Comintern's radical tactics for the Third Period ("Bolshevization" and "proletarianization"), the Comintern itself was about to adopt the flexible tactics of the Popular Front. Before the new ICP line received practical application, it had been outmoded by the Dimitrov line of the Seventh World Congress. Upon Le Hong Phong's return from Moscow in the summer of 1936, yet another Party strategy was published, superseding that of the Macao congress.

The significance of the ICP First National Congress lies not in

---

held in Hanoi in December 1976, was another turning point in the history of Vietnamese communism: the completion of the "national" mission (the complete liberation of the country) and the beginning of "socialist construction" throughout Vietnam.

105. T. C., "Nhin lai," pp. 23–24.

what it actually accomplished, but in what it revealed about the nature and direction of the ICP during this period of infantile communism. The Macao congress was convoked at the explicit instructions of the Comintern and had no formal endorsement by the lower echelons of the Party. Delegates to the congress were either Moscow-trained "professional revolutionaries" (Ha Huy Tap and Hoang Dinh Rong), or those whose revolutionary experiences were outside the confines of Indochina (CCP and Siamese CP) or neophytes from Indochina who had had little previous revolutionary experience. Earlier ICP conferences (February 1930 and October 1930) had focused on the fundamental problems of the Vietnamese revolution (antiimperialism and antifeudalism). These issues were not part of the agenda or resolutions of the Macao congress. Instead, in addition to the problems of organizational restoration, the congress concerned itself with international questions, such as the defense of the Soviet Union and Soviet China. From this point until the formation of the Viet Minh Front in 1941, the strategies, tactics, and revolutionary activities of the ICP were decided more often by non-Vietnamese Communists than by the Vietnamese revolutionaries.

By early 1935, the ICP had thus come to an apparent dead end. With thousands of its most dedicated members still imprisoned by the French and Nguyen Ai Quoc, the Party founder, under some form of preventive detention in Moscow, the Party appeared to be both leaderless and directionless. By sacrificing traditional Vietnamese patriotism to proletarian internationalism, the ICP had of its own volition left the mainstream of Vietnamese politics. As the Party submitted itself totally to the will of the Comintern, it became increasingly isolated from and irrelevant to Vietnam's national experience. Under the command of Moscow-trained left-wing sectarians, the once popular revolutionary movement built by Nguyen Ai Quoc and his comrades in Thanh Nien had become a nonentity among Vietnamese. As we shall see, throughout the Popular Front period, the absence of firm leadership and an independent revolutionary line was to be a great obstacle to the Vietnamese revolutionary movement that the ICP claimed to represent.

CHAPTER FOUR

IN THE INTERNATIONALIST WILDERNESS

> In this period our Party regarded its urban activities as the central task, without, however, neglecting the countryside. It severely criticized "left" deviations, such as isolationism, narrowmindedness, failure to use legal and semi-legal forms to push the movement forward, and right deviations, such as legalism, being intoxicated by partial successes and neglecting the consolidation of secret Party organizations, lack of vigilance against the Trotskyists and unprincipled cooperation with them, too much zeal in seeking the support of the bourgeoisie and landowner class while neglecting to consolidate and develop the revolutionary forces of workers and peasants, and paying insufficient attention to the question of worker-peasant alliance.
>
> *An Outline History of the Viet Nam Workers' Party, 1930–1975*

The evolution of Vietnamese communism during the Popular Front period (1936–1939) further demonstrates the complexity of the relationship between a local Communist party and the international Communist movement. In contrast to the early 1930s, when implementation of the ultra-left line of the Comintern's Sixth World Congress had come close to destroying the ICP, during the latter part of the 1930s the revolutionary line of the Seventh World Congress, the "people's front" policy, created the conditions necessary for the Party's revival. Thanks to the liberal colonial policies promulgated by the left-oriented French Popular Front government, the ICP reemerged to share with other newly constituted Marxist-Leninist factions the leadership of a mass movement unprecedented in scale and scope. Yet even in this instance, the straitjacket of Stalinism allowed the Vietnamese Communists little room for maneuver. For lack of a firm and universally accepted leadership and an independent revolutionary line, the ICP in the end forfeited this favorable opportunity to build a solid party. Instead of unity of the Vietnamese left, there was widespread disunity; instead of dominating the anticolonial scene by dint of its experience and its roots in the masses, the ICP faced dissension from within and the powerful rivalry of the Trotskyists from without. In September 1939, after the collapse of the French Popular Front government, a brutal wave of repression descended on the Vietnamese revolutionaries, Stalinists and Trotskyists alike, preventing the unity of the Vietnamese left and delaying ideological and organizational unity in the ICP itself.

TROTSKYISTS AND STALINISTS

Certain political developments in Vietnam during the "revolutionary ebb" created problems for the ICP during the Popular Front period. During the years 1932–1935 there emerged several Marxist-Leninist factions not previously affiliated with Thanh Nien or under the supervision of the Comintern. Composed of Vietnamese partisans of Trotsky and Stalin, these factions constituted the principal anticolonial forces in Vietnam in this period. Although they proved to be sources of irritation and embarrassment to the ICP during the Popular Front years, these groups made a significant contribution to awareness of Marxism in Vietnam. Indeed, throughout the second half of 1930s it was their efforts, as much as those of the reconstituted ICP, that brought Vietnamese revolutionary activity to a significant level and merged the Vietnamese anticolonial movement with the international working-class movement. Because these groups so strongly influenced Vietnamese politics during the Popular Front period, their evolution and their difficult relationship with the ICP require detailed discussion.

First and most important, the "new" Marxist-Leninist activists had a social and political background similar to that of members of Thanh Nien, Tan Viet, and the VNQDD. All were born during the first decade of the century. They also belonged to the newly emerging petite-bourgeoisie of Vietnam, the vacillating social class that Marxists tend to distrust but consider useful at a certain juncture in the revolutionary process. Finally, they, too, had had their first exposure to anticolonial politics during the mid-1920s: they had undergone the political experience of the catalytic events of 1925–1926—anticolonial demonstrations to demand amnesty for Phan Boi Chau and to mourn the death of Phan Chu Trinh—and helped light the fuse of the Vietnamese revolution.

These similarities notwithstanding, the new activists differed from the members of the other established parties in two fundamental respects. The fact that they came from Nam Ky is important. The members of Thanh Nien, Tan Viet, and the VNQDD, with their center of operations in Bac Ky and Trung Ky, had deep roots in Confucian Vietnam. In contrast, the Nam Ky activists were products of French political culture. Their early education in Vietnam had followed the French curriculum, which tended to encourage them to look to Europe, and France in particular, for inspiration and models. Better versed in French language, literture, history, and philosophy than in the same aspects of traditional Vietnamese culture, they were inspired by the European political and revolutionary experiences.

Their political education also distinguished them from the pre-ICP groups. The new Marxist-Leninist activists were among the hundreds of Nam Ky students who emigrated to France; most had been expelled from schools in connection with their political activities in 1925–1926.[1] While their revolutionary counterparts in

---

1. There are no exact figures for the number of Vietnamese students in France at the time. A police report of January 1929 indicated that approximately 5,000 "Indochinese" (mostly Vietnamese) lived in France. Of these, 1,700 were students, 1,000 sailors, and 1,255 domestic servants. Among the students, 1,100 were in

Trung Ky and Bac Ky smuggled themselves to Canton for political training by Nguyen Ai Quoc, these young Nam Ky students went to France in quest of a new political faith or to continue their Marxist political education, which had begun with *La cloche fêlée, L'Annam,* and the Marxist study circles. Europophile by this time, they went to Europe to find methods to combat European imperialism.

Compared with the Thanh Nien training in Canton, however, the political education of the émigrés to France, though no less intensive, was much less structured. These students acquired their political education while pursuing their studies at French lycées or universities, although for many the political aspect of the French experience appeared to be at least as important as the academic. In France, many of these students joined the Viet Nam Doc Lap Dang (Vietnamese Independence Party), better known as PAI, the abbreviation of its French name, Parti Annamite d'Indépendence. Founded sometime in 1926 by Nguyen The Truyen,[2] a radical patriot and former comrade of Nguyen Ai Quoc, this organization was left-oriented and patriotic, somewhat like the VNQDD in the home country. It maintained contacts with both the PCF and the French branch of the Chinese Kuomintang. PAI published a monthly, *Viet Nam hon* [Soul of Vietnam], and claimed to follow a militant patriotic line, as preached by Phan Boi Chau. As the only Vietnamese political organization in France in 1926 and 1927, PAI had a strange mixture of members from the most varied social

---

Paris, 200 at Aix-en-Provence, and 110 in Toulouse. See Daniel Hémery, "Du patriotisme au marxisme: L'immigration vietnamienne en France de 1926 à 1930," *Le mouvement social,* no. 90 (January–March 1975), pp. 21–23.

2. Nguyen The Truyen was a well-known anticolonial figure in the 1920s and 1930s. Born in 1898 at the village of Hanh Thien, Nam Dinh province, he went to France around 1920. One of the closest collaborators with Nguyen Ai Quoc in Paris in the early 1920s, he agitated within the framework of the Union intercoloniale. A member of the editorial board of *Le paria,* he wrote the preface to Nguyen Ai Quoc's famous *Le procès de la colonisation française* (Paris, 1926). An early member of the Colonial Commission of the PCF Central Committee, he became a leading member of the Union intercoloniale after Nguyen Ai Quoc's departure for Moscow in June 1923. For unknown reasons he left the PCF sometime in 1927 and founded the PAI. After a long career of leftist politics, he turned anticommunist sometime during the early 1940s. Exiled to Madagascar by Admiral Decoux in 1943, he returned to Vietnam in 1949 and became peripherally involved in the French-sponsored scheme to set up the collaborative puppet regime of former Emperor Bao Dai. He died in Saigon in September 1969.

backgrounds—petit-bourgeois students from Nam Ky together with workers and soldiers, most of whom were from Bac Ky and had stayed in France following their service in the French army during the First World War.

The first sign of a Vietnamese Trotskyist-Stalinist debate appeared around 1927–1928. Under the influence of the French left, which then was engaged in a heated Trotskyist-Stalinist conflict, the student members of PAI also split along ideological lines. While the great majority tended toward a moderate "reformist" position, the more articulate and radical elements divided between support for Trotsky and acceptance of the PCF's Stalinist line. When the PAI disintegrated around the end of 1927, some of the more prominent students, such as Ta Thu Thau,[3] Huynh van Phuong,[4] and Nguyen van Luan, joined the French Trotskyist group, Left Opposition (Opposition de Gauche); others, including most of the worker members of PAI, followed Nguyen van Tao to become affiliates of the PCF; the remainder of former PAI members avoided anticolonial politics altogether. While in France, the Trotskyists and Stalinists maintained a peculiar relationship. On account of their ideological differences, heated debates and occa-

3. Ta Thu Thau was born to a poor carpenter on 5 May 1906 in Tan Binh, Long Xuyen province. A student at Collège Chasseloup-Laubat, he earned the *Brevet élémentaire* in June 1923 and the *Baccalauréat indochinois* in June 1925. In 1926 he joined Tran Huy Lieu, Bui Cong Trung, and others to organize demonstrations to demand amnesty for Phan Boi Chau and a "state funeral" for Phan Chu Trinh. He helped found the Dang Thanh Nien (Youth Party), or Jeune Annam. He left for France in September 1927 and became a student at the Faculty of Sciences, University of Paris. Dividing his time among his studies, part-time work as an elevator operator, and politics, he never obtained his degree. One of the most articulate and admired student leaders, he was expelled from France on 30 May 1930 because of his leading role in anticolonial demonstrations by Vietnamese students. Throughout the 1930s he was one of Vietnam's most respected political figures as head of the moderate faction among the Trotskyists and editor of *La lutte*. He died in Quang Ngai in 1945 at the hands of local Viet Minh, but was posthumously exonerated by President Ho Chi Minh.

4. Huynh van Phuong was born on 30 May 1906 to a well-to-do family in My Tho province. One of the student émigrés of the mid-1920s, he studied law at the University of Paris from 1927 to 1930. A member of PAI and then of the Opposition de Gauche, he was among the nineteen students expelled from France on 30 May 1930. Failing as a building contractor in Saigon, he moved in 1936 to Hanoi, where he was again active in Marxist political circles, especially in the Le travail group with Vo Nguyen Giap, Tran Huy Lieu, Khuat Duy Tien, and others. After the Trotskyist-Stalinist split he became editor of his own newspaper, the *Phu nu thoi dam* [Women's tribune].

sional fisticuffs punctuated the meetings of the General Association of Indochinese Students. Despite their bickering, however, they were capable of forming an alliance to protest colonial repression in Vietnam, as they did in the aftermath of Yen Bay.

The Trotskyist-Stalinist controversy was transposed to Vietnam in the spring of 1930, when the French government decided on 30 May 1930 forcibly to repatriate nineteen students[5] who had been charged with "group rebellion" and "political conspiracy." These students had been among the arrested leaders of organized anticolonial activities at the crucial time when the French Chamber of Deputies was in full debate over Yen Bay and the French public was experiencing a first wave of shock and dismay over the brutal repression in Indochina. The decision to expel the students proved to be a fateful one for both French colonial rule and the Vietnamese anticolonial movement. All the repatriated students had been well known for their activities in opposition to French rule. All had openly associated themselves with Marxist-oriented French organizations, such as the PCF and Left Opposition, and had been leaders of numerous "struggle committees" that sprang up at university centers all over France, to break what they called the "criminal" official silence on colonial atrocities committed against Vietnamese in connection with the Yen Bay Mutiny. The injection of these lively and articulate young Vietnamese intellectuals soon helped revitalize the Vietnamese anticolonial movement, which had fallen into disarray after the reprisals of 1930 and 1931. Shortly after their repatriation they were playing an important role in reshaping the outlook, style, and substance of Vietnamese anticolonialism. The cooperation, competition, and disputes among them and the groups they created formed an important part of Vietnamese politics during the 1930s.

The introduction into Vietnam of two new political groups, both of which characterized themselves as "Communist," and "Marxist-

---

5. Among the expelled students were Trotskyists (Ta Thu Thau, Huynh van Phuong, Phan van Chanh); members of the PCF or the PCF-sponsored Federation of Students (Dang Ba Linh, Le van Thu, Tran van Giau, Trinh van Phu, Bui Duc Kien, Vu Lien), and noncommunist leftists (Ho van Nga, Le Ba Cang, Nguyen van Tan). Nguyen van Tao, the most prominent "Stalinist" member of the Colonial Commission of the PCF Central committee, was repatriated in June 1931. See Le van Thu, *Muoi chin sinh vien Viet-Nam bi truc xuat* [The nineteen Vietnamese students who were expelled] (Saigon, 1949).

Leninist," and "Bolshevik," complicated the evolution of Vietnamese communism, for neither group was an outgrowth of the
Party founded by Nguyen Ai Quoc. For one thing, they created a
problem of nomenclature. Until this time neither "Trotskyism" nor
"Stalinism" had existed in the lexicon of Vietnamese communism.
These concepts originated in the conflict after Lenin's death between the partisans of Trotsky and Stalin over an appropriate strategy for the world revolution. Trotsky had opposed Stalin and his
supporters in the Comintern leadership, such as Kamenev,
Zinoviev, and Bukharin, who advocated the doctrine of "socialism
in one country," that is, the necessity of consolidating the Soviet
Union as the center of world communism. Trotsky's theory of
"revolution in permanence," in contrast, postulated that the revolutionary spark in Russia would ignite the latent class conflicts in
Europe; in this way, the bourgeois revolution would be transformed into a proletarian revolution and the proletarian national
revolution into an international one, and thus the cycle of revolution would be complete. After the Sixth World Congress of the
Comintern (1928), which confirmed the final defeat of Trotsky, his
partisans gradually lost the battle to retain the label "Communist."
Meanwhile, members of the various national sections of the Comintern in addition to their Party label were also called "Stalinist" (a
nomenclature that assumed negative connotations only in the late
1930s, apparently in connection with the Great Purges in the
USSR).

Two separate groups of Stalinists existed in Vietnam in the
1930s. The first was composed of those who had been affiliated
with Thanh Nien or one of the Thanh Nien–derived Communist
groups, some of whom had been trained at the KUTV in Moscow.
The second group was composed of the Stalinist returnees from
France, who had not been affiliated with Thanh Nien or any of its
derivatives. This group is best known for its overt political activities during the 1930s, particularly for its collaboration with the
Trotskyists in the La Lutte group and the Indochinese Congress
Movement. Indeed, the rapid expansion of Communist influence in
Nam Ky during the Popular Front years was the work of this
faction rather than of the reconstructed Thanh Nien–derived ICP.
While the ICP tended to maintain strict obedience to instructions
from the Comintern, the other group often made its own decisions

as to the appropriate course of the Vietnamese revolution. For purposes of discussion in this book, members of the Thanh Nien–derived ICP will be designated hereafter as "Communists," the activists deported from France as "Stalinists."

Somewhat more information is available about the Trotskyists than about the Stalinists. The first Vietnamese Trotskyist organization was formed sometime in 1931, after the repatriation of the nineteen students. Founded by Ta Thu Thau, Huynh van Phuong, Le van Thu, and Phan van Chanh, this organization was called Dong Duong Cong San (Indochinese Communism). Though not members of the ICP, the early Vietnamese Trotskyists considered themselves Communists and deemed it their duty to reform the Party. After the colonial regime demolished the ICP in late 1931, the Trotskyists apparently had dreams of remaking Vietnamese communism in accordance with their own ideas. In the autumn of 1932, for example, when false rumors of the death of Nguyen Ai Quoc were widely accepted, an editorial in *Duoc Vo San* [The proletarian torch], the official organ of the Trotskyists in Vietnam, mourned the communist fighter and pledged continuing support for the ICP.

> The Left faction of the Indochinese Communist party learned with much sorrow that Comrade Nguyen Ai Quoc has passed away. It shared its chagrin with all proletarians. We must mourn this man, whose will is indomitable. Comrade Quoc has placed his life in peril for the great service of Indochinese proletarians. . . . The adversary of capitalism and imperialism has so strongly worried the capitalist governments that they found it necessary to arrest him in Shanghai [*sic*]. He finally succumbed to the atrocious tortures which he was made to undergo. Comrade Quoc is dead—dead in the very battlefield, in the decisive struggle against imperialism and capitalism. Bravo, Comrade! Your name is inscribed in revolutionary history for thousands of years.
>
> Comrade Quoc is dead, but the ICP lives. It will live on indefinitely. The Left faction of the Party will follow you, Comrade Quoc. *It will continue its task and make sure that the Indochinese Communist party will be the deserving and only party of Indochinese proletarians.*[6]

In this spirit the Trotskyists called for a change in the ICP's slogans and policies. An article by "Hiep Luc" in *Duoc vo san*

---

6. *Duoc vo san* [The proletarian torch] 1, no. 14 (28 August 193?) (italics added).

appealed for a change in the Party's direction. True to Trotskyist tenets, the article urged less emphasis on peasant struggles and more on workers' struggles.

Our Party has been repressed to the point of being completely destroyed by white terror. We have to change our policy. We ought to abandon the motto "Dictatorship of the Proletariat and Peasantry." We ought to show the Party members that the revolutionary force of the workers is more powerful than that of the peasants, using as example the militant force of the workers of Canton in 1927. Only the workers can practice the theory of Karl Marx.[7]

Like their counterparts in other countries, however, the Vietnamese Trotskyists were gradually divided against themselves, each faction having its own definition of revolutionary strategies and tactics. What united them was their common antipathy toward Stalinism; otherwise, it was difficult to interpret the niceties of their ideological differences. The bitterness of the disputes between the factions was second only to the resentment each felt toward Stalin and his followers. The information now available does not allow identification of all the Trotskyist groups in Vietnam in the 1930s. As far as is known, there were three: Ta Phai Doi Lap (Left Opposition), Ta Phai Doi Lap Thang Muoi (October Left Opposition), and Dong Duong Cong San (Indochinese Communism).[8] Indochinese Communism, the moderate Trotskyist faction led by Ta Thu Thau, emphasized legal and overt means of struggle and eschewed clandestine activities; the Octobrists (so called because of their claim to preserve the spirit of the October Revolution), led by Ho Huu Tuong,[9] in contrast emphasized clandestine activities. Thau's group, derisively called the "Third-and-One-Half

7. Hiep Luc [pseud.], "Cach mang Dong duong" [The Indochinese revolution], ibid.

8. See Anh Van and Jacqueline Roussel, *Mouvements nationaux et lutte de classes au Viet-Nam* (Paris, 1947), p. 53.

9. A vivacious political and literary figure, Ho Huu Tuong was born on 10 October 1910. Son of a poor peasant in Thuong Thanh, Can Tho province, he was expelled from primary school in 1926 because of his role in the student demonstrations of 1925–1926. He continued his studies in France (Aix-en-Provence and Lyons), aided by relatives. An ardent political activist of extreme left tendencies, he returned to Saigon in January 1931 to found the Ta Phai Doi Lap Thang Muoi (October Left Opposition), often derogatorily referred to by more moderate Trotskyists as the "Fourth-and-a-Half International." Leaving Marxist politics in 1949, he turned to his literary interests. He was reportedly arrested in 1977 for leading demonstrations for "human rights" in Ho Chi Minh City. Released from prison following his "reeducation," Tuong died in 1980.

International" by the Octobrists, competed for elections and published *La lutte* in collaboration with the Stalinists. The Octobrists, called the "Fourth-and-One-Half International" or "Left of the Extreme Left" by Indochinese Communism, published their own periodical, *Thang muoi* [October], denouncing both Stalinism and the moderate Trotskyists.

LA LUTTE

Beginning in January 1933, a peculiar kind of "united front" was formed in Nam Ky, composed of several well-known anticolonial activists of different ideological inclinations: two Stalinists (Nguyen van Tao[10] and Duong Bach Mai),[11] two Trotskyists (Ta Thu Thau and Phan van Hum),[12] one self-styled anarchist (Trinh Hung Ngau), one independent anticolonial leader (Nguyen An

10. The leading figure of the "Stalinist" faction throughout the 1930s, Nguyen van Tao was born on 20 May 1908 in Phuoc Loi, Cholon province, into a family of small landowners. He was expelled from Chasseloup-Laubat in 1926 because of student political activities and fled to France the same year. A leading member of the PAI, he left his studies for full-time political agitation, joined the PCF in 1927, and was a delegate at the Sixth World Congress (Moscow, 1928). Expelled from France and forcibly repatriated in June 1931, he led the "overt section" of the ICP in the South throughout the 1930s. As one of the prime movers in the temporary alliance between Trotskyists and Stalinists, he resisted pressure from both the ICP and PCF to break with the Trotskyists. Tao later became North Vietnam's minister of labor and then minister in charge of the prime minister's office. He died in 1972.

11. Duong Bach Mai, a rich man's son, was born 17 April 1904 in Phuoc Le, Baria province. An early student activist, he was expelled from Collège Chasseloup-Laubat and lost his scholarship after participating in a student strike on 9 December 1920. In France, he studied at Aix-en-Provence from 1925 to 1927 and subsequently worked for the National Savings Bank in Paris. Censured for his political activities, he left for Moscow in August 1929 to study at the KUTV (the Stalin School) under the alias "Bourov." He returned to Saigon via Shanghai in September 1931 to become a leading "Stalinist" figure in Cochin China throughout the 1930s. After the August Revolution, Mai became for a time Vietnam's minister of finance.

12. Phan van Hum was born 9 April 1902 in An Thanh, Thu Dau Mot province. Son of a well-to-do family, he was a successful student. As an official in the colonial administration in Hue, Hum often visited Phan Boi Chau and sheltered the striking students in 1927. Forced to resign, he returned to Saigon in 1928 to collaborate with Nguyen An Ninh in organizing the Thanh Nien Cao Vong Dang (High Aspirations Youth Party). He left for France in 1929 to study philosophy at the Sorbonne. Fleeing from the French police because of his political activities, he first went to Belgium and then returned to Saigon in 1933. He became a respected figure in the La Lutte group in the 1930s. He died late in 1945, reportedly killed by the Viet Minh.

Ninh), and one leftist of undetermined political persuasion (Tran van Thach).[13] This *ad hoc* group did not give itself a name, but eventually it became known as the La Lutte Group (*nhom* La Lutte), after their newspaper, *La lutte* [The struggle]. Never before, in Vietnam or anywhere else, had Stalinists and Trotskyists formed a common front. Temporary "issue fronts" may have existed, but as far as is known, never have Trotskyists and Stalinists cooperated within the same organization. Several successful political ventures resulted from this alliance, most notably the election of its members to the Municipal Council of Saigon and the Colonial Council of Cochin China in 1933, 1935, and 1937. Ideological dissension, however, led to the group's disintegration around the middle of 1937.

This united front between Vietnamese Trotskyists and Stalinists was possible for two reasons. First, regardless of their partisan labels, all the original members of the La Lutte group belonged to the same circle of friends and anticolonial activists and had known one another and agitated together since the late 1920s. Influenced by different political tendencies in France, they fell into disagreement and parted ways while there. In the Trotskyist-Stalinist debate that raged among European leftists, they chose different banners under which to fight French imperialism and accepted different international strategies and tactics. The forming of the La Lutte group in Vietnam in January 1933 was thus a regrouping of former comrades who were now directly confronting their common enemy, French colonialism, in their home country. Past differences in ideologies were put aside in order to join in anticolonial activities. The agreement to form a common front, however, did not mean that individuals abandoned their respective ideologies or concurrent affiliation with ideologically opposed groups.

A second factor that made this front possible was the apparent lack of international organizational pressure against its formation.

13. Tran van Thach was born 15 October 1903 to a wealthy family. Completing his early education in Saigon, he went to France in 1926 to obtain a degree in philosophy in Paris. He returned to Saigon in January 1930 and taught at the Institution Huynh Khuong Ninh and other private schools while actively engaged in politics. Thach's ideological orientation was unclear as of 1933, but he veered increasingly toward Trotskyism. Well known as an "intellectual" among southern Trotskyists, he was elected to the Saigon Municipal Council (with Nguyen van Tao) in April 1933 as a candidate of La Lutte. Throughout the Popular Front period he was one of the principal leaders of the Trotskyist faction in Cochin China.

Despite its vehement and comprehensive criticism of the Comintern, Trotskyism did not aspire to the creation of a new International for many years. In fact, Trotsky long opposed the idea of a Fourth International.[14] In his view, the principle objective of Trotskyists was to influence Communist opinion, to effect a realization that usurpers had taken control of the Soviet government and the Comintern, and to encourage a return to pristine Marxism and Leninism. Hence, Trotsky maintained that he and those who followed him owed allegiance to the Third International even though they had been expelled from it. Vietnamese Trotskyists generally accepted this policy in their dealings with Stalinists. They hoped to effect a change in the Vietnamese Communist movement and, if possible, to gain control of and reconstitute it. They were slow to change this general goal even after Trotsky's decision to renounce the Comintern and establish a new International became known late in 1933. Similarly, Vietnamese Stalinists felt no international pressure not to collaborate with the Trotskyists. In those years there were few connections between the Stalinists in La Lutte and the Communists, Vietnamese or non-Vietnamese. Those responsible for the reconstruction of the ICP did not establish contacts with the Stalinist legal activists in Nam Ky until late in 1934, and no official Party policy could have been formulated with regard to the Trotskyists until at least July 1936. Yet, as far as is known, the issue was not raised at the special conference of July 1936. There is one obvious conclusion to be drawn: the decision to form La Lutte was based on personal choice, not on organizational directives, although the ICP leadership's silence on the subject of the La Lutte group could well have been construed as a blessing or at least consent.

Formal collaboration between Vietnamese Trotskyists and Stalinists began as early as 1933. Around the end of January Stalinists, Trotskyists, and "nonpartisan" activists formed a common front "in order to create a legal movement."[15] The formal objective

14. Isaac Deutscher, *The Prophet Outcast* (New York, 1963), p. 43.

15. Ho Huu Tuong asserted in an interview with Nguyen Ngu I that it was the French Communist deputy Gabriel Péri who, through consultation with Nguyen An Ninh and with the approval of Moscow, encouraged the reconstitution of the La Lutte group in 1934; "Song va viet voi Ho Huu Tuong" [Live and write with Ho Huu Tuong], *Bach khoa* 10, no. 27 (25 February 1966), pp. 53–59. That such an event took place is not inconceivable, despite silence on this point by writers in the SRV today. See also Anh Van and Roussel, *Mouvements nationaux*, p. 54.

of the front was quite simple: to use all possible legal means to struggle overtly for the "independent and historical interests of the working class and the oppressed masses, and to make the general masses devote themselves to class struggle."[16] The terms for the collaboration between Trotskyists and Stalinists were equally simple: first, each group would refrain from publicly attacking the other and its policy; second, the two groups would collaborate in efforts to oppose imperialism and capitalist exploitation. More specifically, the following terms were stipulated: "(a) No calumny against the USSR; (b) No hostile attitude toward Communist parties; (c) No press campaigns of a charcter contrary to the program of common action nor criticism against the policy of the allied faction."[17]

There are, however, reasons to suspect that the real motivation behind the formal collaboration was pursuit of a limited goal. In other words, what was intended was an "issue front," or at most a "movement front."[18] The immediate purpose of forming La Lutte in January 1933 had been to compete for electoral seats in the April election of the Municipal Council of Saigon.[19] Ever since the creation of the council, the six seats reserved for Vietnamese (compared with twelve seats for the French) had been more or less the preserve of the Constitutionalist party, whose membership represented large landowners and well-to-do Vietnamese merchants and professionals. To elect people outside the Constitutionalist party to governmental councils was virtually impossible. In 1933, however, Trotskyists and Stalinists who had cooperated in the 1930 demonstrations in Paris decided to join once again in what was anticipated

16. Anh Van and Roussel, *Mouvements nationaux*, p. 54.

17. *Kich bong* [Theater and cinema], no. 2 (2 August 1937). *Kich bong* illustrates the situation of many political publications during the Popular Front period (1936–1939). ICP political prisoners who were on parole and had no legal right to publish would encourage wealthy people to request legal permission to publish a periodical. Ownership of the periodical belonged to the person who received the permit. The activist would then buy the managing editorship and publish the material of his own choice. For that reason, *Kich bong* often dealt more with general political, economic, and social topics than with those suggested by its title.

18. The "issue front" and the "movement front" are variations of the Leninist United Front tactic. Both are temporary alliances. An issue front is a coalition based on a specific issue. A movement front is one formed for a variety of issues. In both fronts, however, the allied groups remain organizationally independent of one another.

19. See Ho Huu Tuong's interview, "Song va viet."

to be a temporary venture. As the April election drew closer, the *ad hoc* group of old political comrades decided to give the French authorities "a hard time." No one in the group, it seemed, seriously expected to see its own members elected. All, however, wanted to "have some fun" *(gion choi)* with the colonial government, with "those with big ears and fat faces" *(tai to mat lon),* or powerful people, and to use the electoral campaign to make Marxist propaganda from legal public forums. It was thought that once the election was over, the coalition would cease to exist.

The group fielded a "workers' slate" composed of "intellectual and manual workers." Like the other parties, they held public forums to discuss their program. Determined to make a nuisance of themselves, they organized takeovers of public rallies organized by other parties to present their candidates.[20] Four large public rallies were held in Saigon prior to the 30 April 1933 election, alternately at the Thanh Xuong and Doi Co theaters. Although the "workers' slate" organized (and paid for the space) only once, it succeeded in dominating all four. Using tactics learned in France, the group packed each of the meetings, elected its people to chair each of them, submitted the candidates of the other parties to tough questioning, and generally succeeded in steering the meetings in their favor. As a result, at each of these rallies the "workers' slate" candidates succeeded in presenting their position and gaining at least as much attention as those of the other parties.

Surprised at its own success and sensing possible electoral victory, the group introduced another new campaign tactic toward the second half of April 1933. It published an electoral propaganda sheet, *La lutte.* The newspaper concentrated on presenting the position of the "workers' slate" and attacking the candidates of the Constitutionalist party. The main objective of the newspaper seemed to be to get people out to vote, on the grounds that a higher turnout would benefit the "workers' slate." *La lutte* folded for lack of funds after only four issues, but not before it had published the appeal of the "workers' slate," summarized its position, and urged

20. Originally, the workers' slate was the only opposition to the Constitutionalist party. Sometime in April 1933, however, there appeared a new "independent slate," or "youth slate" *(liste des jeunes),* composed of Nguyen van Tot, Le Thanh Lu, and Le Trong Dinh. La Lutte and later Tran van Giau accused the "independent slate" of being a creation of the Constitutionalist party designed to divide the opposition vote. See Tran van Giau, *Giai cap cong nhan,* 1: 186.

all eligible voters to go to the polls. *La lutte* also gave full exposure to the group's electoral program, which emphasized demands for democratic human rights (including the right to strike, the right to form unions, and universal franchise) and welfare measures to alleviate the effects of the Great Depression upon hard-pressed Vietnamese workers (including free public housing, lower taxes, free food at public restaurants for the unemployed, and recreational facilities for workers).[21]

In the election of 30 April 1933, two candidates on the "workers' slate"—Nguyen van Tao and Tran van Thach—were elected.[22] This outcome was especially embarrassing to the colonial regime, not only because it attested the vitality of the revolutionary movement, but also because it took place while the administration was conducting a series of mass trials in Saigon.[23] The immediate results of the election were equally significant. Nguyen van Tao managed to be selected as a member of the committee to oversee the Central Prison of Saigon, and Tran van Thach was designated an alternate member of the administrative council of the region. Both were important positions for committed revolutionaries to occupy. The administration, however, was in no mood for a continuation of this political challenge. Within a few weeks of the election, on 20 May, it closed down the left-leaning newspaper *Trung lap* [Neutrality], which the "workers' intellectuals" had used as a platform. The election of Nguyen van Tao and Tran van Thach was annulled on technical grounds.[24]

21. *La lutte*, 24 April 1935.
22. Of the 4,332 eligible voters, 982 voted in the first round of the election. In this round, the "workers' slate" received the most votes: 331 for the candidate with the fewest votes and 457 for the one with the most, compared with 217 and 324 for the Constitutionalists, and 92 and 114 for the "youth slate." At the second round, in early May, with 1,506 eligible voters, Nguyen Minh Chieu, the Constitutionalist, received 633 votes; Tao, 525; and Thach, 509. For details, see Hémery, *Révolutionnaires vietnamiens*, pp. 57–63.
23. The trial of the arrested Trotskyists on 1 May 1933 was followed by a continuous trial on 2–6 May of 121 ICP leaders who had been arrested after the Nghe Tinh Soviet Movement. Among the convicts were some of the best-known, most experienced ICP leaders: Duong Hac Dinh, Ngo Gia Tu, Ha Huy Giap, Ung van Khiem, Nguyen Xuan Luyen, Ngo Duc Tri, Bui Cong Trung, and Bui van Lam. Duong Hac Dinh and Ngo Duc Tri, the members of the Central Committee who had betrayed the Party for several years, were acquitted; ibid., p. 59, n. 63.
24. According to the laws, neither was eligible. To be eligible for election as city councillor, a candidate had to be twenty-seven years old (Nguyen van Tao was only twenty-five) and have paid twenty-five piasters in direct tax (neither had).

The Saigon city council election of May 1935, two years later, again became a testing ground for the "workers' slate." The group, now called La Lutte after its newspaper, was enlarged to include a balance of Stalinists and Trotskyists. In October 1934 *La lutte* appeared as a regular weekly newspaper, issued every Thursday. To promote similar legal anticolonial activities elsewhere in Vietnam, two members of the La Lutte group, Nguyen van Tao (Stalinist) and Ta Thu Thau (Trotskyist), traveled together to Bac Ky. By the time of the 1935 city council election, La Lutte was in a powerful position to compete for council seats. The names of the leaders of the group were well known and its newspaper was widely read. Among the less privileged Vietnamese of Saigon, the group had won a reputation for integrity. Made more politically sophisticated by its experience in the April 1933 election, the group took a further step toward social acceptance. To widen its constitutency, *La lutte* subdued its militant emphasis on the *lumpenproletariat* to appeal to the middle-class voters and the *gagne-petit* (little men).[25] To improve its chance in the election, the group also decided to accommodate the Vietnamese penchant for intellectuals by enlisting professors Duong Bach Mai and Ta Thu Thau in addition to its two proven "intellectual" successes Nguyen van Tao and Tran van Thach. The city council election of May 1935 was a great success for the "workers' slate": the "intellectual workers," Tao and Mai (the two Stalinists) and Thach and Thau (the two Trotskyists), all of whom had been among the repatriated students, captured four of the six Vietnamese seats. In addition to being a rallying point for continuous anticolonial campaigns and a platform for electoral maneuvering, La Lutte acted throughout 1934–1936 as a clearing house for political activities in the South. Its editorial office was a mail drop and rendez-vous where released political prisoners could quickly get their bearings upon release. La Lutte remained a political institution until the end of the decade. The new style of anticolonialist politics introduced by the group—the overt and legal struggle—was to become a regular feature of anticolonial politics.

The Saigon Municipal Council elections in April 1933 and May 1935 had a special significance for the anticolonialist opposition. They provided the politically conscious elements among the Viet-

25. *La lutte,* 4 April 1935.

namese populace in general and anticolonialists in particular with a new perception and style of anticolonialism, and possibly a new meaning. Until this time, the general population had regarded anticolonialist activities as part of the shadowy, illegal, and clandestine realm associated with "secret society" *(hoi kin)* activities and violence (assassinations, kidnappings, extortion, riots) that brought repression (bombings, exile, imprisonment). They viewed fighting colonialism with a mixture of awe and apprehension as something heroic and adventuresome, but outlawed and dangerous—something to stay away from. Anticolonialists themselves tended to perceive their activities in similar terms. Nothing within their experience or memory suggested that effective anticolonial politics could be overt and legal. The most recent attempt at overt struggle, the Dong Kinh Nghia Thuc movement (1905–1907), an outwardly harmless social movement urging the modernization of Vietnam through abandonment of harmful social customs and acceptance of Western education, had been swiftly suppressed. Against this background, the elections of April 1933 and May 1935 stood out in strong relief as something totally new in Vietnamese experience.

Indeed, these elections opened a new world for anticolonial politics. The advantages of legal and overt action were many and obvious. Underground anticolonial activities brought prison terms, exile, or death; overt anticolonialism was respectable and brought power, prestige, and honor. Instead of being hunted down in an alley, a houseboat hidden in a secluded lake, or an antechamber of an abandoned pagoda, the anticolonial activist could now utilize public forums provided by the colonial regime to denounce official abuses and to attack imperialism. No longer restricted to nocturnal activity, anticolonialists could now make propaganda and recruit sympathizers in broad daylight—in the press, at streetcorners, in a public theater, even in governmental council chambers. To their surprise, many activists discovered that their activities were now socially acceptable. They were no longer viewed as dangerous bandits and rebels to be avoided, but as articulate debaters of public issues and parliamentary defenders of the less privileged.

THE FRENCH POPULAR FRONT AND VIETNAM

In addition to the Trotskyist-Stalinist alliance of 1932–1935, Stalin's new "people's front" policy (usually referred to as "popular front," apparently a mistranslation of the French *front populaire*) greatly influenced the evolution of the ICP during the latter half of the 1930s.[26] Popularly designated the "Dimitrov line" after Georgii Dimitrov,[27] who delivered the political report at the Seventh World Congress of the Comintern (25 July–25 August 1935), this new policy advocated a defensive antifascist alliance and flexible revolutionary tactics that appealed for unity of the left, regardless of class background. Reversing the previous ultra-left line of the Sixth Congress, which had governed the world Communist movement from 1928 until 1935, the new line stated clearly that collaboration with the bourgeoisie was not only possible but necessary: the bourgeoisie ought not to be viewed as a single bloc, and Communists everywhere must learn to exploit the differences within the enemy class. They ought to work more closely with sympathetic social democrats and other "progressive" bourgeois elements in order to widen support for the Communist cause and defend the USSR, while isolating the immediate and principal enemy of world communism, fascism. As a corollary to this new revolutionary line, the Comintern also directed the creation of "popular fronts." Communists of all countries were to form the largest possible "united front on a national as well as an international scale" with progressive noncommunists. This extension of the "united front from above" tactic was to ally Communists with not only the working masses and their leaders, but also with nonsocialist democrats who opposed fascism and Germany.

Judging from the increased support for Communist parties around the world during 1936–1939, the Popular Front policy was

26. For a comprehensive study of the French Popular Front, see Georges Lefranc, *Histoire du front populaire* (Paris, 1965). For a brief account of the Communist policy of the "people's front" and its implementation in various countries, see Hugh Seton-Watson, *From Lenin to Khrushchev: The History of World Communism* (New York, 1960), pp. 176–199.

27. Georgii Dimitrov (1882–1949) was one of the earliest Bulgarian Communist leaders. A revolutionist from boyhood, he took part in the bombing of the cathedral of Sophia (1925) and was an obscure exile when, in 1933, he was arrested for alleged complicity in setting fire to the Reichstag. Dimitrov's cool conduct of his own defense and the accusations he directed at the prosecutors during the trial in Leipzig won him worldwide admiration. He was acquitted and went to Moscow, where he was granted Soviet citizenship. Dimitrov was elected secretary-general of the Comintern and held this post from 1934 until the dissolution of the Comintern in 1943. In 1944 he returned to Bulgaria to lead that nation's Communist party and in 1946 succeeded Kimon Georgiev as prime minister. He died in 1949.

the most successful tactic ever adopted by the Comintern in peacetime. For once, the Comintern accurately diagnosed the mood of the masses, and its adoption of the new policy appeared, in the words of Hugh Seton-Watson, to be "a concession made by Moscow to the mood of the masses." Indeed, argued Seton-Watson, "the Popular Front was imposed not by the Communist parties on the masses but by the masses on the Communist parties."[28] The new slogans of various Communist parties appeared to express the genuine feelings of the nonaffiliated—workers, peasants, intellectuals—around the world, who were fearful of Japanese, German, or Italian aggression and wanted to rally to an antifascist cause. Up to this point, these social groups had been either deliberately rejected by the Communists, with their "class-against-class" tactics, or had themselves rejected what they felt to be a dogmatic Communist line. With the new Communist line, however, the PCF, for example, was able to break out of its isolation and reenter the mainstream of French political life. The Spanish elections of February 1936 brought victory to the Popular Front there and allowed its small but well-organized Communist party to play a significant role in Spanish politics. In Britain and the United States, where the unity of the left had been nonexistent for several decades, the Popular Front forged a new unity of purpose. Although the Popular Front had become discredited by the beginning of the Second World War, it succeeded during its limited existence in reestablishing the credibility of communism.

The new Comintern policy had an especially significant effect on the French Communist party. Until late in 1934, the PCF, adhering strictly to the *Proletkult* and "class-against-class" tactics, had persistently denounced French socialists as "social patriots" and "lackeys of the bourgeoisie." In 1935, however, it halted these attacks, called for a broad united front to seal "the alliance of the middle class with the working class," and then campaigned for a "popular front." This was accomplished at a mammoth rally on 14 July 1935, sponsored jointly by the PCF, the French Socialist party (SFIO), and the Radical Party along with their mass organizations, the League of the Rights of Man, General Confederation of Labor (CGT), and United General Confederation of Labor (CGTU). The

28. Hugh Seton-Watson, *From Lenin to Khrushchev,* pp. 177–178.

new political alliance was called the Rassemblement Populaire, later referred to as the Front Populaire. The massive victory of the new alliance in the elections of 3 May 1936 demonstrated its popularity. Whereas collectively all the rightist parties garnered 222 parliamentary seats, the Popular Front won 386. The PCF itself nearly doubled its percentage of votes (from 800,000 votes in the 1932 election to 1.5 million in 1936, or from 8.4 to 15.4 percent) and increased its parliamentary representation sixfold (from 12 deputies in 1932 to 72 in 1936). Thanks to the new policy, PCF membership also experienced a quantum leap. In January 1934, PCF membership stood at 30,000. By January 1936 this had become 74,000, and by December 1937, at the time of the Party's Ninth Congress, it had reached 341,000.[29]

For Vietnam, the French Popular Front government was a source of false hopes. Even before the front came to power, both French colonial circles and Vietnamese anticolonialists had formed their own expectations. Both groups believed that a Popular Front government would promote liberal colonial policies and circumscribe the independent tendencies of the colonial regime. It was generally thought, for example, that a Popular Front government would grant amnesty to all political prisoners, promote equal legal protection for French and Vietnamese, extend to Vietnamese the civil and political rights reserved to French nationals (freedom of travel, of speech, of assembly, and of organization), and give Vietnamese workers guarantees hitherto enjoyed only by French workers.[30] Once the Popular Front came to power, these expectations, nourished by isolated political events, were realized only as self-fulfilling prophecies: convinced that colonial policies would soon be liberalized, Vietnamese militants began acting more boldly and, for fear of their own careers, colonial bureaucrats responded with increasing restraint.

The conviction that important changes were imminent was encouraged by the records of the parties and leaders who formed the

29. Claude Harmel, "France," in Sworakowski, ed., *World Communism; A Handbook*, p. 140.

30. The most complete review of press editorials, statements by prominent French and Vietnamese during this period, can be found in Tran van Giau, *Giai cap cong nhan*, 2: 9–30. The French and Vietnamese alike speculated liberally about the expectations summarized here. See also issues of *La lutte* for 1935–1936.

Popular Front government. First, two of the three major political parties (the Socialist and Communist) that made up the Popular Front government were widely known for their frequent criticisms of past governments' colonial policies. Thus, although the negotiations that led to the formation of the Popular Front gave little attention to the overseas French empire, the colonial issue formed part of the political package agreed upon. In the lengthy program of the Popular Front, the seventh clause promised the creation of "a parliamentary commission to investigate the political, economic, and moral situation in the overseas French territories, especially in French North Africa and Indochina."[31]

Moreover, the men who in the past had been adamantly critical of the colonists in Indochina and active in defense of native civil and political rights were now in power. Léon Blum, a former comrade of Nguyen Ai Quoc and socialist parliamentary leader who had repeatedly denounced colonial abuses in connection with Yen Bay and Nghe Tinh, was now prime minister, and Marius Moutet, that "ringleader of the indigenophiles" (in the language of the *colons*) was now minister of colonies. A militant in the League of the Rights of Man, Moutet had been well known as a "friend of the Indochinese."[32] In the second and third decades of the century Moutet had been the legal sponsor of Phan Chu Trinh, one of the grand old men of Vietnamese anticolonial politics. He had often denounced the miserable conditions of the Indochinese workers. In 1930 he was instrumental in the dissolution of the Haiphong branch of the League of the Rights of Man after its recommendation of reprisals against the Yen Bay revolutionaries. In 1931 Moutet joined with leftists such as Andrée Viollis, André Malraux, Léon Werth, and Paul Rivet in the Committee of Amnesty and Defence of the Indochinese.

The composition of the parliamentary Commission for Inspection of Colonial Affairs also contributed to false hopes about the Popular Front government's policies for Indochina. Created in

31. See "Programme du rassemblement populaire," 14 July 1935, in Lefranc, *Histoire du front populaire,* App. 10, p. 304.
32. For accounts of Moutet's record in defending Indochinese interests, see Stephen R. Lyne, "The French Socialist Party and the Indochina War, 1944–1954" (Ph.D. diss., Stanford University, 1965), pp. 29–31; Lefranc, *Histoire du front populaire,* p. 303; and Tran van Giau, *Giai cap cong nhan,* 2: 23–26.

February 1937 to fulfill a pledge made in the formal program, the subcommittee on Indochina included Andrée Viollis and Louis Roubaud, two authors well known in both France and Vietnam for their provocative exposés of colonial repression and exploitation in Vietnam. Viollis's *Indochine S.O.S.*[33] and Roubaud's *Viet Nam: La tragédie indochinoise*[34] had been and continued to be regarded as evidence of the crimes committed by the colonial authorities in Vietnam. At the time of her appointment to the commission, Viollis was coeditor of the weekly periodical *Vendredi,* which was conducting a public discussion on an "urgent program" to prepare for French evacuation from the colonies and independence for the colonial peoples.

As in France, Spain, Chile, and Central Europe, however, in Vietnam the optimism that had greeted the Popular Front eventually gave way to frustration and disappointment. Compared with previous colonial policies, the accomplishments of the Popular Front government were without doubt considerable. One of its first actions was the release of several thousand political prisoners (most of whom immediately resumed revolutionary activity). This was followed by the replacement of the unpopular governor-general René Robin, who had presided over the repression following the Yen Bay Mutiny and Nghe Tinh Soviet Movement, with Jules Brévié, who had won liberal accolades for his achievements in West Africa. Finally, on 30 December 1936 the government promulgated the first labor code, which among other things would reduce daily working hours, abolish night work for women and children, forbid employment of children under twelve, provide for a six-day work week, and grant an annual leave.[35]

This liberal record pales, however, in contrast to the radical changes the Vietnamese had come to expect. The Commission for Colonial Inspection, for example, proved to be without substance. Despite the efforts of its appointed members, no government funding was made available for its operation. Neither Viollis nor Roubaud nor any member of the commission was allowed to set foot in Indochina. Furthermore, despite his pronative record and

33. (Paris, 1935).
34. (Paris, 1931).
35. For a detailed summary of labor code 30-12-1936, see Tran van Giau, *Giai cap cong nhan,* 2: 150–161.

promising statements made in the early days of the Popular Front government, Marius Moutet proved most disappointing. Under pressure from the colonial government he banned the Indochinese Congress Movement, which had been organized ostensibly to promote support for the Popular Front government. When, after the arrests of three prominent Indochinese Congress leaders—Nguyen van Tao, Ta Thu Thau, and Nguyen An Ninh—appeals were made to Léon Blum and Marius Moutet, neither made an effort to help. By the autumn of 1939, following the collapse of the Popular Front government, Jules Brévié had been recalled, the labor code annulled, and the amnestied political prisoners herded back to Poulo Condore and other inland prisons. Nevertheless, it remains true that the exaggerated hopes for the Popular Front government, as well as some of its actions, were responsible for a colorful period in the political development of colonized Vietnam.

THE CREST OF A MASS MOVEMENT

Regardless of the unfulfilled aspirations associated with it, the advent of the Popular Front government in France inaugurated a new phase in Communist-sponsored politics in Vietnam. There had been no great changes in Vietnamese political development from the destruction of the soviet movement in mid-1931 until the spring of 1936. With the zealous Thanh Nien/ICP members still in prison and KUTV-trained "professional revolutionaries" floundering in confusion, there were few signs of Communist activity. What Marxist influence there was could be seen in the verbal campaign of La Lutte and its members in the Saigon Municipal Council in favor of improved social benefits for the poor and an early amnesty for political prisoners. The victory of the Popular Front in France, however, effected an immediate transformation of Vietnamese politics in general and the evolution of Vietnamese communism in particular. It unlocked a sudden torrent of Communist-sponsored activities that in less than a year engulfed the entire country in a boisterous mass movement.

The Popular Front's victory took effect earliest in the South. Here, antiimperialist politics had been spearheaded from 1933 to 1936 by the popular La Lutte group, supported to some extent by the two clandestine and ideologically conflicting Marxist groups, the Octobrists (Trotskyist) and the ICP, now dominated by KUTV trainees. Immediately after the victory of the Popular Front these Nam Ky Marxist groups united under the leadership of La Lutte to exploit to the utmost the political liberalization anticipated under the Front government. This unification led in a short time to a widespread movement for democratic rights.

The first reaction of the southern Marxists to the advent of the Popular Front government was to "go to the masses." To extend their influence among the people, they made full use of the presumed liberty of the press. Taking advantage of worried colonial bureaucrats who were unsure about the new French government's colonial policies, the various Marxist factions openly published their papers, often without government permission. In July 1936, a Vietnamese version of *La lutte, Tranh Dau* [The struggle], appeared, forming a de facto alliance with two other leftist Vietnamese-language newspapers, *Mai* [Tomorrow] and *Tan van* [News]. In the autumn of 1936 two other Vietnamese newspapers appeared: *Dan quyen* [People's power] and *Saigon*. According to the French police, together these five newspapers dominated the Vietnamese-language press in Nam Ky and formed a "veritable consortium" under the direction of La Lutte. In addition to the use of newspapers, La Lutte and other Communist groups created publishing houses to print political pamphlets. In late 1936, for example, a "Social collection" *(Xa-hoi tong-tho)* (in obvious imitation of the leftist "Collection sociale" of the French publisher François Maspéro) was advertised as "of the La Lutte group" *(cua nhom La Lutte)*.[36] After the breach between the Stalinists and Trotskyists in 1937, two other "collections" appeared: a Trotskyist Cultural Publishing House *(Van hoa tho xa)*[37] and a Stalinist Vanguard Publishing House *(Tien phong tho xa)*.[38] Finally, from June 1936 on, La Lutte also organized several secret Marxist study

36. The best-seller of this collection was Nguyen van Tao, *Mat tran Binh dan o Phap voi nguyen vong cua quan chung Dong duong* [The French Popular Front and the aspirations of the Indochinese masses] (Saigon, 1936).

37. Among the pamphlets of this 'publishing house' were Ta Thu Thau, *Tu De Nhut den De Tu Quoc Te* [From the First to the Fourth International] and Nguyen The Xuong, *Vi sao nhom La Lutte chia re?* [Why the schism of the La Lutte group?], both issued in 1937.

38. Among its publications were Nguyen van Tao, *Ngay Mot thang Nam* [The First of May] and Thanh Huong, *Trotsky va phan cach mang* [Trotsky and the counterrevolution], both printed in 1938.

groups among students and workers to train future cadres. Headed by Nguyen van Nguyen, these study groups were most active among the students and arsenal and tramway workers in Saigon. The government banned them sometime in 1937.

Having learned of the creation in Morocco of a popular congress, the leaders of La Lutte decided to launch a similar "Indochinese Congress." The purpose of this gathering allegedly was to collect "the wishes of the people" in anticipation of the arrival of the commission of investigation. To give the appearance of national unity, the leaders of the group convinced several bourgeois Vietnamese and French personalities to lend their names and influence to the congress. At a meeting on 13 August 1936, several Constitutionalists and other noncommunist Vietnamese personalities were maneuvered onto a Committee to Convoke the Congress, which included representatives of "the intellectuals" (Nguyen Phan Long, Le Quang Liem, Nguyen van Sam, Tran van Kha, Nguyen van Tao, Tran van Thach), "the press" (Ho Huu Tuong, *La lutte;* Nguyen An Ninh, *La lutte;* Bui The My, *Dien tin;* J. B. Dong, *Saigon*), "the workers" (Ta Thu Thau, Trinh Hung Ngau, Dao Huu Long), "the peasants" (Nguyen van Tran, Vo Cong Ton, Tran van Hien), and "women" (Nguyen thi Luu, Mai Huynh Hoa, Nguyen thi Nam). Nguyen Phan Long, head of the Constitutionalist party, was elected chairman of the committee.[39] Because the La Lutte members and their affiliates predominated in number and volubility, however, the committee adopted all the La Lutte proposals.

The Indochinese Congress, according to La Lutte leaders, was organized so that the representatives of all social classes could prepare a "Book of Desiderata" ("Ban Dan Nguyen") to present to the commission of investigation. In reality, however, the leaders used this opportunity to organize the masses into more or less permanent "action committees," coordinated by La Lutte. Like Communist cells, these action committees, organized on geographic and professional lines, were established at the village and

---

39. AOM, SLOTFOM, series 3, carton 148, NPM, September 1936, pp. 28–29. At a meeting on 21 August this committee was enlarged to thirty-three members, with a substantial majority supporting the La Lutte positions. On 15 September, however, five Constitutionalist members, excepting Nguyen Phan Long, resigned from the Committee.

city district levels as well as in factories and by professions. In just over a month after the formation of the Committee to Convoke the Congress, more than six hundred action committees had been created throughout Nam Ky. In Cholon alone there were about forty, and in Gia Dinh, sixty.[40] These committees held daily meetings, ostensibly to collect "the aspirations of the people." The Sûreté estimated that, not counting hundreds of clandestine meetings, within two months of the formation of the Committee to Convoke the Congress, there were two hundred public rallies and meetings in Nam Ky alone, bringing together ten thousand people, and four hundred fifty thousand copies of two hundred different leaflets were disseminated.[41] In most areas this political involvement affected all social strata, and "the great and little notables daily lost further their authority. Tax returns saw a very appreciable reduction. The administrative officials became hesitant in their actions."[42]

In conjunction with the creation of the action committees a wave of workers' strikes was organized by all three groups, but especially by the ICP. In November and December 1936 alone, there were more than forty strikes, affecting eighty factories and enterprises and about six thousand workers or employees.[43] Most noteworthy were the strikes of the arsenal (which affected national defense), tramway, and railway workers. These strikes, occurring simultaneously, affected approximately twenty-five hundred workers. According to French police records, both the ICP and the Trotskyists organized such strikes.[44] The ICP was allegedly most influential in the rural areas, especially where there had been a strong peasant movement 1930–1931. The Trotskyists, in this case the Octobrists, gained most of their support among the workers of the Saigon-Cholon area. "This group had numerous members in many factories, especially at the Arsenal, the Railway, and the Tramways. At the Arsenal, this group clearly had many more members than the Stalinist party (several hundred Trotskyists as against about a hundred Stalinists)."[45]

By the end of 1936, the united action by the various Marxist

40. AOM, SLOTFOM, series 3, carton 52, NPM, December 1936, p. 13.
41. Ibid., p. 14.
42. Ibid.
43. Ibid., p. 17.
44. Ibid., pp. 17–18.
45. Ibid., p. 18.

groups had brought widespread popular support to their movement. A French Sûreté report aptly summarized the situation:

> Knowing how to utilize all the goodwill in making it work in its
> proper domain, without hurrying it or trying to force its convictions;
> knowing in depth the revolutionary techniques learned in Moscow
> or in Paris; possessing the art of infiltrating the working masses;
> finally, knowing marvelously to give to their revolutionary and anti-
> French actions the apparent contours to conform with the principles
> of the Popular Front government, municipal councillors Ta Thu
> Thau, Tran van Thach, Nguyen van Tao, and Duong Bach Mai and
> their friends Nguyen van Nguyen, Nguyen An Ninh, etc., succeed
> amply.[46]

In another report, the Sûreté stated:

> The La Lutte group has attracted a great deal of sympathy among
> the masses, who admire its leaders because they dare attack the
> government and the authorities with a violence unknown up to now
> and because they appear to them to be sufficiently powerful in order
> not to be persecuted [by the government]. They have transformed
> Ta Thu Thau, Nguyen An Ninh, and Nguyen van Tao into legendary
> heroes and always speak of them with much emotion.[47]

The effect of the electoral victory of the Popular Front on Communist activities in Bac Ky, though less immediate than in Nam
Ky, was no less astounding. Throughout the period 1932–1935,
with the exception of some organizing among the Tay ethnic minority in Cao Bang, Communist influence in Bac Ky had been
virtually nonexistent. Beginning in mid-1935, however, procommunist publications, printed by Nha Xuat Ban Dong Duong (Indochinese Publishing House), appeared in Hanoi. These publications
were produced by amnestied communist political prisoners, supervised, paradoxially, by Tran Huy Lieu, who had been chairman of
the Southern Regional Section of the VNQDD but converted to
communism while in prison. According to French police records,
aside from such propaganda activities and Lieu's establishment of
two Communist cells, nothing was known about Communist activities before May 1936. The advent of the Popular Front government, however, facilitated the resurgence of communism in Bac
Ky. Here the ICP's influence was preeminent. Unlike the movement in Nam Ky, which was led by various newer Marxist groups,

46. "Notes mensuelles des sûretés locales d'Indochine pour le mois de
décembre 1936 (Récapitulation de l'activité révolutionnaire au cours de l'année
1936)"; AOM, SLOTFOM, series 3, carton 52.
47. AOM, SLOTFOM, series 3, carton 51, NPM, December 1936.

the mass movement in Bac Ky was monopolized by ICP members released from prison, who had originally been adherents of Thanh Nien and Tan Viet. Emulating the southerners, the northern revolutionaries also attempted to establish action committees at the village level, though with much less success. In the rural areas of the North the ICP created "libraries for revolutionary education."[48] Reminiscing about this period, Hoang Quoc Viet recalled that "a great number of books" appeared,

> dealing with the laws of the development of society, class struggle, the historical task of the working class, communism in brief, the Soviet Union, the French Popular Front, the Spanish Popular Front, the Chinese Revolution, . . . written in an understandable style and openly published by the Party to educate Party members and the masses. Besides these books, I still remember a rather thick book entitled *Three Years in the Soviet Union* by Comrade Tran Dinh Long, published at first in newspapers, then as a book. We can say that this was the first report in book form of the revolutionary literature, greatly appreciated by the readers.[49]

In addition to these books and pamphlets, numerous newspapers were published openly. If one paper was closed down by the authorities, another appeared with a different name but the same editors and revolutionary message. Among the revolutionary newspapers of this period were *Le travail, Rassemblement, En avant, Notre voix, Doi moi* [New life], *Tieng vang* [Echo], *Kien van* [Knowledge], *Hon tre* [Soul of youth], *Tan xa hoi* [New society], *Ban dan* [People's friend], *Nguoi moi* [New man], and *The gioi moi* [New world].[50]

Probably the most noteworthy development among the northern revolutionaries during the Popular Front period was the collaboration of several leading members of the VNQDD with the ICP. According to the French Sûreté, "most of the VNQDD members, who were released from prison in July and November, had been influenced during their detention by their Communist co-detainees."[51] Once out of prison, VNQDD leaders such as Tran

48. Ibid., carton 52.
49. Hoang Quoc Viet, "Our People, A Very Heroic People," in *A Heroic People*, pp. 185–186.
50. Ibid., pp. 178–179.
51. AOM, SLOTFOM, series 3, carton 52, NPM, December 1936, p. 35.

Huy Lieu, To Hieu, and Tuong Dan Bao collaborated enthusiastically with their new Communist comrades. The most significant
convert was Pham Tuan Tai, one of the three founders of the
VNQDD. Before his death at Hanoi's René Robin Hospital, Tai
left his VNQDD comrades a final "Political Testament," in which
he analyzed the causes of the party's defeat, gave reasons for his
adherence to the Communist cause, and urged his former partisans
to follow his example in joining the Communist party, "the only
party capable of leading the masses in their effort of liberation from
the yoke of the imperialists and capitalists."[52]

In Trung Ky, too, the resurgence of Communist activity could be
linked to the formation of the Popular Front government. Ever since
the rout of the ICP in 1931, the Communist movement in Trung Ky
had been virtually nonexistent. From June 1936, however, the
movement began to revive in several Trung Ky provinces, especially in northern Trung Ky. This revival, too, was the work of
former ICP prisoners. After several Communist-sponsored rallies
in Quang Ngai in June, released political prisoners used the cele-
bration of Bastille Day there to speak out on political liberties and
democratic rights, and thus to promote Communist ideas. By the
autumn of 1936 there had been organized throughout Trung Ky
"Committees to Gather the Wishes of the Masses to Submit to the
Commission of Investigation."[53] By September an ICP Provisional
Committee had been formed for Nghi Loc district, Nghe An province, where one of the earliest soviets had been founded in the
1930–1931 movement. By October a Provincial Committee for
Nghe An had also been created.

Probably the most significant indication of the revival of communism in Trung Ky was the preparation for the aborted Indochinese
Congress. By August 1936 the political activism in Nam Ky had
spread to Trung Ky. Here, too, countless political rallies were
held, allegedly to gather the wishes of the masses to present to the
anticipated commission of investigation. Using this pretext, Communists could openly propagate their ideas. According to the
French Sûreté:

52. According to the Sûreté, this political testament was left with Tran Huy
Lieu to be published posthumously. The testament was captured by the French
police during a raid on 24 December 1936 (NPM, ibid.). For the text see Tran van
Giau, *He y thuc tu san*, pp. 597–598.
53. AOM, SLOTFOM, series 3, carton 52, NPM, December 1936, p. 38.

Their unceasingly growing influence permits them to recruit under their banner the nationalist elements, the former [political] prisoners of the 1908 or 1916 [repression], who had stayed away from them until then. In Quang Ngai this collusion has created quite a troublesome situation by the fact that a great number of notables were in fact under the dominating influence of these nationalists.[54]

Sometimes, unconsciously, the old "nationalists" became spokesmen for the Communist cause. Frequently, rallies that had been organized by noncommunist nationalists ended up being dominated by Communist revolutionaries. As the French Sûreté noted, the most applauded speakers were usually those who were introduced as "defender of the people," especially those with the title "political prisoner."[55] This, then, was the background for the restoration of communism in Trung Ky during the Popular Front period.

A PEOPLE'S FRONT FOR VIETNAM

As could be expected, the new Cominterm policy of the Popular Front strongly affected the development of the ICP. This impact was most visible in the liberal colonial policies of the Popular Front government; the release of several thousand political prisoners and the change in political climate gave the Party a new lease on life. The most direct effects of the Popular Front strategy, however, were those on the new ICP revolutionary line. Like other national sections of the Comintern in those years of ideological monocentrism, the strategy of the ICP during the 1936–1939 period was governed by the new "Dimitrov line." Dubbed the "Trojan horse" tactic by anti-Stalinists, this line had called for selective collaboration with all social classes, including the bourgeoisie, in order to widen support for the Communist cause, defend the USSR, and isolate "international fascism." In calling for the formation of the broadest possible "people's front" (*mat tran nhan dan*), it sought to forge an alliance of all social strata under Communist leadership.

In July 1936 Le Hong Phong, ECCI representative with the ICP

54. Ibid., p. 42.
55. Ibid., p. 43.

and head of the Overseas Leadership Committee, explained the new ICP line the first time at a special enlarged conference between representatives of his committee and the Vietnamese delegates to the Seventh World Congress of the Comintern. The new line superseded the previous ultra-leftist line, defined in the ICP's three basic documents: the *Political Theses* (1930), the *Program of Action* (1932), and the *Resolutions of the Macao Congress* (1935). In summary, it covered three basic points: the objective of the struggle, organizational tactics, and operational techniques.

Objective of the struggle. The objective of the Party in the new period was to gain for the Indochinese people elementary democratic rights such as freedom of speech, assembly, organization, and travel. As Nguyen Ai Quoc had put it:

> At this time, the Party should not put forward demands which are too high (independence, parliament, etc.) in order not to fall into the trap set by the Japanese fascists. It ought to confine itself to demanding democratic rights [such as] freedom of association, assembly, press, and speech, amnesty of political prisoners, and it ought to fight for the right to conduct legal activities for the Party.[56]

Organizational tactics. To attain its objectives, the Party was to promote the formation of a broadly based political front that would unify all social classes and political groups in Indochina. This would entail the collaboration of ICP members not only with noncommunist Vietnamese political parties, religious groups, and national ethnic minorities, but also with "progressive elements" among the French in Indochina.

> This front should include not only Indochinese, but also progressive Frenchmen, not only the working people, but also the national bourgeoisie. With regard to the bourgeoisie, the Party ought to use a good deal of tact and flexibility. It ought to do its best to draw [the bourgeoisie] into the front, win over those elements that can be won over, neutralize the wavering elements. None among them ought to be left outside the front; for this would mean pushing them into the hands of the enemies of the revolution and strengthening the reactionaries.[57]

56. Nguyen Ai Quoc's July 1939 report to the Comintern, quoted in Truong Chinh, *President Ho Chi Minh, Beloved Leader of the Vietnamese People* (Hanoi, 1966), pp. 22–23.
57. Ibid., p. 23.

Operational techniques. To implement the new policy effectively, the Party was to use primarily overt and legal means, such as competition for electoral seats, public debates, and legal publications. This would enable the Party to attain its political objectives and restructure its organizational apparatus without sacrificing its illegal and clandestine activities. Several years later, the official ICP history summarized this rationale as follows: "To enable the front to have a broad basis, the forms of mass organization must be changed to have a legal and semilegal character in order to exploit to the maximum the legal and semilegal possibilities to mobilize the masses and to launch a powerful movement of demands for democratic rights."[58]

In subsequent deliberations, however, the ICP decided to abandon its clandestine operations altogether and concentrate on overt and legal political activities. Without prohibiting clandestine mass organizations as such, the Party emphasized that they ought to be used only when all legal and semilegal means had been exhausted.[59] At its March 1937 Central Committee conference, the ICP leadership decided to dissolve the clandestine mass organizations (such as the Red Workers' Unions, the Peasants' Associations, the Communist Youth Corps, and the Red Aid Society), which had been the mainstay of the Party's activities until then. In their place the ICP created innocuous-sounding and legally acceptable groups such as mutual aid associations, cooperatives, and reading societies.[60]

In implementing the new policy, the ICP, which for several years had reserved its harshest vituperation for the "national reformist" parties, now actively sought out reconciliation. Following the July 1936 conference, the Party published an open letter inviting all existing political parties to join in a broad political front based on a twelve-point program. This program contained moderate demands

58. Propaganda Section, *Trente ans,* pp. 52–53. The English edition is entitled *Thirty Years of the Struggle of the Party.* I am using the French version for greater accuracy.
59. Resolutions of the Central Committee Plenum, March 1937. See "Chu truong to chuc moi cua Dang" [The Party's new policy with regard to organization], 26 March 1937, cited in Vu Tho, "Mot so van de lich su Dang thoi ky 1936–1939" [A few problems concerning Party history during the period 1936–1939], *NCLS,* no. 85 (April 1966), p. 7.
60. Ibid., pp. 7–8.

for reforms such as equal eligibility and voting rights for French and Vietnamese, enactment of a labor code (eight-hour workday, social insurance for workers), and general amnesty for political prisoners.[61] Frustrated by lack of response from the other parties, the ICP launched a press campaign to proclaim its goodwill. *Lao dong* [Labor], the "Propaganda Organ of the Provincial Committee of Gia Dinh" (one of many ephemeral clandestine publications), for example, wrote in its issue of 15 August 1936:

> The national reformist parties, such as the Constitutionalist party, accuse us of separatism, and the French authorities of opposition to France. Nothing is more false than these accusations. Communism wishes that Indochina be strong, free, and happy. To this goal it appeals for unity of all parties, all groups, and all social strata in view of realizing a people's front to struggle against the imperialists and to demand Peace, Freedom, and Rice. By imperialism, we mean the minority of French exploiters and oppressors of the colonial peoples. On the contrary, we recognize that the masses of France are our most secure and most faithful ally, for they have always defended us. The Indochinese masses and the French masses ought to unite and help one another. . . .
>
> Here in Indochina we ought to unite with all the French groups and elements which show sympathy toward us. In the same vein, our Central Committee has decided to unite its forces with those of the local sections of the [French] Socialist Party, the [French] Radical Socialist Party, and the [French] League of the Rights of Man and the Citizen.

Having failed in its initial attempts to rally the noncommunist parties, the ICP proposed in March 1938 the formation of another front, the Indochinese Democratic Front (Mat tran Dan chu Dong duong). This was only a variant in name of two earlier ICP-sponsored fronts, the Indochinese Antiimperialist People's Front (Mat tran Nhan dan Phan de Dong duong) and the Indochinese People's Front (Mat tran Nhan dan Dong duong). Its objectives, however, remained identical with those of the earlier fronts, with a moderate political program of political and social reforms. In another open letter published in June 1938, the ICP again appealed to the other political parties and personalities.

61. For the text of the open letter, see Tran van Giau, *Giai cap cong nhan*, 2: 65–66.

All the democratic parties, all strata of the people—whether they are Frenchmen or natives—have the sacred and urgent responsibility to unify all the democratic forces in this country in intimate unity with the French people to demand the democratic rights and reforms in the living conditions of the people. . . .

We in the Communist party never hide the fact that we are a revolutionary party, following the international proletarian ideology, that we fight determinedly for complete independence and emancipation for the peoples of Indochina; but we realize that during the present phase in the mobilization of the Indochinese peoples, the essential and necessary thing is to demand democratic freedoms and the necessary reforms for the progress of the people and the country.[62]

Like the appeals of the earlier fronts, that of the Indochinese Democratic Front met with cogent silence. The ICP had misjudged the current reality of Vietnamese politics. The Constitutionalist party, watchful of its own economic interests and position, refused to have any connection with the Communists. Only with the Trotskyists could the Party have formed an alliance; but by this time, as we shall see presently, any such cooperation was unthinkable.

Under the circumstances, Communist claims notwithstanding, the Indochinese Democratic Front remained little more than a name. In Nam Ky, despite the active agitation of the Stalinists, the front was never organized. The southerners maintained their own "overt operational structure" and simply disregarded the Central Committee's order to form the front.[63] In Trung Ky, except for sporadic workers' strikes in Quang Ngai, Hue, and Vinh, Democratic Front activities during this period were almost nonexistent. Only in Bac Ky were there actual Democratic Front actions, including the organization of workers' strikes, mass demonstrations (the 1938 Labor Day demonstration in Hanoi involved more than twenty thousand people), and the election of Democratic Front representatives to the Hanoi municipal council in April 1939.

62. Quoted in ibid., pp. 360–361.
63. Vu Tho asserts: "During this period, a number of Party members who agitated in the legal realm failed to obey in reality the orders of the clandestine leadership organ of the Party (especially in Nam Ky, where there had been established an entire system of overt organizational structures of the Party at the regional and provincial levels) . . . there was lack of unity between the overt section and the clandestine leadership organ of the Party." See Vu Tho, "Mot so van de," p. 9.

Thus, the Indochinese Democratic Front never succeeded as an organizational tactic. As a "united front from above" with noncommunist parties, it was a failure. As Hoang Quoc Viet saw it, the movement had more breadth than depth.[64] Tran Huy Lieu, one of the principal leaders of the Indochinese Democratic Front in Hanoi, observed later, "Throughout the years from 1936 to 1939, it could be said that the front was still in its formative stage."[65]

For many ICP members, the new Party line and tactics contradicted all the basic premises of the Party's *raison d'être*. Until then, ICP members had been firm believers in the Party's double revolutionary objectives, *bai phong* (antifeudalism) and *phan de* (antiimperialism). The new line had nothing to say on either. Up to this time, ICP members had been trained to despise the "reformism" of the "bourgeois parties" and the "class collaboration" of the socialists. The danger of "reformism," Party members had long learned to accept, was that it focused the attention of the masses on the petty concessions extracted from the capitalists and thus distracted them from the fundamental goals of fighting for national independence and a social revolution. They had long accepted as fact that, at the very least, these "national reformist parties," like "the Constitutionalist crowd in Nam Ky . . . and the constitutional monarchist clique in Bac Ky,"[66] were willing tools of the French colonialists, but more likely they were dedicated collaborators, actively colluding with the imperialists in exploiting the masses.[67] Part of the revolutionary task, up to now, had been to unmask the duplicity and hypocrisy of these "reformist" parties and to denounce to the masses the dangerous role they played.[68]

Given this background, much confusion and dissension followed the introduction of the new Party line. Many ICP members were shocked that the Party now called only for "democratic reforms" identical to those associated with the much denounced "reformist" parties. Worse, the Party itself was actively engaging in the "class

64. Hoang Quoc Viet, in *A Heroic People,* p. 182.
65. Tran Huy Lieu, *Mat tran Dan chu Dong duong* [The Indochinese Democratic Front] (Hanoi, 1960), p. 41.
66. *Chuong trinh hanh dong cua Dang Cong san Dong duong* [Program of action of the Indochinese communist party] (n.p., 1932).
67. Ibid.
68. Ibid.

collaboration" it had for so long deplored. The Brechtian view of communism held that the collective perception and wisdom of the Party was always superior to a single man's vision. The failure of this view to explain such a fundamental shift in the Party's course led many to defect to the more militant Trotskyist factions or to leave revolutionary politics altogether.[69] Moreover, among those who accepted Party discipline, many misunderstood the new policy and collaborated with all political groups regardless of their ideology. This "rightist deviation" appeared to be a serious tendency among many Party members, who "ran after a number of bourgeois and landowning individuals, confusing political merchants with those who were considered by the Party as legitimate representatives of the native bourgeoisie."[70]

Serious problems of Party discipline arose in the South. The entire overt section of the Southern Regional Committee, the most active and best-organized section, refused to obey the command of the Central Committee. The Southern Regional Committee, led by Nguyen van Tao, voted into the resolutions of its December 1936 conference to reject the order of the Central Committee to break with La Lutte, claiming that it was possible to collaborate with the moderate Trotskyists.[71] After being ordered to break with La Lutte in June 1937, this section of the southern Stalinists insisted on its independence. It reserved the right "not to overthrow any native classes or native parties" and "to form an alliance with all native political parties whether reformist or reactionary, to attack severely and overthrow only reactionary *elements*, regardless of the political parties or classes to which they belong."[72] In other words, the southern committee would continue to form alliances

69. *Mat tran do* [The Red front], no. 10 (April 1937), a clandestine ICP paper at the time, complained thus: "In the face of the offensive launched by the government and the sabotage organized by the partisans of the Fourth International, some of our comrades, instead of seeking to understand better the policy of our Party, have taken to criticizing the Popular Front and following the tendency of the Fourth International."

70. Vu Tho, "Mot vai van de," p. 6.

71. "Resolutions of the Southern Regional Committee, December 1936," ibid.

72. T[ri] B[inh], "Tu chi-trich cua nguoi Bon-se-vich," [Self-criticism of the bolshevik], published originally in *Dan chung* [The people], no. 68 (italics added). Cited in Tran Huy Lieu, "Mot vai net ve cuoc dau tranh tu tuong cua Dang tu ngay thanh lap den Cach mang thang Tam" [A few observations on the ideological struggle within the Party from its formation until the August Revolution], *NCLS*, no. 71 (February 1965), p. 5.

with ideological groups disapproved of by the Central Committee
and would have no qualms about criticizing "reactionary elements"
of any Party, the ICP included.

THE DISMEMBERMENT OF LA LUTTE

As it turned out, the new liberal colonial policies, the revival of
the ICP, and especially its close association with Moscow created
many difficulties for the Vietnamese Trotskyist-Stalinist alliance
and led ultimately to the dissolution of La Lutte around mid-1937.
With the more liberal colonial policies, there was no longer need
for mutual support; meanwhile, both the more militant Trotskyists
and the ICP Communists exerted pressure on the members of La
Lutte, with the intention of breaking the alliance. Yet so strong
were the group's bonds of friendship that despite these multiple
pressures, the alliance lingered on for one year after the advent of
the Popular Front government. In the elections to the Saigon city
council in April 1937, La Lutte mounted a slate of two Stalinists
(Nguyen van Tao and Duong Bach Mai) and one Trotskyist (Ta
Thu Thau). As late as June 1938 Duong Bach Mai continued to
defend the alliance and denounced those in the ICP who urged that
he and Nguyen van Tao, the leader of the "legal faction" of the ICP
in Nam Ky, break with La Lutte on the grounds that the latter were
agents provocateurs in the pay of the colonial police who wished to
split the ranks of the Vietnamese working class.[73] These were the
final attempts to salvage a hopeless situation. By the autumn of
1937 the alliance between the Vietnamese Trotskyists and Stalinists had become a part of Vietnamese political history.

The dismemberment of La Lutte originated with the Vietnamese
disillusionment with the Popular Front government, particularly
with Moutet's decision to ban the Indochinese Congress and the
subsequent arrest of the three principal leaders of La Lutte. While
Tao, Thau, and Ninh were in prison, the prestigious *La lutte* came
under the editorial hand of Ho Huu Tuong and the Octobrists, who
used it to denounce the Popular Front government, and often Léon

73. "Reply to Cao van Chanh," *La lutte,* 6 June 1937. Chanh had appealed to
Nguyen van Tao and Duong Bach Mai to break with the moderate Trotskyists,
contending that "the political errors of comrades Tao and Mai can be easily re-
paired."

Blum and Marius Moutet by name.[74] From this point on, a war of words raged between Trotskyists and Stalinists. *La lutte,* now dominated by the former, became increasingly critical of Stalinism and the Popular Front government. In December 1936 it attacked the USSR and the Popular Front for their failure to come to the rescue of the Spanish Popular Front. The same issue attacked the French government for "one of its monstrous acts" in having adhered to a policy of nonintervention regarding the Spanish Civil War and for having given planes and munitions to the Spanish fascist rebels.[75] The paper also insinuated that the Soviets were hypocritical in failing to side unambiguously with the Spanish revolution:

> For one cannot understand very well why the USSR had adhered to the pact of noninterference, which is equivalent to a strangling of the Spanish revolution. France, under the Popular Front, demonstrates its failure to aid the Spanish workers and peasants. The USSR must show the way to the world proletariat.[76]

Pressured by the ICP leadership in Vietnam, the Comintern, and the French Communist party abroad, Duong Bach Mai and Nguyen van Tao, the two prominent leaders of the Vietnamese Stalinists, reluctantly left the La Lutte group, and the alliance came to an end.

The dissolution of the alliance was not the end of the Stalinist-Trotskyist controversy in Vietnam. If anything, the disputes became more frequent and the war of words more shrill. Clandestine ICP publications, which had warned Party members about the erroneous tendencies of La Lutte as early as December 1936[77] and had attacked La Lutte and the Trotskyists for having caused the failure of numerous strikes,[78] now started to call all Trotskyists "lackeys of the fascists." *Mat-tran do* [Red front] stated:

74. Ho Huu Tuong directed *La lutte* from early October to late November 1936. The banner headlines on the paper's front page on 22 October indicated his orientation: "The Fascist Danger Begins in Indochina. Can the Blum-Moutet Government Put an End to It in Time?" and "Mr. Pagès [Cochin China governor] Continues His Reactionary Politics. Is It under the Order of the Blum-Moutet Government?"
75. *La lutte,* 13 December 1936.
76. Ibid.
77. *Su that* [The truth], no. 3, 1 December 1936, in an article entitled "*La lutte* Harms the Communists."
78. *Tan cong* [Offensive], 1 February 1937.

While the Communist party and the Third International seek to realize an Indochinese People's Front, the lackeys of the fascists try by all means to discredit us before the masses. They accuse us of reformism and cover us with abuses. They do not cease to criticize the French Communist party, to demand the dissolution of the Popular Front, and to protest against the formation of an Indochinese People's Front. By obstructing the movement of the proletariat, the Trotskyists Thau, Tuong, Thach [and] Chanh and those fellows in the La Lutte group defend the fascists, whose lackeys they are.[79]

The Trotskyists had their own way of answering such polemics. When *La lutte* published an address by Trotsky in New York City, its editors prefaced the text with certain brutal facts, denouncing Stalin's purge of his colleagues. Part of this preface stated:

July–August 1917: The Sixth Congress of the Bolshevik party elected a central committee of twenty-one members. Of these, seven are dead, six stay away from all political activities. Of the other eight, seven were accused of being "counterrevolutionaries": Bukharin, Zinoviev, Kamenev, Rykov, Smilga, Sokolnikov, and Trotsky. The twenty-first was Stalin.

March 1918: The Seventh Congress of the Bolshevik party elected a Central Committee of fifteen members. Of these fifteen members, nine are dead, two are no longer active politically. Of the other seven, six are accused by Stalinism of being "counterrevolutionaries": Bukharin, Zinoviev, Smilga, Sokolnikov, and Trotsky. The fifteenth is Stalin.

January 1924: Lenin left behind a testament. Six names were mentioned in it. Of these six, five are accused by Stalinism of being "counterrevolutionaries": Bukharin, Zinoviev, Kamenev, Piatakov, and Trotsky. The sixth person is Stalin.

Stalin has led a Thermidorian struggle against the artists of the October Revolution.[80]

La lutte then asked its readers to compare Trotsky's statement and Stalin's speech, printed in *L'avant-garde,* an ICP publication, and make up their own minds: "Either Stalin is a criminal and one must support Trotsky; or Trotsky is a criminal, chief of the terrorists and fascists, and one must support Stalin."[81]

Meanwhile, the extremist "Bolshevik-Leninist" group led by Ho

79. *Mat tran do,* no. 11 (October 1937).
80. Editorial note to "J'Accuse!," a speech given by Leon Trotsky in New York City on 6 February 1937; *La lutte,* 4 July 1937.
81. Ibid.

Huu Tuong had no qualms about mudslinging. It accused the members of the Third International in Indochina of having "betrayed the interests of the proletariat and . . . united with the police against the Trotskyists."[82] *Cach mang vo san* [The proletarian revolution], for example, stated:

> In Indochina, the partisans of the Third International have shown their true faces. These are the reformists. They have made themselves lackeys of the French. They have obstructed the revolutionary movement in Indochina, sabotaged the worker and peasant movement, and are favorable to the imperialist war.[83]

The confused workers in South Vietnam, who had looked to La lutte for leadership since 1933, could not comprehend the intricacies of these quarrels about strange names and strange places. Both sides published numerous pamphlets in Vietnamese to explain their respective positions. This bitter conflict, a war of words, punctuated by a few street fights, persisted until September 1939, when the colonial regime temporarily put an end to it by arresting all known Marxist-Leninists, Trotskyists, and Stalinists. The conflict resumed briefly late in 1945, but, by this time much weakened by repeated repression, the surviving Trotskyist leaders were easily eliminated by reemerging Stalinist members. This marked the end of the two non-ICP Marxist factions.[84]

The issues that led to the break up of La Lutte were the same as those that brought about the schism within the international Communist movement during this period. These issues involved the Comintern's new revolutionary line and its implications. The "Dimitrov line," a reflection of Stalin's "Trojan horse" tactic, had called for the postponement of the class struggle and the formation of a temporary "united front from above" with those noncommunist political parties and nonproletarian classes that shared the Comintern's antifascist apprehensions. This temporary alliance with the "class enemies" had been considered a necessary measure to prevent "class isolation" during a period when the proletariat was

82. *Cong nong hiep nhut* [Worker-peasant unity], 10 May 1938.
83. No. 1, 15 April 1938.
84. Ho Huu Tuong rejected Marxism-Leninism in 1949 for philosophic reasons. Phan van Hum, Huynh van Phuong, and Ta Thu Thau were reportedly murdered by Viet Minh forces during the August Revolution.

not yet powerful enough to carry out the revolution by itself. Ideologically purist, the Trotskyists saw in this new Comintern line another betrayal by Stalin of the Marxist-Leninist revolution. The first had been Stalin's earlier assertion of the need for socialism in one country. The Trotskyists viewed the Comintern's new line as a further step toward accommodation with other classes and a betrayal of the Marxist principle of "class struggle." Trotskyists around the world, and in Vietnam no less, pointed out the dangerous practical implications of the new line: the obvious "reformism" and "class collaboration" practiced by the Popular Fronts of France, Spain, China, and other countries; the refusal of the USSR and the Popular Front government of France to come to the assistance of the Republicans in Spain against fascist forces. Close to home, the failure of the French Popular Front government to aid the Vietnamese workers' movement, and especially Moutet's decision to ban the Indochinese Congress, were regarded as clear examples of the Comintern's betrayal.

To noncommunist Vietnamese, and probably to the rank-and-file ICP members as well, this controversy had all the qualities of a bitter fraternal quarrel, in which seemingly petty and esoteric issues were blown out of proportion. To those involved, however, these ideological issues not only defined the direction and objective of their movement, but also were central to their lives, dedicated as they were to the success of the revolution. Thus, they perceived the existence of a competing ideological interpretation as a threat not merely to the movement, the revolution, but to their very self-definition.

The Trotskyist-Stalinist controversy of the 1930s provides an indication of the ideological distance the Vietnamese anticolonialists had traveled in a decade. By the time of the Popular Front, there was no more talk of *mat nuoc* (loss of the country) or *ai quoc* (loving the country) among Vietnamese revolutionaries; such phrases were out of fashion, condemned as the language of the bourgeoisie. Indeed, the controversy between the Vietnamese Trotskyists and Communists was typical of the worldwide conflict within the Marxist-Leninist movement. If the newspapers of both sides, such as *La lutte, Le peuple* (Stalinist), *Le militant* (Trotskyist), *L'avant-garde* (Stalinist), *Dan chung* [The People] (Stalinist), and *Tranh dau* [Struggle] (Trotskyist), had been transported to a

European country and a few details changed to conform with local situations, the papers would have portrayed the Trotskyist-Stalinist controversy as well there as they did in Vietnam. The issues were identical: Communist power versus ideological purity, conformity to the Comintern's policies versus independence from Moscow. repression of political dissidents in the Soviet Union, and the French and Soviet positions on the Spanish Civil War.

In this sense, Vietnam's intellectual orientation had changed. For certain leading Vietnamese intellectuals during this period, the issues were no longer West versus East, the white race versus the yellow, national independence from Western imperialism—issues that concerned nationalists of the 1910s and 1920s. For them, the most stirring political issues included Stalin versus Trotsky, reformism versus revolution, and class collaboration versus class struggle, and the most important cultural issues included the responsibility of intellectuals and art for the sake of art versus art for the sake of social life. China and Japan, formerly Vietnam's models, were now mentioned in the contexts of the Comintern's new political line and "Japanese imperialism," but were no longer Meccas for Vietnamese revolutionaries. In their place stood the issues, heroes, and villains of European politics. Vietnamese politics and intellect had, indeed, been occidentalized.

By the eve of the Second World War, a confusion of many voices characterized the Vietnamese Communist movement. Comrades and friends who in the mid-1920s had started out together fighting French imperialism for national independence and a social revolution had parted ways in the wilderness of proletarian internationalism. For a while Communist organizational tactics and hatred for the French colonialists had been combined to exploit the liberalism of the Popular Front government and push the antiimperialist movement to a new peak. This high level of political activism, however, belied the narrow organizational base of the various Marxist groups. Although in the long run the experience of the "legal and overt" struggle was to benefit the ICP, in the immediate context of the late 1930s the skillful implementation of organizational and propaganda techniques was not enough to hold the Communist movement together. Blindly accepting instructions from the Comintern, lacking a universally accepted leadership and a revolutionary line suitable to Vietnam's conditions, the Vietnamese Communist movement in general and the ICP in particular foundered in ideological confusion and interfactional disputes. Rectification of these deficiencies was to begin only during the war years, following a second crisis in the survival of Vietnamese communism.

CHAPTER FIVE

A NATIONAL LIBERATION REVOLUTION

> Anything which is in agreement with the people's
> aspirations is supported by them, who will actively
> participate in the struggle. Then, and only then, do
> we have a real movement of the masses. It also
> taught us that we must do our utmost to avoid sub-
> jectivity, narrowmindedness, etc.
>
> Ho Chi Minh at the Second Congress
> of the Vietnam Workers' Party

For students of Vietnamese communism, the period of the Second
World War represents a complicated, major turning point. In the
first years of the war, repeated massive colonial reprisals against
Vietnamese revolutionaries virtually demolished the Communist
organizational networks that had been rebuilt during the second
half of the 1930s. By the end of the war, the former colonial masters found themselves imprisoned and the Communists had come
to power, popularly acclaimed as national liberators. This reversal
reflected Vietnamese political developments during the war years,
molded by the Japanese occupation, the consequent decline of

French authority, and the spectacular rise of the Vietnamese patriotic movement. More significant still was the Communists' political success in the August Revolution of 1945, the result of skillful leadership by the ICP, especially Nguyen Ai Quoc, and of their ideological and organizational strategies. Ultimately, both the objective historical conditions of Vietnam during the war and the subjective situation of the ICP played an important role in establishing communism as a central element of the Vietnamese political organism.

THE WANE OF FRENCH COLONIAL POWER

For the French in Indochina, the Second World War was a time of deepening political crisis. In these five years European colonial hegemony in Southeast Asia met its demise. Cut off from Europe by the defeat of France and isolated as the only surviving Western colonial power in a rising tide of Asian self-assertion, the French discovered that in order to preserve the shell of sovereignty over Indochina, in the hope of recovering colonial power at the end of the war, they would have to allow themselves to be utilized as an instrument of Japanese imperialism. Even this political prostitution, however, did not ensure the preservation of their "civilizing mission." In 1945 these former masters of Indochina watched helplessly as the natives, whom they had proclaimed incapable of self-rule, took over the government. They themselves were soon to become "old Indochina hands," who to their last days would energetically debate the question of who was responsible for the "loss" of Indochina.[1]

The decline of French power in Indochina developed in an unexpected manner. Until the defeat of France in June 1940, Indochina

1. The long-smoldering controversy among France's "old Indochina hands" burst into the open with the publication of the memoirs of Admiral Jean Decoux, *A la barre de l'Indochine: Histoire de mon Gouvernement général, 1940–1945* (Paris, 1949). Thereafter, accusations, justifications, and counteraccusations about the "loss" of Indochina filled the columns of the press and several books. See, for example, Maurice Ducoroy, *Ma trahison en Indochine* (Paris, 1949); General Catroux, *Deux actes du drame indochinois* (Paris, 1959); J. Legrand, *L'Indochine à l'heure japonaise* (Cannes, 1963), and Jean-Michel Pedrazzani, *La France en Indochine: De Catroux à Sainteny* (Paris, 1972).

had experienced a deceptive political tranquillity. The tension that had prevailed in July and August 1939, as the crisis approached, soon gave way to a sense of security and even guarded optimism. Within a few months of the beginning of the war, business had resumed almost as usual. Governor-General Brévié, the Popular Front appointee whom colonial minister Georges Mandel described as a man "of administrative formalism" and not of action,[2] had been replaced by General Catroux, an activist and an old colonial hand of Indochina, North Africa, and the Middle East, who by now had assumed full control. Here and there, some French veterans of the First World War were reenlisted to fight the Germans and reports of draft resistance by Vietnamese appeared daily. Otherwise, fifteen thousand kilometers away, the war in Europe was remote from sight and mind. The sirens for the air-raid drills, which had been begun in August 1939, continued to wail, but few people seemed to pay attention. It was well known that the Molotov-Ribbentrop Pact had been signed in late August and that in September the Soviets and Germans had signed another treaty, dividing Poland between themselves; but Poland, after all, was not France, and although preparations for the evacuation of Paris continued, few French in Vietnam thought them necessary. The Maginot Line was, from all reports, impregnable. *L'Annam nouveau,* a progovernment paper, reflected the general feeling in the European community when it reported, in September 1939:

> Morale in Indochina is excellent. The first emotion, inevitable at the beginning of any cataclysm, has passed. Confidence has been reborn. All the peoples of Indochina are convinced of the invulnerability of the Allies. . . . We are far from the battlefields. We do not need to fear any menace of direct aggression. The calm that we enjoy at this moment will lead quickly to a rebound of business.[3]

The native population, too, had given the French no cause for concern. With the ICP and various Trotskyist groups officially dissolved and banned and thousands of their leaders and members arrested in late September,[4] organized Vietnamese opposition was

2. Quoted in Catroux, *Deux actes,* p. 5.
3. *L'Annam nouveau,* 28 September 1939.
4. Newspaper reports at the time stated that with a few exceptions, "all the Communist leaders" of Nam Ky and "numerous" others elsewhere in Vietnam were arrested. Tran van Giau, citing an "enemy document," stated that approximately

nowhere apparent. The outpouring of supportive sentiment by the Vietnamese elite was reassuring. Less than two weeks after the war started, Emperor Bao Dai issued a proclamation calling upon the Vietnamese population to demonstrate "calmness, discipline, and obedience toward public authorities" and "especially an absolute confidence in the final victory of France."[5] Meanwhile, well-known collaborators such as Le Quang Liem, Bui Quang Chieu, Nguyen Phan Long, and Tran van Kha were waging an active campaign to recruit Vietnamese soldiers and workers for the European fronts. In the pages of *L'Annam nouveau, La dépêche d'Indochine,* and *La tribune indochinoise* these "urban nationalists" gave free play to their loyalty, gratitude, and "patriotism" toward France, appealed to their compatriots to demonstrate similar sentiments, and denounced the Communist "rebels" and "trouble mongers." Finally, there was that minority under all skies who wished they had more than one country to give their lives to and who found in the war an opportunity to show their loyalty toward the "mother country." In addition to the celebrated case of the young scholar Pham Duy Khiem, who enlisted amid much publicity and fanfare (and who appropriately became a few decades later, ambassador to France for the United States–sponsored South Vietnamese government), the few others who volunteered for the European front could not fail to hearten their colonial masters. Looking back two decades later, General Catroux observed:

> Indochina [by 1939] had long been pacified, unified in diversity, and administered, and the troubles that occurred a few years earlier on the banks of the Red River and in the northern region of Annam had left nothing in terms of apparent sequels. The urban and rural masses were docile and peaceful. . . . On the whole, the political situation in Indochina appeared to be favorable and did not harbour any of the disquieting seeds.[6]

Such optimism and confidence, however, proved misguided and short-lived. The defeat of France, the Japanese occupation, aggression by Thailand, and the insurrections of rebellious Viet-

eight hundred were arrested in Nam Ky alone, and about two thousand throughout the rest of Vietnam. See *L'Annam nouveau,* 6, 25, and 26 October 1939; Tran van Giau, *Giai cap cong nhan, 3: 25.*

5. "Proclamation de S. M. l'Empereur d'Annam aux populations annamites," *La tribune indochinoise,* 13 September 1939.

6. Catroux, *Deux actes,* pp. 19–20.

namese—all these crucial tests of the stability of Indochina, occurring in the second half of 1940, shattered the myths of
invulnerability to external menace and of the native population's
support for French sovereignty. Through a combination of compromises with Japan, concessions to Thailand, and repression of
the Vietnamese insurrectionists, the Decoux administration
managed to contain the problems and retain French sovereignty in
the short term; ultimately, however, these events marked the beginning of a deterioration of power that led to the termination of
French colonial rule in Indochina.

CONSEQUENCES OF THE DEFEAT OF FRANCE

The defeat of France profoundly affected the French community
in Indochina and, ultimately, French governance of Indochina.
The news of the armistice, coupled with the imminent Japanese
encroachment, generated disbelief, despair, and massive spontaneous demonstrations by Europeans, civilian and military, expressing their determination to fight until victory. But this initial reflex
of enthusiasm subsided within a few days, as most French quickly
realized that there were more risks than there were profits in either
patriotism or heroism and decided to be reconciled with political
reality.[7] In lamentation and perhaps also in self-justification, Decoux wrote in his memoirs of this "ephemeral" patriotism: "This
great enthusiasm [to fight until victory] was to be as ephemeral as a
fire of straw. Indeed, soon the harsh reality appeared in the eyes of
everybody: the risky position of Indochina, face to face with Japan
at a distance of 15,000 kilometers from a defeated France."[8]

The succession of events in May–June 1940—the rout of the
Allied forces in the "battle of France," the fall of Paris, the evacuation of French government to Bordeaux, the replacement of Reynaud with Pétain, the signing of the armistice on June 22, and, in
Indochina, the Japanese ultimatum, the prelude to a Japanese occupation—created a fissure in the French community in Indochina.

7. For sketches of the reactions of the French in Indochina to the French
defeat and the Japanese threats, see Pedrazzani, *France en Indochine*, pp. 25–46.
See also André Gaudel, *L'Indochine française en face du Japon* (Paris, 1947),
p. 134.
8. Decoux, *A la barre*, p. 36.

On the one hand were those who desired to maintain French sovereignty and economic prosperity at all costs, including following orders from Vichy and the Japanese, on the other were those who wished to retain French sovereignty without collaboration. In its subsequent endeavors to demonstrate loyal collaboration with both the Pétain government and the Japanese, the Decoux regime, apparently with the support of the large majority of the colonial French, launched a determined wave of persecution against the partisans of "Free France" and thereby produced so profound a breach between Vichyites and Gaullists that it appeared never to heal, even long after the war had ended.

The division among the French surfaced soon after Decoux assumed power in July 1940. To the discomfiture of the Gaullists, portraits of Marshal Pétain emblazoned all government offices, streetcorners, hotels, and restaurants. Meanwhile, from late 1941 on, Radio Hanoi and Radio Saigon began celebrating the Japanese victories in Borneo, Malaya, the Philippines, Singapore, Sumatra, and Java. Beginning in 1942, and in imitation of the Vichy government, the Decoux administration organized raids against Freemasons, Jews, and Gaullists.[9] The official hunt of the Gaullists reached a peak early in 1943, when, at the instigation of Decoux himself, French officials had to choose between allegiance to Pétain and dismissal. Indeed, some claimed that the maltreatment reserved for the Gaullists was far more vicious than that for Vietnamese revolutionaries.[10] Yet, while Decoux was openly contemptuous of the Allies and especially resentful of the Gaullists ("These latter are only the traitors, mercenaries, and flunkeys in the service of the Russo-Anglo-American coalition"),[11] members of the Resistance did not remain idle. They were busily organizing an effective intelligence service for the Allies, collecting weapons, cultivating the Vietnamese revolutionaries, and preparing for the "liberation" of Indochina. In the end, the division within the French community could not fail to create a favorable climate for the Vietnamese

9. See Philippe Devillers, *Histoire du Viet-Nam de 1940 à 1952* (Paris, 1952), pp. 86–87; also Legrand, *Indochine à l'heure japonaise,* pp. 160–179.
10. See Legrand, *Indochine à l'heure japonaise,* pp. 160–172; Pedrazzani, *France en Indochine,* pp. 111–113.
11. From an official speech by Decoux delivered in January 1943, quoted in Pedrazzani, *France en Indochine,* p. 111.

revolutionaries. The ICP shrewdly saw political advantages to be gained from the French disunity and by the beginning of 1943 began to exploit it with some success.

THE JAPANESE OCCUPATION AND ITS EFFECTS

As was the case elsewhere in Southeast Asia, the Japanese occupation of Indochina during the Second World War played a determinant role in the country's political development. Though brief in duration, the occupation acted as a catalyst, leading to a fundamental transformation of Vietnamese political configurations. It precipitated an erosion of French colonial power that was never reversed. In the perspective of Vietnamese history, however, it occupied an even more important place. Whatever its pernicious effects on the Western presence in Asia and in Vietnam in particular, the occupation, together with French colonial rule, served the cause of the Vietnamese revolution. Like French colonialism, Japan's role in Vietnamese political development was that of a destroyer rather than a builder. French colonialism, by helping render Confucianism irrelevant and ending the absolute rule of the mandarinate and monarchy, had allowed room for questioning and innovation. By bending the French will, setting limits to their political monopoly, and finally destroying their power, the Japanese exposed, during a period when international relations were interpreted in racialist terms, the hollowness of the myth of the white man's invincibility and, with it, the bankruptcy of the concept of the "white man's burden." Perhaps this psychological liberation was just as important as the political liberation, which in a decisive way was a result of the Japanese occupation.

The Japanese occupation of Indochina, which began in September 1940, was not complete until July 1941. The occupation appeared to be motivated not by political considerations, but by military and economic ones. Possession of Indochina at once ensured the throttling of the southwestern supply routes for the Chungking army and positioned the Japanese within striking distance of the rest of Southeast Asia. In economic terms, the occupation opened up to Japan the natural resources not only of Indochina but also of the neighbouring countries. Thailand, British Burma, and French

Indochina together produced 95 percent of the world's rice export. Possession of other natural resources in the region—rubber, tin, oil, coal, iron, tungsten, zinc, quinine, and phosphate—permitted Japan to go far toward its long-cherished goal of economic self-sufficiency.

On the surface, the occupation did not threaten French sovereignty. The deals struck with Japan appeared to be a good bargain for the French. There were few outward changes in the colonial administration: except for the provision of foodstuffs, transport, and costs of occupation and the agreement to supply Japan with a large quantity of food and other materials, the Decoux administration retained the same control as before the war. French troops moved freely throughout Indochina. Intensive repression against Vietnamese nationalists who, mistaking the Japanese "Asia-for-the-Asian" propaganda for a genuine promise of fraternal support, had agitated against the colonial regime, occurred without Japanese intervention. In return, the French did nothing to interfere with the Japanese expeditions from Indochina base against neighboring countries. Independent Thailand had gravitated toward a pro-Japanese position, and in 1942 the Western colonial territories of the Philippines, Netherlands Indies, British Malaya, and British Burma successively submitted to Japanese control. Given the Japanese treatment of the other colonies in the region, the arguments for patience and collaboration in order to preserve French sovereignty were indeed appealing

Beneath this superficial stability and authority, however, a rapid decline of French power went hand in hand with increased Japanese interference in the domestic and foreign affairs of Indochina. When, in October 1940, just one month after the Japanese entry into Indochina, Thailand launched all-out attacks on the westernmost regions of Indochina, Japan intervened to offer to mediate the conflict. By the terms of this "mediation," signed in Tokyo in May 1941, French Indochina ceded to Thailand the Laotian territories west of the Mekong and the entire Cambodian province of Battambang, a total of seventy thousand square kilometers of territory.[12]

12. For a discussion of the Franco-Siamese conflict over the Indochinese-Siamese borders and the Japanese mediation, see Gaudel, *Indochine en face du Japon*, pp. 94–116.

By the Darlan-Kato Accord of 29 July 1941, Indochina was to be integrated in the Japanese military system, under the pretext of "common defense." By the terms of this accord, the Japanese forces were permitted to use eight airports in southern Indochina (including Nha Trang, Tourane, Bien Hoa, Saigon, and Kompong Trach) and the ports of Tourane, Cam Ranh, and Saigon. The Japanese military occupation, completed in July 1941, was followed by increasingly exacting demands for supplies and costs of occupation. Each Japanese ultimatum brought a French concession, and as the war continued French colonial power became progressively weaker.[13] To be sure, the Japanese continued to protest their respect for French sovereignty over Indochina, the French armed forces retained freedom of movement, and French officials continued to function as previously. By the final year of the war, however, no one doubted the hollow character of French sovereignty over Indochina.

THE GROWTH OF VIETNAMESE NATIONALISM

The rapid growth of the Vietnamese nationalist movement during the Second World War also reflected diminishing French power. In 1939 and again in 1940 the French had suppressed organized Vietnamese opposition, managed for a decade by internationalist revolutionaries. The French were unaware, however, of the groundswell of a more traditionally oriented nationalism that had little to do with international communism. Living apart from the Vietnamese population and mistaking public pronouncements of support by collaborators as representative of native sentiment, most Europeans gave little heed during the war years to private warnings of rising nationalist opposition and continued to delude themselves about Vietnamese support for French sovereignty.[14] Indeed, this self-delusion was so deep-rooted that "old Indochina hands" persisted in it long after the war had ended. As late as 1949, Decoux found it possible to write:

> Not only were there no serious rebellions on the part of our governed against the protective power from 1940 until 1945, but I can

13. Ibid., p. 206–226.
14. Pedrazzani, *France en Indochine*, pp. 28–29.

affirm, without fear of being contradicted, that, in spite of the misfortunes of France, never before were the natives so close to our
fatherland in their spirit and in their heart.[15]

The reality of Vietnamese political development contradicted
Decoux. Except for a few collaborators most Vietnamese either
withheld their backing, lost confidence in French power, or saw
the French difficulties as an opportunity for national liberation.
During the first year of the war, as leaders of opinion among the
urban bourgeoisie refused to espouse the French cause,[16] peasants
and workers joined a widespread draft-resistance movement,
intensified by rumors that ships carrying Vietnamese conscripts to
Europe were being sunk by ghosts or German torpedoes.[17]
France's defeat and the Japanese occupation in the latter half of
1940 only exacerbated these tendencies. The news of the armistice
sent thousands of urban Vietnamese to queue in front of the local
branches of the Bank of Indochina to withdraw their deposits. The
arrival of the Japanese occasioned a mushrooming of political
groups that hoped to make use of Japan to reconquer Vietnamese
independence.

Flagrant political opportunism followed. The noncommunist
Vietnamese nationalists, the Japanese, and the French all schemed
to profit by the presence of the others to bolster their own position.
While several Vietnamese groups attempted to exploit the Japanese presence to undermine French power, the Japanese and the
French outdid each other in appealing to traditional Vietnamese
patriotism. The cumulative effect of these efforts was a progressive
rise in the strength of the Vietnamese nationalist movement as the

15. Decoux, *A la barre,* p. 205.
16. The feelings of the urban bourgeoisie were best expressed in an "inverse La
Fontaine fable" *(ngu ngon La Fontaine nguoc sach),* "The Wolf and the Crane," by
the popular satirist Tu Mo, published in *Ngay nay* [Nowadays], which had a wide
circulation. The fable can be summarized as follows: One day, after a feast, the
wicked, greedy wolf had a huge bone stuck in his throat. In his agony, Wolf saw the
crane leisurely stalking by and groaned for help. Crane, aware of Wolf's notoriety
for turning against friends, said, 'You wicked wolf, whose crimes are well known to
the world, why should anyone save a cruel beast like you and allow you to continue
going after the harmless sheep?" Having spoken, Crane quickly flew away, leaving
Wolf to die in the midst of the forest. Tu Mo's moral tag: "Moralists, don't be so
quick in condemning Crane for pettiness;/killing a wicked beast, thus saving harmless beings/was a virtuous deed deserving praise for ever"; "Con cho soi va con co"
[The wolf and the crane], *Ngay nay,* no. 180 (23 September 1939), p. 6.
17. *La tribune indochinoise,* 15 November 1939.

war continued and as French power gradually dwindled under Japanese pressure. Toward the end of the war, this nationalist movement became an instrument of the Communists in their seizure of power.

The Japanese campaign to win Vietnamese support took many forms. An extensive racialist "Asia-for-the-Asians" propaganda operation was designed to stimulate fear of Japanese power, admiration for Japanese culture, and pride in Asian achievements. The campaign included the opening in Hanoi, Haiphong, and Saigon of cultural centers offering courses in Japanese language and civilization and of exhibition centers publicizing Japanese art, photography, industrial might, and particularly Japan's victorious military campaign. These cultural activities offered covert encouragement to anti-French Vietnamese groups, implying the possibility of Japanese assistance to their efforts. Indeed, from 1943 on, the Japanese actively promoted the formation of pro-Japanese political groups. Japanese political propaganda was most successful in Nam Ky, where anti-French feeling had been strong during and after the Popular Front period and in the draft-resistance movement.

The Japanese connection with the politics of the South during this period was most apparent in the activities of several noncommunist political groups. These groups were characterized by nostalgic, amorphous patriotism, but also by lack of coherent strategies and tactics. Two southern politicoreligious sects—the Cao Dai and the Hoa Hao—best exemplified these groups. Throughout the 1930s, with the VNQDD already suppressed, these sects had been the channels for traditional Vietnamese patriotism. Now, with covert and sometimes overt Japanese support, they became a forceful political influence in Vietnamese society.

Founded around the end of 1925 by Ngo van Chieu, a colonial administrator of Phu Quoc island, in the Gulf of Thailand, Cao Dai (High Tower)[18] is a religion that combines dogmas and philosophies borrowed from the world's major religions (Con-

18. Cao Dai is formally called Dai Dao Tam Ky Pho Do or "Third Amnesty of God." For more information on the Cao Dai religion see Gabriel Gobron, *Histoire et philosophie du caodaisme* (Paris, 1949). Brief discussions of the role of Cao Dai role during the Second World War can be found in Gaudel, *Indochine en face du Japon*, pp. 45–48; Decoux, *A la barre*, pp. 234–235; and Victor L. Oliver, *Caodai Spiritualism: A Study of Religion in Vietnamese Society* (Leiden, 1976), pp. 83–105.

fucianism, Buddhism, Taoism, and Christianity) along with local spiritualist and occult beliefs. Though suspected by the colonial government of harboring political ambitions, Cao Dai was officially recognized by the government as a formal religion in 1926, when it had less than three hundred followers. The new religion quickly became popular in the South, and by 1932 there were already 128 Cao Dai temples and a following of about one hundred thousand. Schism developed by 1933, and soon thereafter seven separate factions vied with one another for converts. The political ambitions of this religious sect became apparent when, in 1938, Pham Cong Tac, the "Pope" of the dominant Tay Ninh sect, prophesied the coming of the war, the arrival of the Japanese, the return of Prince Cuong De from Japan, and Japanese aid for the Vietnamese recon-quest of independence.

Affirming the Tay Ninh sect's connections with Cuong De, the colonial authorities closed the "Holy See" at Tay Ninh and several provincial temples, and in 1941, Decoux exiled Pham Cong Tac and several other nationalist leaders to the Comoro Islands, east of the African continent. In the wake of these incidents, the Japanese placed the Cao Dai temple in Phnom Penh under their protection and overtly aided the Cao Daiists. With the assistance of the *Kempeitai,* the Japanese secret police, Tran Quang Vinh of the Tay Ninh sect reorganized in February 1943 the sect's Leadership Committee, which then began a vigorous campaign to raise funds "to buy weapons for a future insurrectionary movement."[19] Under suspected Japanese sponsorship, the Tay Ninh sect joined with the other Cao Dai sects, the followers of Hoa Hao, and some well-known political personages in May 1943 to form a political organi-zation called the Viet Nam Phuc Quoc Dong Minh Hoi (League for the National Restoration of Vietnam). From this date the activities of these groups reportedly assumed paramilitary forms, and some of the league's members were trained and armed to act as Japanese auxiliaries.[20]

The Japanese also attempted to exploit the Hoa Hao sect's difficulties with the French authorities. Founded in 1939 by Huynh Phu So, the mystic of Hoa Hao village in Chau Doc province, this

19. Devillers, *Viet-Nam de 1940 à 1952,* p. 92.
20. Ibid.

religious sect rapidly acquired a vast following among southern
Vietnamese because of the simplicity of its reformed Buddhist doctrine and possibly also because of nationalist orientation. Huynh
Phu So, "The Master" *(Duc Thay),* combined healing power with
prophecy. As he preached the new doctrine the Master cured the
sick with acupuncture and herbal medicine. His prophecy that
Cochin China was about to experience a series of catastrophic
events, including a French defeat, the arrival of the Japanese, and
the arrival of the Americans, won the sect a great number of converts. In 1940 it had a following of approximately one hundred
thousand.[21]

Alarmed by the popularity of the sect and especially its leader,
the French Sûreté first banned Huynh Phu So from his native Chau
Doc province, and then in August 1940 confined him to the psychi-
atric ward at Cho Quan Hospital in Cholon.[22] But the Master won
new converts wherever he went, including the doctor to whose
care he had been assigned.[23] To make matters even more difficult
for the French police, Hoa Hao followers, believing the French
had martyred their religious leader, made pilgrimages to his various places of exile. When, in the fall of 1942, the French authorities
made plans to banish Huynh Phu So to Laos, the Japanese Kempeitai intervened to force his release and provided him with Japanese protection. Armed by the Japanese, Hoa Hao followers made
preparations to seize power at an opportune moment. Though ex-
cluded from a formal share in power after the Japanese coup
d'état,[24] Hoa Hao followers are alleged to have had military control of most of the territory south and west of Saigon by the time of
the Japanese surrender in August 1945.[25]

Thus, from 1942 until the *coup de force* in March 1945, the
French and Japanese authorities played a sort of tug-of-war with

21. A. M. Savani, *Visage et images du Sud Viet-Nam* (Saigon, 1955), p. 101;
also, Bernard Fall, "The Political-Religious Sects of Viet Nam," *Pacific Affairs* 28
(September 1955): 244–45.
22. See *Tin nguong Viet Nam* by Toan Anh [Nguyen van Toan] (Saigon, 1967),
pp. 392–393. This useful document includes, in addition to general discussion of the
traditional religions of Vietnam, such primary materials as prayers, sermons, and
regulations of each of the religion discussed, including Cao Dai and Hoa Hao.
23. Donald Lancaster, *The Emancipation of French Indochina* (London, 1961),
p. 89.
24. For discussion of the Japanese coup d'état in March 1945, see Chapter 6.
25. Fall, "Political-Religious Sects," p. 246.

well-known activist Vietnamese leaders as the objects of contention. The Japanese Kempeitai and the French Sûreté vied with each other in such principal cities as Saigon, Hanoi, and Hue. French arrests of "pro-Japanese" elements included people suspected of harboring "disloyal" feelings toward France, but who could in no way be considered pro-Japanese. The Japanese Kempeitai, on the other hand, was quick to provide "protection" to well-known Vietnamese, sometimes against their own wishes.[26] When, in July 1943, the French administration wanted to arrest Tran Quang Vinh, Huynh Phu So, and Tran van An, all reputed "pro-Japanese" leaders, the Kempeitai quickly provided them with official Japanese titles. When the Sûreté arrested some known pro-Japanese political leaders such as Tran van Lai, Nguyen Trac, Le Duc, Pham Loi, and Ho Nhat Tan, the Kempeitai quickly exiled other known personages or else put them under Japanese protection. Tran van An was taken to Formosa; Tran Trong Kim (the future prime minister during the Japanese interlude), Nguyen van Sam, and Duong Ba Trac were spirited to Singapore (and then Thailand); Ngo Dinh Diem was "protected" by the Japanese, first in Hue and then in Vinh Long. As it turned out, the Japanese, by encouraging anti-French activities, not only helped undermine French colonial power but also further promoted Vietnamese nationalism, which would be expressed during the Japanese rule of March–August 1945.

FRENCH MANIPULATIONS OF VIETNAMESE PATRIOTISM

The colonial government, too, was responsible in an important way for the revival of Vietnamese patriotism during the war years. In an attempt to contain Japanese influence and channel Vietnamese patriotism to its advantage, the colonial administration competed with the Japanese for Vietnamese support. To offset the Japanese myth of "Greater East Asia," the government put forward that of the "Indochinese nation." According to this myth, Indochina constituted a federation of diversified ethnic groups striving for both solidarity and a maximum of autonomy. Thus, the

26. Tran Trong Kim insisted in *Mot con gio bui* [Whirlwind] (Saigon, 1969), a memoir of his experience in politics in 1945, that the Kempeitai more or less forced its protection on him, claiming that the French were about to arrest him.

French in Indochina and the area's diverse ethnic groups formed one nation in which the French, too, were Indochinese. The native Indochinese states would be given a certain amount of internal autonomy; but the French, because of their experience and position, would act as the cement holding the "Indochinese nation" together. In foreign affairs, the task of defending Indochina against external aggression was not the task of the French alone, but of all Indochinese "patriots."

The dissemination of this myth during the war years involved an unprecedented implementation of the "policy of respect" *(politique d'égards),* which French leaders such as Albert Sarraut, Alexandre Varenne, and Paul Reynaud had encouraged but failed to enforce. In a curious and paradoxical recognition of Vietnamese "patriotism," Vietnamese students were, for the first time in colonial history, allowed to study Vietnamese language and history. Every morning before class, students attended a flag salutation ceremony at which both the tricolor and the yellow emblem of the royal government were raised. Decoux, however, was careful in his definition of patriotism. As he wrote in his memoirs, "If I thus recognized, even encouraged particular 'patriotism,' I formally condemned 'nationalism' of all kinds, because it had a xenophobic and anti-French tendency and received its instructions from abroad."[27]

To flatter the traditional elite, Decoux himself made repeated attempts to increase the prestige of the "sovereigns" of Annam, Laos, and Cambodia. The governor-general made a point of attending all the important traditional ceremonies celebrated by the indigenous kings and even accepted from Emperor Bao Dai the title "Prince Protector of the Empire of Annam." To meet the constant Vietnamese complaints of discrimination in government positions, Decoux moved to end what he called the "flagrant disproportion" in salaries earned by French and Indochinese for the same work. He established a new principle regulating the employment of civil servants: "the same jobs for the same qualifications; the same salaries for the same jobs." As a result of the new policy, more Indochinese and particularly Vietnamese were employed in high-echelon administrative posts, previously reserved for the

27. Decoux, *A la barre,* p. 389.

French.[28] To satisfy the Vietnamese thirst for education, and especially to compete with Japanese cultural activities, the Decoux
administration opened thousands of new elementary and village
schools and admitted hundreds of thousands of new students.[29]

To immunize the workers to Communist appeals, the Decoux
administration promulgated a series of decrees and labor regulations that were astonishingly favorable to workers and constituted
the most radical turnabout in French policy. By the governor-
general's decree of 16 August 1942, Vietnamese workers were
again entitled to an eight-hour workday and forty-eight hour work-
week. (These stipulations had been part of the Popular Front labor
law of 1936, but had been abolished by Governor-General Catroux
in November 1939). By the decree of 21 June, 1943 of the governor
of Cochin China, no employer could dismiss a worker without providing sufficient notice. For a forced dismissal without
sufficient reasons, the employer could be fined, made to pay com-
pensation to the dismissed worker, or both. Whatever its motivations, the new labor policy appeared effective in undercutting Communist appeal among workers. The ICP's success among the rural
population notwithstanding, until the very end of the war the Party
was singularly ineffectual in its attempts to organize urban and
industrial workers.

Of all Decoux's wartime policies, his policy toward Vietnamese
youth contributed most directly and concretely to the awakening of
Vietnamese nationalism. Although he later blamed its creation on
the Japanese, his "sport-and-youth movement" was a logical corollary of the myth of the Indochinese nation. According to J. Lebas,
president of the General Committee of Youth Work under Decoux,
the objectives of the sport-and-youth movement were twofold:
first, to awaken in the French youth in Indochina a consciousness

28. Despite its propaganda value, the new policy actually affected very few
people. In 1941, for example, there were 171 Vietnamese in the middle and upper
ranks (the "European ranks") of the administration, though with lower salaries. In
1943, two years after the new policy was proclaimed, there were 304 Vietnamese in
the European ranks, with salaries comparable to their European counterparts; Tran
van Giau, *Giai cap cong nhan*, 3: 135.

29. The number of village schools increased from 3,143 in 1941 to 9,070 in 1944;
student enrollment in these schools increased correspondingly: from 132,212 to
316,505. During the same period, enrollment at the four vocational schools increased from 553 to 1,329. See Tran Huy Lieu et al., *TLTK*, 9: 35.

of their "solidarity with their comrades in France" and to "combat a widespread slackness and selfishness among them";[30] and second,

> to promote among the young a certain national ideal and a patriotism that generates the most noble virtues. This certainly does not mean to promote the development of subversive ideas, negative to the order that must be realized in this country; but the association of French and Indochinese and their collaboration in the management of public affairs can be carried out only if we can find among our protected people men who are proud of their race and respectful of their traditions, but who know how to appreciate the just value of the work accomplished by France in Indochina.[31]

This movement resulted in the organization of approximately one hundred thousand urban youths[32] into various sports clubs, boy-scout organizations, student and youth associations. Experiencing collective life for the first time, in groups organized in a paramilitary manner and based on patriotic appeal ("Strength for Service"), Vietnamese youth gave this government sponsored program unreserved support. With the permission of the government, the urban students organized movements to visit testimonials of Vietnam's heroic past (the Hung Temple; Hoa Lu; Bach Dang River) and trips to the countryside to teach rural people *quoc ngu* (the national language in roman script), Vietnamese history, general hygiene, and so on. A noteworthy accomplishment was their literacy campaign, which enabled approximately fifty-thousand adults to learn to read and write.[33]

Decoux's youth policy, however, proved to be double-edged. Organized patriotism led easily to organized opposition. Although it momentarily removed Vietnamese youth from possible Japanese exploitation, the patriotism, once aroused, could not easily be oriented toward love of the "mother country." The more politicized among them sought organizations through which to

30. J. Lebas, "Le mouvement de jeunesse en Indochine," *L'Indochine* 2, no. 37 (15 May 1941), pp. 9–10.

31. Ibid.

32. Devillers, *Viet-Nam de 1940 à 1952*, p. 85. Without indicating her source, Ellen J. Hammer claimed that membership in this youth movement reached "over a million"; *The Struggle for Indochina, 1940–1955* (Stanford, 1966), p. 32. I think this is an exaggerated figure.

33. Tran Huy Lieu et al, *TLTK*, 9: 172.

channel their patriotism. The ICP was quick to appreciate the importance of capturing the urban youth movement. In early 1943 it had formulated a specific policy and published its "Prospectus on Vietnamese Culture" *("De cuong van hoa Viet Nam"),* in an attempt to compete with the colonial government for the allegiance of the Vietnamese youth. By the middle of 1944 the Viet Minh Front had established contacts with many student and youth organizations. The ICP also sponsored the formation in June 1944 of the Dang Dan chu Viet Nam (Vietnamese Democratic Party), designed to win Communist support from the urban petit-bourgeoisie, especially the students and intellectuals. In the summer of 1945, the tens of thousands of youths whose patriotism had been aroused by the youth programs of the Decoux administration became the Communist urban vanguards.

AN INSURRECTION THAT MISFIRED

Although the events of the war years hastened the end of French colonial power and enabled the ICP ultimately to seize power, the Communist political success was not a linear development. In fact, this pivotal period was one of the most difficult for the ICP. In addition to the near destruction of the Party and the loss of the majority of its most experienced leaders by the end of 1940, the Party was isolated from the international Communist movement. Yet, despite these misfortunes—or perhaps in some important ways because of them—the ICP experienced an amazing recovery during the last years of the war. In examining the vicissitudes of the ICP during the Second World War , it is worthwhile to distinguish between the 1939–1940 period, which constituted the final glory of the Moscow-oriented Communists, and the 1941–1945 period, which affirmed the reascendancy of Nguyen Ai Quoc and his former comrades in Thanh Nien. In retrospect the latter years of the war had the greatest consequences for the development of the Vietnamese Communist movement. The leadership, revolutionary line, and organizational strategy and tactics that first emerged during this period remained the basic factors of Vietnamese communism for three decades.

The early years of the war, however, were time of crisis for the

ICP similar to the aftermath of the Nghe Tinh Soviet Movement. Like the earlier crisis of survival, this one resulted from a combination of colonialist repression and revolutionary miscalculations. Repression resumed in mid-1939, even before the beginning of the war, as it became obvious that the days of the Popular Front were numbered. With the coming of the war, reprisals against the Communist revolutionaries intensified, in connection with the French government's measures against the antiwar PCF. On 26 September 1939, the French Council of Ministers decided to "dissolve the Communist party and all the groups attached thereto."[34] All properties belonging to the PCF were confiscated, and several French Communists were arrested and subsequently executed for sabotage. Two days later, on 28 September, the governor-general of Indochina dissolved the ICP, outlawed all its publications, and promptly arrested known Communists.

The repression in 1939 took a heavy toll of the ICP despite the Party's precautionary measures to restrict the damage. As the war approached, the Party had ordered its cadres operating overtly or semiovertly to "withdraw into deep cover" *(rut vao bi mat)* and to transfer their center of operations from the cities to the countryside, while maintaining contacts with the masses in the urban areas. These measures went into effect in Bac Ky as early as the autumn of 1938, following the Munich conference, and in Trung Ky immediately after the beginning of the war. Nevertheless, the repression in September 1939 dealt the Party a hard blow. Its urban networks were seriously crippled. Over two thousand Communists were arrested, eight hundred of them in Nam Ky.[35] A second wave launched by the government in November–December 1939 inflicted "heavy damage" on what remained of the Party in the South.[36] Many of its top-level, most seasoned leaders were arrested, including Le Hong Phong, the Comintern's representative to the ICP; Nguyen van Cu, the Party's secretary-general; Ha Huy Tap, Central Committee member and former secretary-general; and other Central Committee members, including Nguyen thi Minh Khai, Le Duan, and Vo van Tan.

34. *L'Annam nouveau*, 28 September 1939.
35. Tran van Giau, *Giai cap cong nhan*, 3: 24; also *L'Annam nouveau*, 5 October 1939.
36. Tran van Giau, *Giai cap cong nhan*, 3: 55.

THE NATIONAL QUESTION REAPPRAISED

Two events in the first two years of the war were fraught with consequences for the ICP. The first involved a radical reorientation of the Party's revolutionary line. Ever since its formation in 1930, following the lead of the Comintern the ICP had adopted positions that emphasized "the social question" (class struggle) at the expense of "the national question" (national liberation), the two basic ingredients in the "bourgeois-democratic revolution." During the ultra-left period of the early 1930s, the Party adopted an anti-nationalist strategy, and during the Popular Front period its official line disregarded both national liberation and the class struggle. In 1939, however, the ICP Central Committee reversed its anti-nationalist position and made an overall reappraisal of the national question. According to the official Party history, they concluded that *"the contradiction between the Indochinese peoples and the imperialist aggressors was the main one of the two fundamental social contradictions then existing in the three Indochinese countries,* and that the national liberation movement was an integral part of the world revolutionary movement."[37]

Although it is not possible to ascertain whether this reemphasis on the national question reflected a new Comintern line or only a local decision (namely, the reassertion of the national liberationists within the Party), this new orientation remained the basic line of the Party throughout the Second World War. On 29 September 1939 the Central Committee issued a directive stressing that "the situation in Indochina will lead to the issue of national liberation" and calling for a radical transformation of the Party's organization and operations to adapt to the new historical conjuncture.[38] At the Sixth Plenum of the Party's Central Committee two months later at Ba Diem, Gia Dinh province, the Party again emphasized the importance of the national question: *"national liberation [was] the foremost task of the Indochinese revolution."*[39] The resolutions of the Plenum stated:

To survive, the peoples of Indochina have no alternative than to overthrow the French imperialists and resist all types of aggres-

37. Commission for Study, *Outline History,* pp. 29–30 (italics in original).
38. *Histoire de la révolution d'août* (Hanoi, 1972), p. 14.
39. Commission for Study, *Outline History,* p. 29 (italics in original).

sors—white or yellow—in order to achieve their national liberation. . . . All questions of the revolution, including the agrarian question, must be resolved with this goal [national liberation] in mind.[40]

This focus on the national question entailed an important new operational tactic: the National United Front. To enable the Party to enlist all available Indochinese forces for the national liberation struggle, the Sixth Plenum decided to postpone the call for an agrarian revolution, and instead "only to oppose high land rents, exorbitant interest rates, and to confiscate land owned by the colonialists and traitors, for distribution to the tillers."[41] This policy, according to the *Outline History of the Vietnam Workers' Party,* was "aimed at rallying all those who opposed the imperialists and their lackeys, winning over progressive elements in the landowner class, and broadening the National United Front."[42] To implement this policy, the Indochinese Democratic Front (1936–1939) was now replaced by the Indochinese Antiimperialist National United Front, which aimed to unite all social classes and peoples of Indochina to fight for "Indochinese" national liberation. November 1939 marks the introduction of the concept of the *National United Front* into the vocabulary of Vietnamese communism. The National United Front was to remain the principal organizational tactic of the ICP for the rest of its existence.

THE NAM KY INSURRECTION

The second momentous event in the first two years of the war was the defeat of the Nam Ky Insurrection, which occurred in November–December 1940. Given the steady decline of French power in France as well as in Indochina, the ICP's Nam Ky Regional Committee had decided to stage an insurrection in order to take advantage of the French weakness. Beginning in March 1940, it circulated a pamphlet entitled *De cuong chuan bi bao dong* [Prospectus on the preparations for the insurrection], which included a directive on the organization and training of revolutionary brigades and the provision of military equipment for the insurrec-

40. *Révolution d'août,* p. 15.
41. Commission for Study, *Outline History,* p. 29.
42. Ibid.

tionary forces.[43] From March until July 1940, several conferences took place in Nam Ky to formulate final plans for the insurrection. Meanwhile, the committee sent Phan Dang Luu, a Central Committe member, to Hanoi to request approval. The Central Committee, meeting for the Seventh Plenum in November 1940 at Dinh Bang village, Bac Ninh province, heard the report from the South, reviewed the overall situation, and ordered postponement of the insurrection. This decision, however, was taken somewhat late and could not halt the rapid developments in the South. The French and Thais were then locked in a territorial dispute over western Cambodia and southern Laos, and Vietnamese conscripts had been mobilized for the conflict. Under pressure from several antiwar units of new conscripts, the date for the insurrection had been moved forward without the Central Committee's instructions.

On the evening of 22 November 1940, the insurrection broke out in several provinces of the South, including Gia dinh, Cho lon, Tan an, My tho, Can tho, Vinh long, Soc trang, and Bac lieu. Due to lack of proper coordination and last-minute haste, Saigon and several provinces had not been informed of the new date and therefore did not participate. For the next month, the scenes of a decade earlier in Nghe Tinh were repeated in the southern provinces. As the local administration disintegrated, the insurrectionists took power, maintained order and security, and meted out revolutionary justice to "counterrevolutionaries." Lacking the necessary leadership, organization, and military equipment, however, the insurgents could not withstand the onslaught of overwhelming French firepower.

The repression that followed rivaled that of 1930–31 in ferocity. A French apologia stated:

> The entire battalion of Foreign Legion troops [freshly brought in from the North for the Cambodian campaign], a company of North Vietnamese, two armored batteries, a mechanized unit, marines . . . were simultaneously ordered to the region north of My Tho and conducted a methodical search there, arresting the suspicious and firing at those who attempted to fight or to flee. The Air Force bombed the nests of resistance with great violence in order to terrorize the dissidents. Within four days, they were subdued. The

43. Tran van Giau, *Giai cap cong nhan,* 3: 68–69.

police [then] sorted out the suspects, and the ringleaders were shot.[44]

A report by the governor of Cochin China to the governor-general of Indochina indicated that within forty days, between 22 November and 31 December 1940, 5,648 people were arrested in the four provinces of My tho, Can tho, Gia dinh, and Long xuyen.[45] Communist sources were more specific. They reported the French use of twenty planes in numerous bombings of the rebellious areas.[46] When all existing prison facilities were full, the French police, with peculiar ingenuity, packed prisoners into dry-docked ships floating in the Saigon River. For want of chains and handcuffs, wires piercing the hands and heels of prisoners were used to hold them in one place.[47] More than a hundred were executed, among them high-level ICP leaders such as Vo van Tan, Phan Dang Luu, and Nguyen van Tien, Central Committee members; and Nguyen van Tu and Ta Uyen, members of the Nam Ky Regional Committee.[48] Several other ICP leaders, including Ha Huy Tap and Nguyen van Cu, both former secretaries-general, and Nguyen thi Minh Khai, the only female Central Committee member, who had been arrested previously but had nothing to do with the current uprising, were also executed. No reports survive of the number of casualties from the indiscriminate bombings. An unknown number of Party leaders, including Le Duan, a Central Committee member, and Le Hong Phong, the ECCI special representative, were dispatched to Poulo Condore, where they suffered the usual inhumane treatment reserved for political prisoners.[49] Jean Charboneau, using the

44. René Bauchar [Jean Charboneau], *Rafales sur l'Indochine* (Paris, 1946), p. 71.
45. Tran Huy Lieu et al., *TLTK*, 10:24. The Nam Ky Insurrection had historic significance in the evolution of the ICP before the Second World War. Two other insurrections of this same period at Bac Son and Do Luong were local in character.
46. Tran Huy Lieu, *Lich su tam muoi nam*, p. 62.
47. Ibid.
48. Ibid., p. 63.
49. Tran Dinh Tri, Le Duan, Duong Bach Mai, Le Hong Phong, and other well-known ICP leaders who survived execution during this repression received the most inhumane treatment, reserved for Vietnamese "politicals" in Con Son. Imprisoned in the now infamous "tiger cages" *(chuong cop)*, or, in the parlance of the political prisoners then, the "lion cages" *(chuong su tu)*, of Poulo Condore, they were regularly beaten entirely at the guards' discretion. There seemed to be a direct relation between revolutionary rank and punishment: the higher the rank in the ICP or Trotskyist party, the more frequent and more severe the punishment. Among

pseudonym René Bauchar in his description of the repression, provides a succinct conclusion to his discussion of the Nam Ky Insurrection: "We were cruel. The obsession with the Siamese threat
explained the rigor [of the repression]. But above all we had to
show our strength to those who thought they could profit from our
reverses."[50]
The course of Vietnamese communism changed as the result of
the Nam Ky Insurrection. The repression of November–December
1940, the ICP's most severe setback since 1931, left an indelible
mark on the Communist organization in Nam Ky.[51] Until Novem-

those who died following these beating sessions was Le Hong Phong, the ECCI
representative. To Vietnamese, the name Poulo Condore or Con Lon is associated
with dread and terror (perhaps comparable to the names Dachau, Auschwitz, or
Babi Yar to Westerners), whether under the French, Japanese, Diem, or Thieu
regime. But it is also associated with nationalist heroism as a "kiln which fired and
created heroes" *(lo nung duc anh hung)*. Huynh Thuc Khang, Ngo Duc Ke, Ngo
Gia Tu, Le Duan, Pham van Dong, Ung van Khiem, and Bui Cong Trung are a few
of the dead and living fighters for Vietnamese national independence who went
through this "kiln." It is rumored that the number of years in Poulo Condore (and
other French prisons) was one of the most important elements of the *curricula vitae*
of the Vietnamese Communist party leaders; it was an important qualification for
advancement in the Party hierarchy. Several revolutionary memoirs contain de-
scriptions of prison life in Poulo Condore and other French prisons in Indochina
(such as Ban Me Thuot, Lao Bao, Son La, and Kontum). See particularly *Guong
chien dau cua nhung nguoi cong san* [The fighting examples of the Communists]
(Hanoi, 1965); and Bui Cong Trung et al., *Len duong thang loi*. See also Demariaux,
Les îles Poulo Condore.
    50. Bauchar, *Rafales*, p. 71.
    51. According to I. Milton Sacks, the ICP was further weakened by an internal
purge of leaders responsible for the Nam Ky Insurrection: "Several members (believed to be police agents) [were] condemned to death" ("Marxism in Vietnam,"
p. 145). Sacks offers no source. Curiously, Duiker, in stating "Communist sources
available to me do not mention this," attributes to Sacks the information (which
Sacks did not provide) that Tran van Giau was purged during this occasion (*Rise of
Nationalism in Vietnam,* p. 270). I have asked two high-level Party officials about
this event, and both denied any knowledge of Giau's purge *in 1940*. Giau became
chairman of the southern committe during the August Revolution (1945–1946). It
would be strange indeed for a purged Communist leader, in Vietnam or anywhere
else, subsequently to have held such a responsible position. The case of Teng
Hsiao-ping of China is one of the rare exceptions. Tran van Giau, Tran Ngoc Ranh,
and several other Stalinists were made to go through *kiem thao* (self-criticism) in
1946 and were subsequently removed from leadership, partly and ostensibly because of the excesses (killings of Trotskyists and nationalists) committed under
their command in the South in the aftermath of the August Revolution. Tran Ngoc
Ranh was assigned to head the DRV delegation in Paris and died there. Tran van
Giau became a professor of history and one of Vietnam's most prolific scholars. He
is currently with the Institute of History, State Commission on Social Sciences,

ber, the Nam Ky section had been the strongest wing of the Party. Despite heavy casualties in the two previous campaigns of repression, the ICP had monopolized the anti-French movement in the South,[52] for the Trotskyist organizations had been eliminated in September 1939. The 1940 repression delayed the ICP's recovery, especially in the South, despite the increasingly favorable political conditions occasioned by the war. More significant still, it helped change the Party's direction. In addition to the Party's isolation from the international Communist movement, the elimination of most of the internationalist-oriented leaders, who had complied closely with whatever line Moscow espoused, facilitated the reascendancy of leaders who had stressed the creative adaptation of Marxism-Leninism to the sociopolitical conditions of Vietnam.

THE VIET MINH FRONT

Beginning in 1941, the much-tested Vietnamese Communist movement embarked on a course that would establish it as the governing power in Vietnam. This departure began at the Eighth Plenum of the Indochinese Communist Party, held 10–19 May 1941 at the cave of Pac Bo, Cao Bang province.

Three aspects of this plenum deserve notice, for they epitomized contemporary conditions in the ICP and, in the long run, had an important influence on the orientation of the Party. First, the fact that the conference had to be held at the mountainous frontier, among ethnic minorities, was a measure of the French success in

---

Southern Section, Ho Chi Minh City. As far as is known, the method of "purification" of the Vietnamese Communist party, at least since 1945, lacks the violent character often associated with the Soviet and Chinese purges. Purged Party leaders are usually made to undergo *kiem thao* and are then retired from decision-making positions. No violent death has been associated with any purged Party leader since 1945.

52. In fact, despite repeated massive reprisals and the imprisonment of a great number of top ICP leaders, Party membership grew rapidly in the South. According to the documents of the Seventh Plenum of the ICP (November 1940), after the defeat of France in Europe, Party membership in the South from June to October 1940 increased 60 per cent. According to the Nam Ky Regional Committee, at this time approximately 30 percent of the Nam Ky population "had come under the influence of the Party." Without actual figures, however, such reports reveal little about the total ICP membership during this period. See Tran van Giau, *Giai cap cong nhan,* 3: 67.

denying the lowland to Communist activities.[53] In the long run, however, this locale proved to be advantageous. The support of the ethnic minorities for Communist revolutionary efforts became a crucial element in the ICP "nationalities" policy.

Nguyen Ai Quoc's position as chairman of the plenum also deserves attention. By February 1941, when he first returned to Vietnam, Nguyen Ai Quoc had been absent from the Vietnamese revolutionary scene for ten years. The first documentary evidence of his rehabilitation appeared in July 1939, when he submitted a report to the Comintern on the ICP's policies during the Popular Front period.[54] Whatever the causes of his eclipse, Nguyen Ai Quoc's reemergence as the leader of the Vietnamese Communist movement, in the wake of the growing irrelevance of the Comintern and the drastic reduction of Stalinist influence within the ICP leadership, represented a new beginning for the ICP.

Finally, the composition of the plenum itself is worth noting: not one Party leader was present who could be identified with the internationalist faction. In addition to Nguyen Ai Quoc, representative of the Comintern to the ICP, four members of the Central Committee were present: Truong Chinh.[55] Hoang Quoc

53. The hamlet of Pac Bo, the site of the Eighth Plenum, is a stone's throw from China. From border marker No. 108, located in a cornfield, a few steps separate Pac Bo from China. The population of this area is composed essentially of the Nung ethnic minority which inhabits both sides of the border. See the preface to Chu van Tan et al., *Dau nguon* (Hanoi, 1975); Chu van Tan, *Reminiscences on the Army for National Liberation,* trans. Mai Elliot (Ithaca: Cornell University, Southeast Asian Program, Data Paper No. 97, 1974), p. 55. General Chu van Tan, a Nung, was one of the architects of the General Insurrection of August 1945. He became minister of national defense in 1946 and in 1956 the secretary of the Party Committee for the Viet Bac Autonomous Region.

54. For the text see Ho Chi Minh, *Ket hop,* pp. 79–81.

55. Truong Chinh was born Dang Xuan Khu in 1907 in Hanh Thien, Nam Dinh province. At age nineteen he was expelled from school for his role in the student movement to demand amnesty for Phan Boi Chau and organize a "state funeral" for Phan Chu Trinh. In 1927 he became a member of Thanh Nien and in 1930, an ICP member. Arrested and imprisoned in Hanoi in December 1930 for burning down the triumphal arches built to welcome the king of Siam, he was released in 1936. During the Popular Front period he was head of the "overt section" of the ICP in Bac Ky. He became the Party's secretary-general in 1941 and held this position until 1951, when the ICP was transformed into the Vietnam Workers' party. He remained secretary-general of the VWP until 1956, when he was removed following the excesses of the Land-Reform Program. He subsequently became vice-premier and chairman of the State Scientific Research Committee. Since September 1960 he has been a member of the Communist party's Political Bureau and chairman of the Standing

Viet,[56] Hoang van Thu,[57] and Phung Chi Kien. There was one representative each from the Trung Ky Regional Committee ("Comrade San") and the Nam Ky Regional Committee ("Comrade Thao").[58] Pham van Dong,[59] Vo Nguyen

Committee of the National Assembly. In July 1981 Truong Chinh became the Chairman of the Council of State (Vietnam's president). Best known as a theoretican, his writings include *Van de dan cay* [The peasant question] (1937) (with Vo Nguyen Giap); *Chien tranh Thai Binh Duong va cach mang giai phong dan toc o Dong Duong* [The war in the Pacific and the national liberation revolution in Indochina] (1942); *Cach mang thang Tam* [The August Revolution] (1946); *Khang chien nhat dinh thang loi* [The resistance will win] (1947); *Chu nghia Mac va van hoa Viet Nam* [Marxism and Vietnamese culture] (1948); *Phuong cham chien luoc cua Dang ta* [The strategic line of our Party] (1960); and *Ve cong tac mat Tran hien nay* [On the front work at present] (Hanoi 1971).

56. Hoang Quoc Viet was born Ha Ba Cang in 1905 to a working-class family. Expelled from school in 1926 for participation in the student movement to demand amnesty for Phan Boi Chau, he worked in mines and industrial workshops and in 1928 became a member of Thanh Nien. He subsequently became a liaison agent for the fledgling Vietnamese Communist movement and the PCF. A founding member of the ICP in 1930, he was arrested and exiled to Poulo Condore. Soon after his release in 1936 he resumed revolutionary activities and became one of the ICP's leading members. In 1941 he was elected to the ICP Central Committee and then became a member of the Party's Political Bureau and chairman of the Viet Minh Central Committee. In 1950 he became president of Vietnam's General Confederation of Labor and since then has held various leadership posts in Vietnam. He is currently chairman of the Vietnamese Fatherland Front.

57. Hoang van Thu was born to a Tay family in 1906 in Van Uyen, Lang Son province. At age twenty he organized the first group of anti-French Tay youth in Lang Son and in 1927 became active among Chinese and Vietnamese revolutionaries in southern China. Becoming an ICP member in 1930, he organized revolutionary cells among the ethnic minorities in the Cao Bang–Lang Son region. In 1932, when the ICP was in disarray, Thu aided Le Hong Phong, the Comintern representative with the ICP, in reviving Communist agitation in Bac Ky. During the early years of the Popular Front he led the revolutionary movement in Cao Bang and in 1939 became secretary of the Bac Ky Regional Committee. Elected to the Standing Committee of the ICP, he led the Communist movement in Bac Ky, especially Hanoi. Arrested in August 1943, he was executed in Hanoi in May 1944.

58. Chu van Tan, *Reminiscences*, p. 41; also Propaganda Section, *Trente ans*, p. 76.

59. Pham van Dong was born in 1906 in Quang Ngai province. Son of a mandarin family, he became a member of Thanh Nien in 1925 and one of Nguyen Ai Quoc's earliest comrades. Elected to the Thanh Nien Central Committee in May 1929, he was arrested in July of that year and incarcerated at Con Son, where he was one of the principal leaders, training other comrades in general culture, history, and geography. Released in 1936, he went to China with Vo Nguyen Giap in 1940 and he resumed revolutionary agitation under Nguyen Ai Quoc's supervision. With Giap he prepared revolutionary bases along the Sino-Vietnamese border. He became the DRV's minister of finance in 1946 and headed the Vietnamese delegation to the Fontainebleau conference. Elected a member of the ICP Central Committee

Giap,[60] and Vu Anh had also been intimately involved with the preparation of the plenum but for some reason were not present at the conference. Except for Nguyen Ai Quoc, then fifty-one years old, the members were in their midthirties and had begun their revolutionary activities in the 1920s as members of Thanh Nien or Tan Viet. Most significantly, all the Central Committee members present were of Bac Ky and Trung Ky origins; their formative political experiences had been in Vietnam or southern China. Whatever the reason for the absence of the internationalists, the decisions made by this plenum permanently altered the development of Vietnamese communism for many decades.

A NATIONAL LIBERATION REVOLUTION

Without doubt the most important aspect of the Eighth Plenum was its reemphasis on the importance of "the national question." Although this was not a new position, this was the first time the

---

in 1949, he was appointed vice-premier of the DRV. At the founding of the VWP in 1951 he was elected to its Political Bureau. In 1954 he headed the Vietnamese delegation at the Geneva Conference and was subsequently appointed prime minister of the DRV, a post he retains today.

60. One of the youngest revolutionaries among the first generation of the Vietnamese Communist leadership, Vo Nguyen Giap was born in 1910 in Quang Binh province and at age sixteen participated in the student movement of 1926. Arrested in 1930 and jailed for two years, he subsequently studied law and became a history teacher. During the Popular Front period he agitated in various semilegal Communist organizations, writing in *Le travail, Notre voix, En avant,* and other periodicals. In 1940 he went with Pham van Dong to southern China to work under Nguyen Ai Quoc. In 1944 he organized and led the Armed Propaganda Brigade for National Liberation, the nucleus of today's Vietnam People's Army. He became minister of interior of the first Viet Minh government after the August Revolution and in 1946, chairman of the DRV's Military Committee. Throughout the Protracted Resistance he was Vietnam's defense minister and commander-in-chief of the VPA. The organizer of the Dien Bien Phu victory in 1954, he later masterminded the war against United States intervention in South Vietnam. Elected to the Political Bureau of the VWP in 1951, he became vice-premier in 1955, while retaining his posts until the Fourth Congress of the Vietnamese Communist party (1976). Gradually giving up his military duties, as minister in charge of science and technology he has devoted himself almost entirely to building up Vietnam's fledgling industrial and technological bases. His books include *People's War, People's Army* (1962); *Le peuple du Sud-Vietnam vaincra* (1965); *La guerre de libération nationale* (1970); *The Military Art of People's War* (1970); *Chien tranh giai phong va chien tranh giu nuoc* [The war of liberation and the war to preserve the country] (1975); and *Suc manh vo dich cua chien tranh nhan dan Viet Nam trong thoi dai moi* [The invincible power of the Vietnamese people's war in the new era] (1975).

Party leadership clearly spelled out the implications of the national question in the proletarian revolution in a colonized society. In what appeared to be a "revisionist" attempt to redefine the Comintern-designated "two-stage revolution" for the colonial countries and at the same time a reversion to the line favored by the much-condemned Thanh Nien, the Eighth Plenum resolved to "employ an especially stirring [*thong thiet*] method of appeal to awaken the traditional nationalism in the people (particularly the Vietnamese people)."[61] Furthermore, it declared that the Indochinese revolution was "no longer a bourgeois-democratic revolution" but "a national liberation revolution" *(cuoc cach mang giai phong dan toc)*.[62] From 1930 on, the ICP had considered its two revolutionary objectives ("antiimperialism" and "antifeudalism") closely interrelated: a successful antiimperialist struggle could result only from the destruction of the remnants of feudalism, which was its native supporting base; at the same time, an antifeudalist social revolution could be carried out only on the basis of a successful national liberation struggle. Until the Eighth Plenum these two objectives had been considered parallel tasks of the Vietnamese revolution. However, to take advantage of the new political situation, the ICP leadership resolved that the two tasks need not be accomplished "evenly, like the two rails on the railroad track, but could progress unevenly according to the levels of achievement."[63] On this point, the resolutions of the Eighth Plenum stated explicitly:

> The Indochinese revolution is at present no longer a bourgeois-democratic revolution that solves the antiimperialist and agrarian problems. Rather, it is a revolution to solve only one urgent problem, that of national liberation. The Indochinese revolution during this period is, therefore, a revolution of national liberation.[64]

Was this conception of the Indochinese revolution a step backward for the Party? Or was it the beginning of a new period in the Vietnamese revolution? In its resolutions the conference ada-

---

61. In the section *"Chinh sach moi cua Dang"* [The new Party policy] of the Resolutions of the Eighth Plenum, quoted in Tran van Giau, *Giai cap cong nhan*, 3: 80.

62. Resolutions of the Eighth Plenum, quoted in Tran Huy Lieu, *Lich su tam muoi nam*, 3: 71.

63. Van Tao, Thanh The Vy, and Nguyen Cong Binh, *Lich su cach mang thang Tam* [History of the August Revolution] (Hanoi, 1960), p. 24.

64. Quoted in Tran Huy Lieu, *Lich su tam muoi nam*, 3: 71.

mantly disavowed either suggestion: the realization of the national liberation revolution meant neither the abandonment of the "anti-feudal" task of the Party nor the beginning of a new period, but the advancement in priority of one of the two traditional revolutionary tasks. Given the specific historical circumstances of Indochina at the time, temporary postponement of the agrarian revolution was necessary. This postponement, the Central Committee emphasized, was only a tactical move and in no way represented a change in the Party's long-term strategy. In the resolutions the Party leaders expressed the rationale thus:

> To put aside the bourgeois-democratic revolution and put forward the national liberation revolution does not mean that the Indochinese proletariat neglects the agrarian tasks, and it also does not mean that it takes a step backward. It means only to take a shorter step in order to try to take a longer one. Everyone knows that, at the present stage, unless the French and the Japanese are overthrown, not only will the nation remain in slavery forever, but the agrarian question will never be solved. Therefore, during this period, in order to solve the task of national liberation, it is not possible to put forward a second task that is not necessary for the entire people, yet is harmful to the first task.[65]

The resolution added specifically:

> At this time, if we put forward the slogan of overthrowing the landlords, distributing lands to the peasants, not only will we lose an allied force who would support us in the revolution to overthrow the French and the Japanese, but we would also push that force to the side of our enemy, as the rear guard of our enemy.[66]

More simply, what the Party leaders recommended at the Eighth Plenum was the principle of *them ban bot thu* (more friends and less enemies) at any one historical period, that is, the idea of fighting one enemy at a time. "Imperialism" and "feudalism" were equally enemies of the Vietnamese revolution, but a wise revolutionary strategist would not fight both these formidable forces at once; rather, realizing that in each specific historical period there are principal and secondary enemies, he would try to form a temporary alliance with the secondary foes in order to "neutralize" them and also to isolate and destroy the principal, concrete, and

65. Ibid., pp. 71–72.
66. Ibid., p. 72.

immediate enemy. Several years after the August Revolution, Truong Chinh, who was secretary-general of the ICP during the Viet Minh Front, explained the Party's strategic thinking thus:

> The imperialists and the feudalists were the two principal enemies of the Vietnamese people; but our enemy number one, the strongest and most dangerous enemy, was the imperialist aggressors. . . . During a particular period (at the beginning of the revolution), *one must concentrate the forces of the revolutionary struggle essentially on the imperialist aggressors,* one must consider the antiimperialist task as the first priority and concentrate all one's forces to realize that task at all costs. The antifeudalist task must always be subordinated to the antiimperialist task.[67]

As a corollary to the decision to emphasize the "national question," the Eighth Plenum resolved to settle the question of national liberation "within the framework of each Indochinese state."[68] Concretely, the conference called for the creation of the League for the Independence of Vietnam, usually called the Viet Minh Front, as a "national united front for Vietnam in particular" and not for the whole of Indochina. In theory, the Viet Minh Front was to help Cambodia and Laos establish their own, separate leagues. Together, the three national fronts would form a federal League for the Independence of Indochina.[69]

The decision to resolve the issue of national independence "within the framework of each Indochinese state" was a significant change of course for the ICP. Throughout its first decade the Party had stressed Indochina as a whole and played down the importance of the three constituent national entities. From October 1930 on, the revolutionary movement in each of these national units had been subsumed in the concept of an "Indochinese revolution." The notion of a "Vietnamese revolution," for example, had been officially condemned as parochial, and "nationalism" denounced as chauvinistic. Given this background, the decision to appeal to patriotism and a national liberation revolution in each of the Indochinese countries amounted to a reconceptualization of the character and tasks of the revolution in Indochina—and those of the ICP itself.

67. Truong Chinh, "Les principes stratégiques directeurs de notre parti," in *En avant sous le drapeau du parti* (Hanoi, 1965), p. 79 (italics in original).

68. Commission for Study, *Outline History,* p. 33.

69. Tran Huy Lieu, *Lich su tam muoi nam,* 3: 76.

It is impossible to exaggerate the practical importance of this new political line for the Communist seizure and retention of power in Vietnam. Just as its previous emphasis on the "class question" had isolated the ICP from the mainstream of Vietnamese nationalist sentiments, whose central concern had always been *danh tay* (fight the French) and *cuu quoc* (save the country), the patriotic emphasis of the new revolutionary line made it possible for the ICP to "find the way back to the nation" *(tim ve dan toc)*. The popularity of the Viet Minh Front during the August Revolution and the years that followed attested the correctness of the new line. For the first time since 1930, the Vietnamese Communists could fire the imagination of the young, rekindle the hopes of the old, and exploit to the fullest the nationalist sentiments aroused by wartime policies of the Decoux regime and the Japanese occupation forces. The thousands of young men and women who left their schools and jobs in Hanoi, Haiphong, and other urban centers to make the trek to the "liberated zone" in late 1944 and early 1945; the outpouring of public support from all social classes during the early years of the Viet Minh government—these were convincing testimonies to the success of the Eighth Plenum's political strategy.[70]

THE NATIONAL UNITED FRONT

In addition to its swift creation of popular support, which enabled the Communists to seize power in August 1945, the success of the Viet Minh Front had a longer-term significance. Although the concept of the National United Front had been presented at the Sixth Plenum in November 1939, not until May 1941 did the ICP resolve to implement it. Throughout its first decade the ICP had advocated several united fronts—the Antiimperialist Front (1930–1931), the Democratic Front (1937–1939), and so on—but because of the Party members' lack of enthusiasm for building front organizations, the earlier fronts had won few converts to communism. In contrast, the Viet Minh Front was exceptionally successful, both

70. Indeed, for more than a decade the name Viet Minh was almost synonymous with "patriotism"—so much so that, until recently, the standard justification of Vietnamese who worked with the Americans was "I, too, used to be with the Viet Minh" *(Truoc day toi cung co chan trong Viet Minh)*.

as an organizational preparation for insurrection and as an instrument for establishing Communist roots in society. The several fronts organized after 1945—such as the Lien Viet Front, the Fatherland Front, and South Vietnam's National Front for Liberation—were only variations of the National United Front policy.

Conceptually, the Viet Minh Front was never a political party, but an organizational front of the ICP, although the Party carefully camouflaged this fact at the time. The front was the organizational nexus of several political and social groups organized, sponsored, and orchestrated by the ICP on professional, ethnic, and religious lines. The Viet Minh bylaws stated in part:

> 2. *Principle:* United all the social classes, revolutionary parties, patriotic groups of the people, in order to expel the Japanese and French, render Vietnam entirely independent, and create a Democratic Republic of Vietnam.
> 3. *Conditions for joining Viet Minh:* Only organizations may be member of Viet Minh. Any political party or organization of the Vietnamese or minority people living in Vietnamese territory—regardless of their social class, religion, or political inclination—which accepts the objectives, principles, and program of the Viet Minh Central Committee is allowed to participate in the Viet Minh Front.[71]

In practice, the ICP created several mass organizations, all of which incorporated the title "National Salvation Association": Peasants' National Salvation Association, Students' National Salvation Association, Women's National Salvation Association, Teenagers' National Salvation Association, and so on. All the mass organizations affiliated with the earlier ICP-sponsored fronts also changed their names and became part of the Viet Minh. Together, these organizations acted as a shield to the Party. Individually, each organization translated esoteric Communist slogans into the everyday language and jargon of its group's members. In theory, then, the Viet Minh Front was the coalition of these National Salvation Assocations.

When put into operation worldwide around the beginning of the Second World War, the National United Front shed the "class" character traditionally associated with Communist-sponsored fronts and adopted a "national" character. Each party's united

71. Tran Huy Lieu et al., *TLTK*, 10: 53.

front was to involve the entire nation, regardless of social classes. Communists, while retaining their separate organizational identity, were temporarily to set aside their antagonism toward such traditional class enemies as capitalists and landlords in order to realize a broad alliance of all social classes and political groups. They were to make a common front not only with the Socialists and their leaders, but also with nonsocialists and even right-wing groups and individuals who were opposed to the Party's principal enemy at the moment: fascism, Nazi Germany, or Japan. This organizational tactic proved to be an efficient one worldwide. Thanks partly to the application of the new front concept, the Communists became a powerful, organized force that seized political power or participated in coalition governments in several European countries after the Second World War.

The creation of the Viet Minh Front in May 1941 was part of this pattern. The Vietnamese Communists called for an alliance not only between the workers and peasants, but of all classes, including the "feudalist elements" who were patriotic. While the Party organization continued to maintain its separate identity, the ICP (which kept its profile low and was rarely heard of during the war) sought to establish organizational control over not only the organized social and political groups, but also the "amorphous" masses. It attempted to win over to the Party's cause supporters from the entire political spectrum. In the hands of the ICP leadership, however, the national United Front was more than a device to control and mobilize the population. It was also a flexible tactic that enabled the Party to neutralize potentially dangerous elements and isolate a particular enemy at a particular time, thereby concentrating all available forces against one enemy. As General Giap put it:

> Our National United Front must be a vast assemblage: it must rally all the forces that are susceptible to being rallied, neutralize all the forces that are susceptible to being neutralized, divide all those who are susceptible to being divided, directing the sharp point of the struggle against the principal enemy of the revolution, the imperialist aggressors. Furthermore, it must be established on the foundation of the alliance of the workers and peasants, and placed under the leadership of the working class.[72]

The front concept, like Marxism itself, is based on an intrinsic-

72. Vo Nguyen Giap, *Guerre du people*, p. 31.

ally optimistic assumption that practical political human action is predictable and calculable. This involves belief in the malleability and manipulability of the inert human masses and in the inevitable defeat of an isolated enemy through a concerted mass action. The concept provides a model for revolutionary strategic calculations in the real political world. In this militarized model there exist two opposing sides: "the people" and "the enemy." Whoever has the support of "the people," whoever is successful in allying "the people" with his cause, whoever is able to control "the people" will inevitably triumph. The actors in the political arena are either friends or foes, allies or neutrals, and the spectators are regarded as potential converts to one's own or the enemy's camp, but must at all costs be drawn into the fray on the side of "the people."

"The people" comprise all the progressive elements led by the "vanguard Party," all their friends, sympathetic spectators, and even neutralized potential foes. It is inevitably the side of the absolute majority. Victory is its destiny. Organizationally, "the people" are aided, organized, and led by the "vanguard Party" of the working class, surrounded by mass organizations and secret allies who together form a "national united front" against the enemy.

The side of "the enemy" is characterized by its isolation from the masses. This side always comprises the principal enemy himself and his lackeys, who may be counterrevolutionaries or opportunists in his pay. The enemy, however, can never escape the hopeless position of being in the minority. In material terms, temporarily, the enemy is powerful. The people should respect this material power. But despite an invincible appearance, the enemy is destined to defeat. Isolated from the masses, abandoned even by his own potential friends who have been either won over or neutralized by the "vanguard Party," the enemy will eventually crumble in the face of a concerted onslaught by "the people."[73]

Characteristically, in this type of revolutionary equation, except

73. The National United Front could also be expanded to become an international united front. This was an important part of the Vietnamese strategy in its war of resistance against the United States. The object, again, was to win the support and sympathy of the entire world against the American "aggressors," "neutralize" the wavering elements, and divide the imperialist camp, thus isolating the principal, concrete, and immediate enemy of the Vietnamese revolution, "the U.S. aggressors." As Truong Chinh put it: "It is necessary to assemble all the forces in the entire world in opposing U.S. imperialism. We are glad to perceive that during

for the working class and the peasantry, led by the "vanguard Party," there is no fixed status for any social class or group. The forces of the revolution, or "the people," include four social classes:[74] the working class, which takes the leading role; the peasantry, which "forms the great revolutionary army"; the petite-bourgeoisie, which is an allied force of the revolution; and the national bourgeoisie, which is a "conditional" allied force of the revolution. Any other group or social class can at any given time be considered an "indirect rear guard" of the revolution or potential enemy agents.

Depending on the objective conditions of a particular historical period and the power needs of the Party, any group or social class may be friend or foe. A friend of the people during one historical period may become a foe during the next; even the principal enemy during one historical stage could be an "objective ally" of the revolution during the next period. Following this strategic calculation, the position of the French and the Japanese shifted rapidly throughout the Second World War. From September 1940, when the Japanese began occupation of Indochina, until March 1945, the "French and Japanese fascists" were considered the principal, concrete, and immediate enemy of the Vietnamese revolution. During this same period, the French Gaullists were considered an ally of the revolution. After March 1945, only the Japanese remained as

recent years, in reality, a *front of the people in the world supporting the Vietnamese people, and the Indochinese peoples to resist the U.S. imperialist aggressors* is being formed. That is a type of front, uniting actions with a concrete and limited goal. . . . The National United Front opposing the Americans in Vietnam, the United Front against the Americans of the Indochinese peoples, and the front of the people in the world opposing American imperialism, to defend national independence and peace—those are the three levels of front, surrounding and conquering U.S. imperialist aggression. Once these three levels of front are established, the American bandits will be tightly besieged within thousands of iron nets, and definitely will not be able to avoid a total defeat"; *Ve cong tac Mat Tran*, pp. 24–26 (italics in original).

74. Truong Chinh, "Les principes stratégiques," pp. 75–76. In the same work (p. 80) Truong Chinh stated: "From the moment a country is enslaved by foreign imperialists, the Communist party and the workers of that country ought to assemble all the national antiimperialist forces, however unimportant they might be, in order to isolate to the maximum the most dangerous enemies, who are the imperialists and their most zealous henchmen. It is necessary to create the Antiimperialist National United Front. In our country, this front is composed of four democratic classes of the people: the working class, peasantry, petite-bourgeoisie, and national bourgeoisie. It may also include democratic personalities and patriots originating from the class of the landowners."

the principal enemy; all French, including the recently defeated Vichy-oriented elements, were considered "objective allies" of the Vietnamese revolution, with whom an alliance could be formed.[75] In August 1945, as soon as the Japanese were defeated, they too ceased to be "the enemy." They had become "neutralized foes" and "objective allies" for a specific period. The French, meanwhile, were approaching "enemy" status.

For Communist revolutionaries this model of the political front is particularly useful for the calculation of revolutionary potential. Like the logistic calculations of any military conflict, it allows the leadership to assess the relative balance of forces, the sources of possible mass support for the movement, and possible enemy weaknesses. The Viet Minh Front's outline of the "balance of forces" at its inception is instructive:

A. REVOLUTIONARY FORCES

1. Vanguard forces: the proletariat of Indochina
2. Direct rear guard:
   a. At home: the peasantry
               all the antiimperialist strata of the entire nation
   b. Abroad: the resistance of the Chinese people
               the national liberation revolution of the peoples under French and Japanese domination
               the USSR

75. The ICP front policy in the immediate aftermath of the Japanese coup d'état of March 1945 was best summarized by Truong Chinh in an article published in July 1945: "In the past we urged 'Fight the fascist Japanese and French' while working for an alliance with Frenchmen who were opposed to fascism and the Axis powers. There was no contradiction in this. For we struggled against the Japanese and French ruling cliques, or the Japanese and French fascists, but not all Frenchmen, without discrimination between fascists and nonfascists. Today we call for a struggle against the Japanese but not a struggle against the Japanese and the French. This does not mean that we form an alliance without condition and without principle with the French Gaullists or approve the return of a French imperialist domination. The fact is, our concrete, immediate, and unique enemy at the moment is fascist Japan. Thus, it is up to us to formulate a slogan that would help solidify all the forces to fight the Japanese, while pulling to our side or neutralizing the other forces, allowing us a free hand to fight the Japanese. At present, the French [colonial government] in Indochina has been overthrown, and it would be superfluous to call for a struggle against the French. However, if for example we are faced with a French Gaullist menace in the future, who will prevent us from calling for a resistance against France?" ("Hay kip di vao duong loi" [Let us quickly follow the Party's line], *Co giai phong* [The liberation banner], 19 July 1945, reprinted in Truong Chinh, *Cach mang dan toc*, 1: 229–230).

3. Indirect rear guard:
   a. the covert and overt conflicts between the French and the Japanese
   b. the covert and overt conflicts within the ranks of the French and Japanese machinery of domination in Indochina
   c. the covert and overt conflicts between the agents of the French and those of the Japanese
   d. the War in the Pacific
   e. the World War

B. COUNTERREVOLUTIONARY FORCES

1. The French oppressors in Indochina and their lackeys
2. The Japanese fascists and their lackeys.[76]

A National United Front is a tactical concept, never a strategic one. Its flexibility permits the Communist party to alter its immediate course quickly, to deviate from its current path when expedient, but not necessarily to modify its strategic goals. The front is to be revised whenever the fundamental historical situation alters. During the "antiimperialist" phase (1941–1945), for example, the Viet Minh Front was the ICP's formulation of the National United Front. During the period of resistance to colonial reconquest (1946–1954), the Party launched the Lien Viet Front. When the ICP finally came to power in Hanoi, the Party launched the Fatherland Front (1955–). Whatever the name or the components, these fronts have all contained the essential elements of the National United Front policy launched in 1941. Understanding the nature and role of the National United Front policy is essential to an understanding of the activities of the Viet Minh Front from its formation until its seizure of power in the August Revolution.

MAKING PREPARATIONS FOR INSURRECTION

The Eighth Plenum resolved that "the preparations for an armed insurrection is the central task *(nhiem vu trung tam)* of our Party during the current period."[77] This emphasis on preparing for an armed insurrection was also a new departure for the ICP. Prior to this conference, decisions had been taken at the Central Commit-

76. Idem, "Chinh sach moi cua Dang" [The new policy of the Party], 23–24 September 1941, reprinted in *Cach mang dan toc*, 1: 144–145.
77. Tran van Giau, *Giai cap cong nhan*, 3: 115.

tee level to establish a workers' and peasants' government (in the *Political Theses* and at the Sixth and Seventh Plenums). These, however, had been only statements of intention: the ICP Central Committee had never before called for preparations for an insurrection, much less considered them a "central task."

To prevent "premature insurrections" such as the Nghe Tinh Soviet Movement and the Bac Son and Nam Ky Insurrections of 1940 (all of which had been initiated regionally without prior approval of the Central Committee) and to guide revolutionary activities during the war years, the "Resolutions" specified the conditions under which a general insurrection would have a reasonable chance of success.

> The Indochinese revolution must culminate in an armed insurrection. The following conditions should be present at the time of an armed insurrection:
>   The National Salvation Front would already have achieved unity throughout the country;
>   The people would no longer tolerate the yoke of domination by the French and the Japanese and be ready to sacrifice and take part in an insurrection;
>   The ruling circles in Indochina would have entered a general crisis affecting the economic, political, and military sectors to the extreme;
>   The presence of the objective conditions favorable for an Indochinese revolution include the following: a great Chinese victory against the Japanese, a revolution in France or in Japan, the victory of the democratic [Allied] side and the Soviet Union in the Pacific, the revolutions in the French and Japanese colonies reaching a boiling point, and especially the invasion of Indochina by either the Chinese, the British, or the Americans.[78]

At the heart of this decision to prepare for an armed insurrection was the strategy of "partial insurrection." It was resolved that before a geneal uprising could occur, there should be local and regional insurrections when the objective conditions were favorable. The "Resolutions" specified:

> We must always be prepared to have a force ready to combat the enemy at the most opportune moment. That is to say, in the near future, when the Pacific War and the resistance of the Chinese people turn out to be completely favorable for the success of an Indochi-

78. Ibid., p. 82.

nese revolution, at that time, with our prepared force, we can lead a partial insurrection, seizing victory from one region to another, opening the way for a general insurrection.[79]

In connection with this resolution, a Party document published after the Eighth Plenum added, "the insurrectionary tactic in this situation must be the guerrilla tactic."[80] Also, in implementing the partial insurrection strategy, the revolutionary force would have to "expand guerrilla warfare" and "establish revolutionary power wherever our guerrilla forces retain control."[81] Professor Tran van Giau, one of the principal ICP leaders during the 1930s and chairman of the Committee for the South (Uy ban Nam Bo) during the August Revolution, later called this strategy "a great, new, and important political thought for the coming evolution of the Vietnamese revolution during the increasingly difficult conditions of the World War."[82] Although the novelty of the strategy is debatable, there can be no doubt about its effectiveness in the August Revolution.

Most of the Viet Minh preparations for insurrection occurred after the spring of 1943. The eighteen months that followed the May 1941 plenum had seen little progress despite all the new plans and strategies. If anything, 1941 and 1942 appeared to be a time of continuing crisis for the ICP. Government repression made it impossible for a revival of Communist activities in the lowland, and the Viet Minh marked time even in the mountainous areas, where their organizational strength was supposed to be at its best. In a mop-up in the second half of 1941, the government forces virtually razed the Bac Son–Vu Nhai revolutionary base (one of the two Viet Minh strongholds), scattering the ragtag Viet Minh guerrilla troops and demolishing Communist organizations there. Beginning in 1943, however, an important new development changed the balance of forces in the world and Indochina. The Soviet victory at Stalingrad, the decline of the Axis military power in Europe, and

79. Ban nghien cuu lich su quan doi thuoc Tong cuc chinh tri, Quan doi nhan dan Viet Nam (Commission for the Study of the History of the Armed Forces of Vietnam of the Central Political Section, the People's Army of Vietnam), *Lich su quan doi nhan dan Viet Nam* [History of the People's Army of Vietnam] (Hanoi, 1977), p. 73.
80. Ibid.
81. Ibid.
82. Tran van Giau, *Giai cap cong nhan,* 3: 83.

Japanese military setbacks in China and the Pacific resulted in a definite deterioration of Axis military power. Within Vietnam itself, the Decoux administration's subservience to the Japanese, the internal conflict within the French community, and the growing isolation of the colonial government greatly reduced its prestige and authority. Meanwhile, Vietnamese would-be politicians who had admired, feared, or wanted to "exploit" Japan had begun to anticipate the possibility of a Japanese defeat.

Facing the new situation, the Standing Committee of the ICP Central Committee (Truong Chinh, Hoang Quoc Viet, Hoang van Thu, and possibly one other person) met in February 1943 to make concrete plans to accelerate the insurrectional preparations and to take advantage of the prevailing climate of suspicion. As it turned out, this conference, second only to the Eighth Plenum in importance, determined the direction and specific tactics of the Viet Minh Front until the Japanese coup in March 1945. To their chagrin the Party leaders observed that the ICP was far from being ready to perform its tasks. Despite the decision of the Eighth Plenum to prepare for insurrection, the Party "did not yet know how to plan itself in an emergency situation."[83] Workers' mobilization, which was supposed to be the spine of a Communist party's activities, demonstrated extreme weakness. The destruction of Party bases among workers in the factories of Hanoi, Haiphong, and Saigon, in the plantations, and in mining areas was so complete that for several years after the repression of 1940–1941 there was not one overt workers' organization in Bac Ky.[84] Even more discouraging, although there were some Party bases in rural areas and among the ethnic minorities in the mountainous areas, the ICP had no urban movement to speak of among the petite-bourgeoisie. Summarizing the condition of the Party at the time, the resolutions of the conference observed:

> There is lacking today in Indochina a national bourgeois revolutionary movement and a movement for youths and students. Consequently, the revolutionary campaign in Indochina is still narrow-based and has a worker-peasant character rather than a national character.[85]

83. Quoted in Van Tao et al., *Lich su Cach mang thang Tam*, p. 53.
84. Ibid., p. 59.
85. Quoted in ibid., p. 58.

THE URBAN PETITE-BOURGEOISIE AND
THE CULTURAL FRONT

After the February 1943 conference the ICP made a determined
drive to expand Viet Minh influence among the population. The
objective was to establish mass organizations among various social
strata and thus involve them in Communist-directed activities. The
workers' mobilization campaign was intensified under the direct
supervision of Hoang van Thu, a member of the Standing Committee of the ICP Central Committee.[86] This campaign, however, reg-
istered little success until the Japanese action in March 1945. Government repression, the low level of political awareness among the
workers, and the immunizing effects of Decoux's labor policy all
combined to render the Communist efforts largely futile. Success
in recruiting peasants, though greater, was limited largely to some
mountainous areas of Viet Bac, remote from effective government
administration. Until the end of 1943, Communist organizational
efforts in rural areas were limited to the three border provinces of
Cao Bang, Bac Can, and Lang Son (usually known as Cao-Bac-
Lang). Only late in 1944 and early in 1945 did Communist influence
begin to take hold among the peasants in these areas.

Paradoxically, the most significant political success of the Viet
Minh Front during these years involved its policy toward the urban
bourgeoisie. The ICP leadership, it will be recalled, had consisted
mainly of petit-bourgeois intellectuals who entered the Party as a
consequence of their participation in various patriotic movements
during the 1920s. Yet, throughout the 1930s, because of the ICP's
antinationalist and antibourgeois policies, which emphasized recruitment among the proletariat, the Communists had failed on the
whole to attract students, intellectuals, and other urban elements.
In a radical turnabout at the February 1943 conference, the Party
decided to launch a methodical campaign to enlist the support of
these urban elements. In the enthusiastic response of Vietnamese
youth to the government-sponsored "sport-and-youth movement,"
the ICP recognized an important source of potential support that,
left untapped, could be an instrument for the colonial government
or a rival, noncommunist political organization. A "cultural front"

---

86. Hoang van Thu was arrested in Hanoi in August 1943, while engaging in
workers' mobilization. He was executed on 24 May 1944.

(mat tran van hoa) was thus launched. The conference resolved that

> the Party ought to dispatch members who specialize in cultural matters to launch a movement of progressive culture, a national salvation culture, to oppose the retrogressive fascist culture. National salvation cultural organizations must be established in the cultural centers such as Hanoi, Saigon, Hue, etc., and [we ought to] make use of all the overt or semiovert forms [of organization] to unify the writers and intellectuals. For example, it is possible to organize such groups as "vanguard culture," "Marxist studies," "Vietnamese historical studies," etc.[87]

The campaign to enlist "the superstructure" of Vietnamese society has a much larger historical significance than Communist writers today, for reasons known to themselves, assign it. By the beginning of 1944 the ICP had assembled several well-known writers and artists to discuss the Party's cultural program and subsequently to form a Cultural National Salvation Association (Hoi Van Hoa Cuu Quoc), attaching itself to a popular literacy campaign called the Movement to Propagate Quoc Ngu (Phong Trao Truyen Ba Quoc Ngu). In June 1944 the ICP sponsored the creation of a mass organization for intellectuals (writers, artists, engineers, doctors, and other professionals). This was the Vietnamese Democratic Party.[88] Throughout 1944 the cultural front enlisted intellectuals, students, and urban youths in the Viet Minh. The majority of well-known intellectuals in the Tan Viet Nam (New Vietnam) Group leaned toward supporting the Viet Minh by the end of 1944.[89] The students and youth in various government-sponsored scout, youth, and student organizations were also steered gradually into supporting Viet Minh positions. Urban youths became Viet Minh "vanguards" during the "preinsurrectional period" in 1945. In August 1945 the powerful General Association of Students of Hanoi, heavily infiltrated by Viet Minh vanguards, played an important role in bring about Emperor Bao Dai's abdication. These

---

87. Quoted in Tran Huy Lieu, *Lich su tam muoi nam,* 3: 105.
88. The Vietnamese Democratic party and the Socialist party (formed in 1946) claim to represent the noncommunist voice in today's Vietnamese political system.
89. The Tan Viet Nam (New Vietnam) group included virtually all the best-known intellectuals in Bac Ky at the time. Several of its prominent members, such as Nguyen van Huyen, Phan Anh, Vu van Hien, Nghiem xuan Thien, and Phan Huy Quat later held responsible positions in various Communist and noncommunist Vietnamese governments.

were among the important results of the Viet Minh's "cultural front."

THE ETHNIC MINORITIES

Viet Minh preparations for insurrection during the war years centered on a so-called revolutionary base *(chien khu)* in Cao Bang, on the border of Kwangsi, China. Most of the population of this province consisted of minority ethnic groups such as the Tay, Nung, Man, Meo, and a small number of Vietnamese. The people in this region often have relatives and friends on both sides of the border. The proximity to China and the deep roots of communism in this area lay behind the Viet Minh choice of the area as its initial base. Since the late 1920s, the people of this region had been exposed continuously to Communist influence from both China and Vietnam. In 1929 the CCP had set up a short-lived soviet in the Lungchow area (southern Kwangsi) which left a deep impression on the people. As early as 1930 there had been ICP cells in Cao Bang. During the difficult days of 1932–1935, Cao Bang was one of the few regions of Vietnam where the ICP could continue to function, and it served as a link to the CCP across the border. Throughout the Popular Front period, Cao Bang generated the highest number of Communist-inspired activities among the mountainous provinces.

From late in 1940, the Communists could claim some political control of two areas that became revolutionary bases as the war continued and government control became progressively weaker: Bac son–Dinh Ca and the Cao-Bac-Lang, whose center of activities was Cao Bang. Having established almost complete control of Cao Bang in 1942–1943, the Viet Minh Front laid the foundations for an embryonic state within colonized Indochina. By mid-1943 a Viet Minh administrative apparatus had supplanted the local government administration. A postal system, complete with Viet Minh stamps, provided communication within the region. A public educational system was instituted. In the *chau* (the administrative unit in highland areas, equivalent to a county in the lowlands) of Ha Quang alone, the revolutionary government established ten primary schools in 1943. These public services went hand in hand with political activities. The revolutionary regime published a newspaper, the *Viet lap* (an abbreviation of Viet Nam doc lap, or Independent Vietnam) and countless political pamphlets, often prepared in three-word lines *(tam tu kinh)* or five-word lines *(Ngu tu kinh)*. Public demonstrations were organized frequently. Mobile teams brought propaganda materials to remote areas. In addition, the revolutionary regime established short-term, month-long courses in political and military tactics for its members.

All these activities were based on a specific combined political and military strategy. After political agitation (propaganda and organization), a military force was created on the foundation of the mass organizations already established. The results of this operation were firm revolutionary bases, in which a parallel Viet Minh administration could replace the government administration at will. In 1942 there were 235 militiamen in Ha Quang alone; in 1943 this figure reached 1,184 including 180 who belonged to "fighting squads" *(tieu doi chien dau)*. In 1942 there were "complete villages" *(xa hoan toan)*, that is, villages whose entire population belonged to one Communist-sponsored organization or another. By 1943 there were several "complete districts" *(tong hoan toan)* and "complete counties" *(chau hoan toan)*. By then the Viet Minh Front had 5,453 members of various mass organizations and 1,184 militiamen.[90] The residual strength of the Viet Minh "state" was tested when, in November 1943, the Decoux administration launched a systematic mop-up of Communist activities in this region. Although Viet Minh activities were somewhat weakened, in 1944, the front still had 4,000 members of mass organizations and 812 militiamen.[91] Cao-Bac-Lang remained a Viet Minh stronghold until the Japanese coup in March 1945, when revolutionary activities quickly spread from this region to the rest of Bac Ky and northern Trung Ky.

Behind the Communist success in developing the Cao-Bac-Lang region into a revolutionary base was the ICP's nationality policy *(chinh sach dan toc)*. From time immemorial, population settlement in Vietnam has followed a pattern observable throughout Southeast Asia, that is, a tendency for the more vigorous ethnic group to occupy the lowland, driving the less aggressive groups into the higher regions. This is the background of the difficult rela-

90. Vien Su hoc, To Lich su Cach mang thang Tam (Institute of Historical Studies, History of the August Revolution Cell), *Cach mang thang Tam (Tong khoi nghia o Ha-noi va cac dia phuong)* [The August Revolution (general insurrection in Hanoi and other localities)], 2 vols. (Hanoi, 1960), 1: 93 (hereafter cited as *CMTT*).
91. Ibid.

tions between the Vietnamese majority, which inhabits the low-lands, and the ethnic minorities, who make up 13 percent of the Vietnamese population[92] and who inhabit the middle plains and highlands of northwestern Bac Ky and the central highlands of Trung Ky.

Colonial policies deliberately exacerbated these ethnic difficulties. As the French conquered Vietnam, they employed a vicious racial policy as part of a divide-and-rule strategy. As defined by Galliéni, "the pacifier of Tonkin," this *politique de races* favored the use of latent racial hatreds to set one ethnic group against another to the advantage of the conqueror. Galliéni explained this racial strategy in the following terms:

> The study of the races that occupy a region determines the kind of political organization to give to it, and the means to use for its pacification. An officer who has succeeded in preparing a sufficiently exact ethnographic map of the territory under his command is well-nigh close to having obtained its complete pacification.
>
> Every agglomeration of individuals, race, people, tribe, or family represents a sum of either common or opposed interests. . . . There are hatreds, rivalries, that we should know how to disentangle and utilize to our profit, by opposing one against the other and by leaning on one the better to conquer the other.[93]

In implementing this racial policy, the conquerors sought, as early as the nineteenth century, to exploit the existing antagonisms among the various ethnic minorities, and especially those between the highland minorities and the lowland Vietnamese majority. To join the new colonial administrative apparatus with that of the traditional Vietnamese administration, they used Vietnamese personnel and tactics. Vietnamese mandarins and sheriffs were used to control the minorities; chiefs and notables of the more important minorities were employed to maintain control over the weaker races; meanwhile, minority troops were used in suppressing Vietnamese rebellions or as prison guards.[94]

The practical objective of the French policy was twofold: first to rigidify the ethnic boundaries, thereby promoting mutual hostility

92. Viet Chung, "National Minorities and Nationality Policy in the DRV," *Vietnamese Studies*, no. 15 (1968), p. 4.

93. H. Deschamps and P. Chauvet, *Galliéni pacificateur* (Paris, 1949), p. 239, as quoted in Isoart, *Phénomène national vietnamien*, pp. 153–154.

94. Isoart, *Phénomène national vietnamien*, p. 154; Viet Chung, "National Minorities," p. 8; Van Tao et al., *Lich su Cach mang thang Tam*, p. 21.

among the various groups and facilitating the task of pacification; second, and equally important, to transform the ethnic minorities into hostile communal barriers, thus isolating the lowland Vietnamese from Chinese assistance for their anticolonial resistance.[95] Until the end of the 1920s this policy proved quite successful. The Muongs, for example, in rallying to the French, delivered the rebellious Vietnamese King Ham Nghi and later the anticolonial leader Doc Ngu.[96] Meanwhile, the Thais, Yaos, Meos, Nungs, and Tays of the mountains of northwestern Bac Ky effectively isolated anti-French Vietnamese from southern China, where they had sought refuge and assistance.[97]

The Communist Vietnamese very early recognized the importance of the ethnic minorities to the Vietnamese revolution.[98] While the French, the traditional Vietnamese elite, and the Vietnamese population in general continued to treat the minority people as "savages" (*moi* or *man* or *tho*), the Communists were the first to advocate joint action by all the ethnic groups with a view to national independence and self-determination. This recognition is based on an understanding of both the strategic importance of the midland plains and highlands that frame Vietnam's rice-growing lowlands, and the important role of the ethnic minorities in a postcolonial multiethnic social system. Immediately after its founding, the ICP made its nationality policy explicit: "to achieve the unity of all nationalities on the basis of equality and mutual assistance with a view to winning together independence, freedom, and happiness."[99] In the "Resolutions" of the Macao Congress (1935), the Party reiterated its nationality policy, emphasizing the right to self-determination of the ethnic groups in Indochina in the following terms:

> The Congress recognizes the right of the minority people to self-determination as was expounded in 1932 in the Party's program of action with the full approval of the Communist International. It reminds all Party branches of their task of explaining to the Viet-

95. David G. Marr, *Vietnamese Anticolonialism, 1885–1925* (Berkeley, 1971), p. 72.
96. Isoart, *Phénomène national vietnamien*, p. 154.
97. Ibid.
98. For discussion of the ICP's policies toward the ethnic minorities, see Viet Chung, "National Minorities," pp. 11–21; see also Mai Elliot's introduction to Chu van Tan, *Reminiscences*, pp. 15–18.
99. Quoted in Viet Chung, "National Minorities," p. 11.

namese laboring masses and to the national minorities the important significance of the watchword "self-determination" and of close unity against the imperialists. The Communist party recognizes the right of all nationalities to full liberty. It opposes all colonial systems and all forms of oppression and exploitation, direct or indirect, of one nationality by another.[100]

The ICP succeeded in turning the French-erected barriers into shelters for communism. First, it recruited members from the minority communities themselves. In the case of the Tay and Nung especially, this recruitment was made much easier by the fact that many in these communities had relatives and friends living across the Chinese borders in southern Kwangsi, where Communist agitation had been strong throughout the late 1920s and early 1930s. Hoang van Thu, for example, a Tay who had gone to Kwangsi late in 1927 while studying in Hanoi and later an active ICP militant. In returned in 1930 to organize the first ICP section in Cao Bang.[101] Hoang Dinh Rong, another Tay, became a member of Thanh Nien in 1927 while studying in Hanoi and later an activie ICP militant. In 1932, at one of the lowest ebbs of the Communist movement in Vietnam, Hoang van Thu and Hoang Dinh Rong, accepting orders from the Overseas Leadership Committee, recruited Party members from the minority groups of the Lang Son and Cao Bang regions and sent them to China for training.[102] Bases of support in the Tay and Nung communities were expanded and later extended to the Yao (Man) and the Meo (Hmong). This expansion was most rapid during the Popular Front period and was later consolidated when Vietnamese Communist cadres became active in the region. To overcome language problems and cultural barriers, Viet Minh members learned the local dialects, wore local dress, followed the local customs, and often lived with local people.[103]

100. Ibid., pp. 11–12.

101. *Nhung nguoi cong san,* pp. 126–128; also *Nhan dan,* 20 January 1965. Patriotic activities began in the Cao Bang–Lang Son region in the second half of the 1920s. Hoang van Thu and Luong van Chi organized the first "patriotic youth group" in 1926, after a memorial service for Phan Chu Trinh (*Nhung nguoi cong san,* p. 126). By 1929 a Thanh Nien section had been established in this region. See Vien Su hoc, *CMTT,* 1: 82.

102. "Dong chi Le Hong Phong" [Comrade Le Hong Phong], *Nhan dan,* 27 January 1965.

103. Vo Nguyen Giap, for example, learned to speak Tay and Yao, and Pham van Dong became fluent in Tay. See George McT. Kahin, "Minorities in the Democratic Republic of Vietnam," *Asian Survey,* 12 (July 1972): 583.

Thus, the northwestern midlands and highlands of Bac Ky, instead of being anti-Vietnamese barriers as the French had hoped, from an early date became a frontier station at the Chinese border, where Communist cadres could rest and obtain necessary information before proceeding in either direction. From 1940 on, this region gradually became a solid Communist revolutionary base. The Bac Son Insurrection in September 1940, for example, was staged largely by Tay and Nung revolutionaries. The first National Salvation Army units were composed mainly of ethnic minority troops of Tay, Nung, and Yao origins and led by such men as Chu van Tan, a Nung (who became minister of national defense in 1946), and Le Quang Ba, a Tay (who later became a member of the Central Committee). In June 1945 this region became the cradle of the Democratic Republic of Vietnam with the founding of a "liberated zone" *(vung tu do)* governing six provinces of the midlands and highlands of northwestern Bac Ky. From Tan Trao, a village in Tuyen Quang province, the National Congress of the Viet Minh front officially launched the General Insurrection in August 1945. On 16 August 1945 General Vo Nguyen Giap led the first National Liberation Army units, composed mainly of minority troops, toward Hanoi to light the fuse of the August Revolution, in a symbolic reversal of tradition and a new beginning for ethnic minorities in Vietnamese national life.

MILITARY PREPARATION: POLITICS TAKES COMMAND

One question that has occupied students of the Vietnamese August Revolution is the importance of the role of the armed force in the Viet Minh preparations for insurrection.[104] The consensus appears to be that although the armed force played a considerable

104. During 1963 there was debate in North Vietnam on the different aspects of the August Revolution, culminating in a conference organized by the Historical Studies Institute on the occasion of the eighteenth anniversary of the August Revolution. The role of the military was one of the main topics of discussion. See Truong Chinh, "Mot so van de ve Cach mang thang Tam Viet Nam," *Hoc tap,* no. 92 (September 1963), pp. 1–10; Le Quoc Su, *NCLS,* no. 50 (May 1963), pp. 10–20; To Minh Trung's response to Le Quoc Su in *NCLS,* no. 53 (August 1963), pp. 16–24; and Nguyen Cong Binh, "Khoi dau va ket thuc cua Cach mang thang Tam" [The beginning and conclusion of the August Revolution], *NCLS,* no. 51 (June 1963), pp. 17–28.

role after the Japanese coup, especially in the creation of propaganda, the expansion of the Liberated Zone, and the intimidation of collaborators, its role was a limited one in the period before the Japanese coup.

Although the actual decision to create a Communist armed force originated at the Eighth Plenum, the policy of establishing a Communist military force dates to the beginning of the ICP. The *Political Theses* (1930), for example, called for the creation of a "worker-peasant army"; the Macao Congress (1935) repeated the resolution five years later; and the Sixth Plenum (1939) adopted a similar resolution when it called for the creation of a "National Revolutionary Army" (Quoc dan Cach mana Quan). What was new and important about the Eighth Plenum decisions was its determination of the specific character of the armed force and the concrete steps required to create it. More than just a statement of aspiration, this resolution formulated a specific strategy for building a Vietnamese army.

> We must choose the healthy, enthusiastic, and agile elements in the national salvation associations and the self-defense militia and organize them into guerrilla cells. . . . At present, the guerrilla cell is the fundamental form that will develop into regular guerrilla units.[105]

The plenum also recommended a step-by-step strategy to arm guerrilla fighters and give them experience.

> We must progress from acts of destroying Vietnamese traitors to ambushing enemy patrols and to attacks on the guard posts of the enemy. We must follow the motto "Seize the enemy's weapons" and "Arm ourselves while we fight!" in order to advance to big battles.[106]

Two important principles, borrowed from the Chinese People's Liberation Army (PLA), guided the building of the Viet Minh armed force.[107] First, as a logical extension of the strategy of partial insurrection, the guerrilla armed force must function on the

105. Quoted in Van Tao, "Mot vai nhan dinh ve qua trinh phat trien cua luc luong vu trang cach mang Viet-Nam, vai tro va tinh chat cua no trong giai doan gianh chinh quyen cach mang" [Some observations on the history of the development of the Vietnamese revolutionary armed force: Its role and character during the period of seizure of revolutionary power], *NCLS*, no. 93 (December 1966), pp. 17–18.

106. Quoted in ibid., p. 18.

107. Vo Nguyen Giap, *Tu nhan dan ma ra* [Born of the people] (Hanoi, 1964), pp. 64–65.

principle of mutual dependence and support between political and military development. That is, the armed force had to rely on the mass organizations to develop itself, and the mass organizations had to participate directly in armed struggles. As in the relationship between the fish and the water in the well-known Maoist formula, the guerrilla forces were to depend on the local population for sustenance and growth, to be extremely mobile and endlessly versatile. When necessary, they were to disperse themselves and blend with the population in order to build revolutionary organizations among the masses. When conditions permitted, they were to regroup, train themselves, and prepare for combat.[108] The Viet Minh guerrilla force was to be composed of local forces *(dia phuong quan)* capable of waging insurrection to seize and defend political power in a particular region, assist in the consolidation of that power, and expand Viet Minh influence to surrounding regions.

The primacy of politics was the second principle in the strategy of building the armed force. That is, the guerrilla armed force was to play a supporting political role and not necessarily a primarily military one. The motto of the Viet Minh guerrilla force was "Political actions are more important than military actions; propaganda is more important than fighting" *(Chinh tri trong hon quan su; tuyen truyen trong hon tac chien)*. This principle remained the guideline for all Viet Minh military activities at least until the Japanese coup.

The Chinese PLA contributed much to the initial efforts to create the guerrilla armed force. As early as 1940, both Pham van Dong and Vo Nguyen Giap had been sent to Yenan for political and military training.[109] Although, through a change of plans, they never reached Yenan and had to return to Vietnam to help build the Viet Minh movement, Chinese assistance continued in the form of military advisers and training. Chinese guerrilla warfare principles permeated the plans for building the Viet Minh force, and exchanges of Vietnamese and Chinese military cadres took place in the early 1940s. In 1942, for example, Yeh Chien-ying (today the

108. For the principles and practice in the construction of the Cuu Quoc Quan (National Salvation Army), see Ban nghien cuu lich su, *Lich su quan doi*, pp. 81–91.
109. Vo Nguyen Giap, "Ho Chi Minh, père de l'armée revolutionnaire du Vietnam," in Bui Lam et al, *Souvenirs sur Ho Chi Minh* (Hanoi, 1965), p. 183.

minister of national defense of the People's Republic of China) was in Cao bang as part of the Chinese effort to help the Viet Minh Front build its armed force.[110] In addition, to improve the quality of military cadres the ICP in the same year sent one hundred youths, most of them from the two *chau* (prefects) of Ha Quang and Hoa An, Cao Bang province, "to study for a period of two years at the Liu ch'iao Military School in China."[111]

Until March 1945 Viet Minh military activities were limited to two areas: Bac Son–Vu Nhai and the Cao-Bac-Lang. A National Salvation Army was established at the *chien khu* at Bac Son–Vu Nhai early in 1941. Led by Phung Chi Kien, a member of the Central Committee; Huy Com, a graduate of the Whampoa Academy; and Chu van Tan, this was the first local force of the ICP.[112] Attacked and harassed continuously during its first few years of existence, this unit had no more than propaganda value, which was not always favorable for the Viet Minh. Its activities often brought reprisals by the colonial army to the areas that sheltered it. In October 1944 (with an army of three hundred men and a total of fifty-six guns of all sorts), the National Salvation Army waged a local insurrection. In the ferocious repression that followed, the remaining force of 200 was dispersed to Yen The, Phu Luong, Dai Tu, and Cho Chu, with only a small contingent remaining in the Bac Son–Vu Nhai area to keep in touch with the local people.[113]

At the *chien khu* at Cao-Bac-Lang an entirely different situation existed. Here, under the direct supervision of Nguyen Ai Quoc, assisted by Vo Nguyen Giap, the local guerrila force was developed methodically, step-by-step. Initially the force had neither men or weapons, and a specific strategy was devised to gain both. Soon, when it became evident that men were easier to come by than weapons, it was decided to select fighters from the enthusiastic and able-bodied members of the various mass organizations, and to obtain weapons gradually from combat. First, a self-

110. Vien Su hoc, *CMTT,* 1: 88.
111. Ibid.
112. Phung Chi Kien was killed in battle in July 1941; Huy Com was arrested in the same battle and died later in the Cao Bang prison.
113. Chu van Tan, *Reminiscences,* pp. 193–195; see also Vien Su hoc, *CMTT,* 1: 69–71.

defense militia *(tu ve)* was selected from the male and female members of the mass organizations; they remained with the population to defend their own areas. Second, units of "fighting self-defense militia" *(tu ve chien dau)* were formed from the best elements of the local militia. Using their own home areas as bases, they expanded their military and political activities into neighboring areas. These so-called semi-separation units *(doi quan ban thoat ly)* formed the regional force. According to General Vo Nguyen Giap,

> the Party organized the units of fighting self-defense militia from the bravest elements of the self-defense militia in the villages; virtually all the male and female youths in the "complete village" [villages under complete Viet Minh control] participated in the various self-defense militias and went through military training. Every village had about one or two sections of fighting self-defense militia.[114]

Third, the "separation units" *(doi quan thoat ly)*, the first of the ICP "regular" guerrilla army, were developed. These units fought away from their home base and were involved in agricultural production for self-sustenance. By 1942 there were nineteen such "separation units" under the leadership of Vo Nguyen Giap. These units formed the "Southward March" *(Nam Tien)* Brigade, whose function was to keep open the "safe corridor" between Cao Bang and the Red River delta. Although on paper this force sounded impressive and although it did play a considerable role in propaganda after the Japanese coup, its activities were limited to the Cao-Bac-Lang region.

DIPLOMACY

Closely connected with the Viet Minh Front's political preparations of the Vietnamese population was the conduct of relations with the non-Vietnamese anti-Japanese forces (the Gaullists in Vietnam, the American OSS in southern China, and the Kuomintang). These efforts were part of the Viet Minh application of the National United Front to widen its circle of support and at the same time isolate its principal enemies, the Japanese and the Decoux regime. Although from today's perspective these diplomatic

114. Vo Nguyen Giap, *Tu nhan dan*, p. 64.

efforts appear to be a historical curiosity and, in terms of concrete material assistance for the Viet Minh, deserve no more than a few footnotes, they help illumine both the conditions under which the Viet Minh Front labored to power and the Viet Minh strategy in dealing with the international forces that shaped the destiny of Vietnam.[115]

The Viet Minh decided at its February 1943 conference to forge amicable relations with non-Vietnamese anti-Japanese forces. In view of the altered world situation since the Eighth Plenum, the Party resolved:

> . . . whichever War does a disservice to fascist Germany and aids the Soviet Union is progressive; on the contrary, whichever war benefits Germany and opposes the interests of the Soviet Union and her allies is reactionary. For that reason, the Party is resolutely opposed to the Pacific war.[116]

This decision led to a skillful attempt to exploit the advantageous political conditions created by the conflict between the Vichyites and Gaullists. Under the direct leadership of Truong Chinh, the Party's secretary-general, the ICP attempted to create an "Indochinese Democratic Front to Oppose Fascist Japan" (Mat tran Dan chu Dong-duong Chong Phat-xit Nhat), whose main objective was to form an alliance with the French Gaullists in Indochina.

In February 1944 the Party proposed the following conditions for collaboration with the Gaullists:

> 1. The French Gaullists and the Indochinese revolutionary parties will coordinate their activities against their common enemies, namely the French and Japanese fascists;
> 2. The French Gaullists must recognize the rights to freedom and independence of the Indochinese peoples.[117]

---

115. Several works have dealt competently and in detail with these relationships. For the relations between the Viet Minh Front and the French Gaullists, see Philippe Devillers, *Viet-Nam de 1940 à 1952*, pp. 96–113; and Jean Sainteny, *Histoire d'une paix manquée: Indochine 1945–1947* (Paris, 1954). The most detailed account of the relationship between the Viet Minh Front and the OSS is in Archimedes L. A. Patti, *Why Viet Nam? Prelude to America's Albatross* (Berkeley, 1980); see also Charles Fenn, *Ho Chi Minh: A Biographical Introduction* (London, 1973), pp. 65–84. For a detailed and comprehensive account of the relationship between the Viet Minh Front and the Kuomintang and affiliated anti-French Vietnamese groups in southern China, see King Chen, *Vietnam and China, 1938–1954* (Princeton, 1969), pp. 33–98.

116. Tran Huy Lieu et al., *TLTK*, 10: 79.

117. *Co giai-phong* [Banner of liberation], 3 (15 February 1977).

For their part, the Viet Minh Front agreed to recognize the French right to protection of life and property, and to residence and livelihood in Indochina upon the success of the revolution.[118] In November 1944 a delegation of the Central Committee of the Viet Minh Front met with representatives of a French Socialist-Communist group (Nhom Xa hoi–Cong san) in Hanoi. The Viet Minh delegates reportedly warned the French of the inevitability of the Japanese attack on the colonial government and proposed close collaboration between the Gaullists and the Viet Minh Front. They also put forward three demands:

1. Help bring about a cessation of the collection of paddy;
2. Help effect a release of political prisoners;
3. Give weapons to the Viet Minh Front to fight the Japanese.[119]

Although the Gaullists rejected the third demand outright, they apparently did take some action on the other two. One hundred fifty political prisoners were released in Hanoi and "tens of others" were released in Hoa Binh after this meeting. There were no other concrete results of the negotiations between the Viet Minh and the Gaullists in Vietnam.

In addition to the attempt to form an alliance with the French Gaullists, little else of a diplomatic character occurred prior to the Japanese coup. In 1944 the Viet Minh Front approached the Office of Strategic Services (OSS), a clandestine American group operating intelligence, counterintelligence, undercover propaganda, and sabotage in southern China; but there were no relations between the two organizations until May 1945. A complex relationship between the Kuomintang government and the Vietnamese community in exile in southern China led to the formation of several Kuomintang-supported groups and also involved the arrest of Nguyen Ai Quoc in 1942 (he was suspected of being a "French-Japanese spy")[120] and his detention for more than two years. These events, however, were not part of the Viet Minh preparations for an insurrection. In short, although the establishment of relations between the Viet Minh Front and non-Vietnamese anti-Japanese organizations succeeded in advertising the front's existence as an

118. Ibid.
119. Tran Huy Lieu et al., *TLTK*, 10: 84.
120. Chen, *Vietnam and China*, p. 56.

effectively organized Vietnamese political group, there was little significance to the relationships in the period before the Japanese coup d'état of March 1945.

AN ABORTED INSURRECTION

By mid-1944 the world situation had changed rapidly, favoring Allied forces in both Europe and Asia. The destruction of the Axis was only a matter of time. In Indochina, the Decoux administration was becoming more isolated than ever from both the native population and the French community. At the same time, as it became more subservient to the Japanese, its authority sank progressively lower. Facing this new situation, on 7 May 1944 the Central Committee of the Viet Minh issued a "Directive on the Preparation for Insurrection" ("Chi thi ve sua soan khoi nghia"). This important directive approached pragmatically all the basic questions of an armed insurrection.

> 1. Who will fight the enemy? Our entire people. . . . We ought to have the basic revolutionary armed units, which have been well prepared . . . to forge ahead, supported by the masses of the population.
> 2. With what can we fight the enemy? . . . There are two ways to obtain weapons: fabricate them by ourselves and buy or seize them from the enemy. . . . Our people must fabricate some of the weapons, with which we can destroy the enemy. . . . Whatever we cannot fabricate we must buy or seize from the enemy. . . . We must attack military outposts, weapons sheds, and enemy patrol units in order to seize their weapons. . . . We must try our best to mobilize the troops of the enemy, . . . awaken their political consciousness, so that they would bring enemy weapons to us.[121]

As the next few months brought ever more favorable events (the fall of the Pétain-Laval government, the Allied entry into France, the bombardment of important Japanese naval bases, the movements of Vietnamese peasants opposed to French and Japanese agricultural policies), the ICP's Interprovincial Committee for Cao-Bac-Lang believed a "revolutionary situation" to be imminent and decided to launch an armed insurrection and local guerrilla warfare in this region in preparation for a general insurrection. The

121. Tran Huy Lieu et al., *TLTK,* 10: 98, 101–102.

committee was about to hold a final meeting to decide on the date and time for the general insurrection, when Nguyen Ai Quoc returned from China[122] and, upon hearing the plans, vetoed the entire project.

In Nguyen Ai Quoc's view, a revolutionary situation did not yet exist in the country.[123] Although the movement had reached its height in Cao-Bac-Lang, no other region in the country was in any way prepared to engage in supportive military action. Under such conditions, it would be easy for the French to crush the revolutionary guerrilla forces. Nguyen Ai Quoc reportedly emphasized:

> The phase of the peaceful revolution is already past, but the hour of a general insurrection has not yet arrived. The political struggle [alone] is no longer sufficient, but an armed insurrection is still too dangerous for us. The struggle will thus have to pass from politics to military action. But in the immediate future political agitation must carry more weight than military activities.[124]

Nguyen Ai Quoc recommended the creation of an Armed Propaganda Brigade for the Liberation of Vietnam (Doi Viet Nam Tuyen Truyen Giai Phong Quan), whose military activities were to help mobilize the population but not necessarily to engage in combat for position. On 22 December 1944, the Armed Propaganda Brigade for the Liberation of Vietnam was formally established under the command of Vo Nguyen Giap. Composed of thirty-four fighters (thirty-one male and three female), this brigade was initially divided into three squads. For weapons, this army had a total of two Chinese-made automatics *(pac-hoocs),* seventeen rifles, fourteen rear-loading rifles, one submachine gun with 150 bullets, and six time bombs. It had a military budget of 500 piasters.[125] The slogan "Politics takes command" remained the governing principle of this Army. Today, 22 December is celebrated as the birthdate of the Vietnamese People's Army.

By the end of 1944 the Vietnamese Communist movement had

---

122. Nguyen Ai Quoc was arrested in August 1942 in Chinghsi by the Kuomintang and was released only in September 1943. For a detailed discussion of Nguyen Ai Quoc's experience in China during this period, see Chen, *Vietnam and China,* pp. 55–85.
123. See Chapter 6.
124. Quoted in Vo Nguyen Giap, "Ho Chi Minh, père de l'armée," p. 209.
125. Tran Huy Lieu et al., *TLTK,* 10: 164.

made an amazing recovery. Although in actual membership the ICP was still minuscule, it had reestablished itself as a credible revolutionary organization. This reversal had been made possible to a large degree by favorable "objective historical conditions"— the Japanese occupation, the erosion of French colonial authority, and the resurgence of Vietnamese patriotism. The "subjective factor," however, was equally important. By the end of 1944 the ICP once more had a central leadership commanding the loyalty of Party members throughout the nation, although admittedly such allegiance may have been less than complete in the far South. By this time, too, perhaps thanks in part to its isolation from the Comintern and fraternal parties, the Party had put aside sectional interests and evolved a flexible, independent revolutionary line that appealed to a national constituency. Revolutionary patriotism had resumed importance at the expense of proletarian internationalism. Finally, thanks to its National United Front policy, the ICP, through its Viet Minh Front, could involve large numbers of people in the activities of workers' unions and youth, professional, and other organizations that were formally outside the Party but operated under Party guidance and the supervision of disciplined ICP members. At the beginning of 1945, as the war entered its final phase, the Communists of Vietnam were poised to stage a general insurrection whenever an "opportune moment" *(thoi co)* presented itself. That moment arrived in the summer of 1945, following the destruction of French colonial power in a Japanese coup d'état on 9 March 1945.

CHAPTER SIX

THE AUGUST
REVOLUTION

The French have fled, the Japanese have
capitulated, Emperor Bao Dai has abdicated. Our
people have broken the chains of colonialism which
have fettered us for nearly a century in order to
create an independent Vietnam. Our people have at
the same time overthrown the monarchical regime
which has reigned supreme for dozens of centuries
to establish a democratic republic.

Declaration of Independence (1945)

Until 9 March 1945 Vietnam was a French colonial possession governed by the repressive regime of Governor-General
Decoux, who considered all Communists subversive rebels to be
hunted out, arrested, and imprisoned. Six months later, in late
August, the French rulers were in prison and the Communist
Vietnamese controlled the government. Virtually unknown when
the year began, their leaders carried death sentences or were still
under indictment for treason when they came to power. With the
possible exception of Russia's October Revolution, there has
rarely been such a sharp turn in history. This dramatic reversal
resulted from a combination of events in the final months of the
war: the Japanese coup d'état of 9 March 1945; the general political confusion and institutional breakdown in its aftermath, and a

devastating famine. In the midst of this political malaise a mass movement led by the Vietnamese Communists materialized and gained momentum daily. Within ten days of the Japanese surrender the Communists were in control of the country. In Leninist terminology, the events between 9 March 1945 and the Japanese surrender in August 1945 could be labeled a "revolutionary situation." In Vietnamese history the events of the second half of August 1945 are called the August Revolution.

THE JAPANESE INTERLUDE

By March 1945, France and Japan had uneasily coexisted on Vietnamese soil for more than four years. Two conditions made this collaboration possible: the colonial government's continued loyalty to Vichy; and Japan's military superiority in the Pacific.

The situation changed abruptly on the evening of 9 March 1945. Without waiting for a response to an ultimatum to Governor-General Decoux, which demanded the virtual transformation of French Indochina into a Japanese possession,[1] Japanese troops attacked every center of French power throughout Indochina at nine P.M. In less than twenty-four hours most of the French Indochina army had been put out of combat. All major cities were placed under Japanese control. Saigon surrendered during the night; Hue fought back but surrendered at around seven the next morning; Hanoi held out until the afternoon of March 10. The French colonial system, which had lasted more than eighty years, thus came tumbling down. Nearly all French civilian and military

---

1. The Japanese *aide-mémoire* to Decoux "solicit[ed] . . . the Governor-General of Indochina to show proof of the expressed willingness to defend Indochina to the end, by collaboration with Japan against the eventual invasion of the Anglo-American forces." It demanded that the French armed forces—army, navy, air force, and armed police—be put under Japanese command; and that all movement, organization, and armament of French troops be put under Japanese supervision. The ultimatum was delivered to Decoux at 7:00 P.M. He was given two hours to reply. At 9:05 that evening, Captain Robin, the French messenger for the governor-general, telephoned Ambassador Matsumoto to request an extension of the deadline. The Japanese diplomat replied in an angry tone that he considered the request a negative reply to the ultimatum. By 9:20 the Japanese had occupied the government palace without firing a shot. A few hours later, Saigon was taken. Decoux, *A la barre*, p. 330; also Gaudel, *Indochine en face du Japon*, pp. 141–155.

leaders, including Governor-General Decoux and the well-known Generals Mordant and Aymé, were made prisoners. On 10 March Radio Tokyo announced that "the colonial status of French Indochina has ended." The traditional elite of Indochina, who had made a profession of loyal collaboration with whichever foreign imperialists were in power, quickly transferred their loyalty. On 11 March Emperor Bao Dai, who had just returned from a hunting trip, declared the independence of Vietnam, the reunification of Tonkin with Annam, the abrogation of the Treaty of Protectorate with France, and Vietnam's willingness to collaborate with Japan. On 13 March King Norodom of Cambodia announced his kingdom's independence from France and sincere collaboration with Japan. King Sisavang Vong of Laos followed suit with a similar declaration on 8 April. Indochina ceased to be French.[2]

The rationale for the Japanese action was quite apparent. By late 1944 the Decoux regime had outlived its usefulness to the Japanese. In France the Vichy government had collapsed, and General de Gaulle had long declared his government's intention to "liberate" Indochina. In the Pacific, General MacArthur had already entered the Philippines, and there was a clear possibility of an imminent Allied invasion of Indochina to truncate Japanese connections with the rest of Southeast Asia. Within Indochina itself, the opportunism of the colonial government and the French nationals had become insupportable. During the heyday of the Vichy regime, the colonial government and a sizable number of Frenchmen had put aside their fair-weather patriotism and openly supported the Axis powers and the Pétain-Laval government, resolutely persecuting the Gaullist Resistance movement in Indochina.[3] By mid-1944, when the situation in Europe had changed in favor of "Free France," the French of Indochina had quickly changed their political allegiance. Decoux ordered the removal of portraits of Marshal Pétain from roads and public buildings and publicly expressed his support of liberated France. While the portrait of General de Gaulle now emblazoned some government offices, Generals Mordant and Aymé were making plans to oppose the Japanese in

---

2. This discussion of the Japanese *coup d'état* is based on Gaudel, *Indochine en face du Japon*, pp. 141–155; Legrand, *Indochine à l'heure japonaise*, pp. 263–281; and Decoux, *A la barre*, pp. 160–179.

3. See Legrand, *Indochine à l'heure japonaise*, pp. 160–172; Pedrazzani, *France en Indochine*, pp. 111–113.

the event of an Allied intervention. Meanwhile a French information service in Indochina, provided the Allied forces with military intelligence, and French Resistance forces were accumulating supplies by parachute.[4]

Faced with the new situation, the Japanese decided to activate "Operation Mei," the code name for a contingency political and military plan prepared in December 1943–January 1944, to "disarm" the French Indochina army.[5] Although available information indicates that the Japanese would have preferred to keep the Decoux regime in place until the end of the war, they were forced to act to protect themselves. In an interview with the author in 1966, former Ambassador Yokoyama, Japan's plenipotentiary representative to Vietnam during the "Japanese interlude," dwelt at some length on this issue:

> As long as the French cooperated with our armed forces, we found it more practical to assure for ourselves this cooperation. As long as we had the French cooperation, we did not want to occupy the country.
>
> This entente continued for a number of years. But the Japanese defeat had then become imminent, and the French attitude in Indochina also changed, in the sense that they now received orders from the French Resistance and wanted to resist cooperation with us. Although their communications with the French Resistance were secret, we knew all about their exchanges.
>
> When the French intentions were clear, that they did not want to continue cooperation with us, and there was a possibility that they would work with the Allied forces, we decided that we had to overthrow them. The main reason was to avoid being caught between two fires. We were afraid the French forces would cooperate with the Allies behind our back.[6]

---

4. According to André Gaudel, the intelligence supplied by the French information service in Indochina was so precise that "four cruisers, five destroyers, eight transport ships, six oil tankers, three escort ships, two cargo ships, and thirteen other ships, or a total of forty-one ships, were sunk or severely damaged between 14 October 1944 and 9 March 1945, while 1,800 enemy troops were eliminated during these attacks." See Gaudel, *Indochine en face du Japon,* p. 136.

5. For a discussion of the Japanese political and military plans for Indochina and especially "Operation Mei," see Kenneth E. Colton, "The Influence of Japanese Wartime Policy on the Independent Political Movement in Vietnam after March 1945" (Paper delivered at the 1971 Annual Meeting of the American Political Science Association), pp. 2–4.

6. Interview with Ambassador Yokoyama, Paris, 3 March 1966. Ambassador Yokoyama was then on an official Japanese mission to France to find a peaceful solution to the U.S.–Vietnam War.

The period of Japanese military rule from March until August 1945 is now called the Japanese Interlude.

DOC LAP BANH VE

From 9 March until the Japanese surrender in August 1945, Vietnam enjoyed what was popularly called a *doc-lap banh ve,* or pseudo-independence,[7] which brought little change in political life. Except that Asian faces had replaced European ones in the top administrative posts, there were no perceptible changes in Indochinese political structures, at least in the early months after the coup. In Nam Ky, which was placed under the direct control of the Japanese military authorities, a Japanese "governor," Minoda, had replaced the French governor; in Trung Ky, Ambassador Yokoyama assumed the functions of the former French *résident supérieur* in advising the Vietnamese Emperor on political matters; in Bac Ky, a Japanese diplomat, Tsukamoto, took the place of the former French resident. Meanwhile, Indochina remained under the supervision of General Tsuchihashi as governor-general, in fact though not in title.

It would, however, be a mistake to claim that Japan tried to transform Vietnam into a Japanese possession. Aside from trying to prevent anti-Japanese elements (such as the Viet Minh Front) from causing security problems, the Japanese did not seem to have any definite political program for Vietnam. After the coup, the Japanese did everything possible to minimize changes in internal Indochinese politics, for such changes would have affected their military objectives. To the disappointment of many Vietnamese, the Japanese initially retained the five separate French administrative structures for Indochina. Of the three Vietnamese *pays* only Trung Ky (Annam) and Bac Ky (Tonkin) were placed under the direct administration of the Emperor of Annam, while Nam Ky (Cochin China) and the three enclaves of Hanoi, Haiphong, and Danang were placed under Japanese military administration. More

7. The term *banh ve* (make-believe cake) comes from the term *ca ve* (make-believe fish) and has a similar meaning. The story is told of a family who had little else to eat at mealtimes but rice. Thereupon the father hit upon a brilliant idea. He sketched the figure of a salty dry fish and hung it on the wall at dinnertime. As they ate their food, the children were supposed to look at the fish *only a few times* during the meal. One day the littlest complained that his older brother looked at the fish too often. "Don't worry, son," said the father. "He will be thirsty the whole day."

disappointing still, in the wake of the coup the Japanese appealed for French functionaries to return to their posts, reflecting the Japanese intention only to "disarm" the French and detain top civilian French leaders but otherwise to retain the services of the rank-and-file French bureaucrats. Contrary to widespread expectations, the Japanese did not bring back Prince Cuong De, whom they had groomed since 1905 for such an occasion, but instead kept Bao Dai on the throne.[8] Twice Bao Dai asked the Japanese to transmit an invitation to Ngo Dinh Diem, a reputed pro-Japanese and pro–Cuong De partisan, to form a government. Diem never received Bao Dai's invitations. Instead, the Japanese brought back to Hue Tran Trong Kim, a well-known Confucian scholar whom they had placed under "protective custody," first in Singapore and then in Thailand. On 17 April 1945, having waited in vain for Ngo Dinh Diem's response, Tran Trong Kim reluctantly agreed to form a government.[9]

The accomplishments of the Tran Trong Kim cabinet were mea-

8. Ambassador Yokoyama told the author in March 1966 that Prince Cuong De had been brought back to Hong Kong, waiting to assume a position as head of state of Vietnam, but "for reasons of age and health" he did not proceed to Vietnam. There were two reasons, said he, for keeping Bao Dai: first, he was much younger; and second, "il était là sur place." According to Komatsu Kiyoshi, however, Prince Cuong De never left Japan, was in good health, and was waiting anxiously to return to Vietnam. In July 1945, following a successful intervention by Tran Trong Kim, Cuong De was allowed by Bao Dai to return to Vietnam for a sentimental, not political, journey. Cuong De reportedly sat at Tokyo's Haneda Airport for three consecutive days, awaiting a Japanese military plane to take him to Hanoi and then Hue. No plane ever arrived for him. Komatsu Kiyoshi, *Betonamu* (Tokyo, 1955), cited in Colton, "Japanese Wartime Policy," p. 19. Komatsu's work is a history of Vietnamese-Japanese relations in the Vietnamese nationalist movement.

9. I am grateful to Mr. Hoang Xuan Han, Dr. Ho Ta Khanh, Mr. Nguyen Manh Ha, and Ambassador Yokoyama for having granted me a series of in-depth interviews on the situation in Vietnam during the Japanese interlude. My discussion of the Tran Trong Kim cabinet is based on these interviews and on the memoirs of Tran Trong Kim. Mr. Hoang Xuan Han, in his interview, and Mr. Tran Trong Kim, in his memoirs, both insisted that Bao Dai had written to Ngo Dinh Diem twice, offering him the premiership. Former premier Tran Trong Kim reported, "I was waiting [for Diem's response] for nearly ten days. I came to see the Japanese Supreme Adviser [Yokoyama] every three or four days. At the beginning the Japanese Adviser said he did not know where Mr. Diem lived. Later he said Mr. Diem was ill and could not come" (*Mot con giu bui*, p. 50). Diplomatic illness, it appears, must have been on the rise in those days. Meanwhile, Dr. Diem's relatives in Hue were waging an energetic campaign by leaflets and whispers, calling for a Ngo Dinh Diem cabinet (ibid., p. 64). As for Mr. Diem himself, it was widely known that he wandered between his brother's bishopric in Vinh Long and the Japanese commandant's headquarters in Saigon, futilely awaiting an invitation to form a government.

ger. Whatever it achieved in terms of wresting Vietnamese
sovereignty from the Japanese appeared to be a consequence of
Japanese policy, not the result of Vietnamese pressure (although it
was doubtful if a government led by pro-Japanese hands such as
Prince Cuong De and Ngo Dinh Diem would have done any better).
Three months after the coup, the Japanese government had neither
officially recognized Vietnamese independence nor signed any
treaty with the new government. Among the Vietnamese who had
enthusiastically hailed the Japanese action as the beginning of Vietnamese independence and freedom, some now voiced doubts
about Japanese sincerity. *Ngay nay* [Nowadays], a Hanoi periodical,
wrote, for example:

> Three months have passed since the coup d'état, yet the situation
> remains in limbo and nothing is clearcut. There has been no treaty
> signed between Japan and Vietnam to set the limits of power and
> responsibility of the two governments on the questions of territory
> and the organization of this country. . . . The essential thing is for
> the Japanese government to declare its recognition of the indepen-
> dence of Vietnam and sign treaties with the Vietnamese government
> in the near future.[10]

Until its surrender in August, Japan never formally recognized the
Bao Dai–Tran Trong Kim government. As their defeat became
increasingly apparent, however, the Japanese did make concessions. In July 1945, one month before the surrender, they agreed to
return Haiphong, Hanoi, Danang—the extraterritorial cities—and
Nam Ky, the colony, to Vietnam. This concession then allowed
Emperor Bao Dai to issue an imperial decree on August 14 abolish-
ing the treaties of 6 June 1862 and 15 August 1874 ceding Nam Ky
to France, and to unite it with the rest of the country. However, by
the time Nguyen van Sam, the Vietnamese imperial delegate,
reached Saigon to oversee the reintegration of Nam Ky with Vietnam, the August Revolution had already swept the entire country.
There are no other known accomplishments of the Tran Trong Kim
cabinet. At the time of the Japanese surrender, it was on the verge
of self-dissolution without a replacement.

The outburst of Vietnamese political participation was one of the
most curious phenomena of the Japanese administration. Frustrated for so many decades by having to stand on the sidelines and
observe the shaping of their nation's destiny, the urban elite of

10. *Ngay nay*, 2 June 1945.

Vietnam had been quietly yearning for an opportunity for political participation. Although the political appetite of some had been whetted by the liberal colonial policies of the Popular Front period, it had been dampened by the repressive Catroux and Decoux regimes. The comparative political freedom under the Japanese thus encouraged an unprecedented blossoming of political activity.

The initial reaction of the Vietnamese was that of stupified spectators. The coup was accomplished with all the ease of a military drill, and the "independence" announced by the Japanese was too good to be true. Vietnamese who were well known for cherishing and fighting for independence showed few signs of jubilation. Although people welcomed the defeat of the French, they expressed little enthusiasm for collaboration with Japan. Public demonstrations, organized by pro-Japanese groups in Hanoi, Saigon and other cities to generate approval for the coup, soon ceased. Would-be Vietnamese politicans were as noncommittal as the general population. One week after the coup, a group called the Alliance for a Great Viet State (Dai Viet Quoc Gia Lien Minh), a coalition of several supposedly pro-Japanese political parties, published an "Appeal to Men of Talent to Shoulder State Affairs" *("Hieu-trieu Nhan-tai ra ganh vac viec nuoc")*. The response to this appeal was eloquent silence. *Tin moi* [New information], for example, soon complained:

> It has been seven long days since the heartfelt appeal was published. Unfortunately, there has not been one voice of support. By today, not one group has publicly emerged to accept the responsibility for this new period. . . . The sadder part is that our country has more than a sufficient supply of men of talent . . . yet all of them choose to guard their silence, folding their arms, watching the situation with the cold attitude of spectators.[11]

The noncommital attitude toward the Japanese-granted "independence" did not necessarily indicate unconcern or lack of interest in politics. Initial reservation soon gave way to the activities of a myriad of political organizations, representing the entire ideological spectrum. At first these activities were sparse, hesitant, and always restrained for fear of possible Japanese repression. Long years of experience with the French had conditioned the Vietnamese to distrust foreigners' promises of political freedom. Once

11. *Tin moi* [New Information], 24 March 1945; quoted in Tran van Giau, *Giai cap cong nhan*, 3: 201.

they were assured of Japanese indifference to political activities that were not overtly anti-Japanese, however, political participation became increasingly varied, enthusiastic, and better organized. For some time the urban Vietnamese appeared to be intoxicated with the newfound political freedom. Political rallies, public demonstrations, spontaneous and not-so-spontaneous political discussions occurred daily at public squares, marketplaces, and streetcorners. Throughout Vietnam, according to the periodical *Ngay nay*, "after a brief storm of bullets on March 9, political parties, groups, and associations shot up like mushrooms."[12] Some, like the "Viet Nam Thanh Nien Doan" (Vietnamese Youth Corps), were officially sponsored by the Tran Trong Kim cabinet; many more were self-generated. Most, however, were paper organizations, having neither a clearcut ideological orientation, organizational structure, program of action, nor any substantial mass following. A survey made by a newspaper at that time revealed that in Bac Ky alone, there were more than thirty such "parties."[13] Among the better known were: Dang Tan Viet Quoc Dan (New Viet People's Party); Dang Dai Viet Quoc Xa (Great Viet National Socialist Party); Dang Phung su Quoc gia (National Service Party); Hoi Tan Viet Nam (New Vietnam Association); Dang Phuc Viet (Restoration of Vietnam Party); and Viet Nam Quoc gia Doc lap Dang (Independent Vietnamese State Party). These groups appeared to be motivated by patriotic sentiments. Their members obviously wished to do something for the country but were hampered by their meager political experience.[14] A few of these groups, such as the Phuc Quoc (Restoration of the Country) or the Hoa Hao, had reputedly been encouraged and possibly even materially supported by the Japanese prior to the coup. Even if this is true, it is doubtful that their political activities during the Japanese interlude deserve the label "pro-Japanese."

12. *Ngay nay*, 5 May 1945.
13. *Tin moi*, 10 May 1945.
14. In an interview with the author in January 1966 in Paris, Mr. Nguyen Manh Ha, the labor commissioner for the Haiphong region during the Decoux regime and the earliest minister of national economy of the DRV, described the Japanese interlude as the "cleanest moment" of the urban bourgeoisie. High-ranking Vietnamese civil servants temporarily abandoned their habitual interest in bribes, gambling casinos, and houses of prostitution to take an active part in political groups.

THE FAMINE

A devastating famine, which reached emergency proportions around the time of the Japanese coup, had far greater political implications than most short-sighted politicians at the time cared to consider. While the French were nursing their political wounds, the Japanese worrying about their future, and the educated Vietnamese minority in urban centers jockeying for power, millions of Vietnamese in Bac Ky and northern Trung Ky were struggling just to stay alive.

Even before the Second World War starvation had been a more or less permanent condition of peasant life in Bac Ky and northern Trung Ky. For three to four months of any normal year the peasant diet consisted of rice supplemented by corn, beans, or sweet potatoes. To meet the needs of the North, rice had been regularly brought up from Nam Ky. Wartime policies worsened this situation. By the agreement of 19 August 1942, the Decoux regime agreed to supply to Japan the entire exportable surplus of rice and corn during the harvests of 1942–1943, or a minimum of 1,050,000 tons of the highest quality white rice and at least 250,000 tons of corn.[15] To meet these Japanese demands, the colonial regime exacted a quota from all the farmers of Bac Ky.[16] Meanwhile, to fulfill military requirements, farmers in Bac Ky were made to plant oil seeds and peanuts (to produce hydrocarburants), cotton, and jute instead of rice.[17] Ironically, most of the conversion occurred in Bac Ky, which had to depend on rice supply from Nam Ky. Only early in 1944 was the conversion mandated in Nam Ky.

15. Gaudel, *Indochine en face du Japon*, pp. 208–209.
16. In 1945 farmers who owned five *mau* or less of rice land were required to sell to the government 20 kilograms per *mau;* those who owned five to ten *mau*, 80 kilograms per *mau;* and those who owned over fifteen *mau*, all their surplus. In 1944, when the crops were ravaged by a terrifying flood, this ratio was increased even further. Those farmers who owned up to ten *mau* were required to sell the government 72 kilograms per *mau;* those who owned from ten to fifteen *mau*, 120 kilograms per *mau;* and those who owned fifteen *mau* or more, 200 kilograms. (One *mau* equals 360 square meters.) See Tran van Giau, *Giai cap cong nhan*, 3: 122–123.
17. In 1939 there were 17,500 hectares of oil seeds; in 1944 this surface had been multiplied fourfold to 68,000 hectares. During the same period the surface of cotton growing increased more than seven times, from 7,000 hectares to 52,000 hectares, and the surface devoted to jute planting increased from 600 to 1,700 hectares. See Gaudel, *Indochine en face du Japon*, pp. 227–228.

The effects of this conversion on the rice supply began to be felt in Bac Ky in the autumn of 1943, when Allied bombardment added to the misery. In 1944, while the railroad became virtually unusuable, a combination of aerial and submarine attacks reduced shipping between Nam Ky and Bac Ky from the usual sixteen ships with a total of fourteen thousand tons to a mere five ships with thirty-five hundred tons.[18]

Starvation had begun in late 1943 and became progressively worse. By late 1944, the peasants of Bac Ky and northern Trung Ky had to eat ground paddy husks, roots of banana trees, grass, herbs, clover leaves—all the feed that had previously been given to cattle and pigs, all nonpoisonous plants—in fact, anything that could be swallowed. *Viet Nam tan bao* [Tribune of Vietnam] reported on 28 April 1945:

> A dead dog or a dead rat was an occasion for the entire hamlet to get together and share a few bits. An old man refused to eat and died a slow death, trying to save his share of rice porridge for his four- and ten-year-old grandchildren. A group of peasants demanded to be put in prison; when rejected, they declared, "If you do not put us into custody, we will have to steal."[19]

Death by starvation became common throughout the Bac Ky countryside, affecting entire families. In some villages, people managed to sow paddy but did not survive to harvest it. The village of Thuong Cam in Thai Binh province shrank from four thousand in 1944 to less than two thousand by May 1945.[20] Starvation drove the peasants to urban areas to become beggars, where their fate was not much better. On the streets of Hanoi, Haiphong, and other large cities parents tried to sell or give away their children; when this failed, children were abandoned on the streets. Rows of naked peasants, little more than skeletons, lined the walls, awaiting

18. Ibid., p. 230.
19. For a discussion of the 1945 famine, see Ngo Vinh Long, *Before the Revolution: The Vietnamese Peasants under the French* (Cambridge, Mass., 1973), pp. 122–135.
20. Pham Gia Kinh reported, "In a recent investigation, we discovered that in the village of Thuong Cam, Thai Ninh district, Nam Dinh province, there were 900 grown men last year, but as of 20 May this year only 400 were still alive. The village used to have four thousand persons, males and females, young and old; more than two thousand of them, however, have died from starvation"; in "Nhung ruong bo hoang" "The abandoned ricefields], *Thanh nghi* [Impartial opinion] 5, no. 110 (26 May 1945), p. 5, n. 2.

death. At noon and 5:00 P.M. daily, oxcarts collected the dead and
dying piled up on the pavement and at streetcorners. They were
then dumped—sometimes still protesting—into mass graves outside the city limits. By March 1945 approximately two million Vietnamese had died of starvation.[21] "Independence" under the Japanese, however, brought no relief. A popular two-line verse of that
period encapsulated the Vietnamese view of the entire situation

> *Nhat cuoi, Tay khoc, Tau lo;*
> *Viet Nam Doc lap chet co day duong.*
> (The Japanese laugh, the French weep, the Chinese worry;
> Independent Vietnamese curl up and die all over the streets.)

The reactions of Vietnam's colonial leaders to the famine would
have made cynics of the most politically innocent. For all its solici-
tude in courting the Vietnamese elite, the Decoux regime showed
an unconcern verging on callous contempt for the Vietnamese as
humans. It did nothing to help the famine victims. Except for author Gaudel, who was anxious to refute the Vietnamese charge that
the French deliberately fostered the famine, leading French
officials of Indochina (including Decoux, Catroux, and Legrand)
who wrote voluminous memoirs presenting their cases and justifying their actions during the war seemed unaware that a famine even
occurred. No mention of it appeared in their books. After the coup,
the Japanese likewise did nothing to alleviate the situation. On the
contrary, the Japanese commandant insisted at his initial meeting
with Bao Dai that the newly "independent" Vietnamese government
guarantee regular food supplies to his army. Though well-
intentioned, the Tran Trong Kim cabinet could do nothing practical
to ameliorate the situation. The only political group to effect any
relief was a procommunist organization, the Thanh Nien Tien
Phong (Vanguard Youth), which collected more than one million

21. This figure of two million Vietnamese deaths from starvation is generally
accepted in Vietnam. It is derived from estimates in newspaper reports at the time.
No official statistics are available. In the absence of any contradictory figure, I
accept it for the purpose of this discussion. See *Trung Bac Chu Nhat* [Center and
northern Sunday magazine], 29 July 1945; also, Vo Nguyen Giap, *Nhung nam
thang khong the nao quen* [The unforgettable months and years] (Hanoi, 1970), pp.
14, 37. This memoir by General Giap has been translated into English by Mai Elliot
and published by the Cornell University Southeast Asian Studies Program, Data
Paper No. 99, *Unforgettable Months and Years* (Ithaca, 1975). Hanoi's FLPH has
also published a translation of this book entitled *Unforgettable Days* (1975).

302   Vietnamese Communism, 1925–1945

piasters and 1,595 tons of rice in the South to send to the North in June 1945.[22] Indeed, no political party except the Communists had any concrete plans to alleviate the suffering or understood the political implications of the tragedy.

The Japanese coup, the vacuum in national leadership, the aroused Vietnamese interest in politics, and the famine formed the background for the "General Insurrection of August" (Tong Khoi Nghia thang Tam). In Leninist parlance, these were some of the "objective material conditions" of the revolutionary situation. Whether a political organization could make profitable use of such conditions would depend upon its strategies and tactics, its leadership, and its ability to adapt itself to the social and political environment. In 1945 the Indochinese Communist Party was the only party capable of turning the new situation to its political advantage.

PRELUDE TO INSURRECTION

For the ICP, the interval between 9 March and the Japanese surrender, now called "the preinsurrectional period," was a hectic and exhilarating time of visible fruition of all the years of theoretical, organizational, and agitational preparation. It was a testing time for both the leadership and the members—a time when a correct assessment of the situation and a slogan correctly attuned to the feelings of the masses would help carry the Party to power, and an incorrect assessment and inappropriate slogan would doom the efforts of two decades of revolutionary agitation. It was a time that required sharp political vision to determine strategies and tactics. What line was to be taken toward the French, the Japanese, the Tran Trong Kim cabinet, the various noncommunist parties, the noncommittal intellectuals, and especially the famished masses? How were they to gain power when many of the Party's five thousand members[23] were still in jail? How were they to seize power when the Liberation Army had only a few hundred combatants and less than a hundred pieces of assorted weaponry? Finally, what social and political conditions would indicate that the situa-

22. Tran van giau, *Giai cap cong nhan*, 3: 233.
23. The ICP membership figure of five thousand at the time of the August Revolution has often been mentioned by Vietnamese Communist leaders. See, for example, Hoang Tung, *Dang cua giai cap*, p. 16.

tion was opportune for an insurrection? These were among the problems that faced the ICP leadership at the time of the Japanese coup.

THE "HISTORIC DIRECTIVE"

The ICP Central Committee, perhaps having advance intelligence of Japanese intentions, held a special "enlarged conference" on the evening of 9 March to determine the Party's plan of action. The conference met for three days at Tu Son village, Bac Ninh province, about twenty kilometers from Hanoi. When the conference ended on 12 March the ICP Central Committee published what is now called the "Historic Directive," entitled "Our Action in Relation to the Franco-Japanese Conflict" *("Nhat Phap Ban Nhau va Hanh Dong cua Ta")*.[24] As the core document in the ICP's plan for the general insurrection, it analyzed the new situation and outlined all the basic strategies, tactics, and forms of activity to be undertaken by the Party. This directive was to have a practical influence on political events in a way few other such documents had ever had. In August 1945, after studying the document carefully, ICP members throughout Bac Ky and northern Trung Ky would launch an insurrection in response to the Japanese surrender, in many cases without having received final instructions from the Central Committee.

After briefly describing the coup, the directive predicted that "the French will lose" because they lacked fighting spirit, modern weapons, and support from the Indochinese masses. In the view of the ICP Central Committee, then, the "nature and objective of the political event" was that of "a coup d'état [*dao chinh*] (that is to say one ruling clique seizes power from another in order to supplant it), whose objective is to deprive the French of all power, thereby turning Indochina into an exclusive colony of Japanese imperialism."

The Central Committee identified three principal causes of the coup d'état: first, the "two imperialist wolves" could not share "a fat prey like Indochina"; second, now that China and the United

24. For the text, see Nguyen van To, *Chat xieng*, pp. 10–18. Unless otherwise indicated, all quotations of the directive in this section are derived from this text. Italics, when they appear, are from the original document.

States were about to attack Indochina, the Japanese had to eliminate the French in order to forestall a potential rearguard action; and third, the Japanese would have to fight a "life-and-death" struggle to maintain the "land bridge linking Japan with the colonies in the Indonesian region, now that their maritime lines had been cut due to the American occupation of the Philippines." The coup, according to the directive, constituted a significant political development, for it had produced "an acute political crisis," as reflected in a combination of factors in which "(1) the two aggressors are engaged in a mortal combat; (2) French political power is disintegrating; (3) Japanese political power is not yet consolidated; (4) the intermediary strata of the population are in confusion; (5) the revolutionary masses are eager for action."

The directive also recommended a bold shift in the Party's perceptions of "friends and enemies." For decades, French colonialism had been considered one of the principal enemies of the Vietnamese revolution. Now that the French were sure to be defeated they were "no longer our concrete and immediate enemy." Indeed, the French Resistance movement in Indochina should be considered "progressive" and an indirect, "objective ally" of the Vietnamese revolution in the new period. Instead "the principal, *concrete,* immediate, and unique enemy" of the Vietnamese revolution after the coup was the Japanese; therefore, whoever fought the Japanese was automatically to be considered an "objective ally." In more practical terms, the directive called for collaboration with the French Resistance and urged attempts to get weapons from them. On the other hand,

> if the French Resistance refuses to help us with weapons to fight the Japanese, we still have the obligation to try to mobilize a union with their infrastructure, attracting the resolutely antifascist elements, who have an internationalist inclination, to unite in action with us against the Japanese, or to come to our side with weapons of the French imperialists, over the head of their selfish and irresolute officers. They can form with us an anti-Japanese Democratic Front in Indochina.

Thus, the basic element in the new strategy was a rejection of any collaboration with or dependence on Japan to regain Vietnamese independence. This anti-Japanese policy remained official until the Japanese surrender in August.

Without doubt the most important aspect of the directive was its stipulation of the appropriate time to launch a general insurrection. This involved what Lenin called a "revolutionary situation," or, in ICP nomenclature, the "opportune moment" *(thoi co)*. The issue of whether a "revolutionary situation" existed had seriously affected the ICP during the Second World War. At least three times before the August Revolution several ICP leaders had thought the Party was facing a "revolutionary situation." Both the Bac Son and Nam Ky Insurrections, for example, had been launched with the misconception that a revolutionary situation existed, and both ended in bloodbaths for the insurrectionists. It was to prevent another premature insurrection that the ICP Central Committee specified in the resolutions of the Eighth Plenum (1941) the conditions for an armed insurrection. Nevertheless, another misjudgment occurred in the autumn of 1944, when Vo Nguyen Giap and his comrades in the Viet Minh Central Committee made serious plans to launch a general insurrection, plans that were vetoed by Nguyen Ai Quoc only in the nick of time. All these efforts had been or would have been premature insurrections, given the political situation of the country and especially the imbalance between the revolutionary and the counterrevolutionary forces.

In Leninist theory, making a revolution is a science involving specific laws and requiring long-term preparation and judicious planning. Therefore, one of the central tasks of the revolutionary Party during its prepower phase is to gauge the propitious moment for launching the revolution. This propitious moment, what Lenin called "the revolutionary situation," occurs when social conditions and the mood of the masses combine to raise the spontaneous will for action to its highest point. At such a time a vigilant and well-prepared revolutionary Party can ride the waves of mass spontaneity to power. As Lenin put it in his letter of September 1917 to the Central Committee of the Russian Social Democratic Labor party:

> To be successful, insurrection must rely not upon conspiracy and not upon a Party, but upon the advanced class. That is the first point. Insurrection must rely upon a *revolutionary upsurge of the people*. That is the second point. Insurrection must rely upon that *turning point* in the history of the growing revolution when the activity of the advanced ranks of the people is at its height, and when the

vacillations in the ranks of the enemy and *in the ranks of the weak, half-hearted and irresolute friends of the revolution* are strongest. That is the third point.[25]

Thus, in Lenin's view, a revolution can occur only when there exist both insurrection and conspiracy, both spontaneous mass action and organizational work, both irrational forces and rational preparations.[26] A conspiracy without the participation of the masses can lead to a successful coup d'état, but in this case one group of leaders would merely replace another, and the masses would lack any sense of involvement. Without their participation or consciousness there can be no revolution. Similarly, insurrections without conspiracies are seldom victorious and never lasting. A leaderless insurrection, even if it overturns the government, provides nothing to replace that government, and power will pass from the insurrectionists to other, organized factions. Thus, again there is no revolution. The repeated failures of spontaneous peasant revolts are examples of insurrection without conspiracy.

In Lenin's view, the moment of the insurrection is the most important in the life of a revolutionary party. It unites leadership, organization, and propaganda. The success or failure of an insurrection depends largely upon the ability of the revolutionary leadership to gauge the *mood of the masses,* the *objective social conditions,* and the *subjective conditions of the Party,* weigh them against one another, and on the basis of this diagnosis select the most opportune moment for action. If the masses are not ready, the result will be a premature insurrection and a "revolutionary miscarriage." If it occurs too late, the enthusiasm of the masses may have spent itself. Trotsky summarized the Leninist theory of "the revolutionary situation" thus:

25. Lenin, "Marxism and Insurrection," a letter to the Central Committee of the RSDLP, 13–14 September 1917, in *Selected Works,* 2: 365.
26. As Lenin put it in 1920: "Certainly, without a revolutionary mood of the masses, and without conditions facilitating the growth of this mood, revolutionary tactics will never develop into action. In Russia, however, lengthy, painful, and sanguinary experience has taught us the truth that revolutionary tactics cannot be built on a revolutionary mood alone. Tactics must be based on a sober and strictly objective appraisal of all the class forces in a particular state (and of the states that surround it, and of all states the world over) as well as the experience of revolutionary movements." " 'Left-Wing' Communism—An Infantile Disorder," ibid., 3: 373–374.

But if it is true that an insurrection cannot be evoked at will, and that nevertheless in order to win, it must be organized in advance, then the revolutionary leaders are presented with a task of correct diagnosis. They must feel out the growing insurrection in good season and supplement it with a conspiracy. The interference of the midwife in labor pains—however this image may have been abused— remains the clearest illustration of this conscious intrusion into an elemental process. . . .

Between the moment when an attempt to summon an insurrection must inevitably prove premature and lead to a revolutionary miscarriage, and the moment when a favorable situation must be considered hopelessly missed, there exists a certain period—it may be measured in weeks, and sometimes a few months—in the course of which an insurrection may be carried out with more or less chance for success.[27]

In the days immediately after the Japanese coup, the ICP leadership carefully weighed the various theoretical and practical aspects of the Vietnamese political situation to see if, and when, a revolutionary situation would occur. Anxious to avoid another aborted insurrection, the Central Committee sharpened its definition of "the opportune moment" in the directive. It placed a special importance on warning Party cadres not to act hastily. In the view of the ICP leadership, although the political situation in the country was becoming increasingly favorable to the revolutionary side, the "objective conditions" were not yet "ripe" *(chin muoi)*. First, French resistance to the Japanese coup had been so feeble that the Japanese retained virtually all their military strength. Second, the noncommittal population had necessarily to go through a period of disillusionment with the Japanese-granted pseudo-independence before they would turn whole-heartedly to the revolutionaries. Finally, except for a few localities where topographical conditions were favorable for guerrilla actions and where the Party had some fighting units, in the country as a whole, Party cadres and combatants were still "floundering" *(lung tung)* in their preparations for insurrection. The leadership, however, foresaw "three good opportunities" that would aid the "rapid ripening of the conditions for an insurrection":

27. Leon Trotsky, *The Russian Revolution: The Overthrow of Tzarism and the Triumph of the Soviets,* trans. M. Eastman, ed. and comp. F. W. Dupee (New York, 1959), pp. 309–310.

(a) The political crisis (the enemy's hands are tied, preventing them from dealing with the revolution);
(b) The terrible famine (the masses will have profound hatred for the aggressors);
(c) The decisive stage of the War (imminent Allied landing in Indochina to attack the Japanese).

The directive then specified three conditions as indications of the "ripeness" of the revolutionary situation: first, the ranks of "the enemy" were to be "divided in consternation, and indecisive to the ultimate level"; second, the masses were to be "leaning completely to the side of the revolution" and were to be "determined to support the vanguard forces"; and third, the revolutionary cadres were to be "ready to fight and determined to sacrifice to the end."

In concrete terms, the directive considered a "Japanese surrender to the Allies" or a "firm hold and powerful advance of the Allies in our country" as a sure indication of the presence of a revolutionary situation. On the whole, however, the Central Committee leaders leaned toward the probability of an Allied invasion. In fact, they appeared to count on an Allied invasion as a prelude to the end of the conflict. An entire section, entitled "Be Ready to Rally to the Allied Power," admonished Party cadres to be careful in selecting the moment to rise up against the Japanese when (*not* "if") the Allies arrived. The directive stated in part:

1. We cannot launch the general insurrection immediately upon the arrival of the Allied forces in Indochina to fight the Japanese. We should not only wait for the Allied forces to gain a firm foothold, we must also wait until they are advancing. At the same time we must wait until the Japanese send forces to the front to intercept the Allied forces, thus relatively exposing their rear, before we launch the general insurrection: only then will the situation be favorable to us.

2. Wherever the Allied forces land, we should mobilize the people to organize demonstrations to welcome them and at the same time arm the masses and form people's militia forces to fight the enemy side by side with the Allied forces. In localities where our guerrillas are active, they should enter into contact with the Allied forces and together with them fight the Japanese according to a common plan. *But in any case, our guerrillas must always keep the initiative in the operations.*

The directive repeatedly emphasized the need for self-reliance and keeping the initiative. To count on an Allied invasion "as the

essential condition for our general insurrection would be a total
reliance on others and to tie our own hands while the situation
develops in our favor." The directive exhorted further:

> We are determined not to be caught unprepared when the situation
> changes in our favor. It is possible that towards the end of the World
> War, a Japanese revolution might burst out [in Japan] and succeed in
> establishing people's revolutionary power before the Allies could
> enter Indochina; it is also possible that Japan might be occupied in
> the same way that France was in 1940 and the Japanese expedi-
> tionary forces would be dispirited. In such instances, *even if the
> Allies have not yet invaded* [Indochina], *our general insurrection
> could still be launched and be successful.*

Ironically, the directive appears to have weighed all possibilities
except those that actually facilitated the Viet Minh seizure of
power: first, the collapse of the war party in Japan without revolution or an Allied invasion of either Japan or Indochina, and second,
the nonresistance of the dispirited Japanese troops to the Viet
Minh takeover. When the time came for the August Revolution,
the Viet Minh took power almost effortlessly.

"ADVANCE TO A GENERAL INSURRECTION!"

In the five months that followed the Japanese coup, Viet Minh
activities consisted essentially in practical elaboration and application of the strategies and tactics outlined in the "Historic Directive." The ICP expanded its influence among the populace and
strengthened its forces while awaiting anxiously that elusive "revolutionary situation."

These five months were the most important period in the history
of the ICP. Indeed, they were the culmination of twenty years of
Communist agitation, when the lessons of propaganda and organization, of conspiracy and insurrection from the days of Thanh
Nien, the Nghe Tinh soviets, the Democratic Front, to the Nam
Ky and Bac Son Insurrections were reanalyzed and carefully
adapted to the new situation; when all the experiences of illegal,
clandestine activities were combined with those of legal, overt
activities; and, most important, when Nguyen Ai Quoc's strategy
of partial insurrection enjoyed methodical application.

As the ICP thus strengthened the "subjective conditions," the "objective material conditions" were becoming increasingly favorable. "The enemy," the Japanese, preoccupied with the increasing likelihood of a general defeat, were uninterested in Vietnamese affairs. Meanwhile, the inexperienced puppet regime of Bao Dai–Tran Trong Kim was flailing helplessly in a gathering political crisis. The numerous noncommunist parties were occupied with high-level problems such as national policies on the design and colors of a national emblem and securing foreign diplomatic recognition. These parties deserved Nguyen Ai Quoc's condemnation of Tam Tam Xa twenty years previously: they knew "nothing about politics, and much less about organizing the masses." The Vietnamese political arena was thus wide open to the Viet Minh's agitprop operations, organizing "the bottom"—the hungry masses, the peasants, and the workers. Such activities went hand in hand with diplomatic negotiations and military preparations. All these activities were governed by one slogan, "Advance to a General Insurrection!" *(Tien toi Tong Khoi Nghia!).*

The five-month Japanese interlude was a time of feverish organizational and military activity by the Viet Minh. The motto now was to fuse the political and military forms of struggle; that is, propaganda and organizational work were to accompany military action. Military activities were to aid propaganda and organizational activities in spreading the Viet Minh influence; in turn, propaganda and organizational work, were designed to bring in fighters and possibly weapons to bolster military activities.

A two-pronged military and political campaign went into effect. On the military front, the two separate guerrilla forces—the National Salvation Army (Cuu-quoc Quan) of the Bac Son–Vu Nhai region and the Army of Propaganda and Liberation of Vietnam (Viet Nam Tuyen Truyen Giai Phong Quan)—were united into a single army, the Vietnamese Liberation Army (Viet Nam Giai Phong Quan). Within a few days of the coup they were able to recruit three thousand troops of the disbanded Indochina army.[28] The Liberation Army also acquired weapons and ammunition, including heavy machine guns and mortars, from the fleeing French troops. Because at this time the Viet Minh Front still expected an Allied invasion and possible heavy fighting with the Japanese, it gave priority to military activities. A special Revolutionary Mili-

28. Tran van Giau, *Giai cap cong nhan,* 3: 235.

tary Conference was held in the middle of April (15–20 April 1945), which divided Vietnam into seven fighting zones: four in Bac Ky, two in Trung Ky, and one in Nam Ky. The conference also decided that "in view of the present situation, the military task must have priority over all other important and urgent tasks for the time being. We must actively intensify guerrilla warfare, set up anti-Japanese resistance bases, and prepare ourselves for a timely launching of the general insurrection."[29]

The Viet Minh forces gained in military strength and virtually controlled the mountainous regions within three months of the Japanese coup. Japanese convoys were ambushed, roads were cut, Japanese posts in remote mountain areas were attacked and sometimes taken. These guerrilla activities continued until the Japanese surrender. Though limited in number, these daring attacks gave considerable political prestige to the Viet Minh Front as the only Vietnamese political organization with a military force that dared to stand up to the all-powerful Japanese.

The Viet Minh political mobilization was more substantial. The application of Nguyen Ai Quoc's partial insurrection strategy led to a "spreading oil stain" *(vet dau loang)* pattern of activities. This pattern involved several steps: first, spread out from the mountain strongholds to seize power in areas out of reach of the Japanese army; consolidate it; then, spread from the mountains to the plains *(trung du);* and finally, from the plains to the delta of the Red River. In the first three months after the coup Viet Minh activities quickly expanded from the two *chien khu* of Cao-Bac-Lang and Bac Son–Vu Nhai into the surrounding areas. In these places, where there had been Communist activities for several years, local government authorities crumbled before the Viet Minh military and organizational advance. For more than sixty years the centuries-old traditional power structure in these rural areas had based its legitimacy on its connections with the colonial system. In the new situation this structure lost whatever legitimacy it had possessed. Local notables, who for decades had relied on central government power to rule, either turned over village documents and seals of office to Viet Minh representatives or continued to function nominally, at the discretion of the members of the Front, while a parallel Viet Minh political structure was created and actually

29. Tran Huy Lieu et al., *TLTK*, 11: 46.

governed. Those few who resisted were called *Viet gian* (Viet-namese traitors) or *tho phi* (bandits) and were executed by "armed propaganda" teams as examples. By late May and early June 1945, it could be said that the Japanese had lost control of the mountainous and the plains regions. Viet Minh propaganda and organization were carried out in these regions without interference.

In the first week of June 1945, just three months after the coup, the Viet Minh Front formally inaugurated a "liberated zone" *(khu giai phong)*. This zone contained six provinces (Cao Bang, Lang Son, Ha Giang, Bac Giang, Phu Tho, Yen Bay), with approximately one million people. This was an attempt to consolidate all the Front's political and military gains and to streamline activities, in preparation for further expansion of Communist influence and the general insurrection.[30] The Liberated Zone was governed by a sort of government, the Provisional Leadership Committee, headed by Nguyen Ai Quoc. Under this provisional committee there existed a collection of administrative committees, which formed the skeleton of a future government. It included a Department of Politics, responsible for both administering the zone and mobilizing the people (propaganda and information); a General Staff; a Department of Finance and Economy; a Department of Communications; and a Department of Culture and Social Welfare. The Provisional Leadership Committee proposed a three-month emergency plan to govern the Liberated Zone as if it were a small state. This plan dealt with political, military, economic, cultural, and communications problems. Once established, the Liberated Zone became the Viet Minh–directed center for the revolutionary movement throughout the country. In addition to governing the nearly "liberated" areas, the zone had short-term, intensive-training schools for military, political, and administrative affairs. From the Liberated Zone newly trained cadres were sent to the lowland areas of Bac Ky and northern Trung Ky, where they quickly organized "Liberation Committees."

SOLVING THE PROBLEMS OF FAMINE

Mobilizing the peasant masses to solve the problems of famine was no less important than any other Viet Minh activity during this

30. For documents and detailed discussion on the creation of the Liberated Zone, see Tran Huy Lieu et al., *TLTK*, 11: 62–69.

period. Indeed, the ICP considered combatting the famine "the principal point" of its activities in the rural areas of the lowlands.[31] Communist-instigated "rice struggles" had begun sometime in 1944. Until the coup, however, such struggles had remained in the "preventive" phase, restricted to the prevention of forced sales of paddy or forced planting of industrial crops. As the famine became widespread, however, the Communists mobilized peasants to storm granaries or to "borrow" rice from landlords.[32]

Initially the famine had caused a number of difficulties for revolutionary mobilization. In some northern provinces, some Viet Minh members, following the command of the Party to stay close to the masses, died of starvation together with those in their charge; others, because of hunger, neglected Party activities.[33] Furthermore, a famished population struggling to stay alive was no material for a revolutionary movement. The ICP, however, quickly realized that the famine could become a useful instrument to arouse hatred against the French and the Japanese, to give people political consciousness, and to involve them practically in revolutionary politics. Already in late 1944 and early 1945, the Viet Minh Front had put forward the slogan, "Destroy the granaries, solve the danger of the famine!" In the "Historic Directive," the Party leadership urged consideration of antifamine organizing as one of the "central" tasks of Viet Minh activities. Two out of three points under "On Struggle" (in the section entitled "Urgent Tasks") in this directive dealt with the question of the famine:

(a) *Slogans for the Struggle:* link the slogans relating to the questions of demanding food, opposing paddy and tax collection with the slogan of "people's revolutionary power."
(b) *Method of Mobilizing the Struggle:* make use of the famine to mobilize the masses and lead them to struggle (organize demonstrations to demand rice and food or destroy the granaries of the imperialists).

The Viet Minh Front then decided to solve the problem of hun-

31. Tran Huy Lieu, *Lich su tam muoi nam*, 3: 133.
32. For details, see Tran Huy Lieu et al., *TLTK*, 11: 97–115.
33. In the directive of the Viet Minh Provincial Committee of Thanh Hoa, dated 5 March 1945, Viet Minh members were specifically chastised for inactivity due to hunger. "A majority of our comrades have become lazy because of hunger. . . . Comrades, put aside inappropriate thoughts, such as being lazy and putting off revolutionary work. Only by struggling against the Japanese and the French—and when absolutely necessary, with the rich—can we solve the problems of the famine for our compatriots and comrades"; ibid., pp. 100–101.

ger by "revolutionary methods." Granaries of the Japanese and those of the French that had been confiscated by the Japanese (and sometimes granaries of rich Vietnamese landowners) were attacked by peasants led by Viet Minh cadres. By mid-1945 the Viet Minh considered the struggle against the famine "the key" to all other political problems, as well as the most important challenge it faced. Aside from being an immediate solution to the problems of hunger, it was also one way to expand further the prestige of the Viet Minh Front among the population. Furthermore, it was a way to bring people within and outside the organization into a widespread movement of social concern led by the Viet Minh Front (and thus indirectly emphasize the inadequacy of the Tran Trong Kim cabinet and the other parties). Finally, it trained the people and emboldened them to fight for their own lives.

It is not an exaggeration to say that the campaign against the famine was largely responsible for the Viet Minh rise to power in Bac Ky and northern Trung Ky. These areas, where the population was hardest hit by the famine and where the Viet Minh led the most daring attacks on the Japanese granaries and rice transports, were also the areas where the Front's influence was most extensive. Here, "people's committees" and "liberation committees" mushroomed and governed local affairs for several months before the general insurrection. In September 1946, one year after the August Revolution, Truong Chinh wrote:

> The March 9 [event] occurred at a time when the famine was torturing our people in a horrid way. Hundreds of thousands of our people lay dying next to Japanese and French granaries which were filled to the top. At the time, the essential task was the leadership of the masses for armed attacks on the Japanese granaries and the French colonialists' plantations, stocking all kinds of agricultural products. The Communist and Viet Minh cadres did grasp and solve this problem, causing the vast masses, either organized or unorganized, to participate eagerly in the movement against the Japanese. The more they participated in these activities, the more they saw the hideous face of the enemy and felt their own strength.
>
> It was thanks precisely to the attacks against the granaries and the plantations that the national salvation movement developed in an effervescent way. The people armed themselves rapidly. The self-defense militia was established quickly in places where there had never been a [political] movement, and liberation committees blossomed in several provinces.[34]

34. Truong Chinh, *Cach mang thang Tam*, p. 25.

This kind of political vision and strategy never characterized those opposing the Viet Minh people at the time. Even many years later, when they assessed and reminisced about those stormy days of Vietnamese history, none of the "nationalist" leaders who have written about the period seem to have been aware of the political implications of the famine.[35] Indeed, it is debatable whether they ever gained sufficient political sophistication to comprehend how the Communists had been able to turn a national tragedy into a political instrument while feeding the people.

DIPLOMATIC EFFORTS

The Viet Minh's "diplomatic" efforts during the Japanese interlude proved almost as important as the Front's political and military preparations at home. Despite persistent efforts, the Viet Minh Front, which was suspected of Communist connections, had been unable until the coup to gain the confidence and concrete support of the non-Vietnamese groups that could assist it in the most effective way—the American OSS, the French Gaullists in southern China, and the Chinese Kuomintang. These efforts, however, began to meet with success after the Japanese coup. Whatever their anticommunist misgivings, these groups needed the Viet Minh as the only organization in Vietnam that could provide them with information on Japanese movements and activities, now that the French intelligence and meteorological networks within Indochina had been destroyed. Subsequent relations between the Viet Minh and the Allied forces in southern China eventually helped establish Viet Minh authority among the Vietnamese population.

Of the three Allied groups, the Americans had the greatest effect

35. Nghiem Ke To, a VNQDD leader during the August Revolution, referred to the famine in one part of one sentence in a 524-page study of the 1945–1954 period; *Viet Nam mau lua* [Vietnam in blood and fire] (Saigon, 1954), p. 23. Tran Trong Kim devoted less than nine lines of his memoirs to this national tragedy. This fact alone reveals the level of political sophistication of the nationalists at the time. Also, although the neglect by Western historians (Bernard Fall, Joseph Buttinger, Dennis Duncanson) is explicable, it is more difficult to understand the fact that Vietnamese historians of the South during the U.S.–Thieu era also appeared to be unaware of the famine. Pham van Son, for example, in two separate works dealing with this period—*Viet Nam tranh dau su* [History of the struggles of Vietnam] (Saigon, 1959) and *Viet su tan bien* [Modern History of Vietnam], 7 vols (Saigon, 1968–1972), made no reference to the famine of 1944–1945.

on the Viet Minh preparations for insurrection. This appears to have been a consequence of both an official United States policy toward Indochina and mutual feelings of friendship between the OSS officers and Viet Minh members. Under Franklin D. Roosevelt American policy was geared to the notion that Indochina should be groomed for eventual self-government and should not be returned to French control after the war. As early as March 1943, Roosevelt had communicated this idea to British Foreign Secretary Anthony Eden when the latter came to Washington for a meeting.[36] He reiterated a similar idea in a note dated 24 January 1924 to Secretary of State Cordell Hull:

> France has had the country—thirty million inhabitants—for nearly one hundred years, and the people are worse off than they were at the beginning. . . . France has milked it for one hundred years. The people of Indochina are entitled to something better than that.[37]

Roosevelt later revealed at a press conference aboard the U.S.S. *Quincy Adams* on 23 February 1945 that he had approached Chiang Kai-shek at the Cairo Conference (November 1943) to see whether China would want Indochina as a prize for her part in the war. Since Chiang did not want it—"They are not Chinese. They would not assimilate into the Chinese people"[38]—Roosevelt thought of an international trusteeship scheme, whereby Indochina would have been temporarily governed by a board of trustees, composed of "a Frenchman, one or two Indochinese, and a Chinese and a Russian, because they are on the coast, and maybe a Filipino and an American, to educate them for self-government."[39]

Official United States policy aside, the OSS and the Viet Minh members who worked together in the jungles of Cao-Bac-Lang in the spring and summer of 1945 developed mutual respect and friendship.[40] As a result of negotiations between Nguyen Ai Quoc

36. Cordell Hull, *The Memoirs of Cordell Hull*, 2 vols. (New York, 1948), p. 1598.

37. Ibid., p. 1997.

38. *The Public Papers and Addresses of Franklin D. Roosevelt, 1944–1945*, vol. 13, *Victory and the Threshold of Peace*, as cited in Hammer, *The Struggle for Indochina*, pp. 562–563.

39. Ibid.

40. The discussion of the Viet Minh–OSS relationship in this section is based on Fenn, *Ho Chi Minh*, 74–84; Robert Shaplen, "The Enigma of Ho Chi Minh", *Reporter*, 27 January 1955, and Tran Huy Lieu et al., *TLTK*, 11: 80–83.

and the OSS in Kunming, several Americans had parachuted "into an area in the Liberated Zone,"[41] and the Americans continued to maintain contacts with the Viet Minh during the Japanese administration. During this time, a friendly working relationship developed between Americans and Vietnamese. An OSS lieutenant who had parachuted into Nguyen Ai Quoc's jungle headquarters in May 1945 later reported that Nguyen Ai Quoc and his men had an "unrestrained affection for all Americans."[42] Charles Fenn, the OSS officer who had introduced Nguyen Ai Quoc to General Chennault, reminisced about the affection and admiration that he and his fellow OSS members had for "Old Man Ho," or "Agent Lucius."[43]

Concrete American assistance to the Viet Minh Front was negligible; the Americans "presented the Vietnamese revolution with a number of weapons."[44] But the moral support provided by the presence of Americans among the Viet Minh and the latter's ability to profit politically by such "Allied connections" proved significant when the time came for the general insurrection. While the OSS Radio in Kunming broadcast Viet Minh articles, American planes dropped over eighty thousand Viet Minh leaflets in Bac Ky, appealing to the Vietnamese to "rise up to fight the Japanese."[45] A "Joint American-Vietnamese Brigade" (Lien quan Viet My) included seven American officers, and American officers reportedly trained some Vietnamese guerrilla fighters in the Liberated Zone. According to one Vietnamese source:

> According to the plans of cooperation between the American forces and the Viet Minh Front during this period, the liberation forces ought to be organized as special forces units *(doi biet dong)*, emphasizing sudden guerrilla tactics to destroy isolated enemy posts. When necessary, [these guerrilla attacks] would be supported by [American] airplanes. . . . Such was the plan of action, but actually there were few results, for the Americans were not sincere in help-

41. Tran Huy Lieu et al., *TLTK*, 11: 82.
42. Shaplen, "Enigma of Ho Chi Minh," p. 11.
43. Fenn, *Ho Chi Minh*, pp. 74–84.
44. Tran Huy Lieu et al., *TLTK*, 11: 82. This was confirmed in a report prepared by the U.S. Department of State dated December 1945: "Annamites, inspired by the anti-enemy activities of the leftist Viet Minh party, cooperated in guerrilla bands with American infiltration forces which supplied them with weapons, ammunition, and tactical leadership." Papers of general Philip E. Gallagher, Office of the Chief of Military History, U.S. Army Archives, Washington, D.C. (hereafter cited as Gallagher papers).
45. Tran Huy Lieu et al., *TLTK*, 11: 81–82.

ing us and, in fact, did not help us much, except for a number of weapons.[46]

Mutual friendship between American officers in southern China and members of the Viet Minh persisted despite the important change in United States policy toward Indochina as a result of the death of Roosevelt and his succession by Harry S. Truman. In a reversal of its earlier policy the United States decided in the spring of 1945 not to interfere with the French position in Indochina. Yet, until several months later, U.S. officers on the scene continued, in public and private reports, to espouse the cause of Vietnamese independence. American officers and journalists sometimes spoke at Viet Minh rallies, supporting Vietnamese independence and the Viet Minh Front ("the liberator of the Vietnamese people"),[47] and reports to the State Department and military headquarters generally sided with the Vietnamese.[48]

The Viet Minh leaders, though disappointed in the new American policy of noninterference, still looked to the United States as a source of aid against a possible French attempt at colonial reconquest. General Vo Nguyen Giap's speech on Independence Day (2 September 1945) stated what appeared to be not only an official policy, but also the private feelings of the Viet Minh leaders at the time: "As to America, that is a democratic country, which has no territorial ambitions, yet bore the greatest burdens in defeating fascist Japan, our enemy, and therefore we consider America a good friend."[49] Although the Viet Minh tended to exaggerate greatly the Front's connections with the "Allies" in order to gain prestige and influence among the Vietnamese public, only the uninformed or the malicious could say that such claims had no basis.

46. Ibid., p. 82.

47. Devillers, *Viet-Nam de 1940 à 1952*, p. 152.

48. For instance, in the report by General Gallagher to Maj. Gen. Robert McClure, dated 20 September 1945 from Hanoi, there are such blunt statements of American opinions as "The French are a pain in the neck, as you know. . . . The smart man, and the one who is stirring up trouble, is Major [Sainteny]. He is the instigator of a lot of propaganda, trying to stir up trouble between the Annamites and ourselves and between the Chinese and the Annamites. . . . The Annamite party, Viet Minh, led by Ho Chi Minh, is definitely in the saddle. This Ho Chi Minh is an old revolutionist and a political prisoner many times, a product of Moscow, a Communist. . . . They now claim their independence. . . . Confidentially, I wish the Annamites could be given their independence. . . ." Gallagher Papers.

49. General Vo Nguyen Giap's speech is reprinted in Tran Huy Lieu et al., *TLTK*, 12: 107–121.

Besides these friendly relations with the Americans, the Viet Minh Front had few meaningful relations with the French Gaullists or the Kuomintang Chinese during the five months under the Japanese. Sporadic contacts were maintained with the French Gaullist mission in Kunming through the OSS.[50] They added little to the Viet Minh plans for insurrection in Vietnam. There had been many more contacts between the Kuomintang leaders in southern China and the Viet Minh Front through Nguyen Ai Quoc during the days before the Japanese coup. On the whole, Viet Minh relations with the Kuomintang during the Japanese interlude, like those with the Gaullists, had little influence on the actual process of the general insurrection.

REVOLUTIONARY ACTIVITIES

The five months of Japanese rule were a time of revolutionary ferment throughout the country. Bolstered by Party members who had escaped from prisons in the confusion of the days after the coup, the Viet Minh increased its "armed propaganda" and organizational activities among the rural and urban masses. Most noticeable were Viet Minh activities in the villages of the Red River delta, which followed a pattern: first the "liberation committee" took over the administration of the villages, then the county seats, then the provincial seats, and finally, the large urban areas such as Nam Dinh, Hai Duong, Haiphong, and Hanoi. With a general institutional breakdown occurring throughout most rural areas, the Viet Minh encountered practically no resistance. Where they failed to take over completely, the liberation committees became a sort of parallel administrative structure. Documentary evidence is lacking, but it appears from various revolutionary memoirs that the Provisional Leadership Committee of the Liberated Zone had decided to center the activities of the prospective general insurrection in Hanoi.[51] By June virtually all the villages surrounding

50. Sainteny, *Histoire d'une paix manquée*, pp. 66–69.
51. Although the Viet Minh considered that "it was in the big cities: Hanoi, Hue, and Saigon that the August general insurrection . . . [would win] victories of a main and decisive meaning" (Propaganda Section, *Thirty Years*, p. 94), judging from documents and memoirs it is obvious that within the limits imposed by available human and organizational resources, Hanoi and Saigon were considered the main centers of the insurrection.

Hanoi had been transformed into *co-so* (bases) of Viet Minh activity.

Meanwhile, Japanese indifference had permitted Viet Minh cadres to carry out increasingly bold agitprop activities in the urban areas. In Hanoi, for example, speeches on soapboxes at street-corners became daily affairs, while Viet Minh propaganda publications flooded the city. Selective terrorism also sowed fear, demonstrated Viet Minh power, and confirmed the rumors, deliberately exaggerated, about daring Viet Minh attacks on the Japanese. Japanese soldiers who wandered around alone often found themselves roughed up, their weapons "confiscated"; a Viet Minh assassination squad roamed the city, giving "warnings" to the so-called *Viet gian* (Vietnamese traitors), or reputed pro-Japanese elements or well-known collaborators with the French. Some people in this category were murdered in Hanoi (including Hoang si Nhu on 18 June; Cat Long on 20 June; and a certain Sinh, allegedly a French secret police agent, on 7 July).[52] The killings were not numerous, but sufficient to cow adversaries and to advertise the Viet Minh presence. New forms of propaganda were invented: Viet Minh flags mysteriously appeared atop buildings and floated on rafts in rivers; young pupils were taught to sing Viet Minh songs in unison in schools; and theater and movie audiences often found themselves in total darkness, while a mysterious voice commanding a loudspeaker explained the Viet Minh program. By July 1945 the Viet Minh presence was ubiquitous, especially in Bac Ky. Prior to the general insurrection, Viet Minh activities appeared to be weakest in Trung Ky, where there had been little militant anticolonial activity since 1931.

Thus, by the final month of the war, the objective conditions had become extremely favorable for an insurrection. One of the conditions laid down in the "Historic Directive" was being fulfilled: "the enemy" was now placed in an untenable position. Expecting defeat, the Japanese became increasingly dispirited and were in no mood to suppress a Vietnamese independence movement, as long as it did not pose a threat to them. After nearly four months in office, the Tran Trong Kim cabinet was still floundering. No vertical connections existed between it and the civil bureaucracy.

52. Tran van Giau, *Giai cap cong nhan*, 3: 255.

Within the cabinet, conflicts of political viewpoints and personal interests so hampered its functioning that by the end of July the cabinet itself was on the verge of distintegration.[53] With only a few cabinet ministers still remaining with the government, Prime Minister Tran Trong Kim submitted his resignation the first week of August.[54] Meanwhile, in the countryside in Bac Ky and northern Trung Ky, more and more notables at the county *(phu)* and district *(huyen)* levels, unprotected by the Japanese and pressured by the Viet Minh armed propaganda squads, either chose to collaborate with the various people's committees or else left their posts to go into hiding.

As the situation of the Japanese and the Tran Trong Kim cabinet became more and more desperate, the subjective conditions of the Viet Minh Front became increasingly favorable. By late July, most of the rural areas around Hanoi and some of the counties outside of Hue had come under de facto Viet Minh control. Viet Minh-sponsored mass organizations multiplied. In Hanoi alone "the number of members of various mass organizations reached tens of thousands."[55] By this time the Viet Minh Front had also succeeded in infiltrating government services, especially the Security Militia Corps (Bao An Doan) and the police. In his memoirs, Tran Trong Kim recalled that during his last month in power, the Security Militia Corps in Hue, the only "armed force" available to the Bao–Dai–Tran Trong Kim government, began taking orders from the Viet Minh.[56] An official Communist account of the situation in those days in Hanoi also reported: "Our cadres could now circulate more easily. There were those comrades who were caught carrying weapons and documents, but the police looked the other way. We also knew beforehand of several Japanese raids, thanks to our brothers in the police."[57]

53. Tran Trong Kim, *Mot con gio bui*, pp. 89–90.
54. Ibid., pp. 90–91.
55. Bui Huu Khanh, based on materials supplied by Viet Minh activist-participants in the insurrection in Hanoi, in Vien su hoc, *CMTT*, 1: 31.
56. Tran Trong Kim, *Mot con gio bui*, pp. 85–86.
57. Vien su hoc, *CMTT*, 1: 31: "The confidence of the Hanoi people vis-à-vis the revolution was clearly expressed, even among the upper classes. Several bourgeois families bought Viet Minh bonds by the tens of thousands of piasters. Children of the upper-class families who wished to participate in revolutionary activities were no longer discouraged [by their parents] as before. In the government offices [revolutionary] newspapers such as *Cuu quoc* [National salvation],

By July, the General Association of Students and Youths (Tong Hoi Sinh Vien Thanh Nien), probably the best organized and most effective noncommunist force in Bac Ky, organized by Phan Anh, minister of youth in the Tran Trong Kim cabinet, was leaning toward the Viet Minh, as was the General Association of Civil Servants (Tong Hoi Cong Chuc), which was heavily infiltrated. Tan Viet Nam (New Vietnam), an organization of well-known writers and intellectuals, under pressure from the Viet Minh Front, dissolved itself, making it possible for many of the leading intellectuals to join the Viet Minh–sponsored Democratic Party.

THE AUGUST REVOLUTION

On 6 August 1945 an atomic bomb was dropped on Hiroshima. On 8 August the Soviet Union declared war on Japan and commenced a powerful invasion of Manchuria. Two days later, Japan offered to surrender. These events, which terminated the Second World War, unleashed in Vietnam a general insurrection that led to the seizure of power by the Viet Minh Front.

When, on 13 August, the news of Japan's offer to surrender reached Vietnam, the Viet Minh Provisional Leadership Committee of the Liberated Zone issued Military Order No. 1, which called upon the Vietnamese people and the officers and men in the Vietnamese Liberation Army to rise up, "concentrate your forces, urgently attack the cities and the important centers of the enemy; block their paths of withdrawal, disarm them!"[58] On 16 August, as Vo Nguyen Giap led a detachment of the Vietnamese Liberation Army toward Thai Nguyen, twenty kilometers north of Hanoi, Viet Minh–sponsored "People's Revolutionary Committees" in villages and counties throughout Bac Ky and northern Trung Ky began to take over the government administrative apparatus and to exercise power (see Map 2). The entire nation appeared to be caught in a political frenzy. In the ten days following the Japanese surrender, political demonstrations and rallies erupted in every urban area,

---

Doc lap [Independence] could be circulated almost openly. In several factories, the workers openly disseminate propaganda and lent the newspaper *Co giai phong* [The liberation flag] to their bosses."

58. Tran Huy Lieu et al., *TLTK*, 12: 21.

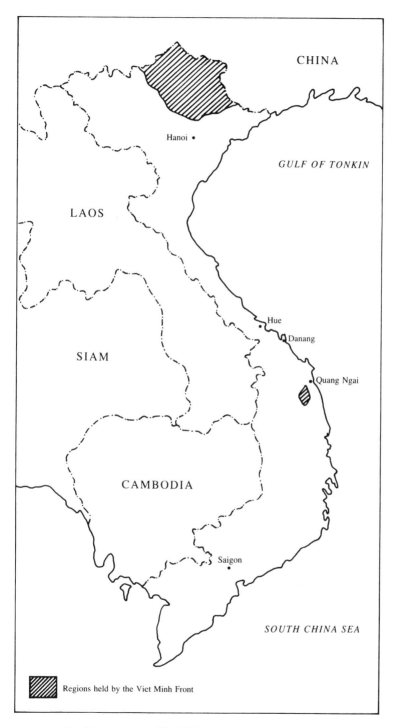

CHINA

Hanoi •

GULF OF TONKIN

LAOS

Hue
Danang

SIAM

Quang Ngai

CAMBODIA

Saigon

SOUTH CHINA SEA

Regions held by the Viet Minh Front

Map 2. Areas under Viet Minh control as of 17 August 1945

administrative center, and provincial seat of power. In places like Hanoi, there were on some days several demonstrations at once in different quarters of the city. Viet Minh flags, slogans, songs, and publications were everywhere. And wherever they appeared, Viet Minh speakers were warmly applauded and their slogans shouted.

In this wave of popular enthusiasm, power simply fell into Viet Minh hands. With few exceptions, there were no haggles, no fights, and little shooting. It was an insurrection by street demonstrations. Hanoi was taken on 19 August with a mass demonstration and three revolver shots—to salute the Viet Minh flag; Hue, on 23 August with a mass demonstration; Danang, on the same day with two people with rifles leading a mass demonstration; and Saigon, on 25 August with an enormous demonstration. On 30 August Bao Dai, the last monarch of the Nguyen dynasty, formally abdicated in favor of the Viet Minh. Three days later Nguyen Ai Quoc, now known as Ho Chi Minh, proclaimed the success of the Vietnamese revolution, pronounced the Declaration of Independence, and presented to the Vietnamese nation a government of the Democratic Republic of Vietnam.

As it turned out, few of the ICP Central Committee leaders involved in the final planning for the general insurrection played much of a role in the insurrectionary activities themselves. When the news of Japan's surrender arrived on radio, the Central Committee held an emergency three-day meeting (13–15 August) at Tan Trao to decide how to deal with the immediate situation. An urgent appeal was published declaring:

1. The very favorable opportunity for the conquest of independence has arrived.
2. We are in an extremely urgent situation. All our operations must be based on the following three principles:
   a. Concentration–concentration of our forces on the essential tasks;
   b. Unity–unity of action and of command in political and military matters;
   c. Timeliness–acting in good time and not letting any opportunity slip by. . . .
5. Occupy immediately those areas where we are sure to win, regardless of whether they are urban or rural. Establish People's Committees wherever we have established control.[59]

59. Ibid., p. 9.

Following the ICP Central Committee meeting, a parallel conference of the "People's Congress," with sixty delegates representing various social and ethnic groups, met for two days. To legitimize their actions, the People's Congress created a provisional government, headed by Ho Chi Minh.[60]

Meanwhile, Vo Nguyen Giap, chairman of an Insurrection Committee and head of the Vietnamese Liberation Army, was leading the insurrectionary armed forces toward Thai Nguyen, opening the official Viet Minh–led insurrection. On 19 August, when Giap had just reached the village of Thinh Dan, west of Thai Nguyen, he received news of the liberation of Hanoi.[61] Several delegates who were on their way to Tan Trao for the People's Congress received orders to return to their own areas to lead the insurrection. By the time Hanoi was liberated, Ha Dong, Ha Tinh, Quang Ngai, and several other cities and provincial seats had fallen into the hands of local "people's revolutionary committees."[62] In some places insurrectional activities began as early as 13 August, immediately after the Japanese surrender. Having studied the "Historic Directive" and waited eagerly for the "revolutionary situation" to arrive, ICP members in most places acted before receiving final instructions from the Central Committee. The strategy of partial insurrection was particularly effective in Bac Ky and northern Trung Ky. Here, the rural areas were taken over first, then the provincial seats or cities. This pattern was reversed in Nam Ky and southern Trung Ky, where the ICP forces had largely been destroyed in 1940 and Viet Minh influence was very weak. In these areas the Viet Minh Front, claiming Allied support, was able to form coalitions with existing political groups and to manipulate them to support the provisional government in a show of national unity. By the time Saigon was under nominal Viet Minh control on 25 August, most of the country was already in Communist hands.

60. Ibid., pp. 27–28.
61. Tran Huy Lieu, *Lich su tam muoi nam,* 3: 160.
62. For a complete account of the August general insurrection, province by province, read both volumes of *CMTT.*

Chronology of the August Revolution 1945

INSURRECTIONS IN CITIES AND PROVINCIAL CAPITALS

August 18: Bac Giang, Hai Duong, Ha Tinh, Quang Nam
19: Hanoi, Yen Bay, Thai Binh, Phuc Yen, Thanh Hoa, Khanh Hoa
20: Bac Ninh, Thai Nguyen, Ninh Binh
21: Cao Bang, Tuyen Quang, Son Tay, Nghe An, Ninh Thuan, Bac Can
22: Hung Yen, Quang Yen, Nam Dinh, Kien An
23: Hue, Hoa Binh, Haiphong, Ha Dong, Quang Tri, Quang Binh, Binh Dinh, Lam Vien, Gia Lai, Tan An, Bac Lieu
24: Ha Nam, Dac Lac, Phu Yen, Binh Thuan, Go Cong, My Tho
25: Saigon, Cholon, Gia Dinh, Soc Trang, Long Xuyen, Vinh Long, Ba Ria, Thu Dau Mot, Chau Doc, Tra Vinh, Bien Hoa, Ben Tre, Sa Dec, Cong Tum, Tay Ninh, Lang Son, Phu Tho
26: Hong Gai, Son La, Can Tho
27: Rach Gia
28: Quang Ngai, Ha Tien, Dong Nai Thuong

OTHER EVENTS OF IMPORTANCE

August 30:   Abdication of Emperor Bao Dai
September 2:   Declaration of Vietnamese independence and establishment of the Democratic Republic of Vietnam
November 11:   "Self-dissolution" of the Indochinese Communist party

THREE SIGNIFICANT EVENTS

The numerous insurrectionary activities throughout Vietnam in the autumn of 1945 were capped by three events of symbolic importance: the abdication of Emperor Bao Dai, the pronouncement of the Declaration of Vietnamese Independence, and the "self-dissolution" of the Indochinese Communist party.

On 30 August, Emperor Bao Dai abdicated in favor of the provisional government. The last emperor in the Nguyen dynasty, which had ruled since 1802, he had been placed on the Vietnamese throne in 1932 at age eighteen in a French gesture to placate certain segments of the Vietnamese population, as part of the "reforms" made in the aftermath of Yen Bay, the Nghe Tinh soviets, and the visit of Paul Reynaud. Although there had originally been much hope in Bao Dai's supposed youthful idealism and progressive ideas, there were no signs of reforms in the years following the young emperor's accession. Constrained by the French, who had placed a dedicated agent, Pham Quynh, next to him as prime minister, he was unable to put his idealism to the test. From 1932 until the Japanese coup Bao Dai spent much of his time hunting or at the card tables. With the Japanese coup he quickly switched his allegiance, kept the throne, and continued to serve the new foreign masters.

Yet, for all his servility to foreign rulers, Bao Dai held an important position. As the last figure in the imperial succession of the Nguyen dynasty, he represented a sort of legitimate continuity of the Vietnamese state, and at the same time, for a sizable number of Vietnamese who looked to the monarchy, Bao Dai continued to be the sacred symbol of the nation. Thus, his voluntary abdication was an event of symbolic importance. In handing over the imperial seals and sword, symbols of sovereignty, to the representatives of the Provisional Government of the Democratic Republic, Bao Dai conferred legitimacy on the new government. At the same time, his abdication represented the end of the centuries-old monarchical institution. In the aftermath of this event, Emperor Bao Dai became "First Citizen" Nguyen Vinh Thuy. He was later elevated to the ceremonial position of "supreme adviser" to the government. This was neither the first nor the last time that Bao Dai assumed the role of a puppet.

The pronouncement of the Declaration of Independence on 2 September was another event of symbolic importance. In front of a mass meeting of half a million people gathered in Hanoi's Ba Dinh Square, a smallish, thin, older man named Ho Chi Minh read an official pronouncement declaring an end to French colonial rule, Japanese control, and the monarchy. It would be another six years before it was acknowledged officially that this older man and the famed Vietnamese revolutionary Nguyen Ai Quoc were one and the same person. Meanwhile, the declaration was more than just a declaration of independence. It was also a declaration of the victory of a party, whose revolutionary objective was *bai phong, phan de* (antifeudalism and antiimperialism). The declaration stated in part:

The French have fled, the Japanese have capitulated, Emperor Bao Dai has abdicated. Our people have broken the chains of colonialism which have fettered us for nearly a century in order to create an independent Vietnam. Our people have at the same time overthrown the monarchical regime which has reigned supreme for dozens of centuries to establish a democratic republican regime. . . .
For the reasons mentioned above, we—the Provisional Government of the Democratic Republic of Vietnam—solemnly declare to the world that:
Vietnam has the right to enjoy freedom and independence, and has in reality become a free and independent country. The entire people of Vietnam are determined to mobilize all their physical and mental strength, to sacrifice their lives and property to preserve their right to freedom and independence.[63]

The second of September is today celebrated by the Socialist Republic of Vietnam and its supporters throughout the world as Vietnam's Independence Day. This date is officially considered the formal end of the August Revolution, which is seen as the climax of the century-long Vietnamese struggle for independence from Western imperialists. For the Communists, the reading of the Declaration of Independence at Ba Dinh Square formally established the end of French colonial imperialism, the end of the Confucian-oriented monarchical regime, the regaining of Vietnamese independence, and the beginning of the Democratic Republic of Vietnam.

The "self-dissolution" of the ICP was the third significant event during this period. Whereas the abdication of the monarchy and the emergence of an independent republic represented turning points for the Vietnamese state as a whole, self-dissolution, however formalistic it may have been, was an important event in the evolution of Vietnamese communism. On 11 November 1945 the Central Executive Committee of the ICP declared that, "ready to put the interests of the nation above class interests," the Party had voluntarily decided to dissolve itself. The ICP resolution states:

2. Whereas the essential condition for the completion of the great task of national liberation is the solidarity and unity of our entire people regardless of class or party;
3. To demonstrate that the members of the Communist party are the vanguard fighters of the nation, ready to put the interests of the nation above class interests and to sacrifice partisan interests for the sake of the common interests of the Nation;

63. Tran Huy Lieu et al., *TLTK*, 12: 106–107.

4. To destroy all misunderstandings outside and inside the country which may obstruct the prospect of liberating our country;

The Central Executive Committee of the Indochinese Communist Party, met on 11 November 1945, resolved that the Indochinese Communist Party dissolve itself.

The faithful *(tin do)* of Communism who wish to go on with their ideological study shall adhere to "the Indochinese Association for the Study of Marxism."[64]

This was an exceptional act. Communist parties do not shed their appellation lightly. Save for the self-dissolution in 1944 of the American Communist party at a time of extreme internal schism, never had a Communist party previously disbanded itself voluntarily. In the entire history of international communism, there has been no other example of a Communist party dissolving itself following a successful seizure of power.

Although official and semiofficial historical accounts of the ICP today have in general maintained a studious silence concerning the 1945 "self-dissolution,"[65] it is possible to accept at face value the argument that this action had been forced upon the Party by the pressure of political isolation.[66] Aside from the overwhelming support of the Vietnamese population, the regime was virtually friendless. Three months after an incredibly easy victory, the Party nominally governed a country occupied by the armies of three powerful nations—Great Britain, China, and France—all of which

64. "Dang Cong san Dong duong tu y giai tan" [The Indochinese Communist party voluntarily dissolves itself], text of the resolution of the Executive Committee of the ICP, dated 11 November 1945. In Nguyen Kien Giang, *Viet-Nam nam dau tien sau Cach mang thang Tam* [Vietnam during the first year after the August Revolution] (Hanoi, 1961), p. 129, n. 1 (italics in original).

65. Except for the study by Nguyen Kien Giang, cited above, Communist Vietnamese accounts of ICP history usually ignore this important event. Neither the official history by the Commission for Study, *Outline History*, nor *Hoi va Dap*, the catechism on the Party's history, mentions the 1945 self-dissolution. The recently published collection of official Party documents (Vu bien soan, Van kien Dang) also passes over the document on the 1945 self-dissolution.

66. See Nguyen Kien Giang, *Nam dau tien*, p. 130. Harold R. Isaacs conjectures that the ICP decision to self-dissolve might have been motivated by a desire to "avoid any responsibility at a time when responsibility was the heaviest" (*No Peace for Asia* [New York, 1947]). Although this may have been one of the motivations, it would not have been the most important. For a Communist party such as the ICP, which had twice previously—in 1931 and again in 1940—been suppressed by colonial authorities, organizational survival would always have to be the prime and central motivation.

would have preferred a different Vietnamese regime. Since September 1945, British troops had occupied southern Indochina, south of the sixteenth parallel, to disarm the Japanese in accordance with the Potsdam Agreement. They had done everything possible to rearm the resident French and otherwise help the returning French troops to reconquer Indochina. Chinese Kuomintang troops, in the meantime, had come to disarm the Japanese in the northern part of the peninsula. They did their best to install an anticommunist Vietnamese regime friendly to Kuomintang China. International support for the new Vietnamese government was nowhere to be found. The Chinese Communists were preoccupied at home in a struggle for power with the Kuomintang. The Soviets, in the words of an ICP leader then, had already exhibited "an excess of ideological compromise" and shown no interest in the Vietnamese revolution.[67] The French Communists, too, had proved themselves loyal French first and Communists second. While in France the PCF itself wasted no time on the ICP, the small group of French Communists in Indochina urged upon their Vietnamese comrades a policy of "patience" and avoidance of "premature adventures."[68]

Under such circumstances, "self-dissolution" was an expedient tactic. Its leaders perceived it as the best measure to preserve the Party's survival as a political force. As Nguyen Kien Giang put it:

67. Recounting his personal experience in Vietnam during the August Revolution, Isaacs reported extreme bitterness among Vietnamese Communist leaders, who felt they had been abandoned by their Russian and French comrades. He attributed the quoted phrase to Tran van Giau, then chairman of the Committee of the South (see Isaacs, *No Peace for Asia*, p. 172). Another Vietnamese Communist stated bitterly, "The Russians are nationalists for Russia first and above all. They would be interested in us only if we served some purpose of theirs. Right now, unfortunately, we do not seem to serve any such purpose" (ibid., pp. 172–173).

68. Ibid., p. 173. One year later when, on 23 November 1946, the fleet of the French Expeditionary Force shelled Haiphong, thus opening the "First" Indochina War, the PCF—according to Communist sources—was debating whether to attribute responsibility for the war to "Vietnamese troublemakers." For the next several months, as PCF members took the limelight in the French government with five ministers, including the minister of defense and the vice-president of the Council of Ministers (who was also secretary-general of the PCF), the French Chamber of Deputies voted in favor of military credits for the French war efforts in Vietnam. Although the PCF members of the Chamber abstained, all their ministers voted in favor—in order to maintain "ministerial solidarity"! See Claudin, *The Communist Movement*, 2: 338–339.

Faced with the threatening pressure of the Chiang Kai-shek gang against the survival of our Party, [self-dissolution] was a very good measure for our Party to escape the butt of their attack. At that time, either the Party continued to agitate publicly, thus inviting a suppression of the Vietnamese revolution and a destruction of our Party by the Chiang Kai-shek gang which would use the "anticommunist" excuse, or else the Party had to sacrifice its appellation in order to preserve its forces and continue to lead the revolution. The Party's Central Committee, headed by President Ho, quickly decided on the second course of action.[69]

There were Communists who later contended that the ICP's 1945 public renunciation of its ideological badge was an erroneous policy that set a bad example.[70] The Vietnamese Communists have always based their justification on the need to preserve the Party's organizational network, albeit in secret, in order to maintain its revolutionary leadership. The 1945 "self-dissolution," in the words of Nguyen Kien Giang, was a "beautiful gesture." It demonstrated that Vietnamese Communists "were ready to sacrifice temporarily their appellation—and only their appellation—for the sake of the revolution."[71]

In reality, self-dissolution occurred only on paper. The ICP merely went underground, or, to use Communist jargon, "withdrew into clandestinity" *(rut vao bi mat)*. In the meantime, it continued to consolidate its hold on political power and reinforce itself with a determined membership drive. In the provisional government, supposed to be a coalition government, Communists controlled all the crucial ministerial posts. In addition to Ho Chi Minh, who was both president and minister for foreign affairs, other Communists held key Cabinet positions: Vo Nguyen Giap (interior), Chu van Tan (national defense), Pham van Dong (finance), Tran Huy Lieu (propaganda), and Le van Hien (labor).[72] The Party also sought to extend its influence in Vietnamese society. In its "Directive on Resistance and National Construction," issued 25 November 1945, two weeks after the publication of the self-dissolution resolution, the Central Executive Committee in-

69. Nguyen Kien Giang, *Nam dau tien,* p. 130.
70. Ibid.
71. Ibid.
72. Devillers, *Viet-Nam de 1940 à 1952,* p. 142, n. 4.

structed Party members on the tasks of consolidating the Party apparatus. The directive reads in part:

> *On the Party:* We must preserve the Party's clandestine and semiclandestine organizational network. Recruit more Party members. . . . We must organize cells for the Association for the Study of Marxism, under the direction of Communists, for those who have Communist inclination or sympathy. At the same time, we must avert Party members from being contaminated with petit-bourgeois habits and by the disease of legalism often seen in all countries where legal actions are feasible. Party organs must function regularly, and there is no excuse for their activities to be incoherent and uncoordinated.[73]

In the following five years the Party experienced an unprecedented growth in membership. From five thousand members in August 1945, Party membership had already reached "several hundred thousand"[74] by the summer of 1950, when the Party decided to halt temporarily its recruitment drive.

In the context of Vietnamese communism, however, the ICP decision to self-dissolve was more than just a tactic to preserve the Party's survival. This supple political expedient actually represented the final victory of a political line within the Party. As we have seen, from its very beginning the Vietnamese Communist movement had always contained within itself two contrary tendencies. One, which may be labeled the "Vietnamese" faction, consistently emphasized the primacy of Vietnamese independence and the necessity of a political strategy that would appeal to national unity and patriotism. The other, the "Indochinese" faction, emphasized the importance of an Indochinese, not Vietnamese, revolution and the class struggle and downgraded patriotism, sometimes condemning it as a manifestation of petit-bourgeois chauvinism. The conflict between the two political lines had already flared up in 1930, first over the question of the necessity of having a Communist party to lead the revolution and then over an appropriate strategy, and name for the Party. The establishment of the Indochinese Communist party in October 1930 as a replacement for the Vietnamese Communist Party, founded by Nguyen Ai Quoc in February 1930, had been a temporary victory of the Indochinese faction. This victory also led to the eclipse of Nguyen Ai

73. "Chi thi Khang chien Kien quoc" [Directive on resistance and national construction], in Vu bien soan, *Van kien Dang* 2: pp. 12–13.
74. Hoang Tung, *Dang cua giai cap cong nhan*, p. 16.

Quoc and the domination of Party affairs by the Indochinese faction throughout the 1930s. With the return of Nguyen Ai Quoc to
Vietnam in the spring of 1941 and the subsequent formation of the
Viet Minh Front, however, a reemphasis on Vietnamese patriotism
and national liberation and the self-effacement of the ICP marked
the beginning of the erosion of the Indochinese faction's influence
and the resurgence of the Vietnamese faction to leadership. "Self-
dissolution" and the expurgation of the term *Indochinese* were thus
consistent with the dominant political line within the Party.

As a victory of this political line, the August Revolution had an
indelible influence on the evolution of Vietnamese communism.
The publication of the self-dissolution resolution was one of the
last occasions when the appellation "Indochinese Communist
Party" appeared during the turbulent period of Vietnamese history.
Since the August Revolution, Vietnamese Communist strategy has
placed special stress on national independence, patriotism, and the
need for national unity. When, in 1951, the Communist party
reemerged in public view, it called itself the Vietnam Workers'
Party (Dang Lao Dong Viet Nam). At its Fourth National Congress in December 1976, the Party renamed itself once more the
Vietnamese Communist Party (Dang Cong San Viet Nam), the
same name that Nguyen Ai Quoc gave the Party in February 1930.

AN ASSESSMENT OF THE AUGUST
REVOLUTION

Among the questions that arise about the origins, nature,
and forms of revolutionary action in the August Revolution, the
one asked most often is why the ICP, and not any other Vietnamese political party, succeeded in winning power and popular
support in August 1945. To this question several answers have
been given. According to some analyses, the ICP succeeded because it was more cunning, had better liars, or was the only political organization on the scene. Historical facts easily dispose of
these explanations. Cunning people and liars are not the exclusive
characteristics of Communist parties in Vietnam or anywhere else.
As to political parties, there were no less than thirty noncommunist
parties during that period.[75]

75. Pham van Son, *Viet-nam tranh dau su,* pp. 251–252.

Two explanations deserve special consideration. One, often put forward by ICP detractors, sees the success of the Viet Minh in August 1945 as a result of fortuitous circumstances. According to this argument, there was a vacuum of power in Vietnam following the Japanese surrender. The Japanese had destroyed the French colonial regime in March. When they in turn capitulated to the Allies, their troops were in confusion and became dispirited. Taking advantage of the situation, the Viet Minh Front easily took power in the face of Japanese indifference,[76] or even with their connivance.[77] The Viet Minh Front, following this theory, had gained mass support by its connections with the Allied forces.

A second explanation, often presented by Vietnam's historians today, views the Communist success in August 1945 as a result of skillful analysis of the revolutionary situation and long-term planning and preparation. The success of the August Revolution must accordingly be seen as a result of the "correct revolutionary line" and of the "creative application of Marxist-Leninist principles to the revolutionary conditions of Vietnam" by the ICP leadership. Following this argument, the origins of the August Revolution go back to the Eighth Plenum of the ICP Central Committee in May 1941, when it decided to set aside temporarily the program of class struggle in favor of national unity in the struggle against French colonialism, when the Viet Minh Front was created, and when plans for insurrection were first put forward.[78] The success of the ICP in August 1945, in other words, was the result of long-term revolutionary preparation involving propaganda and organizational work. As Tran van Giau, one of the best-known ICP leaders, would have it, the success of the August Revolution was the result of both an art and a science of insurrection.[79] The scientific principles of insurrection were already laid down by Lenin, and it was the ICP artists who made the insurrection.

Although there is sufficient evidence to support either of the explanations, by itself each is inadequate. Chance alone explains

76. See Joseph Buttinger, *Vietnam: A Dragon Embattled*, 2 vols. (New York, 1967), 2: 298. Buttinger stated, "The Japanese, who were indeed the only ones in a position to prevent the Viet Minh from taking, remained ostentatiously neutral. Thus it might be said that they made the victory of the Viet Minh feasible."

77. See John T. McAlister, *Viet Nam: The Origins of Revolution* (New York, 1969), p. 190.

78. See Tran Huy Lieu, *Lich su tam muoi nam*, 3: 127.

79. Tran van Giau, *Giai cap cong nhan*, 3: 277.

little. The element of chance in the peculiar combination of factors in the Vietnam of August 1945—the Japanese capitulation, the absence of French and Allied forces—offered itself not only to the Viet Minh Front but to all other political parties. At best, the theory of chance explains the obvious, that is, that the conditions of political flux of August 1945 were extremely favorable for an insurrectional attempt. It fails to explain how an organized political force could obtain and maintain political power. The explanation of "revolutionary skills," often smugly propounded by Vietnamese Communists, is equally unsatisfactory. The ICP's skills in revolutionary analysis, organization, propaganda, and leadership were undoubtedly superior to those of the other Vietnamese political parties. These skills, however, would have been useless without a favorable "revolutionary environment." Specifically, if the Japanese army in Indochina had not destroyed French colonial power, it is doubtful whether revolutionary skill would have brought the ICP close to any of its desired objectives. By the time of the Japanese coup, several of the most seasoned, Moscow-trained ICP leaders had already been killed or captured, and most of those who were still alive were in French prisons or "concentration camps" *(trai tap-trung)*. Every Vietnamese insurrectional uprising, Communist-initiated or otherwise, had been swiftly and brutally suppressed by the colonial regime. It is difficult to see how, without the Japanese coup, any insurrectional attempt could have succeeded.

In retrospect, historical fortuity and revolutionary ability played equally important roles in the victory of Vietnamese communism. Yet theorists on both sides have been inclined to ignore the fact that both elements came into being well before the climatic events of August 1945. More than any other single event, the Japanese coup served as the catalyst and contributed decisively to the success of the August Revolution. Its most obvious and important contribution was the elimination of the French colonial regime, which was the most dangerous, implacable, and capable enemy of the Vietnamese revolution. The destruction of French colonial forces was a *conditio sine qua non* for the success of any Vietnamese revolution. Unexpectedly, the coup and the subsequent Vietnamese "independence" awakened patriotism and a sense of social concern among urban Vietnamese, who were soon to swell the revolutionary ranks. Thus, the Japanese coup may be considered the turning point in the fortunes of both French colonialism and Vietnamese nationalism. The resultant collapse of the old order and the Japanese preoccupation with the war created a vacuum of power in areas remote from administrative and military centers—a vacuum that the Viet Minh–created "liberation committees" quickly filled.

Favorable circumstances were, however, only one of the requirements for a successful insurrection. In destroying French colonialism, the Japanese coup merely provided the Vietnamese revolution with an opportunity. The rest was up to the Vietnamese revolutionaries. The ICP's activities on the very night of the Japanese coup demonstrate clearly that they correctly perceived the "acute political crisis" and the "favorable conditions" for revolutionary action, both of which had just been created by the coup. The ICP also wisely perceived that the conditions were not yet "ripe" for an insurrection. The French had been destroyed, but Viet Minh forces were far from able to challenge the Japanese army. It was also doubtful whether the majority of the population knew, at this stage, who the Viet Minh were. Except for the famine, which initially caused many difficulties for the local, rural-based Viet Minh organizations—difficulties that the Viet Minh Front managed to overcome and even exploit to their advantage—political conditions during the five-month Japanese interlude became increasingly favorable for an insurrectional attempt. In urban areas, where Viet Minh influence was the weakest, Viet Minh members secretly infiltrated existing political groups and eventually either took control or weaned away the most active and susceptible elements. In the countryside, the Viet Minh led daily attacks on the granaries and rice convoys. Everywhere secret "liberation committees" were formed. In July large areas of Bac Ky and northern Trung Ky were either overtly or secretly under some form of Viet Minh influence. In most places throughout Vietnam, the Viet Minh capture of power was received with enthusiasm, or at worst, unopposed.

In addition to tactical flexibility, another of the Communists' "subjective conditions" was crucial to their political success: the predominance of the political line of the Vietnamese faction, led by Nguyen Ai Quoc, with its emphasis on the primacy of Vietnamese national liberation, patriotism, and national unity. The adoption of this line in May 1941 led to the concealment both of the Party's Commmunist label and of the personal identity of its leader. In 1945, Communist activities were carried out in the name of the Viet Minh Front, the ICP reemerged only to abolish itself, and its leader was known as Ho Chi Minh, not the legendary Nguyen Ai Quoc. Thanks to the flexibility of this national liberationist line, the Communist party was able to gain the support of the broad masses of the Vietnamese population regardless of social class. It is not inaccurate to say that in the August Revolution the Communist party rode to power on a wave of Vietnamese patriotism.

Finally, the irrelevance of the Communist International to the Viet Minh success in the August Revolution deserves emphasis. For all the material and psychological benefits, connections with international communism were not always conducive to the advancement of Communist power in Vietnam. The 1930s, a period in which the ICP closely aligned its policies with Comintern objectives, saw the nadir of Communist fortunes. On the contrary, the Viet Minh's popularity during the early 1940s, just as Thanh Nien's during the late 1920s, occurred when the Vietnamese Communist movement was isolated from its international network. Most noteworthy, unlike their comrades in Central Europe, the Vietnamese Communists seized political power in 1945 without any external Communist assistance. They retained power and popular support with policies contradictive to international advice. Their success, it may be said, was achieved in spite of, and not because of, their ties with international communism.

The August Revolution was the first of three significant turning points in recent Vietnamese history (the other two being the victory at Dien Bien Phu in May 1954 and the American defeat in April 1975). This event marked the end of direct foreign domination in internal Vietnamese affairs, formally abolished the centuries-old monarchical-mandarinate political system, brought large numbers of Vietnamese into the political process, and finally, fulfilled the Vietnamese wish to make independent Vietnam a part of the global political configuration.

The success of the August Revolution belongs, in the first place, to the indomitable spirit of the Vietnamese people, who reject domination by foreign imperialism and struggle determinedly for their national independence. It belongs more particularly to the generation of revolutionary patriots of the 1920s who had the daring, courage, and tenacity to search for teachers and ideas for a revolution and map a new direction for Vietnamese politics. These were the members of Thanh Nien, Tan Viet, the Vietnamese Nationalist Party (VNQDD), the Nguyen An Ninh "secret society," and Vietnamese Independence Party (PAI), many of whom would continue their political mission under different ideological labels—ICP, Trotskyist, Vung Hong, and others. The success belongs no less to the Indochinese Communist party, which provided the Vietnamese revolution with an ideological orientation, organization, and leadership. Finally, it belongs to one man—Nguyen Ai Quoc, alias Ho Chi Minh—whose devotion to the cause of Vietnamese national liberation and whose political perspicacity made it possible for the Communist party to seize power in the autumn of 1945.

Without question, however, the August Revolution was less than a total success. Foreign imperialism remained in Vietnam in different forms and under different pretexts. Vietnamese independence and unity were not realized completely until April 1975. If anything, the August Revolution represented a beginning. The process of social and political change that began with the events of August 1945 effected a definite transformation of Vietnamese society and politics. That process is still going on.

For Vietnamese communism, too, the August Revolution represented a new beginning. This event was an important turning point in the process of transplanting Marxism-Leninism to the Vietnamese sociopolitical environment. The Communist party had ceased to be an illegal organization; it became a party in power. The grafting of Marxism-Leninism in Vietnam had taken place; "indigenization" had yet to begin.

EPILOGUE

On 30 April 1975, Vietnam's thirty-years' war of national resistance came to an abrupt end. As a result of the seven-week "Ho Chi Minh Campaign," the "Republic of Vietnam," which had been supported with American dollars, troops, and equipment, collapsed. Thus ended nine years of French attempts at colonial reconquest and twenty-one years of American neocolonial enterprise. Vietnam was finally decolonized. Vietnamese independence declared during the August Revolution of 1945, finally became a reality.

There was a *déjà vu* quality to the Communist victory. As in the August Revolution, the Communist Vietnamese took over South Vietnam almost as if it were an empty house. There was not much opposition. The Americans had been first to take flight, with their troops in 1973, and then with their dollars. The war-profiteering Saigon generals followed. Deprived of active support from their foreign masters, these collaborators, who had long styled themselves "nationalists" and defenders of Vietnamese self-determination, abandoned their native land and the people they were supposed to lead as quickly as they could gather their loot. Meanwhile, beset with self-doubt about their mission and suspicious of their leaders' motive, most of the South Vietnamese troops simply abandoned the battlefields and their uniforms and fled, even before the arrival of the adversary troops. Left behind was a bewildered, battered population that, long imbued with anti-communist propaganda, was both relieved by the coming of peace and uncertain about its fate under the victors. Many fled the country empty-handed; most others stayed and were "reeducated" to be members of the new society. Again, as in August 1945, there were mass demonstrations to welcome the Communist victory; but the demonstrations this time lacked the earlier spontaneity and festive spirit. As in 1945, Vietnamese national unity was reasserted, but in reality only an administrative unity had been imposed as a factual consequence of military victory. Meanwhile, spiritual unity remained an aspiration.

Whatever else the judgment of history will be, the events of April 1975 were a turning point in the history of Vietnam and of Vietnamese communism. The defeat of the United States effected the complete decolonization of the country, the culmination of 117 years of resistance against continuous Western attempts to mold Vietnamese national destiny and arbitrate the country's internal affairs. For Vietnamese Communists, the victory in April 1975 was more than the acquisition of complete power, of which they had been deprived in August 1945 and which they had believed to be their due after the victory at Dien Bien Phu in 1954. It was the completion of an important phase in the ICP's evolution. Having defeated foreign imperialism, henceforth the Party would have to lead a social revolution. This victory would fundamentally modify not only the appearance but also the substance of Vietnamese communism. Up to this point the Communists had trod familiar ground. From 1930 to 1975 the ICP had had double, parallel objectives: national liberation and a social revolution. As long as foreign intervention was a factor in Vietnamese politics, however, the goal of national liberation had remained preeminent. Indeed, for the previous half century the fight against foreign imperialism for national independence had been the defining factor and *raison d'être* of the Communist movement. It was this struggle that helped it gain popular support, justifying the sacrifices it demanded of its people and the postponement of deserved material rewards for hard work. It also helped keep the Communist leadership virtually free of factionalism.

The Communist movement now faces the problems of success.

What will happen to Vietnamese communism now that foreign intervention is no longer a factor in Vietnamese politics and national liberation is an accomplished fact? Will the Vietnamese Communists do as well in reconstructing the country as in repulsing foreign aggressors? Given radical change in the international context—in which increasing Sino-Soviet confrontation has destroyed the long-empty semblance of an international Communist movement—and the evolving character of Vietnamese patriotism as a result of liberation, where will Vietnamese communism go from here?

Another important question pertains to the evolving character of Vietnamese communism. This book has viewed the process of transplanting communism into Vietnam as the grafting of a scion of Marxism-Leninism onto the stock of Vietnamese patriotism. The phenomenal growth of Vietnamese communism during the last half century attests to the success of that grafting process. At this point, in considering the relationship between Vietnamese patriotism and international communism, it is relevant to raise the ultimate Bolshevik question: *kto kogo?* (who is using whom?); or another question, often heard among Communist Vietnamese in discussing international developments: *ai thang ai?* (who is winning over whom?). In the union of Communist ideology and patriotism in the development of Vietnamese communism, has Marxism-Leninism been a vehicle for Vietnamese patriotism? Or has patriotism been exploited for the sake of expanding the Communist ideology? Finally, as communism *in Vietnam* is transformed into communism *of Vietnam*—or, as Vietnamese Communists become Communist Vietnamese—to what extent will the movement be suffused with cultural characteristics drawn from the deep roots of Vietnamese history and tradition, and to what extent will it absorb the imported qualities of its internationalist connections?

These are among the basic questions that await further consideration.

ORGANIZATIONAL CHARTS

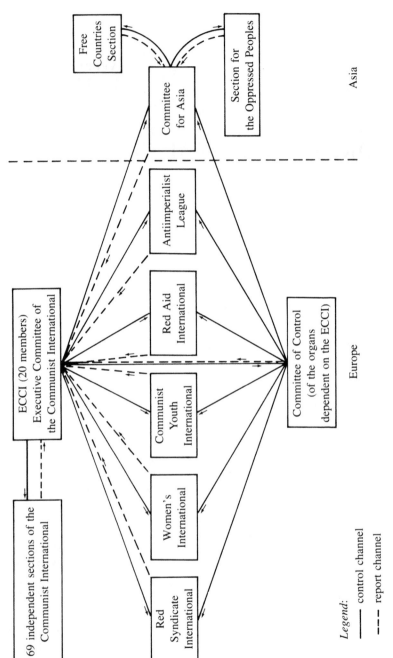

Chart 1. Organization of the Communist International, 1930

Legend:

—— control channel

- - - report channel

Asia

Europe

Free Countries Section

Section for the Oppressed Peoples

Committee for Asia

Antiimperialist League

Red Aid International

Communist Youth International

Women's International

Red Syndicate International

ECCI (20 members) Executive Committee of the Communist International

69 independent sections of the Communist International

Committee of Control (of the organs dependent on the ECCI)

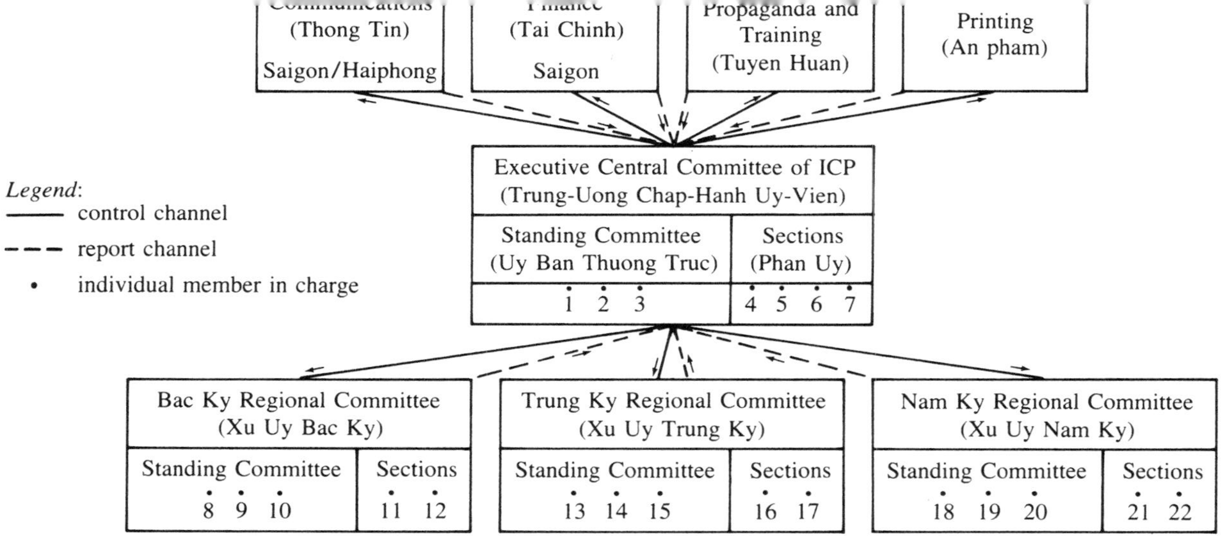

Printing
(An pham)

Propaganda and
Training
(Tuyen Huan)

(Tai Chinh)
Saigon

Communications
(Thong Tin)
Saigon/Haiphong

Executive Central Committee of ICP
(Trung-Uong Chap-Hanh Uy-Vien)

Standing Committee (Uy Ban Thuong Truc)	Sections (Phan Uy)
• • • 1 2 3	• • • • 4 5 6 7

Bac Ky Regional Committee (Xu Uy Bac Ky)	
Standing Committee	Sections
• • • 8 9 10	• • 11 12

Trung Ky Regional Committee (Xu Uy Trung Ky)	
Standing Committee	Sections
• • • 13 14 15	• • 16 17

Nam Ky Regional Committee (Xu Uy Nam Ky)	
Standing Committee	Sections
• • • 18 19 20	• • 21 22

Legend:

——— control channel

– – – report channel

• individual member in charge

Central Committee

1 Tran Phu
2 Ngo Duc Tri
3 A Chinese
4 Giap
5 information unavailable (from Bac Ky)
6 Thanh (Le van Sac) (from Trung Ky)
7 information unavailable (from Trung Ky)

Bac Ky Regional Committee

8 Nghiem Thuong Bien (alias Thang)
9 Pham van Ngo (alias Ngan)
10 Khuat Duy Tien (alias To Dau)
11 Hoang (Pham van Phong; Lan)
12 information unavailable

Trung Ky and Nam Ky Regional Committees

(13–22) The only member known as of
March 1931 was Nguyen Duc
Canh, on the Standing Committee
for Trung Ky; otherwise all were
unknown to the informers
(apparently Nghiem Thuong Bien
and Ngo Duc Tri).

Chart 2. Special organs of the ICP Central Committee, 1930

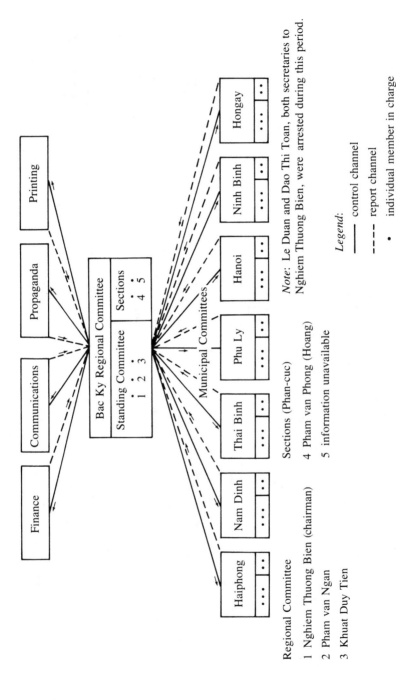

Regional Committee

1 Nghiem Thuong Bien (chairman)

2 Pham van Ngan

3 Khuat Duy Tien

Sections (Phan-cuc)

4 Pham van Phong (Hoang)

5 information unavailable

Note: Le Duan and Dao Thi Toan, both secretaries to Nghiem Thuong Bien, were arrested during this period.

Legend:

―――― control channel

‑ ‑ ‑ ‑ report channel

• individual member in charge

Chart 3. Organs of the Bac Ky Regional Committee, March 1931

BIBLIOGRAPHY

PRIMARY SOURCES

ARCHIVES

Paris, Archives Nationales de France, Section Outre-Mer. Service de Liaison avec les Originaires des Territoires de la France Outre-Mer.
Washington, D.C. U.S. Army Archives, Office of the Chief of Military History. Papers of General Philip E. Gallagher.

DOCUMENTS

"Ban nghi quyet cua Toan Quoc Dai Bieu Dai Hoi Lan Thu Nhat cua Dang Cong san Dong duong, Ngay 27–31 thang Ba 1935" [Resolutions of the First National Congress of representatives of the Indochinese Communist party, 27–31 March 1935].
Cahiers des voeux annamites. Saigon: Imprimerie de l'Echo Annamite, 1925.
"Le *chi bo:* Methode de travail d'une cellulle annamite." *Extrême-Asie* 7, no. 75 (April 1933), pp. 163–174.
Chuong trinh hanh dong cua Dang Cong san Dong duong [Program of Action of the Indochinese Communist party]. n.p., 1932.
Degras, Jane, ed. *The Communist International, 1919–1943: Documents.* 6 vols. New York: Oxford University Press, 1956–60.
Gouvernement de la Cochinchine, Service de police. *Recherche de condamnés dangereux évadés du pénitencier de Poulo-Condore. Tap na tu loi hai da vuot nguc Con non.* Saigon: Imprimerie de l'Union, 1935.

Gouvernement-général de l'Indochine. *Discours de M. Paul Reynaud, 16 novembre 1931.* [Hanoi?] 1931.

"Lettre ouverte du Comité central du P. C. de Chine aux membres du P. C. de l'Indochine." *Cahiers du bolchévisme* 11, no. 16 (15 August 1934), pp. 957–968.

Luan cuong chinh tri cua Dang Cong san Dong duong [Political theses of the Indochinese Communist party]. n.p., 1930.

Nguyen van To [Ung Hoe], ed. *Chat xieng: Nhung lai lieu lich su tu chinh bien thang Ba den cach mang thang Tam 1945* [Breaking our chains: The historical documents from the political crisis of March until the August Revolution 1945]. 2d ed. Hanoi: Su That, 1955.

Orgwald [pseud.]. "Entretiens avec les camarades indochinois." *Internationale communiste,* 15 October 1933, pp. 1150–70.

"Thu cua Quoc te Cong san gui cho cac nhom cong san o Dong duong (1929)" [Letter of the Communist International to the diverse Communist groups in Indochina (1929)]. Reprinted in *Hoc tap* [Study], no. 61 (1960), pp. 42–49.

"Ve viec thanh lap mot dang cong san o Dong duong (thu chi thi cua Quoc te cong san ngay 27-10-1929)" [On the formation of a Communist party in Indochina (directive of the Communist International, 27 October 1929)]. *Hoc tap,* no. 48 (1960), pp. 9–12.

Vu bien soan, Ban tuyen huan trung uong (Editorial Section, Central Committee for Propaganda and Education). *Lich su Dang Cong san Viet Nam: Trich van kien Dang* [History of the Vietnamese Communist party: Extracts from Party documents]. 3 vols. Hanoi: NXB sach giao khoa Mac-Le-nin, 1979.

MEMOIRS AND BIOGRAPHIES

Ba Phuong Lan [Bui The My]. *Nha cach mang Ta Thu Thau, 1906–1945* [The revolutionary Ta Thu Thau, 1906–1945]. Saigon: Khai Tri, 1974.

Bui cong Trung, Van Tien Dung, Xuan Thuy, and others. *Len duong thang loi* [Onward to victory]. Hanoi: Van Hoc, 1960.

Bui Lam, Nguyen Luong Bang, Vu Anh, Vo Nguyen Giap, and others. *Souvenirs sur Ho Chi Minh.* Hanoi: 1965.

Catroux, General [Georges]. *Deux actes du drame indochinois.* Paris: Librairie Plon, 1959.

Chang Kuo-t'ao. *The rise of the Chinese Communist Party.* Vol. 2, *1928–1938.* Lawrence: University Press of Kansas, 1972.

Chu van Tan. *Reminiscences on the Army for National Liberation.* Translated by Mai Van Elliott. Cornell University Southeast Asian Program, Data Paper No. 97. Ithaca, 1974.

Chu van Tan, Hoang Quoc Viet, Hoang van Hoan, Nguyen Luong Bang, Vo Nguyen Giap, and others. *Dau nguon* [Fountainhead]. Hanoi, Van Hoc, 1975.

Decoux, Admiral [Jean]. *A la barre de l'Indochine: Histoire de mon Gouvernement général, 1940–1945.* Paris: Librairie Plon, 1949.

Drachkovitch, Milorad M., and Branko Lazitch, eds. *The Comintern: Historical Highlights*. New York: Frederick A. Praeger, 1966.

Ducoroy, Maurice. *Ma trahison en Indochine*. Paris: Editions Internationales, 1949.

Fenn, Charles. *Ho Chi Minh: A Biographical Introduction*. London: Studio Vista, 1973.

Figuères, Leo, and Charles Fourniau, comps. and eds. *Ho Chi Minh, notre camarade*. Paris: Editions Sociales, 1970.

Guong chien dau cua nhung nguoi cong san [The fighting examples of the Communists]. Hanoi: Su that, 1965.

A Heroic People: Memoirs from the Revolution. [Hoang Quoc Viet, Le van Luong, Pham Hung, and others] Hanoi: Foreign Languages Publishing House, 1965.

Hoang van Tam, Hong Chuong, Luu Quy Ky, Nguyen Duy Trinh, and others. *Trong kham tu vi thanh nien* [In the juveniles prisons]. Hanoi: Thanh Nien, 1965.

Huong Nam [pseud.], ed. *Trai tim bat khuat cua mien Nam* [The indomitable spirit of the South]. Hanoi: Van hoa–Nghe thuat, 1962.

Lacouture, Jean. *Ho Chi Minh: A Political Biography*. New York: Vintage Books, 1968.

———. "Ho Chi Minh et la tradition révolutionnaire française." In *Cinq hommes et la France*. Paris: Editions du Seuil, 1961.

Legrand, J. *L'Indochine à l'heure japonaise*. Cannes: Aegitna, 1963.

Le Manh Trinh, Nguyen Khanh Toan, Nguyen Luong Bang, Vo Nguyen Giap, and others. *Bac Ho* [Uncle Ho]. Hanoi: Van Hoc, 1960.

Le van Thu. *Muoi chin sinh vien Viet-Nam bi truc xuat* [The nineteen Vietnamese students who were expelled]. Saigon: Nam Viet, 1949.

Neumann-Hoditz, Reinhold. *Portrait of Ho Chi Minh*. New York: Herder, 1972.

Nguyen Hai Ham. *Tu Yen-Bay den Con-Lon* [From Yen Bay to Con Lon]. Saigon: Phan Vy 1970.

Nguyen Khanh Toan, Nguyen Luong Bang, Le Manh Trinh, and others. *Avec l'Oncle Ho*. Hanoi: Foreign Languages Publishing House, 1972.

Nhung nguoi cong san [The Communists]. Hanoi: Thanh Nien, 1977.

Nhuong Tong. *Nguyen Thai Hoc, 1902–1930*. Saigon: Tan Viet, 1949.

Patti, Archimedes L. A. *Why Vietnam? Prelude to America's Albatross*. Berkeley and Los Angeles: University of California Press, 1980.

Pham van Dong. *Ho Chu Tich, lanh tu cua chung ta* [President Ho, our leader]. Hanoi: Su That, 1963.

Phan Boi Chau. *Tu phan* [Self-judgment]. Hue: Anh Minh, 1956.

Rageau, Christiane Pasquel. *Ho Chi Minh*. Paris: Editions Universitaires, 1970.

Reynaud, Paul. *Mémoires*. 2 vols. Paris: Flammarion, 1960–63.

Sabattier, G. *Le destin de l'Indochine: Souvenir et documents, 1941–1951*. Paris: Librairie Plon, 1952.

Sainteny, Jean. *Histoire d'une paix manquée: Indochine 1945–1947*. Paris: Fayard, 1954.

T. Lan [Ho Chi Minh]. *Vua di duong vua ke chuyen* [Anecdotes on the road]. Hanoi: Su That, 1963.

The Nguyen. *Phan Boi Chau, 1867–1940.* [Saigon?] Tan Viet, 1956.

Tran Dan Tien. *Glimpses of the Life of Ho Chi Minh.* Hanoi: 1958.

Tran Huy Lieu. *Dang Thanh Nien, 1926–1927* [The Youth party, 1926–1927]. Memoirs. Hanoi: Su Hoc, 1961.

———. *Mat tran Dan chu Dong duong* [The Indochinese Democratic Front]. Memoirs. Hanoi: Su Hoc, 1960.

Tran Huy Lieu and the History of the August Revolution Cell, eds. *Cach mang thang Tam: Tong khoi nghia o Ha-noi va cac dia-phuong* [The August Revolution: The general insurrection in Hanoi and other regions]. 2 vols. Hanoi: Su Hoc, 1960.

Tran Trong Kim. *Mot con gio bui* [A whirlwind]. Saigon: Khai Tri, 1970.

Vo Nguyen Giap. *Nhung nam thang khong the nao quen* [The unforgettable years and months]. Hanoi: Quan doi nhan dan, 1970. Translated by Mai Van Elliott. *Unforgettable Years and Months.* Cornell University Southeast Asia Program, Data Paper No. 99. Ithaca, 1975.

———. *Tu nhan dan ma ra* [Born of the people]. Hanoi: Quan doi nhan dan, 1964.

OFFICIAL STUDIES

Ban nghien cuu lich su Dang (Commission for the Study of the History of the Party). *Chu tich Ho Chi Minh* [President Ho Chi Minh]. Hanoi: Su That, 1970.

———, comp. *Buoc ngoat vi dai cua lich su cach mang Viet Nam* [The great turning point in the history of the Vietnamese revolution]. Hanoi, 1961.

Ban nghien cuu lich su quan doi thuoc Tong cuc chinh tri, Quan doi nhan dan Viet Nam (Commission for the Study of the History of the Armed Forces of the Central Political Section, the People's Army of Vietnam). *Lich su quan doi nhan dan Viet Nam* [History of the People's Army of Vietnam]. Hanoi: NXB Quan doi nhan dan, 1977.

Commission for the Study of the History of the Vietnam Workers' party. *An Outline History of the Vietnam Workers' Party (1930–1975).* Hanoi: 1976.

The Democratic Republic of Viet Nam. Hanoi: 1960.

Direction fédérale de l'information. *La situation en Indochine (mars 1945–juin 1946).* Saigon, 1946.

Gouvernement générale de l'Indochine, Direction des affaires politiques et de Sûreté française. *Contribution à l'histoire des mouvements politiques de l'Indochine française.* 5 vols. Hanoi: IDEO, 1930–35.

Hoi va Dap ve lich su Dang [Catechism on the Party's history]. Hanoi: Thanh Nien, 1977.

Métin, Albert. *L'Indochine et l'opinion.* Paris: H. Dunot and E. Pinat, 1916.

Pham van Dong and Commission for the Study of the History of the Vietnam Workers' Party. *President Ho Chi Minh.* Hanoi: 1970.

Propaganda Section, Central Committee of the Vietnam Workers' Party and Commission for the Study of the Party's History. *Trente ans du Parti de la classe ouvrière.* Hanoi: 1960.

Sacks, I. Milton. *Political Alignments of Vietnamese Nationalists.* Washington, D.C.: Office of Intelligence Research, U.S. Department of State, 1949.

Sakai, Lt. Colonel Tateki. "French Indo-China Area Operations Record." Japanese Monograph No. 25. Headquarters, Far Eastern Command, Military History Section [n.p.], n.d.

Service d'information, République democratique du Viet-Nam. *Le Président Ho-Chi-Minh.* Paris, 1947.

Les soviets du Nghe Tinh de 1930–1931 au Vietnam. Hanoi: 1960.

Tran Huy Lieu, Van Tao, Nguyen Luong Bich, Nguyen Cong Binh, Huong Tan, and Nguyen Khac Dam. *Tai lieu tham khao lich su cach mang can dai Viet Nam* [Research materials on the history of the contemporary Vietnamese revolution]. 12 vols. Hanoi: Van Su Dia, 1955–58.

PERIODICALS AND NEWSPAPERS

Argus indochinois (Hanoi). 1922–30.
L'Asie française (Paris). 1909–40.
Bao cong nong [Workers' and peasants' news] (Canton). 1926–27.
La cloche fêlée (Saigon). 1923–26.
Dai doan ket [Great solidarity] (Ho Chi Minh City). 1977–80.
Dong Phap thoi bao [The times of French Indochina] (Saigon). 1923–28.
Hoc tap [Study] (Hanoi). 1959–76.
L'Indochine (Saigon). 1941.
L'Indochine enchainée (Saigon). 1924–25.
Lao dong [Labor] (Paris). 1932–33.
Lao nong [The toiling peasant] [n.p.]. 1928.
Linh kach menh [Revolutionary soldier] (Canton). 1927–28.
La lutte (Saigon). 1933–38.
Mat tran do [The red front] (Saigon). 1937–38.
Nam phong [Southern wind] (Hanoi). July 1917–November 1934.
Ngay nay [Nowadays]. (Hanoi). 1939–45.
Nghien cuu lich su [Historical studies] (Hanoi). 1959–74.
Le nha que [The rural hick] (Saigon). 1927.
Nhan dan [The people] (Hanoi). 1955–80.
Phu nu tan van [Women's news] (Saigon). 1929–34.
La presse indochinoise (Saigon). 1924–41.
Quan chung [The masses] [m.p.]. 1936.
La résurrection (Aix-en-Provence), 1928.
La revue indochinoise (Hanoi). 1937–43.
Su that [Truth] [n.p.]. 1936–37.
Tan cong [Attack] [n.p.]. 1938.
Tap chi Bon-so-vic [Bolshevik review] [n.p.], 1934.
Tap chi cong san [Review of communism] (Hanoi). 1977–80.

Tap chi dan toc hoc [Review of ethnography] (Hanoi). 1978–80.
Thanh nghi [Impartial opinion] (Hanoi). 1944–45.
Thanh nien [Youth] (Canton). 1925–30.
La tribune indochinoise (Saigon). 1926–30, 1936–39.
Triet hoc [Philosophy] (Hanoi). 1979–80.
Van su dia [Literature, history, geography] (Viet Bac, Hanoi). 1949–59.
Vietnamese Studies. 1964–78.
Viet Nam hon [Soul of Vietnam] (Paris). 1926.
Vo san [Proletariat] [n.p.]. 1936–37.

WORKS BY COMMUNIST LEADERS

Capitan-Peter, Colette, comp. and ed. *Ho Chi Minh: Action et révolution, 1920–1957.* Paris: Union Générale d'Editions, 1968.
[Ho Chi Minh] *Duong kach menh* [The road to revolution]. 1926; reprinted in Vu bien soan, Ban tuyen huan trung uong (Editorial Section, Central Committee for Propaganda and Education). *Lich su Dang Cong san Viet Nam: Trich van kien Dang* [History of the Vietnamese Communist party: Extracts from Party documents]. 3 vols. Hanoi, 1979. 1: 7–16.
Ho Chi Minh. *Ecrits (1920–1969).* Hanoi: FLPH, 1971.
————. *Ket hop chat che long yeu nuoc voi tinh than quoc te vo san* [Fusing intimately patriotism with proletarian internationalism]. Hanoi: Su That, 1976.
———— [Nguyen]. "Ky niem lan thu 4 ngay thanh lap Dang cong san Dong duong" [Commemorating the fourth anniversary of the formation of the Indochinese Communist party]. 1934; reprinted in *Hoc tap*, no. 85 (February 1963), pp. 4–6.
————. *Oeuvres choisies.* 4 vols. Hanoi: FLPH, 1960.
———— [Nguyen Ai Quoc]. *Le procès de la colonisation française.* First series, *Moeurs coloniales.* Paris, 1926.
————. *Tuyen tap* [Selected works]. Hanoi: Su That, 1960.
———— [Nguyen Ai Quoc]. "The Party's Military Work among the Peasants." In *Armed Insurrection.* edited by A. Neuberg [Franz Neumann]. London: New Left Books, 1970.
Le Duan. *Chu nghia Le-nin va cach mang Viet-Nam* [Leninism and the Vietnamese revolution]. Hanoi: Su That, 1960.
————. *Forward under the Glorious Banner of the October Revolution.* Hanoi: FLPH, 1969.
————. *Giai cap cong nhan Viet-Nam va lien minh cong nong* [The Vietnamese proletariat and the worker-peasant alliance]. Hanoi: Su That, 1976.
————. *On the Socialist Revolution in Vietnam.* Vols. 1 and 2. Hanoi: FLPH, 1965.
————. *The Vietnamese Revolution: Fundamental Problems, Essential Tasks.* Hanoi: FLPH, 1970.
Lenin, V. I. *The National Liberation in the East.* Moscow: Progress Publishers, 1954.

———. *Selected Works*. 3 vols. Moscow: Progress Publishers, 1967.

Stalin, Joseph. *Problems of Leninism*. Moscow: Foreign Languages Publishing House, 1940.

Truong Chinh. *Cach mang dan toc dan chu nhan dan Viet-Nam* [The people's national democratic revolution in Vietnam]. 2 vols. Hanoi: Su That, 1975–76.

———. *Cach mang thang Tam* [The August Revolution]. Hanoi: Su That, 1955.

———. *En avant sous le drapeau du parti*. Hanoi: FLPH, 1965.

———. *Forward along the Path Charted by K. Marx*. Hanoi: FLPH, 1969.

———. "Mot so van de ve Cach mang thang Tam Viet-Nam" [A number of issues concerning the Vietnamese August Revolution]. *Hoc tap*, no. 92 (September 1963), pp. 1–10.

———. *President Ho Chi Minh, Beloved Leader of the Vietnamese People*. Hanoi: FLPH, 1966.

———. *Selected Writings*. Hanoi: FLPH, 1977.

———. *Ve cong tac mat tran hien nay* [On the front work at present]. Hanoi: Su That, 1972.

Vo Nguyen Giap. *Guerre du peuple, armée du peuple*. Paris: François Maspéro, 1966.

———. *Nhung chang duong lich su* [Stages on the historical road]. Hanoi: Van Hoc, 1977.

———. *Selected Writings*. Hanoi: FLPH, 1977.

SECONDARY SOURCES

WESTERN-LANGUAGE MATERIALS

Ajalbert, Jean. *L'Indochine par les français*. Paris: Librairie Gallimard, 1931.

Anh Van and Jacqueline Roussel. *Mouvements nationaux et lutte de classes au Viet-Nam*. Marxisme et Colonie, Publications de la IVe Internationale. Paris: Imprimerie Réaumur, 1947.

An [Nguyen van Tao]. "Le mouvement révolutionnaire en Indochine." *Cahiers du bolchévisme* 5 (May 1930): 467–474.

Arendt, Hannah. *On Revolution*. New York: Viking Press, 1963.

Avtorkhanov, Abdurakhman. *The Communist Party Apparatus*. Cleveland and New York: Meridian Books, 1966.

Azeau, Henri. *Ho Chi Minh, dernière chance: La conférence franco-vietnamienne de Fontainebleau, 1946*. Paris: Flammarion, 1968.

Ball, William MacMahon. *Nationalism and Communism in East Asia*. Carlton, Australia: Melbourne University Press, 1956.

Barthouet, Arnaud. *La tragédie franco-indochinoise*. Paris: Delmas, 1948.

Bauchar, René [Jean Charboneau]. *Rafales sur l'Indochine*. Paris: Fournier, 1946.

Bell, Daniel. *The End of Ideology*. New York: Collier Books, 1961.

Bernard, Paul. *Nouveaux aspects du problème économique indochinois.* Paris: Fernand Sorlot, 1937.

―――. *Le problème économique indochinois.* Paris: Nouvelles Editions Latines, 1934.

Bidault, Jean. *La paix au Viet Nam.* Paris, 1947.

Brower, Daniel R. *The New Jacobins: The French Communist Party and the Popular Front.* Ithaca: Cornell University Press, 1968.

Brunschwig, Henri. *French Colonialism, 1871–1914: Myths and Realities.* London: Pall Mall, 1966.

Buttinger, Joseph. *Viet Nam: A Dragon Embattled.* 2 vols. New York: Frederick A. Praeger, 1967.

―――. *Viet Nam: A Political History.* New York: Frederick A. Praeger, 1968.

―――. "The Ethnic Minorities in the Republic of Vietnam." In *Problems of Freedom: South Vietnam since Independence.* Edited by Wesley Fishel. Glencoe, Ill.: Free Press, 1961.

Camus, Albert. *The Rebel.* New York: Vintage Books, 1961.

Carrère d'Encausse, Hélène, and Stuart R. Schram. *Marxism and Asia: An Introduction with Readings.* London: Allen Lane, 1969.

Caute, David. *The Fellow Travellers.* London: Weidenfeld and Nicholson, 1973.

Chen, King. *Vietnam and China, 1938–1954.* Princeton: Princeton University Press, 1969.

Chesneaux, Jean. *Contribution à l'histoire de la nation vietnamienne.* Paris: Editions Sociales, 1955.

Chesneaux, Jean; Georges Boudarel; and Daniel Hémery, eds. *Tradition et révolution au Vietnam.* Paris: Editions Anthropos, 1971.

Chow Ts'e-tsung. *The May Fourth Movement: Intellectual Revolution in China.* Cambridge: Harvard University Press, 1960.

Claudin, Fernando. *The Communist Movement: From Comintern to Cominform.* 2 vols. New York and London: Monthly Review Press, 1975.

Colton, Kenneth E. "The Influence of Japanese Wartime Policy on the Independent Political Movement in Vietnam after March 1945." Paper delivered at the 1971 Annual Meeting of the American Political Science Association.

Cook, Megan. *The Constitutionalist Party in Cochinchina: The Years of Decline, 1930–1942.* Clayton, Australia: Monash University Center of Southeast Asian Studies, 1977.

Coulet, Georges. *Les sociétés secrètes en terre d'Annam.* Saigon: Ardin, 1926.

Cowley, Malcolm. *Think Back on Us.* Edited by Dan Piper. Carbondale: Southern Illinois University Press, 1967.

Crossman, Richard H. S. *The God That Failed.* New York: Bantam Books, 1959.

Cucherousset, H. "La famine au Nghe Tinh: Ce qu'en dit la presse." *Eveil économique de l'Indochine,* no. 700 (23 August 1931).

Dallin, David J. *Soviet Russia and the Far East.* New Haven: Yale University Press, 1948.

Demariaux, Jean-Claude. *Les secrets des îles Poulo-Condore, le grand bagne indochinois.* Paris: J. Peyronnet, 1956.

Deutscher, Isaac. *The Prophet Outcast.* New York: Vintage Books, 1963.

Deux ans d'Indochine: Un fleuve de sang. Cannes: Aegitna, 1934.

Devillers, Philippe. *Histoire du Viet-Nam de 1940 à 1952.* Paris: Editions du Seuil, 1952.

Do Duc Ho. *Réponse des étudiants indochinois de Paris à M. Alexandre Varenne.* Paris, 1937.

Dorsenne, Jean. *Faudra-t-il évacuer l'Indochine?* Paris: Nouvelle Socièté d'Edition, 1932.

———. "Le péril rouge en Indochine." *Revue des deux mondes,* 1 April 1932, pp. 519–556.

Drachkovitch, Milorad M., ed. *The Revolutionary Internationals, 1964–1943.* Stanford: Stanford University Press, 1966.

Duiker, William J. "The Red Soviets of Nghe Tinh: An Early Communist Rebellion in Vietnam." *Journal of Southeast Asian Studies* 4, no. 2 (September 1973), pp. 186–198.

———. *The Rise of Nationalism in Vietnam, 1900–1941.* Ithaca: Cornell University Press, 1976.

Dumarest, André. *La formation des classes sociales en pays annamite.* Lyon: Imprimerie Ferreol, 1935.

Duncanson, Dennis J. *Government and Revolution in Vietnam.* London: Oxford University Press, 1968.

Durtain, Luc [André Robert Gustave Nepreu]. *Dieux blancs, hommes jaunes.* [Paris] Flammarion [1930].

Elsbree, Willard E. *Japan's Role in Southeast Asian Nationalist Movements.* Cambridge: Harvard University Press, 1953.

Ennis, Thomas. *French Policy and Developments in Indochina.* Chicago: University of Chicago Press, 1956.

"L'épilogue des troubles communistes dans le Nord-Annam." *Illustration,* no. 4591 (22 February 1931), p. 243.

Fall, Bernard B. "The Political-Religious Sects of Vietnam." *Pacific Affairs,* 28, no. 3 (September 1955), pp. 235–253.

———. *The Viet Minh Regime.* Cornell University Southeast Asia Program, Data Paper No. 14. Ithaca, 1954.

Fanon, Frantz. *Les damnés de la terre.* Paris: François Maspéro, 1966.

Fitzgerald, Frances. *Fire in the Lake: The Vietnamese and the Americans in Vietnam.* New York: Vintage Books, 1973.

La France en Indochine. Paris: Nouvelles Editions Latines, 1950.

Gaudel, André. *L'Indochine française en face du Japon.* Paris: J. Susse, 1947.

Gautherot, G. *Le bolchévisme aux colonies et l'impérialisme rouge.* Paris: Librairie de la Revue Française, 1930.

Gobron, Gabriel, *Histoire et philosophie du caodaisme.* Paris: Derby, 1949.

Gorz, André. "Mai et la suite." *Les temps modernes*, August–September 1968.
———. *Socialism and Revolution*. Garden City, N.Y.: Doubleday, Anchor Press, 1973.
Goudal, Jean. *Labour Conditions in Indochina*. Geneva: International Labour Office, 1938.
Gourou, Pierre. *Les paysans du delta tonkinois; étude de géographie humaine*. Paris: Editions d'Art et d'Histoire, 1936.
Gros, Louis, *L'Indochine française pour tous*. Paris: Albin Michel, 1931.
Gruber, Helmut. *Soviet Russia Masters the Comintern: International Communism in the Era of Stalin's Ascendancy*. Garden City, N.Y.: Doubleday Anchor Press, 1974.
Guérin, Daniel. *Au service des colonisés, 1930–1953*. Paris: Editions de Minuit, 1954.
———. *Front populaire: Révolution manquée*. Paris: Editions Internationales, 1964.
Hammer, Ellen J. *The Emergence of Viet Nam*. New York: International Secretariat, Institute of Pacific Relations, 1947.
———. *The Struggle for Indochina 1940–1955*. Stanford: Stanford University Press, 1966.
Harmel, Claude. "France." In *World Communism: A Handbook, 1918–1965*. Edited by Witold S. Sworakowski. Stanford: Hoover Institution Press, 1973.
Hémery, Daniel. "Du patriotisme au marxisme: L'immigration vietnamienne en France de 1926 à 1930." *Le mouvement social*, no. 90 (January–March 1975), pp. 3–54.
———. *Révolutionnaires vietnamiens et pouvoir colonial en Indochine*. Paris: François Maspéro, 1975.
Hertrich, Jean-Michel. *Doc lap: L'indépendence ou la mort*. Paris: Vigneau, 1946.
Hoang van Chi. *From Colonialism to Communism: A Case History of North Vietnam*. New York: Frederick A. Praeger, 1964.
Hong The Cong. "La révolution indochinoise." *Cahiers du bolchévisme* (1 July 1932): 866–872.
———. "Le travail du parti communiste indochinois." *Cahiers du bolchévisme* 8 (1 February 1932): 177–190.
———. "Troisième anniversaire de l'unification du parti communiste indochinois." *Cahiers du bolchévisme* 8 (1 March 1933): 275–283.
Hu Shih. *The Chinese Renaissance*. 2d ed. New York: Paragon Book Reprint, 1963.
Hull, Cordell. *The Memoirs of Cordell Hull*. 2 vols. New York: Macmillan, 1948.
Huynh Kim Khanh. "The August Revolution Reinterpreted." in *Journal of Asian Studies* 30, no. 4 (August 1971), pp. 761–782.
"The Indochinese Democratic Front (1936–1939)." *Vietnam Advances*, no. 3 (March 1963), p. 8.
Isaacs, Harold R. *No Peace for Asia*. New York: Macmillan, 1947.

Isoart, Paul. *Le phénomène national vietnamien: De l'indépendence unitaire à l'indépendence fractionnée.* Paris: Pichon et Durand-Auzias, 1961.

Johnson, Chalmers. *Revolutionary Change.* Boston: Little, Brown, 1966.

Kahin, George McT. "Minorities in the Democratic Republic of Vietnam." *Asian Survey* 12 (July 1972): 580–586.

Komor, I. "Ten Years of the Comintern." In *The United Front.* New York: Rand School Press, 1933.

Krivitsky, Walter G. *In Stalin's Secret Service.* New York: Harper, 1939.

Lancaster, Donald. *The Emancipation of French Indochina.* London and New York: Oxford University Press, 1961.

Langlois, Walter G. *André Malraux: The Indochina Adventure.* New York: Frederick A. Praeger, 1965.

Lebas, J. "Les mouvements de jeunesse en Indochine." *L'Indochine* 2, no. 37 (15 May 1941).

Lefranc, Georges. *Histoire du front populaire.* Paris: Payot, 1965.

———. *Le mouvement socialiste sous la Troisième République (1875–1940).* Paris: Payot, 1963.

Le Thanh Khoi. *Le Viet Nam: Histoire et civilisation.* Paris: Editions de Minuit, 1955.

Luethy, Herbert. *France against Herself.* Cleveland and New York: Meridian Books, 1968.

Lyne, Stephen R. "The French Socialist Party and the Indochina War, 1944–1954." Ph.D. diss. Stanford University, 1965.

Mannheim, Karl. *Ideology and Utopia.* New York: Harcourt, Brace, and World, 1963.

Marc, Henry, and Pierre Cony. *Indochine française.* Paris: Editions France-Empire, 1946.

Marr, David G. *Vietnamese Anticolonialism, 1885–1925.* Berkeley and Los Angeles: University of California Press, 1971.

McAlister, John T. *Vietnam: The Origins of Revolution.* New York: Alfred A. Knopf, 1969.

McAlister, John T., and Paul Mus. *The Vietnamese and Their Revolution.* New York: Harper & Row, 1970.

McKenzie, Kermit. *Comintern and the World Revolution, 1928–1943.* New York: Columbia University Press, 1964.

McLane, Charles B. *Soviet Strategies in Southeast Asia.* Princeton: Princeton University Press, 1966.

Meyer, Alfred G. *Leninism.* New York: Frederick A. Praeger, 1962.

Mills, C. Wright. *The Marxists.* New York: Dell, 1962.

Monet, Paul. *Les jauniers.* Paris: Gallimard, 1930.

Mus, Paul. "The Role of the Village in Vietnamese Politics." *Pacific Affairs* 22 (September 1949), pp. 265–272.

———. *Viet Nam: Sociologie d'une guerre.* Paris: Editions du Seuil, 1950.

Naville, Pierre. *La guerre du Viet Nam.* Paris: Editions de la Revue Internationale, 1949.

Newfield, Jack. *A Prophetic Minority.* New York: New American Library, 1967.

Ngo Vinh Long. *Before the Revolution: The Vietnamese Peasants under the French*. Cambridge: MIT Press, 1973.

―――. "The Indochinese Communist Party and Peasant Rebellion in Central Vietnam, 1930–1931." *Bulletin of Concerned Asian Scholars* 10, no. 4 (December 1978), pp. 15–34.

Nguyen Khac Vien. *Expériences vietnamiennes*. Paris: Editions Sociales, 1970.

―――. *Histoire du Vietnam*. Paris: Editions Sociales, 1974.

Nguyen Kien Giang. *Les grandes dates du parti de la classe ouvrière du Viet Nam*. Hanoi: FLPH, 1960.

North, Robert C. *Moscow and the Chinese Communists*. Stanford: Stanford University Press, 1953.

O'Harrow, Stephen. "French Colonial Policy towards Vernacular Language Development in Vietnam and the Selection of Pham Quynh." In *Aspects of Vietnamese Language in Asian and Pacific Societies*. Edited by Nguyen Dang Liem. Honolulu: University of Hawaii Press, 1973.

Oliver, Victor L. *Caodai spiritualism: A Study of Religion in Vietnamese Society*. Leiden: Brill, 1976.

Osborne, Milton. "The Faithful Few: The Politics of Collaboration in Cochinchina in the 1920s." In *Aspects of Vietnamese History*. Edited by Walter Vella. Honolulu: University of Hawaii Press, 1973.

―――. *The French Presence in Cochinchina and Cambodia: Rule and Response (1859–1905)*. Ithaca: Cornell University Press, 1969.

Paillat, Claude. *Dossier secret de l'Indochine*. Paris. Presses de la Cité, 1964.

Panikkar, K. M. *Asia and the Western Dominance*. London: George Allen and Unwin, 1959.

Parti communist français. *Un an de terreur et de lutte révolutionnaire en Indochine*. Paris, 1931.

Pedrazzani, Jean-Michel. *La France en Indochine: De Catroux à Sainteny*. Paris: B. Arthaud, 1973.

Petrus, Joseph. "Marxism, Marxists, and the National Question." Ph.D. diss., University of Texas, 1966.

Pham Quynh. *Essais franco-annamites*. Hue: Bui Huy Tin, 1937.

Pham thi Ngoan. "Introduction au Nam phong." *Bulletin de la Société des Etudes Indochinoises* n.s. 48 (1973): 175–473.

Priestley, Herbert. *France Overseas: A Study of Modern Imperialism*. New York: D. Appleton-Century, 1938.

Robequain, Charles. *L'Indochine française*. Paris: Armand Colin, 1952.

―――. *The Economic Development of French Indochina*. London, New York, and Toronto: Oxford University Press, 1944.

Robin, René. "La situation politique de l'Indochine." *Revue du Pacifique*, February 1935, pp. 69–88.

Rodinson, Maxine. *Marxisme et monde musulman*. Paris: Editions du Seuil, 1972.

Rogger, Hans, and Eugen Weber, eds. *The European Right: A Historical Profile*. Berkeley and Los Angeles: University of California Press, 1965.

Roth, Andrew. *Japan Strikes South*. New York and San Francisco: American Council, Institute of Pacific Relations, 1941.

Roubaud, Louis. *Viet Nam: La tragédie indochinoise*. Paris: Valois, 1931.

Rousset, Pierre. *Le parti communiste vietnamien*. Paris: François Maspéro, 1973.

Sacks, I. Milton. "Marxism in Vietnam." In *Marxism in Southeast Asia: A Study of Four Countries*. Edited by Frank N. Trager. Stanford: Stanford University Press, 1959.

Sarraut, Albert. *La mise en valeur des colonies françaises*. Paris: Payot, 1953.

Savani, A. M. *Visage et images du Sud Viet-Nam*. Saigon: Imprimerie Française d'Outre-Mer, 1955.

Selznick, Philip. *The Organizational Weapon*. Glencoe, Ill.: Free Press, 1960.

Seton-Watson, Hugh. *From Lenin to Khrushchev: The History of World Communism*. New York: Frederick A. Praeger, 1960.

Shaplen, Robert. "The Enigma of Ho Chi Minh." *Reporter*, 27 January 1955, pp. 11–18.

"La situation en Indochine: Soumission des communistes." *Monde colonial illustré*, no. 91 (March 1931), pp. 62–63.

Smith, Ralph. "Bui Quang Chieu and the Constitutionalist Party in French Cochinchina, 1917–1930." *Modern Asian Studies* 3, no. 2 (1969), pp. 131–150.

Starobin, Joseph R. *Eyewitness in Indochina*. New York: Cameron and Kahn, 1954.

Sworakowski, Witold S., ed. *World Communism: A Handbook, 1918–1965*. Stanford: Hoover Institution Press, 1973.

Tédral, Pierre. *La comédie indochinoise*. Paris: Editions Vox, 1926.

Tersen, Emile. *Histoire de la colonisation*. Paris: Presses Universitaires de France, 1950.

Thai Nam Van. "Le communisme en Indochine." *Extrême-Asie* 7, no. 76 (May 1933), pp. 244–246.

Thep Moi. "The Birth of the Indochinese Communist Party." *Vietnam courrier*, nos. 34 (March 1975), pp. 3–7, and 35 (April 1975), pp. 21–25.

Thomazi, A[uguste A.]. *La conquête de l'Indochine*. Paris: Payot, 1934.

Thompson, Virginia. *French Indo-China*. 1937; reprint ed., New York: Octagon Books, 1968.

Thompson, Virginia, and Richard Adloff. *The Left Wing in Southeast Asia*. New York: William Sloane Associates, 1950.

———. "Vietnamese Nationalism and French Policies." In *Asian Nationalism and the West*. Edited by William L. Holland. New York: Macmillan, 1953.

Thorez, Maurice. *La France du front populaire et les peuples coloniaux*. Paris: 1938.

Tournoux, J.-R. *Secrets d'état*. Paris: Librairie Plon, 1960.

Touzet, André. *L'économie indochinoise et la grande crise*. Paris: Marcel Giard, 1934.

Trotsky, Leon. *The Russian Revolution: The Overthrow of Tzarism and the Triumph of the Soviets*. Translated by Max Eastman. Selected and edited by F. W. Dupee. Garden City, N.Y.: Doubleday, 1959.

Tucker, Robert C. *The Marxian Revolutionary Idea*. New York: W. W. Norton, 1969.

——. *The Soviet Political Mind: Stalinism and Post-Stalin Change.* Rev. ed. New York: W. W. Norton, 1971.

Ulam, Adam B. *The Bolsheviks*. New York: Macmillan, 1965.

Viet Chung. "National Minorities and Nationality Policy in the DRV." *Vietnamese Studies*, no. 15 (1968), pp. 3–21.

Villemotier, L. "Le patriotisme et le mouvement révolutionnaire en Indochine française." *Mercure de France* 45, no. 872 (15 October 1934), pp. 225–250.

Viollis, Andrée [Ardenne de Tizac]. *L'Indochine S.O.S.* 2d ed. Paris: Editeurs Français Réunis, 1949.

Woddis, Jack. *New Theories of Revolution*. New York: International Publishers, 1972.

Woodside, Alexander B. *Community and Revolution in Modern Vietnam.* Boston: Houghton Mifflin, 1976.

Xuan Thuy. "La politique de front national uni." *La nouvelle critique*, March 1962, pp. 82–95.

Yacono, Xavier. *Histoire de la colonisation française*. Paris: Presses Universitaires de France, 1969.

VIETNAMESE-LANGUAGE MATERIALS

Bui Dinh Thanh. "Dau tranh vu trang trong Cach mang thang Tam" [The armed struggle in the August Revolution]. *NCLS*, no. 17 (August 1960), pp. 16–26.

Chiem-Te. "Cach mang thang Tam, mot bo phan cua cach mang the gioi" [The August Revolution is a part of the world revolution]. *NCLS*, no. 18 (September 1960), pp. 21–30.

Chuong Thau. "Anh huong cach mang Trung Quoc doi voi su bien chuyen cua tu tuong Phan Boi Chau" [The influence of the Chinese Revolution upon the changes in Phan Boi Chau's thinking]. *NCLS*, no. 43 (October 1962), pp. 12–26, 36.

——. "Nguon goc chu nghia yeu nuoc cua Phan Boi Chau" [The origins of Phan Boi Chau's patriotism]. *NCLS*, no. 88 (July 1966), pp. 21–24.

Chu Quang Tru. "Tim hieu Phan Chu Trinh trong lich su can dai Viet-Nam" [Understanding Phan Chu Trinh in the context of modern Vietnamese history]. *NCLS*, no. 72 (March 1965), pp. 50–56, 62.

"Coi trong hon nua cong tac Mat Tran" [Pay more attention to the Front work]. Editorial. *Hoc tap*, no. 64 (May 1961), pp. 1–4.

Dang Viet Thanh. "Cach mang thang Tam va cach mang van hoa" [The August Revolution and the Cultural Revolution]. *NCLS*, no. 18 (September 1960), pp. 31–37.

Dong Tung. "Nguoi Viet Nam o Thai lan." *Nghien cuu su dia*, 1970, pp. 17–18.

Hai An. "Tinh chat cua Cach mang thang Tam [The nature of the August Revolution]. *NCLS*, no. 54 (September 1963), pp. 10–17.

Hoang Ho. "Ban them ve bai 'Tim hieu qua trinh hinh thanh va phat trien cua Mat tran dan toc thong nhat Viet Nam' cua ong Van Tao" [Let us discuss further the article "Understanding the Formation and Development of the Vietnamese National United Front" by Mr. Van Tao]. *NCLS*, no. 5 (July 1959), pp. 47–62.

Hoang Nhat Tan. "Gioi thieu cuon sach 'Buoc ngoat vi dai cua lich su cach mang Viet-Nam'" [Introducing the Book "The Great Turning Point in the History of the Vietnamese Revlution"]. *Hoc tap*, no. 65 (June 1961), pp. 60–62.

Hoang Nhat Tan and Le Quoc Su. "Neu mot so van de can di sau trong viec nghien cuu ve Cach mang thang Tam" [Introducing a number of issues concerning the August Revolution which require careful study]. *NCLS*, no. 47 (February 1963), pp. 3–21.

Hoang Tung. *Dang cua giai cap cong nhan* [The party of the working class]. Hanoi: Su That, 1960.

Hoang van Dao. *Viet-Nam Quoc-Dan Dang* [The Vietnamese Nationalist party]. Saigon, 1970.

Hong Quang. "May y nghi ve van de nghien cuu y nghia va tac dung lich su cua Xo-viet Nghe Tinh" [Some reflections on the meaning and the historical import of the Nghe Tinh soviets]. *NCLS*, no. 35 (February 1962), pp. 5–10.

Huynh van Tong. *Lich su bao chi Viet Nam tu khoi thuy den nam 1930* [History of Vietnamese newspapers from the beginning until 1930]. Saigon: Tri Dang, 1973.

Le Manh Trinh. "Bai hoc dau tranh de cung co va tang cuong su doan ket thong nhat noi bo Dang trong thoi ky 1939–1945" [Lessons of the struggle to solidify and strengthen the internal unity of the Party during the 1939–1945 period]. *Hoc tap*, no. 91 (August 1963), pp. 9–15.

———. "Xuc tien hon nua viec nghien cuu lich su Dang" [Intensify the research on the Party's history]. *Hoc tap*, no. 73 (February 1962), pp. 16–19.

Le Quoc Su. "Vai y-kien gop ve bai hoc: Kheo ket hop cac hinh thuc dau tranh chinh tri va vu trang trong Cach mang thang Tam" [Some opinions contributing to the lesson: Skillfully fusing the political and military forms of struggle in the August Revolution]. *NCLS*, no. 50 (May 1963), pp. 12–20.

Le Thi. "May van de phuong phap luan cua tac pham 'Duong Kach Menh' cua Ho Chu Tich" [On some methodological issues of *Duong kach menh* by President Ho]. *Triet hoc* 1, no. 28 (March 1980), pp. 22–45.

Mau Ung. "Ho Chi Minh, ten nguoi tren nhung chang duong lich su cuu nuoc" [Ho Chi Minh: His names in the stages on the road to national liberation]. *NCLS*, no. 156 (May–June 1974), pp. 11–18.

"May van de khoa hoc cua Cach mang thang Tam" [Some scientific issues

concerning the August Revolution]. *NCLS*, no. 18 (September 1960), pp. 1–20.

Nghiem Ke To. *Viet Nam mau lua* [Vietnam in blood and fire]. Saigon: Mai Linh, 1954.

Nguyen Cong Binh. "Ban ve tinh chat cuoc Cach-mang thang Tam" [On the nature of the August Revolution]. *NCLS*, no. 17 (August 1960), pp. 5–15.

———. "Khoi dau va ket thuc cua Cach-mang thang Tam" [The beginning and conclusion of the August Revolution]. *NCLS*, no. 56 (June 1963), pp. 17–28.

Nguyen Hong Phong. "Cach-mang thang Tam va chu-nghia xa-hoi" [The August Revolution and socialism]. *NCLS*, no. 29 (August 1961), pp. 1–6.

———. "Su thanh-lap Dang Cong-san Dong-duong la mot buoc ngoat vi dai" [The formation of the Indochinese Communist party was a great turning point]. *NCLS*, no. 10 (February 1960), pp. 6–29.

Nguyen Khanh Toan. *Van de dan toc trong cach mang vo san* [The national question in the proletarian revolution]. Hanoi: Su That, 1962.

Nguyen Kien Giang. *Viet-Nam nam dau tien sau Cach Mang thang Tam* [Vietnam during the first year after the August Revolution]. Hanoi: Su That, 1961.

Nguyen Nghia. "Cong cuoc hop nhat cac to chuc cong san o trong nuoc sau hoi nghi Huong-cang va viec to chuc ban Trung uong lam thoi dau tien" [The unification of the Communist organizations in the country after the Hong Kong conference and the formation of the first Provisional Central Committee]. *NCLS*, no. 62 (May 1964), pp. 54–59.

———. "Gop them mot it tai lieu ve cong cuoc hop nhat cac to chuc cong san dau tien o Viet-Nam va vai tro cua dong chi Nguyen-ai-Quoc [Some new materials on the unification of the first Communist organizations in Vietnam and the role of Comrade Nguyen ai Quoc]. *NCLS*, no. 59 (February 1964), pp. 3–8.

———. "Gop them mot it tai lieu ve to chuc va phat dong phong trao dau tranh o Nam-ky sau khi Dang ta nua moi thong nhat ra doi" [Some new materials on the organization and launching of the struggle movement in Nam Ky following the founding of the unified Party]. *NCLS*, no. 67 (October 1964), pp. 58–64.

Nguyen Thanh Nam. "May nhan xet ve Phan Chu Trinh" [Some observations on Phan Chu Trinh]. *NCLS*, no. 71 (February 1965), pp. 40–42.

Nguyen The Anh. *Viet Nam duoi thoi Phap do-ho* [Vietnam under French domination]. Saigon: Lua Thieng, 1970.

Nguyen The Xuong. *Vi sao nhom La Lutte chia re?* [Why the schism of the La Lutte group?]. Saigon: Van hoa tho xa, 1937.

Nguyen Thuong Huyen. *Cach menh* [Revolution]. n.p.; 1925.

Nguyen Trong Con. "Nhung hinh thuc to chuc va dau tranh cua thuy thu Viet Nam tu nam 1929 den 1935" [The forms of organization and struggle of the Vietnamese sailors from 1929 until 1935]. *NCLS*, no. 151 (July–August 1978), pp. 26–32.

Nguyen van Dinh. *Ta Thu Thau: Tu quoc gia den quoc te* [Ta Thu Thau:

From nationalism to internationalism]. Saigon: Sang, 1939.

Nguyen van Hoan. "Phong trao 'vo san hoa' nam 1930" [The "proletariani-zation" movement in 1930]. *NCLS* no. 134 (September–October 1970); pp. 10–17.

Nguyen van Tao. *Mat tran Binh dan o Phap voi nguyen vong cua quan chung Dong duong* [The French Popular Front and the aspirations of the Indochinese masses]. Saigon: La Lutte, 1936.

———. *Ngay Mot thang Nam* [The First of May]. Saigon: Tien phong tho xa, 1937.

Nguyen van Tay. *Staline co doc tai khong?* [Is Stalin a dictator?] My Tho: Dong phuong tho xa, 1938.

Nguyen van Trung. *Chu nghia thuc dan Phap o Viet-Nam: Thuc chat va huyen thoai* [French colonialism in Vietnam: Reality and myths]. Saigon: Nam Son, 1963.

———. *Pham Quynh.* 2 vols. Saigon: Trung tam Alpha, 1972–1973.

Pham van Son. *Che do Phap thuoc tai Viet-Nam* [The French colonial regime in Vietnam]. Saigon: Khai Tri, 1972.

———. *Viet-Nam tranh dau su* [History of the struggles of Vietnam]. Saigon: Viet Cuong, 1959.

———. *Viet-su tan-bien* [Modern History of Vietnam].. 7 vols. Saigon: Khai Tri, 1968–72.

Phan van Ban. "Dang Cong san Phap voi cach mang Viet-Nam" [The French Communist party and the Vietnamese revolution]. *NCLS,* no. 23 (February 1961), pp. 39–53.

Ta Thu Thau. *Tu de nhat den de tu quoc te* [From the First to the Fourth International]. Saigon: Van hoa tho xa, Collection Hieu biet moi [New knowledge], 1937.

Tam Vu. "Ve vai tro cua tri thuc trong lich su dan toc ta" [On the role of intellectuals in the history of our people]. *Dai Doan Ket,* nos. 18 (4 June 1977), 20 (18 June 1977), and 21 (28 June 1977).

T. C. "Nhin lai cac lo so bi mat cua co quan lanh dao Dang Cong san Dong duong (tu 1930 den 1935)" [Retrospective view on the secret bases of the leadership organs of the Indochinese Communist Party (from 1930 to 1935)]. *NCLS,* no. 37 (April 1962), pp. 20–26.

Thanh Huong. *Trotsky va phan cach mang* [Trotsky and the counter-revolution]. Saigon: Tien phong tho xa, 1937.

———. *Vi sao phai ung ho mat tran binh dan ben Phap* [Why we must support the Popular Front in France]. Saigon: Tien phong tho xa, 1937.

Thao Giang. "Dang ta la con de cua giai cap cong nhan" [Our party is the offspring of the working class]. *Hoc tap,* no. 73 (February 1962), pp. 20–25.

———. "Chu nghia yeu uoc trong lich su Viet Nam" [Patriotism in Viet-namese history]. *Dai doan ket* [Great solidarity] 3, no. 27 (1979), pp. 16–17 and 20; and no. 28 (1979), pp. 20–21.

Thep Moi. *Thoi dung Dang* [The Party-building period]. Paris: Doan Ket, 1976.

The Tap and Thanh Nam. "Ten cua chu-tich Ho Chi Minh va cuoc hanh trinh vi dai cua Nguoi" [The names of President Ho Chi Minh and His great odyssey]. *Tap chi cong san* [Review of communism] (May 1980), pp. 77–85.

"Tiep tuc phat huy truyen thong cach mang ve vang cua Cach mang thang Tam" [Continue to develop the heroic traditions of the August Revolution]. Editorial. *Hoc tap*, no. 91 (August 1963), pp. 1–3.

Toan Anh [Nguyen van Toan]. *Tin nguong Viet-Nam* [Vietnamese religions]. Saigon: Kim Lai, 1967.

To Minh Trung. "Chung quanh bai hoc: 'Kheo ket hop cach hinh thuc dau tranh chinh tri va vu trang trong Cach mang thang Tam'" [On the lesson: "Skillful fusion of the political and military forms of struggle in the August Revolution"]. *NCLS*, no 53 (August 1963), pp. 16–24.

Ton Duc Thang. "Can lam tot hon nua cong tac Mat Tran" [It is necessary to improve the Front work]. *Hoc tap*, no. 75 (April 1962), pp. 6–10.

Ton Quang Phiet. *Phan Boi Chau va mot giai doan lich su chong Phap cua nhan dan Viet Nam* [Phan Boi Chau and a period in the history of the anti-French resistance of the Vietnamese people]. Hanoi: Van Hoa, 1958.

"Tranh dau tren hai mat tran" [Struggle on two fronts]. *Tap chi bon-so-vich* [Bolshevik review], no. 4 (September 1934).

Tran Huy Lieu. "Bai hoc lich su ve Xo Viet Nghe Tinh" [The historical lessons of the Nghe Tinh Soviets]. *Van su dia* [Literature, history, geography], no. 32 (September 1957), pp. 1–8.

———. "Ba muoi nam dau tranh cua phu nu Viet Nam duoi su lanh dao cua Dang" [Thirty years of struggle of Vietnamese women under the leadership of the Party]. *NCLS*, no. 13 (April 1960), pp. 1–12.

———. "Cach mang thang Tam voi viec hoan thanh cuoc cach mang dan toc dan chu trong toan quoc" [The August Revolution and the completion of the national democratic revolution in the entire country]. *NCLS*, no. 47 (August 1962), pp. 1–2.

———. "Dang Cong san Viet Nam thanh lap trong boi cach lich su nao?" [In what historical context was the Vietnamese Communist party founded?]. *NCLS*, no. 47 (February 1963), pp. 1–2.

———. "Di du Quoc dan Dai hoi o Tan trao" [Attending the National People's Congress at Tan trao]. *NCLS*, no. 17 (August 1960), pp. 35–43.

———. "Diem qua qua trinh cong tac tu tuong va van hoa cua Dang" [A review of the past accomplishments of the ideological and cultural work of the party]. *NCLS*, no. 6 (August 1959), pp. 1–10.

———. "Gop y kien vao viec xay dung lich su Dang" [A contribution to the elaboration of the Party's history]. *NCLS*, no. 51 (June 1963), pp. 1–2.

———. "Hoat dong cua thanh nien Viet Nam duoi su lanh dao cua Dang" [The activities of Vietnamese youths under the leadership of the Party]. *NCLS*, no. 22 (1961), pp. 6–17.

———. *Lich su tam muoi nam chong Phap* [History of the eighty-year anti-French resistance]. 3 vols. Hanoi: Van Su Dia, 1957–61.

———. "Mot vai net ve cuoc dau tranh tu tuong cua Dang tu ngay thanh lap den Cach mang thang Tam 1945" [A few observations on the ideological struggle within our Party from its formation until the August Revolution in 1945]. *NCLS*, no. 71 (February 1965), pp. 1–6.

———. "Phan dau de tro nen mot dang vien Cong san" [Striving to become a Communist party member]. *NCLS*, no. 10 (February 1960), pp. 77–90.

———. "Tuoc an kiem cua Hoang de Bao Dai" [Dispossessing Emperor Bao Dai of the seal and sword]. *NCLS*, no. 18 (September 1960), pp. 46–51.

———. "Van de chinh quyen Xo-viet" [The problems of Soviet power]. *NCLS*, no. 33 (December 1961), pp. 1–7.

———. "Y nghia lich su cua Dai-hoi Dang lan thu Ba" [The historical significance of the Third Party Congress]. *NCLS*, no. 15 (June 1960), pp. 1–3.

Tran Trong Kim. *Viet Nam su luoc* [An outline history of Vietnam]. 1929; reprint ed., Saigon: Tan Viet, 1958.

Tran van Giau. *Giai cap cong nhan Viet Nam: Tu dang cong san thanh lap den cach mang thanh cong* [The Vietnamese working class: From the formation of the Communist Party until the success of the revolution]. Vol. 1, 1930–1935; vol. 2, 1936–1939; vol. 3, 1939–1945. Hanoi: Vien Su hoc, 1962–63.

———. *Su phat trien cua tu tuong o Viet Nam tu the ky XIX den cach mang thang Tam* [The development of Vietnamese thought from the nineteenth century to the August Revolution]. vol. 2, *He y thuc tu san va su bat luc cua no truoc cac nhiem vu lich su* [Bourgeois thought system and its incapacity in the face of historic tasks]. Hanoi: NXB Khoa hoc Xa hois, 1975.

Tran van Ty. "Tim hieu nhung kinh nghiem va hinh thai dau tranh cach mang thang Tam" [Understanding the experiences and forms of struggle in the August Revolution]. *NCLS*, nos. 29 (August 1961), pp. 7–13, and 30 (September 1961), pp. 6–12.

Tri Binh. *Lien bang Xo-viet ngay nay* [The Soviet Union today]. Cholon: Tan Van Hoa tong tho, 1938.

———. *Van de phong thu Dong duong* [The problems of defense of Indochina]. Saigon: Nhom dan Chung, 1939.

Tri Thanh. *Cac quyen tu do dan-chu voi nhan dan Dong duong* [The rights of freedom and democracy and the people of Indochina]. Saigon: Tan Van Hoa tong tho, 1938.

Trung Chinh. "Pham Hong Thai hy sinh ve viec nuoc" [Pham Hong Thai sacrificed for the country]. *NCLS*, no. 158 (September–October 1975), pp. 16–26.

———. "Tam Tam Xa la gi?" [What was Tam Tam Xa?]. *NCLS*, no. 134 (September–October 1970), pp. 5–9.

———. "Thu tim xem Ho Chu tich tiep thu chu nghia Lenin va truyen ba vao Viet Nam nhu the nao?" [How did President Ho receive Leninism and propagate it in Vietnam?]. *NCLS*, no. 132 (May–June 1970), pp. 5–21.

————. "Tinh chat doc dao cua Xo-viet Nghe Tinh" [The originality of the Nghe Tinh soviets]. *NCLS*, no. 32 (November 1961), pp. 7–14.

————. "Tinh chat tu phat cua Xo-viet Nghe Tinh" [The spontaneity of the Nghe Tinh soviets]. *NCLS*, no. 31 (October 1961), pp. 1–6.

Trung Thuc and Ho Hai. "Quan he giua tinh Dang va tinh khoa-hoc trong viec nghien cuu lich su Dang" [The relationship between the party character and scientific character in the research on Party history]. *NCLS*, no. 51 (June 1963), pp. 12–16.

Truong Chinh and Dang Duc Sieu. *So tay van hoa Viet Nam* [Handbook of Vietnamese culture]. Hanoi: NXB Van Hoa, 1978.

Truong Ngoc Phu. "Tu vu am-sat Bazin nam 1929 den cuoc khoi nghia Yen Bay nam 1930 cua Viet Nam Quoc Dan Dang" [From the assassination of Bazin in 1929 to the Yen Bay Insurrection in 1930 of the Vietnamese Nationalist party]. *Su dia* 9, no. 26 (January –March 1974), pp. 98–118.

Van Phong and Nguyen Kien Giang. *Chien tranh the gioi lan thu hai va cuoc van dong giai phong dan toc Viet Nam* [The Second World War and the campaign for national liberation in Vietnam]. Hanoi: Su That, 1962.

Van Tao. "Ket thuc cuoc thao luan ve Phan Chu Trinh." [Concluding the discussions on Phan Chu Trinh]. *NCLS*, no. 76 (July 1965), pp. 11–26.

————. "Lien minh giai cap trong cach mang Viet Nam tu sau 1930" [The class alliance in the Vietnamese revolution since 1930]. *NCLS*, no. 10 (February 1960), pp. 50–67.

————. "Mot vai nhan dinh ve qua trinh phat trien cua luc luong vu trang cach mang Viet-Nam, Vai tro va tinh chat cua no trong giai doan gianh chinh quyen" [Some observations on the history of the development of the Vietnamese revolutionary armed forces: Its role and character during the period of seizure of revolutionary power]. *NCLS*, no. 93 (December 1966), pp. 16–27.

————. "Tim hieu qua trinh hinh thanh va phat trien cua Mat tran Dan toc Thong nhat Viet Nam" [Understanding the history of the formation and development of the National United Front in Vietnam]. *NCLS*, no. 7 (March 1959), pp. 27–41.

Van Tao, Thanh The Vy, and Nguyen Cong Binh. *Lich su cach mang thang Tam* [The history of the August Revolution]. Hanoi: Su Hoc, 1960.

"Ve dac diem va ban chat cua nong dan lao dong Viet-Nam" [On the nature and special character of the agrarian proletariat in Vietnam]. *Hoc tap*, no. 89 (June 1963), pp. 53–61, and no. 92 (September 1963), pp. 59–67.

Vien Su hoc (Institute of Historical Studies). "Van de Dang su" [On the issues of Party history]. *NCLS*, no. 10 (February 1960), pp. 1–5.

Vien Su hoc, To Lich su Cach mang thang Tam (Institute of Historical Studies, History of the August Revolution Cell). *Cach mang thang Tam (Tong khoi nghia o Ha-noi va cac dia phuong* [The August Revolution (general insurrection in Hanoi and other localities)]. 2 vols. Hanoi: NXB Su hoc, 1960.

Vo Khac Thieu. *Go mat na bon gia danh cach mang loi dung quan chung: Ta Thu Thau* [Unmasking the fake revolutionaries who exploit the masses: Ta Thu Thau]. Saigon: Imprimerie Testellin [1935?].

Vu Tho. "Mot so van de lich su Dang thoi ky 1936–1939" [A few problems concerning Party history during the period 1936–1939]. *NCLS*, no. 85 (April 1966), pp. 3–10.

———. "Qua trinh thanh lap dang vo san o Viet-Nam da duoc dien ra nhu the nao?" [What happened in the process of the formation of the proletarian party in Vietnam?]. *NCLS*, no. 71 (February 1965), pp. 15–22.

———. "Tu 'Duong cach menh' den 'Luan cuong chinh tri cua Dang Cong san Dong duong'" [From "The Road to Revolution" to the "Political Theses of the Indochinese Communist Party"]. *NCLS*, no. 72 (March 1965), pp. 14–19.

INDEX

A Chau Bi Ap-buc Dan-toc Lien-hiep
Hoi. *See* League of the Oppressed
Peoples of Asia
AFIMA (Association pour la Formation Intellectuelle et Morales des Annamites), 42, 97
Allied invasion of Indochina, 292, 308–
309
ancestor worship, 30–32, 30n17
Annamese communism, 120–122,
120n57, 124
L'Annam nouveau, 234
anticolonialism, 37, 194, 204–205; in
France, 143, 147–149
anticolonial movements (Vietnamese):
Can Vuong (Support the King), 54,
153; Dong Du (Eastern Travel), 54;
Dong Kinh Nghia Thuc (Free School
of Dong Kinh), 54. *See also* Tam
Tam Xa
apparatchiki (organization men), 172,
173–175, 176–177
armed insurrection, 269–272
armed propaganda, 310, 319–320
Asiocentrism, 56n35

August Revolution, 322–326; assessment of, 333–338; chronology of,
326; in Danang, 324; in Hanoi,
321n57, 324; in Hue, 324; origins of,
334; role of chance, 334–335; role of
the Japanese, 334, 334n76, 336; role
of the military, 280n104; in Saigon,
324
Ayme, 292

Bac Son–Vu Nhai revolutionary base,
271, 283
Ban Chi huy o Ngoai. *See* Overseas
Leadership Committee
Bank of Indochina, 145, 145nn5, 6, 8
Bao Cong Nong (Worker-Peasant), 24,
67
Bao Dai, 235, 292, 295, 296; abdication
of, 87n80, 274, 324, 326–327; ab-
rogated treaties with France, 292,
296; supreme adviser of Viet Minh
government, 327
Bazin, Hervé, 94; assassination of, 94–
95, 94n7
Bell, Daniel, 51

One Step Forward, Two Steps Back,
135n83; "Theses on the National and
Colonial Questions," 56, 56n35;
What Is to Be Done?, 137n90
Le Quang Ba, 280
Le Quang Liem, 43, 45, 97, 235
Le van Phan. *See* Le Hong Son
Le van thu, 196
Levy Pau, 168n56
liberated zone *(vung tu do),* in north-
western Bac Ky, 280, 312, 319, 322
Liberation committee, 319
Lien Viet Front, 269
Likwe. *See* Tran Phu
Linh kach menh (Revolutionary sol-
dier), 67, 79
literati mandarins, Vietnamese, 40
Loseby, Frank, 179n85
Luethy, Herbert, 148n14
Luong van Chi, 279n101
Luu Su Phuc, 65n50
Ly Nhan Dang, 159
Ly Thuong Kiet, 28
Ly Tu Trong, 79

mandarin institution, 34, 40, 41n14. *See
also* boy-mandarins
Mannheim, Karl, 69
Marty, Louis, 42, 62n17, 67n55
Marxism, 102, 100–104, 103n22
Marxism-Leninism, 36, 54, 75, 89, 100
Marxist study groups, 36
mass organizations, 77–79, 133, 137–
140, 138nn91, 92, 220
Mat tran Dan chu Dong duong. *See* Indochinese Democratic Front
Mat tran Dan chu Dong duong chong
phat xit Nhat (Indochinese Democratic Front to Oppose Fascist Japan), 285
me min (the witch), 94, 94n8
Merlin, Martial, 65n50
Metin report, 151
Mills, C. Wright, 103n22
Minoda, Japanese official in Nam Ky,
294
monarchy, Vietnamese, 50–51, 54, 326–
327

Mordant, General, 292
Moutet, Marius, 151, 209, 209n32, 211
movement front, 138n91, 201n18. *See
also* United Front

Nam Dong Thu Xa (Nam Dong Publishing House), 36n4, 45, 92
Nam Ky Insurrection, 252–255, 254n45
Nam phong (Southern wind), 42,
42n17, 97
national heroes, veneration of, 32
nationalism, 27, 27nn9, 10, 39n10, 262
national liberation, 39
"national liberation revolution," Marx-
ist concept of, 85, 116, 259–263
"national question," Marxist concept
of, 86, 86n78, 116, 251–252, 259–263
National Revolutionary Army (Quoc
dan Cach mang Quan), 281
National Salvation Army. *See* Cuu
Quoc Quan
National Salvation Associations, 264
National Service Party. *See* Dang
Phung Su Quoc Gia
"National United Front," ICP organi-
zational tactic, 252, 263–269, 266n73,
267n74, 268n75
New Viet People's Party. *See* Dang
Tan Viet Quoc Dan
Ngay Nay (Nowadays), 296, 298
Nghe Tinh Soviet Movement, 151–171;
origins of, 163–171, 164nn46, 47,
165n50; role of Nguyen Ai Quoc,
167–170; role of the Comintern, 167
Nghia. *See* Nguyen Thieu
Nghiem Thuong Bien, 24, 160
Ngo Dinh Diem, 245, 295, 295n9
Ngo Duc Ke, 254n49
Ngo Duc Tri, 24, 77, 126n69, 160,
176n77, 203n23
Ngo Gia Tu (alias Ngo Si Quyet), 110,
110n35, 115, 115n47, 117–118, 162,
203n23, 254n49
Ngo Si Quyet. *See* Ngo Gia Tu
Ngo van Chieu, 242
Nguyen Ai Quoc (alias Ho Chi Minh),
35, 56n35, 57–66, 92n2, 115n47,
126n69, 129n76, 149–50, 232; "Agent

Lucius," 317; aliases, 58n37; and armed forces, 283–284; arrest of, 160, 179, 286, 288n122; and August Revolution, 325, 327; autobiography: [T. Lan] *Vua di duong vua ke chuyen*, 88n83; birth, 58, 58n37, 59; as Comintern agent, 126n69, 168n69, 181n91, 257; conflict with ICP leaders, 183–185; criticism of, 183–185; "death" in 1932, 25, 179, 179n85; *Duong kach menh*, 67, 83, 84–85, 115; on the masses, 83; in Moscow, 168n58, 180–181; and Nghe Tinh Soviet Movement, 167–171; and orthography, 63n48; "partial insurrection," strategy of, 168–170, 270–271, 309, 311, 325; "The Party's Military Work among the Peasants" (1927), 168, 168n58; "The Party's Strategies in Summary" (1930), 125; political orientations of, 60–62; return to Vietnam, 161, 257
Nguyen An Ninh, 48, 49, 49n26, 53, 150, 198–199, 200n15
Nguyen An Ninh Secret Society, 46–47
Nguyen Cong Vien (alias Lam Duc Thu), 65n50, 117, 118
Nguyen Duc Canh, 110, 110n36, 117, 125
Nguyen Duy Trinh, 48, 170
Nguyen Khac Nhu, 95, 96
Nguyen Khanh Toan, 49, 176n78
Nguyen Kien Giang, 329n65, 330–331
Nguyen Luong Bang, 79
Nguyen Manh Ha, 295n9, 298n14
Nguyen Nghia. *See* Nguyen Thieu
Nguyen Ngoc Vy, 32n18
Nguyen Phan Long, 43, 43n19, 44, 45, 98, 98n16, 235
Nguyen Phong Sac, 115, 115n47
Nguyen Thai Hoc, 48, 92, 95, 95n10, 96n12
Nguyen The Truyen, 150, 192, 192n2
Nguyen Thieu (alias Nghia), 117, 120n57, 125
Nguyen Thuong Huyen, 82, 82n73
Nguyen Trong Nha, 126n69

Nguyen Tuan (alias Kim Ton), 117–118, 117n49
Nguyen van Cu, 101n19
Nguyen van Nguyen, 213, 215
Nguyen van Tao, 147, 150, 194n5, 198n10, 215; role in Trotskyist-Stalinist controversy, 224–226; Saigon elections (1933), 203–204, 203nn22, 24; Saigon elections (1937), 224
Nguyen van Trung, 42n17
Nguyen van Vinh, 39nn9, 10, 41, 41n15, 48
nha cach nang (respectable revolutionaries), 52, 96, 161
Nhuong Tong (alias of Hoang Pham Tran), 91n1, 92, 92n2
noncommunist parties, 298, 310, 315
Nong Hoi. *See* Peasants' Association
Norodom, king of Cambodia, 292

"objective ally," Communist concept of, 267–268
October Revolution, Russian, 75, 290
O'Harrow, Stephen, 41n15
"Old Indochina hands," 233, 233n1, 240
OMS (International Communications Section). *See* Comintern
Operation Mei, 293
"opportunism," Communist concept of, 131, 132; left-opportunism, 132n79, 133; right-opportunism, 132n79
organization, Leninist concept of, 135n84; of Thanh Nien, 77–79. *See also* ICP, organization of
organizational front. *See* ICP, organizational front of
OSS (Office of Strategic Services), 286, 315–318, 317n44, 318n48
Overseas Leadership Committee (Ban Chi huy o Ngoai), 175, 178, 185, 187

Pac Bo, 256, 257n53
PAI (Parti Annamite d'Independence, Viet Nam Doc Lap Dang, Vietnamese Independence Party), 192–193

quoc dan (nation), 27
quoc gia (state), 27, 27n9; *chu nghia
quoc gia* (statism), 27n9

radicalism, 49–51; Vietnamese, 51–53
Red Peasant Associations, 154–155
red villages ("soviets"). *See* Nghe Tinh
Soviet Movement
"reformism," Communist attitude toward, 132, 132n80, 223
revolution, 82, 306; traditional Vietnamese understanding of, 82n73;
Western conception of, 82, 82n74
Revolutionary Party of the New Vietnam. *See* Tan Viet
revolutionary patriotism, 47–53, 91–99;
revolutionary patriots, 36n2, 39,
40n11, 45–53, 178, 337
"revolutionary situation," Leninist concept of, 287, 291, 305–308
revolutionary upsurge of 1930–1931,
152, 161, 164
Robin, René, 210
Roosevelt, Franklin D., 316
Roy, M. N., 56n35

Sacks, I. Milton, 255n51
Sarraut, Albert, 42, 42n17
Second International, 60
Self-Defence Militia (Doi Tu Ve), 139
Serrati, Giacinto, 56n35
Seton-Watson, Hugh, 207
Siamese Communist Party, 173
Sisavang Vong, king of Laos, 292
Smith, Anthony, 27n10
socialism, 36, 55
Socialist Republic of Vietnam, 328
Soviet Union, 188, 330, 330n67
Spanish Civil War, 101, 226, 229, 230
Sport-and-youth movement, 247–248,
348n32
Stalinists, 195–196, 255n51
students, Vietnamese, exodus overseas
of, 38, 191n1; repatriation from
France, 194n5; and revolt of, 38n24
Summit Colonial Council, 151
Sun Yat-sen, 89; *Three Principles of*

the People, 36, 75
Sûreté, French, 25, 177n80, 217n52,
244–245

Tagore, 36
Tam Tam Xa (Heart-to-Heart Associa-
tion), 54, 64–66, 65n50
Tam Xa (Heart Association), 65n50
Tan Trao, 324
Tan Viet (Tan Viet Cach Menh Dang)
(Revolutionary Party of the New
Vietnam), 46, 92n21, 122–123,
122n64
Tan Viet Nam, 274, 274n89, 298, 321
Tan Viet Thanh Nien Doan (Youth
Corps for a New Vietnam). *See* Tam
Tam Xa
Ta Thu Thau, 47, 53, 143n3, 193, 196,
212n37, 228n84
Tax Protest Movement of 1908, 46, 83,
153
Thai van Giai, 100, 159n36
Than chung (Morning bell), 96, 161
Thanh Nghe Tinh tan van (News of
Thanh Hoa, Nghe An, and Ha Tinh),
159
Thanh Nien (Viet Nam Thanh Nien
Kach Menh Hoi) (Vietnamese Revo-
lutionary Youth Association), 63–88,
113–119, 182n93
Thanh Nien Cao Vong Dang (High As-
pirations Youth Party). *See* Nguyen
An Ninh Secret Society
Thanh Nien cong San Doan. *See* CYC
Thanh Nien Tien Phong (Vanguard
Youth), 301
Thanh Nien (Youth), 24, 67, 67n55, 79,
83
Thayer, Carlyle, 168n58
thien menh (heavenly mandate), 81
Third International, 60. *See also* Com-
intern
thoi co, 289, 305–309
Thomazi, Auguste, 148n14
Togliatti, Palmiro (Comrade Ercoli),
109
To Hieu, 98

Vietnamese Communism, 1925–1945

Designed by G. T. Whipple, Jr.
Composed by Coghill Book Typesetting Co.
in 10 point Times Roman, 2 points leaded,
with display lines in Times Roman.
Printed offset by Thomson-Shore, Inc.
on Warren's Number 66 text, 50 pound basis.
Bound by John H. Dekker & Sons, Inc.
in Holliston book cloth
and stamped in Kurz-Hastings foil.

Library of Congress Cataloging in Publication Data

Huỳnh, Kim Khánh.
 Vietnamese communism, 1925–1945.

 Bibliography: p.
 Includes index.
 1. Communism—Vietnam—History. I. Title.
HX400.5.A6H89   335.43′09597   81-70696
ISBN 0-8014-1369-9 (cloth)   AACR2
ISBN 0-8014-9397-8 (paper)